ALLY McCOIST
PORTRAIT OF A HERO

ALLY McCOIST
PORTRAIT OF A HERO

ALISTAIR AIRD

JOHN BLAKE

Published by John Blake Publishing Ltd,
3 Bramber Court, 2 Bramber Road,
London W14 9PB, England

www.johnblakepublishing.co.uk

First published in hardback in 2008
This edition published in paperback in 2009

ISBN: 978-1-84454-841-5

British Library Cataloguing-in-Publication Data:

A catalogue record for this book is available from the British Library.

Design by www.envydesign.co.uk

Printed in Great Britain by CPI Bookmarque, Croydon CR0 4TD

3 5 7 9 10 8 6 4 2

Papers used by John Blake Publishing are natural, recyclable products made from
wood grown in sustainable forests. The manufacturing processes conform to the
environmental regulations of the country of origin.

Every attempt has been made to contact the relevant copyright-holders,
but some were unobtainable. We would be grateful if the appropriate people
could contact us.

ACKNOWLEDGEMENTS

There are a number of people that I would like to extend a vote of thanks to, as without their help or support, this project might never have got off the ground – far less into print.

Firstly, I'd like to say a heartfelt thanks to my mum and dad, Sheena and Tom, who have always believed in me and given their unstinting support from the day and hour that I was introduced to this wonderful, if often complex, world in which we live. Both also lent a hand in the proofreading of the final manuscript, with their advice and guidance a huge benefit in helping to smooth off any rough edges that existed. My wife Sharon has also been a rock throughout the preparation of the book, providing love and understanding as I attempted to pull together this tribute to my all-time hero.

For the construction of the book itself, I would like to thank Paul Smith, Rob Mason and Richard Cairns, who each provided me with some indispensable information on Ally's career with St Johnstone, Sunderland and Kilmarnock respectively. Also the staff at The Mitchell Library were always polite and helpful as I trawled through the archives in my attempts to unearth as much information as I could about one of Scotland's greatest and most popular footballers. I'd like to give special thanks too to Michelle Signore and Allie Collins at Blake Publishing for believing that this project was worthy of publication and for their help and support throughout.

For Eva, Daddy's little angel

CONTENTS

CHAPTER ONE

THE EARLY YEARS: 1962–78

In 1962, the 24th of September fell on a Monday. The players and staff of Rangers Football Club were on their travels, destination Seville, for the second leg of their first-round European Cup-Winners' Cup tie against the local side. They arrived in the Spanish city in fine fettle, defending a four-goal lead from the first leg at Ibrox and having thrashed Hibernian 5-1 at Easter Road in the Scottish League Championship two days earlier.

This was a Rangers team maturing into one of the club's greatest-ever sides. Under the astute stewardship of James Scotland Symon, they had reached the last four of the European Champions Cup, the continent's premier club competition, in the 1959/60 season (where they lost heavily to Eintracht Frankfurt), and had become the first British side to contest the final of a major European tournament when they lost 4-1 on aggregate against Italian cracks Fiorentina in the 1960/61 European Cup-Winners' Cup.

At that time, Rangers boasted players of the calibre of Jim Baxter, Davie Wilson, John Greig, Ralph Brand and Jimmy Millar, and while they had not won the League Championship in 1961/62 (they were runners-up, finishing three points behind Dundee), they had secured the Cup

Double by winning the Scottish Cup and Scottish League Cup. The current season, 1962/63, would witness the reclamation of the championship and the retention of the Scottish Cup, but the following season would surpass all of those achievements, as Symon's men went on to sweep the board in Scotland to complete the domestic Treble for only the second time in the club's ninety-year history.

Away from football matters, the early autumn of 1962 saw Elvis Presley topping the UK singles chart with his rendition of 'She's Not You', while boxing fans were at fever pitch as they looked forward to the world heavyweight title fight between champion Floyd Patterson and the fearsome Charles 'Sonny' Liston on 25 September. Elsewhere in 1962, cinema-goers willing to part with the equivalent of 14p were able to take in the blockbuster movies *Dr No*, *Cape Fear* and *Lawrence of Arabia*, although all the talk in Hollywood was of matters off-screen following the death on 5 August of the iconic actress Marilyn Monroe, who passed away after taking an overdose of sleeping pills.

Oblivious to all these goings-on was a new arrival into the world. At Bellshill Royal Infirmary in North Lanarkshire, proud parents Jessie and Neil McCoist announced the birth of their second child, a son they named Alistair Murdoch McCoist. Little did anyone know at the time, particularly the Rangers people in Seville, but the arrival of young Mr McCoist would ultimately prove an extremely significant event in the history of Rangers Football Club. The new addition to the McCoist family shared a birthday with the famous American author F. Scott Fitzgerald and Jim Henson, creator of the Muppets, who were born on this day in 1896 and 1936 respectively. McCoist's birthday also coincided with the anniversary of the world's oldest horse race, with the St Leger Stakes being run at Doncaster for the first time on 24 September 1776, thus providing an early indication that the 'Sport of Kings' would play a significant role in the life of the new arrival.

Incidentally, Rangers' pre-match confidence was somewhat misplaced, as they got an almighty scare in the city famous for its orange crop. The Light Blues lost by two goals to nil in the Ramon Sanchez Pizjuan stadium, but still managed to progress to the next round 4-2 on aggregate. The tie was marred by an ugly brawl that unfolded in the closing stages. All twenty-two players were involved in the fracas, prompting the referee to call time on the match before the ninety minutes had elapsed. Elsewhere, in the boxing bout, Liston ruthlessly hammered Patterson, knocking him out inside two rounds to become world heavyweight champion, a crown he would hold until a young upstart named Cassius Clay took it from him some three years later.

The McCoist family were from East Kilbride, the first of Scotland's 'new towns'. Prior to the Second World War, the city of Glasgow was overcrowded and poor housing standards were rife, so the Clyde Valley Regional Plan was drawn up in 1946 with the purpose of alleviating the congestion through the building of satellite 'new towns'. East Kilbride, located approximately ten miles south of Glasgow, had swelled from a small village to a large burgh in 1930, and became one of the sites chosen to handle the overspill. In 1947, it was the first town to be awarded 'new town' status and set the benchmark for the others that followed in Glenrothes, Cumbernauld, Livingston and Irvine.

McCoist's parents, Neil and Jessie, set up home in the Calderwood district of the town, one of the largest areas of East Kilbride and one which is famous for being the birthplace of two of the eighteenth century's medical pioneers, the Hunter brothers, William and John. Both were outstanding anatomists, with John, in particular, credited with innumerable medical advances, and sited at the place of their birth today is the Hunter House Museum.

McCoist's father worked as a fitter with Weir Pumps of Cathcart, while his mum was a secretary. Ally and his older sister Allison, who completed the family unit, enjoyed an excellent upbringing, with their parents grafting hard to provide a comfortable life for them. 'My dad did constant night shifts for twenty years to provide for me and my sister,' said Ally some years later. 'We [he and Allison] were brought up to appreciate the value of money.'[1]

Both parents were also hugely supportive of Ally's early football career. Neil eventually took over the running of the local boys' club that McCoist played for, but there was no favouritism where his son was concerned, with young Ally being treated the same as the other players in the team in a bid to ensure that he kept his feet firmly on the ground. Jessie also lent a hand by providing some much-needed sustenance for the aspiring footballers after games and training sessions, and the McCoist residence would often double as a dormitory for the players. After McCoist elected to pursue a career as a professional, Neil and Jessie would also make regular trips to watch their son in action, with Jessie still a regular in the Ibrox stands every other Saturday.

That unstinting parental support was welcome, because it was apparent from an early age that young McCoist had a penchant for the game of football. 'The Beautiful Game' was popular in the family, as both his mother and father were avid football followers. Neil followed Rangers and was involved in the running of a local boys' club team, while Jessie had been an ardent supporter of Hibernian in her younger days. She idolised Gordon Smith, one of the quintet that made up the Edinburgh side's 'Famous Five' forward line that terrorised Scottish defences when Hibernian won the Scottish League Championship three times between 1948 and 1952, and had been a football devotee ever since her teenage years.

In those early years of his life growing up in East Kilbride, seldom was young McCoist seen without a football at his feet. His mum still has his first pair of football boots – 'They're so small they look like toys,'[2] she told Sue Mott in an interview for her son's testimonial programme in 1994 – and she was sure from an early stage that her boy was destined for greatness. She wasn't alone either. 'I admit he looked like a budding star to me, but I might have been biased,' she said. 'I knew, though, that he had something special when a gentleman that stayed across our street in East Kilbride told me that when Alistair played with the ball he suddenly looked so much older and more capable than all the other children.'[3]

It was clear that Ally was a bit special, and he began to look the part too when, at the age of six, he won a competition in the local evening newspaper, the now-defunct pink paper called *The Citizen*. The first prize was a football strip of his choice, and it came as no surprise when young McCoist plumped for that of his favourite team, Rangers. The royal blue jersey at that time was the one with the famous crew-neck design with the large white RFC crest on the breast, and McCoist used to strut with great pride around the streets of East Kilbride, kicking a ball and sporting his new attire. Although Rangers were the team he followed, McCoist also had a soft spot for the all-conquering Liverpool side of that era who, under the astute leadership of Bill Shankly, would go on to conquer Europe over the course of the next decade.

In addition to enjoying regular kick-arounds in the streets with his friends, McCoist also played football at his primary school, Maxwellton, where the headmaster, a gentleman called Mr Petrie, ran the team and also refereed the matches. One of McCoist's earliest football memories is of playing for his primary school in a crucial match against rival school,

St Kenneth's. If Maxwellton won the match they would win the league, but any other outcome would mean the trophy going to St Kenneth's. With the game balanced on a knife-edge at 3-3 and with only a few minutes left on the clock, McCoist thundered in a shot from long range. He and his team-mates watched as it bounced once, twice and then for a third time. The third bounce took the ball out of the reach of the goalkeeper and into the goal, making the score 4-3 to Maxwellton. They were champions ... or so they thought.

Amid much back slapping and congratulatory gestures in the dressing room, Mr Petrie came in accompanied by a teacher from St Kenneth's and a spectator who was claiming that instead of bouncing under the crossbar, McCoist's effort had in fact bounced over it. The pitch on which the school matches were played did not use goal nets, so confusion reigned before Mr Petrie, in his role as match referee, took the decision that the goal should not have stood and ruled that the final score was 3-3. His decision handed the title to St Kenneth's, much to the disappointment of his own school, but while his verdict may have annoyed McCoist at the time, he would look back in later life and remark that he found his headmaster's attitude refreshing, for Mr Petrie had no concern over whether his team won or lost, merely that his boys enjoyed themselves and got a game of football.

In addition to his school-team commitments, McCoist also turned out for a local boys' club side called Calderwood Star, representing their Under-12 side at the age of nine. Albert England ran the team (McCoist's father took over a few years later), and he gave McCoist his debut against Villa Star, handing him the number seven jersey and placing him in the outside-right position. It proved a very productive and lucrative debut, as McCoist claimed a hat-trick in a 3-2 win, a treble that earned him the princely sum of fifteen pence since his father had promised to reward him with five pence for every goal he scored. This financial incentive continued throughout his school days; although McCoist later re-negotiated the deal to take into account the rate of inflation, earning himself a 100 percent raise to ten pence a goal!

On leaving Maxwellton, McCoist moved on to secondary school at Hunter High in Calderwood, East Kilbride. As a rising star in the game, football played a large part in McCoist's time at Hunter, with his chemistry teacher, Archie Robertson, having a huge influence on him. Robertson, who had played for and managed Clyde and won five caps for

Scotland, took charge of the school football team and nurtured his young protégé through his later school years. He died in January 1978, a few months before McCoist left school, and his passing at the age of forty-eight left his star pupil devastated: he regarded Robertson as one of the key figures to have inspired him to pursue a career in professional football. It was such a shame, therefore, that Robertson never saw McCoist fulfil his early potential and make the grade as a professional before going on to achieve such greatness in a glittering career.

Although he focused the majority of his attention on football, McCoist also tried his hand at other sports during his school days, most notably handball and rugby. He enjoyed swimming too, and the pool was actually where young McCoist obtained the first of what turned out to be a vast array of sporting honours, picking up the bronze medal when he finished third in a school race. He was only six years old, and he maintains to this day that he would have claimed the gold medal had he not been hampered in his pursuit of first place when his water wing fell off, forcing him to alter his course to retrieve it!

In addition to his sporting achievements, McCoist, a highly respected pupil who was both a prefect and school captain at secondary school, also gained some respectable academic qualifications, leaving Hunter with Highers in English and Chemistry and O-Grade passes in Arithmetic, English, Mathematics, Physics, Chemistry, Economics, French and Biology. 'I was lucky my football never put me off my other subjects and I did well at exams,'4 he said. Although Ally boasted a decent scholastic record, the brains of the McCoist clan belonged to his sister Allison. She was recognised as being the conscientious student in the family, and would go on to gain a degree in mathematics and computing science. Like her younger brother, she had an aptitude for sport too, and she represented Great Britain at handball.

It was clear, though, that Ally McCoist had that 'special something' in the shape of his football ability. By now he had graduated from Calderwood Star to the East Kilbride District side and then on to Fir Park Boys' Club in Motherwell. At that time Motherwell were managed by former Rangers utility player Roger Hynd and he was keen to tie McCoist to the Lanarkshire club on schoolboy forms. This was not something that interested McCoist, though. 'I couldn't then, and still can't see the benefit of committing yourself to a club with an "S" form,' he said some years later. 'It is great for the club … they have the youngster well and truly tied up, but not so good for the player himself. I've heard stories of boys who have signed "S" forms and the managers haven't even bothered to register them with the SFA, they've just stuck the completed form away in a drawer somewhere.'[5]

Instead of pledging himself to Motherwell, McCoist pursued other avenues, which included spending time training at Love Street with St Mirren under the watchful eye of their manager, who in those days was none other than Alex Ferguson (now Sir Alex, of course). Although McCoist did well in the trial matches he participated in, scoring in one game against Eastcraigs, he did not do enough to impress Fergie, who felt that McCoist was too small to make it as a footballer. Evidently Ferguson had not yet perfected the knack of spotting talented young players and this was the first of two rebuffs McCoist would suffer at the hands of the future Manchester United manager during his playing career.

Ferguson's rejection did not discourage the determined youngster, though, and the next step for McCoist was to take up an offer to play in a couple of trial matches with Perth side St Johnstone. At the time, the Saints were struggling in the lower reaches of the Scottish First Division, having deteriorated badly since the early seventies when the club had enjoyed their most successful era. Their standing in the Scottish game bore little consequence to McCoist, though: he was simply on the lookout for the opportunity to showcase his talents in the hope that someone would make him the offer that would help to accomplish his mission to earn a living as a professional footballer.

Unlike his experience with the Paisley Saints, McCoist's encounter with their Perth equivalents was much more fruitful. The sixteen-year-old made a real impression in the trial matches, prompting manager Alex Stuart to offer him semi-professional terms with the guarantee of regular reserve-team football coupled with opportunities to break into the first team if he made good progress.

McCoist was tempted with the idea of senior football. It was, after all, what he had dreamed about for as long as he could remember, but showing remarkable maturity for his age, and conscious of the massive step he was about to take, he asked the St Johnstone officials if he could take a couple of days to mull things over and discuss the offer with his family before reaching his final decision.

The conclusion drawn from that discussion was that McCoist would sign up at St Johnstone, but then, out of the blue, he received a phone call from a gentleman called George Runciman. Runciman was the scout for McCoist's boyhood heroes, Glasgow Rangers, and he had watched him play for Hunter High in a Lanarkshire schools cup-tie against St Ambrose of Coatbridge. The match had ended 5-5, with McCoist netting four of Hunter's goals and playing a part in the move that set up the fifth. Having been suitably impressed with McCoist's display, Runciman telephoned the youngster and asked if he would be interested in coming along to Ibrox to talk to Willie Thornton, who at that time was assistant manager at the club. Thornton was a legendary centre-forward who had played for Rangers in the halcyon days of the forties and fifties, and he had played a significant part in one of the club's great teams alongside players of the ilk of Willie Waddell, Jock 'Tiger' Shaw and Bobby Brown. However, the offer was only to go to Ibrox for a chat and there was no guarantee a concrete proposal like the one McCoist had received from St Johnstone would be made.

Whether there ever would have been will never be known: Ally McCoist had already made his mind up to sign for St Johnstone. The discussion with Thornton never took place. Instead, he decided to take the first fledgeling steps of his senior football career with St Johnstone at Muirton Park, Perth, under the stewardship of Alex Stuart. He signed on 1 December 1978 at the age of sixteen to open up the first chapter of his professional football career. The fairytale was only just beginning.

CHAPTER TWO

THE SAINTS: 1978–81

Formed by a group of young local cricketers who sought a winter pursuit to fill the void left by the off-season of their traditionally fair-weather activity, St Johnstone Football Club came into existence in early 1885. The club's name was derived from Saint John's Toun, the ancient name of Perth, the city in which the club is based. The team played their first match on 7 March 1885 and emerged victorious, defeating Caledonian Railway 1-0.

Their first ground was a vacant piece of land called Craigie Haugh. This was later named Recreation Grounds and was officially opened on 15 August 1885 when Queen's Park hammered Our Boys from Dundee by six goals to nil. St Johnstone contested their home matches at Recreation Grounds until 1924 at which time, after outgrowing the ground, they moved on to Muirton Park at the north end of Perth.

Muirton Park would be home to St Johnstone for the next sixty-five years, and the inaugural match at the ground was a Scottish First Division fixture against Queen's Park on Christmas Day of 1924. The Saints had returned to the top flight of Scottish football the previous May after winning the Second Division championship, their first major honour, and finished a respectable eleventh in the First Division in

1924/25. They remained in the top division for five years until they were relegated after finishing bottom of the heap in 1929/30.

Under the management of former Rangers stalwart Tommy Muirhead, St Johnstone regained their place among Scottish football's elite in 1932 when, aided by thirty-six goals from top goalscorer Jimmy Benson, they finished runners-up to East Stirlingshire in the Second Division. The club held on to their top-flight status until the outbreak of the Second World War in 1939, finishing as high as fifth in seasons 1932/33 and 1934/35, and scored some fine victories in that period, notably against Rangers, who were the dominant side of that era. They defeated the Ibrox giants twice in successive seasons at Muirton Park, winning 3-1 on 18 November 1933 and 2-0 on 23 March 1935.

Another noteworthy success recorded by St Johnstone in the 1930s was the achievement of reaching the semi-finals of the Scottish Cup in 1934. The Perth outfit defeated Vale of Leithen in round two and, having received a bye in the third round, despatched Queen of the South in the quarter-final to set up a last-four showdown with First Division champions Rangers at Hampden Park. St Johnstone lost narrowly on the day, with a goal from James 'Doc' Marshall giving the Glasgow giants a 1-0 victory. Rangers then proceeded to hammer the other Saints, St Mirren, 5-0 in the final one month later.

When the Scottish League was reconstructed into an 'A' and 'B' division in the wake of the war, St Johnstone ended up in the latter and, despite further reconstruction in 1955, they remained in the lower tier until manager Bobby Brown, a man who had kept goal for Rangers with great success during the 1940s and '50s, guided them to the Second Division title in the 1959/60 season. However, the spectre of relegation haunted Muirton Park once again at the end of the 1961/62 season when they finished second bottom of the First Division. During the campaign, the Saints gave Rangers an almighty scare in the semi-final of the League Cup, storming into a 2-0 lead before succumbing by three goals to two after extra-time, but they failed to reproduce that form over a sustained period in the league and were relegated on goal average.

A third Second Division title saw St Johnstone bounce straight back up to the higher echelons of Scottish Football in 1962/63, and the club also made their second successive appearance in the semi-finals in the League Cup. On this occasion, though, Hearts comprehensively defeated the Perth side by four goals to nil.

After a successful spell at the helm, Bobby Brown vacated the manager's chair in 1967 to take over the reins of the Scottish national team and Willie Ormond took charge at Muirton Park. Over the next few years, Ormond, a celebrated member of Hibernian's much-lauded 'Famous Five' forward line that had terrorised defences in the late forties and fifties, began to sculpt one of the most celebrated sides in the club's history.

For the majority of the 1960s, St Johnstone had finished in the lower half of the First Division table, but Ormond managed to steer them to a sixth-place finish in 1968/69 and, a season later, took his charges to Hampden to contest the League Cup final. It was the first time the Saints had appeared in the final of one of the major competitions in Scotland.

Drawn in Section Three alongside Kilmarnock, Partick Thistle and Dundee, the Perth side romped into the quarter-finals, topping the group with a 100 percent record. They scored a magnificent twenty-two goals over the course of the six sectional matches, with Partick bearing the brunt, shipping twelve goals in the two matches between the sides. The Firhill outfit were pummelled 8-1 on their own ground and 4-0 at Muirton Park, with Henry Hall hitting a hat-trick for the Saints in the first match. In the last eight, St Johnstone drew Falkirk and the Perth side continued their free-scoring run over the two-leg tie, comprehensively sweeping aside the Brockville Bairns 11-3 on aggregate.

Goals from McCarry and Aitken took care of Motherwell in the semi-final and now only Jock Stein's Celtic stood in the way of the silverware. However, this was one of the greatest-ever Celtic teams, one that was on its way to a fifth successive League Championship crown and a second European Cup final appearance in four years. Nevertheless, they found it tough against Willie Ormond's side, and only a Bertie Auld goal separated the teams at the final whistle. St Johnstone drew praise from the national press for their performance and, but for a couple of great saves from Celtic custodian John Fallon, may well have at least forced extra-time.

This was arguably the greatest era in St Johnstone's history. Captained by Benny Rooney, they had star turns like Henry Hall, a prolific striker who would score 114 goals in 253 appearances for the Saints, John Connolly, a cultured left-sided player, and a full-back partnership of John Lambie (later to make a name for himself during his time in charge of Partick Thistle) and Willie Coburn.

ALLY McCOIST

Buoyed by their success in reaching the League Cup final, St Johnstone took the First Division by storm in 1970/71, finishing third, three points ahead of Rangers and only twelve points behind champions Celtic. They defeated the blue half of the Old Firm both home and away in the league, winning 2-1 at Muirton Park in December and 2-0 at Ibrox in the penultimate match of the season in April. The third-place finish earned St Johnstone a UEFA Cup place for 1971/72, the first time they would take part in European competition in the club's history. And it turned out to be relatively successful, too: victories over Hamburg and Vasas Budapest took them into the third round where they eventually succumbed to Yugoslav outfit Zeljeznicar.

Like Bobby Brown before him, Willie Ormond left St Johnstone to become manager of Scotland in 1973, and he proceeded to enjoy great success with the national team, leading the nation through arguably their finest World Cup campaign in West Germany in the summer of 1974. Drawn alongside holders Brazil, Yugoslavia and Zaire, the Scots drew 1-1 with the Yugoslavs, 0-0 against Brazil and beat the Zairians 2-0 courtesy of goals from Joe Jordan and Peter Lorimer. Unfortunately, the Scots were robbed of a place in the next round on goal difference, thus becoming the first country to be eliminated from the World Cup with an unbeaten record.

After Ormond left Muirton Park, the excellent side he had built began to break up, although St Johnstone remained in the top flight until the end of the 1975/76 season. The Scottish League had undergone a facelift in the summer of 1975, with the First and Second Divisions being split into three leagues, the Premier Division, the First Division and the Second Division. The Saints were one of the original ten to make up the Premier Division, but their stay among the elite was short-lived: they won only three of their thirty-six fixtures and were left rooted firmly to the foot of the table with only eleven points on the board.

When Ally McCoist arrived at Muirton Park in December 1978, St Johnstone were still enduring life in the First Division. The giddy highs of the early part of the decade were now becoming a distant and fading memory, with the club finishing eleventh in the league in 1976/77 and eighth in 1977/78.

The St Johnstone squad at that time was a mixture of youth and experience. The side was captained by Drew Rutherford, a man who would go on to make 298 appearances for the Saints, and contained the rugged striker John Brogan, the fans' favourite. Signed in 1977, Brogan was a proven goalscorer and he ended up having an enormous influence on the career of the young sixteen-year-old who was cutting his professional football 'teeth' at Muirton Park. 'I learned so much just playing beside him,' McCoist recalled some years later. 'He taught me how a striker, more than any other player, has to think quickly. He could see an opportunity before it had happened, and when it did happen his reactions were like lightning.'[1]

McCoist thoroughly enjoyed his early experiences of the professional game, even if the trip to training two nights a week was both arduous and tiring. When the bell sounded at the end of the school day, McCoist would make his way to his mother's workplace in East Kilbride where he would grab some much-needed sustenance before boarding the bus to Glasgow. On arrival at Glasgow's Queen Street station, he jumped on to the 17:35 train bound for Perth, which arrived at quarter to seven. The final leg of the journey was a short taxi ride to Muirton Park, where he would undergo a hard training session before repeating the journey in reverse. The result was a midnight return to East Kilbride, but although fatigued at the end of the day, McCoist knew his commitment would reap its own rewards in the longer term.

At least he wasn't alone on the journey. Team-mates such as John Pelosi, Tam McNeill, Jackie O'Brien and Danny Scullion also made the same train journey, and while McCoist passed the time catching up with his school homework, his colleagues would run a card school to help while away the seventy-minute train ride to Tayside. Although his companions were quick to take the rise out of the young upstart, as most professional footballers are prone to do, they were also very protective of McCoist and looked out for him, particularly in his early days in the game.

As he had been told when he signed for the club, McCoist spent much of his early days plying his trade in the reserves in the now-unfamiliar role of midfielder. He made his first senior appearance in Scottish football on 7 April 1979, donning the St Johnstone number eight jersey in a 3-0 victory against Raith Rovers. The young debutant played well, and was involved in the move that led to the Saints' second goal scored by Pat Ward.

McCoist kept his place in the starting line-up for the next three league games, but St Johnstone lost all three, going down 4-2 to Ayr United at

Somerset Park, 1-0 against Clydebank at Kilbowie and then suffering a 2-0 reverse against Stirling Albion at home. This terrible run of results sucked St Johnstone into the relegation quagmire at the foot of the First Division. With McCoist still only sixteen, manager Alex Stuart felt that he required the experience of his older players for the remainder of the campaign and the youngster was left out of the action for the last four league matches.

Three wins from those four games was enough to preserve St Johnstone's First Division status and they finished the 1978/79 season in twelfth position in the table, one place above the drop zone, managing to stave off relegation to the Second Division by finishing six points clear of second bottom Montrose. The club's form in the cup competitions was nothing to write home about either, with exits at the first hurdle of both the League Cup (a 2-0 aggregate loss to Second Division Berwick Rangers) and the Scottish Cup (a 4-2 defeat to Premier Division Morton in a replay after the first game away from home at Cappielow had ended 1-1).

With his promising career still very much in its infancy, the appearance of the name A. McCoist on the team-sheet for the first eleven was sporadic. In his second season at Muirton Park in 1979/80, he made his first appearance as a substitute in the first league match, a 2-2 draw with Hamilton Academical, and over the course of the campaign made a total of fifteen league appearances, nine as part of the starting eleven and six as a substitute. He also made his Scottish Cup debut in January 1980, but St Johnstone lost in the third round for the second successive season, going down 3-1 to the eventual First Division runners-up Airdrie. The result was disappointing to say the least, as the winners of the tie had been drawn to meet Premier Division pacesetters Aberdeen at Pittodrie in round four.

In addition to their early demise in the Cup, St Johnstone endured yet another poor season in the First Division, languishing in the bottom half of the table and ending the campaign in eleventh place, six points clear of relegation. The poor finish effectively cost Alex Stuart his job, and he was succeeded in the close season by Alex Rennie. The arrival of Rennie, part of the playing staff at Muirton Park during the sixties and seventies, would prove a pivotal moment in Ally McCoist's football career.

Although he now had several first-team appearances under his belt, McCoist was still without a goal in competitive football. He had netted a double in a friendly match against Dundee on 16 January 1980 and another in a pre-season friendly with Hartlepool that ended in a 2-2 draw, but in the competitive matches he had appeared in he had played mainly in a midfield role and, although he did like to get forward, opportunities to get on the scoresheet had so far eluded him. That was all about to change, though, thanks to the foresight of Alex Rennie.

St Johnstone were rocked in the summer of 1980 when club legend John Brogan walked out on the Muirton Park side after a clash with the club's board over wages. Arguably the best goalscorer outside the Premier Division at that time, Brogan had netted twenty-nine goals in the season just finished (he would go on to score 222 goals in a career that also took him to Albion Rovers, Hibernian, Hamilton and Stirling Albion, and his 115 goals for St Johnstone is still a club record today), so his departure left a huge void to be filled. Rennie felt that the man to step into Brogan's shooting boots was McCoist, so the youngster was moved forward from his midfield berth with the hope that he could take over Brogan's mantle until the dispute was settled. It proved an inspirational piece of management.

McCoist revelled in his new role and settled in immediately, scoring his first senior goal in St Johnstone's second league game of the season on 16 August 1980, volleying in a cross from Brannigan in the seventy-third minute of a 3-0 win over Dumbarton at Boghead. Having waited almost two years to score his first competitive goal he did not have to wait much longer for his second, as he netted the only goal of the Tayside derby the following weekend as the Saints defeated Dundee by one goal to nil at Muirton Park.

Despite losing 1-0 to Stirling Albion in their opening league match and falling to Clydebank over two legs in the first round of the League Cup, St Johnstone were showing no ill-effects from the loss of Brogan and made a promising start in the First Division title race. They were in the top half of the table for most of the early months of the season, and only some wretched home form prevented Rennie's men from pushing early pacesetters Hibernian for top spot.

Their excellent start had much to do with McCoist's electrifying goal-scoring form. The eighteen-year-old was 'on fire' in the early matches, netting a brace against Dunfermline at East End Park on 20 September and following this with goals against Berwick Rangers (1-1), Motherwell (2-2) and Clydebank (2-0), with the latter result going some way to avenging the League Cup exit the team had suffered at the hands of the Bankies.

McCoist's form was winning him a whole host of new admirers; none more so than Andy Roxburgh, who was in charge of the Scotland Under-18 side. Indeed, Roxburgh was so impressed with the striker's early-season exploits that he selected McCoist for the Under-18 side due to travel to Reykjavik in October to face Iceland in the first leg of the European Youth Championships qualifying match. Roxburgh had the feeling that McCoist was on the cusp of becoming the next household name in Scotland, believing he had the ability to follow in the footsteps of the likes of Charlie Nicholas, John Wark and Ray Stewart, who had all enjoyed a solid grounding at Under-18 level before graduating to the Under-21s and beyond.

The manager's lofty opinion of the St Johnstone star did not appear to be misplaced either when, on a freezing cold October evening on a public park in the Icelandic capital (the match was supposed to be played in the national stadium, but was switched at the last minute by the Icelandic FA), McCoist marked his first appearance for his country by netting a crucial goal, the only one of the game, after nineteen minutes, when his shot from thirty-five yards deceived the Iceland goalkeeper.

McCoist retained his place for the return leg ten days later, and was among the goals again as the Scots booked their place at the following summer's European Youth Championships with a comfortable 3-1 victory at Parkhead. A meagre 500 supporters, including national team manager Jock Stein, turned out to cheer on the colts, and they watched Manchester United's teen sensation Scott McGarvey fire the Scots in front, before home favourite Dave Kenny doubled the lead. The Icelanders reduced the arrears after the interval, but McCoist secured the victory in the sixty-second minute when he thundered a low cross from Ayr United's Colin Hume into the net.

Further recognition followed at the end of October when McCoist won his third cap in a 3-1 victory over Northern Ireland at Somerset Park in Ayr – inevitably his name found its way on to the scoresheet – and in mid-November he journeyed with Roxburgh and his squad to Monaco to represent Scotland in the Monaco Youth Tournament. Eight teams entered the event, with the participants being split into two sections of four. The winning team from each section would then meet to contest the final.

The squad was littered with some of the best young talent Scotland had to offer. Under the watchful eye of Roxburgh and his assistant, Walter Smith, McCoist was joined by Neale Cooper and Eric Black of

Aberdeen, Davie Bowman of Hearts, Iain Ferguson of Dundee and goalkeeper Nicky Walker of Leicester City. Having now left school, McCoist had taken up a part-time business studies course in Hamilton, but his involvement in the tournament in Monaco brought that to a premature end. Faced with the decision of either sitting his exams or travelling to Monaco, there was only going to be one winner: the course was abandoned and McCoist boarded a plane bound for the principality.

The Scots were grouped with West Germany, Switzerland and France, but they got off to a poor start when they lost 1-0 to the Germans in their opening fixture. Eintracht Frankfurt's Ralf Faulkenmayer scored the only goal of a game in which McCoist had the dubious honour of becoming the first Scottish player to cool off in the 'sin bin' that was under trial at the event. Two minutes into the second half, he was guilty of fouling a German player by the name of Herdst, an offence for which he was duly admonished by the referee and banished to the sin bin for the statutory period of six minutes.

Two days later, Roxburgh's side faced the Swiss, but they had to do so without the services of their captain Neale Cooper, who was recalled by his club side Aberdeen, who required him to sit on the bench for their Premier Division fixture against Partick Thistle. The Scots played very well against a Swiss side that had forced a 1-1 draw against France in their opening fixture, and could well have been a few goals ahead at the interval but for the reflexes of the Switzerland goalkeeper. He denied McCoist twice in the opening period, but the eighteen-year-old eventually got the better of him in the fiftieth minute when he nudged home a cross from Hearts midfielder Dave Bowman at the far post. A second goal from stand-in skipper David Moyes in the seventy-eighth minute gave Scotland a 2-0 win, and that success, coupled with France's 5-0 thrashing of West Germany, suddenly gave rise to the prospect of Roxburgh's side making it through to the final. A 1-0 win in their final group fixture against the French would suffice, provided the West Germans did not conjure up a six-goal victory against the Swiss.

For twenty-two minutes of the match against France the dream of meeting Italy in the final looked like becoming a reality. In the fifty-fifth minute, McCoist maintained his excellent record in a dark blue jersey by netting his fifth goal in only his sixth appearance in Scotland colours with a fine volleyed finish, but just when the end was in sight, the French scored a controversial equaliser to eliminate the gallant young Scots. A disputed free-kick was awarded against Scotland, which was quickly taken and the ball found its way to the Nantes sweeper Michel der Zakarian who beat Nicky Walker with a fine header. It was a devastating finale, and many of the youngsters wept in the dressing room at the end of the match. 'Our dressing room was gutted at full time,' recalled McCoist. 'I don't mind admitting I cried my eyes out. I couldn't believe football could be so cruel.'[2]

McCoist's involvement in Monaco meant that he missed out on St Johnstone's league match against Dunfermline Athletic at Muirton Park, and his presence was sorely missed as the Saints were defeated by four goals to two. Normal service was soon resumed, though, and McCoist was on the scoresheet again in late November, with Motherwell once again on the wrong end of his sharp-shooting skills as the young striker bagged another double in a 2-2 draw at Muirton Park. The following weekend his solitary goal against third-placed Ayr at Muirton Park was enough to halt a six-match winless run at home, although he was powerless to prevent a heavy 4-0 defeat against Hibernian at Easter Road in the next league match that ended the Saints' unbeaten away record. Despite this result, though, St Johnstone were still handily placed in the league, lying fifth, which was a far cry from the relegation struggle the club had endured for the previous two seasons.

McCoist's scoring exploits at club and international level had suddenly thrust him into the limelight, and he was beginning to attract interest from other clubs. His free-scoring start to the season had not gone unnoticed and no fewer than five scouts watched him score that winning goal against Ayr United. At the age of eighteen, he was regarded as being one of the hottest young players in the Scottish game, with a market value of anywhere between £150,000 and £300,000 being touted.

With McCoist in such prolific form it was no surprise that St Johnstone were among the post-Christmas favourites for promotion to the Premier Division. And the young striker started the New Year just as he had ended the old one, grabbing the only goal of the game in the home match with Berwick Rangers. He was among the goals again in an epic match with fellow promotion chasers Ayr United at Somerset Park a fortnight later, scoring twice in a pulsating 3-3 draw.

League business was placed to one side the following Saturday, the penultimate weekend of January, for the opening round of the Scottish Cup. St Johnstone were drawn against Hamilton Academical at Douglas

Park and they progressed to the next round courtesy of a comprehensive 3-0 win. The prize for the Perth side was a plum draw against the mighty Glasgow Rangers (McCoist's boyhood heroes) in the fourth round at Muirton Park. Although he had played, and scored, against sides with experience of playing in Scotland's top flight, the match against Rangers would undoubtedly be the biggest of McCoist's career to date.

Although still a formidable force in the Scottish game, Rangers were in the middle of a lean spell in the early 1980s. After having ended the 1979/80 season without a trophy, they were enduring a terrible run in the Premier Division, having won only four of their previous twelve league matches, and the week before travelling to Perth to face St Johnstone they had gone down 2-1 to Dundee United at Tannadice to fall further behind the leaders in the chase for the championship. Thus, in the midst of growing disquiet among the Rangers faithful, their manager, John Greig, was looking at the St Valentine's Day cup-tie in Perth as a means of restoring some confidence in his battered and bruised squad.

And initially, at least, it looked as though Rangers would do just that, as goals from Colin McAdam and Ian Redford saw them race into a 2-0 lead, but what followed took St Johnstone to the verge of one of the biggest giant-killing acts in Scottish Cup history. The plucky home side refused to be overwhelmed by their illustrious opponents, and goals from Jim Docherty and John Brogan, back in the line-up after resolving his pay dispute shortly before Christmas, restored parity, and when Brogan scored again to put St Johnstone ahead for the first time, Rangers were on the ropes and rocking. The scoreline remained at 3-2 as the game entered its closing moments and pulses were racing on the terraces, in the dugouts and on the pitch. It took an injury-time goal from Redford, his second of the game, to spare Rangers' blushes and force a replay at Ibrox four days later.

McCoist, no doubt overwhelmed by the occasion, did not play well in the match, but he was intent on rectifying that when he turned out at Ibrox the following Wednesday for the replay. However, there was to be no glory for the visitors, as Rangers took command of the match, eventually running out 3-1 winners and going on to win the trophy by defeating Dundee United in the final in May. McCoist, though, playing in the Ibrox amphitheatre for the first time, made an impression on both the club's hierarchy and the home fans, as he grabbed St Johnstone's consolation goal, forcing the ball over the line after the

Rangers goalkeeper Peter McCloy had parried a long-range shot from Tam McNeill.

In addition to success at club level and youth international level, McCoist gained further recognition in the international arena when he was selected in Scotland's semi-professional squad for a four-team tournament in Holland. Although McCoist did not play in any of the games against either England, Italy or the host nation, the whole experience was a valuable one and it represented yet another step up the professional game's steep learning curve. His selection for the semi-professional squad was further acknowledgment that his stock was on the rise and, in the wake of the cup-tie with Rangers, he added to his league tally when he netted his fourteenth league goal of the season in a 4-1 home win over Dunfermline Athletic, a result that stretched the Saints' unbeaten run in the league to eight matches and pushed them up to fourth in the table.

Next on the agenda were relegation-threatened Berwick Rangers at Muirton Park, and with the match being filmed by a television unit from Scottish Television, McCoist chose this match against the 'wee Rangers' to showcase his burgeoning talents to a wider audience. He opened the scoring after four minutes when he slotted home a pass from John Brogan and doubled his tally seven minutes later with a firm header before completing his first professional hat-trick in the twenty-sixth minute when he knocked in a rebound after the Berwick goalkeeper had parried his rasping drive from 25 yards. Although Berwick pegged the score back to 3-2 early in the second half, goals from Kilgour and Brogan restored St Johnstone's three-goal cushion before McCoist added some extra shine to the final result by firing in his fourth goal in the dying seconds of the game.

St Johnstone, now lying third in the First Division, were in with a really good chance of finishing in one of the two promotion spots and they cemented their claim for one of those places when they travelled to Easter Road in mid-March and beat the league leaders Hibernian by two goals to one, thanks to goals from Brogan (his fifth in three games) and Docherty. A 4-1 reverse at Dens Park in April – McCoist netted the visitors' only goal – against fellow challengers Dundee threatened to derail their promotion charge, but a 2-0 win over Raith Rovers helped steer the Saints back on course, and when goals from McCoist and Brogan forced a 2-2 draw with East Stirlingshire in their penultimate league match, Alex Rennie's side leapfrogged Raith to occupy the coveted second promotion place for the first time that season. All they had to do now was stay there.

With Hibernian confirmed as champions, there was effectively a three-way fight for second place between St Johnstone, Dundee and Raith Rovers. St Johnstone were now in pole position going into the final round of fixtures, and they retained their position when they narrowly won their last game of the season by one goal to nil against already relegated Stirling Albion at Muirton Park. With Raith drawing their last fixture, only Tayside rivals Dundee stood between St Johnstone and a return to the big time. The Dens Park side lay one point behind, but had a game in hand over the Perth side, which was scheduled to take place a week after St Johnstone had completed their fixture list. As they had a superior goal difference, Dundee only needed to take a point from their final match against East Stirlingshire to clinch promotion to the Premier Division, but they claimed both points courtesy of a 1-0 victory. It was a bitter end to what had been a tremendous season for St Johnstone. They finished the campaign on fifty-one points, six behind champions Hibernian and an agonising one point adrift of Dundee.

Although disappointed at missing out on the prospect of Premier Division football, McCoist could at least take consolation from his own form during the season. He missed just one league match over the course of the campaign – the 4-2 home defeat by Dunfermline in November as a result of his trip to Monaco with the Scotland Youth team – and his goal in the 2-2 draw with East Stirlingshire was his twenty-second in thirty-eight league appearances. His strike against Rangers in the Scottish Cup took his final tally to twenty-three goals in forty-three appearances, and he was rewarded for his outstanding contribution when the St Johnstone Sports and Social Club voted him as their Player of the Year for the 1980/81 season, his first individual accolade in the professional game.

However, there was no rest for the prodigious youngster. Just days after the curtain fell on the domestic season, McCoist joined up with the Scotland Under-18 squad bound for West Germany, where they were taking part in the European Under-18 Championships. Having previously been run under the guise of the FIFA Junior tournament and the European Junior tournament, this was the first year the competition had operated as the European Under-18 Championships, and the Scots were one of sixteen nations taking part.

The entrants were split into four groups of four, with the group winner progressing to the knockout stages of the tournament. Scotland found themselves pitched into one of the toughest groups alongside Spain, Austria, and defending European champions England, with the Austrians providing the opposition in the Scots' opening match of the competition. Orchestrated by sixteen-year-old Paul McStay, the Scots produced a 'superb display of open, attacking football'[3], but despite their best efforts, Andy Roxburgh's side were thwarted by an inspired display by the Austrian goalkeeper. Even the prolific McCoist was denied a goal when the keeper blocked his close-range effort in the forty-sixth minute. Scotland's industry eventually paid off, though, when Manchester United's Scott McGarvey struck the only goal of the game with five minutes remaining.

Forty-eight hours later, a staggering crowd of 35,000 turned up at the Tivoli Stadium in Aachen to watch Scotland's second match, an encounter with the Auld Enemy, England. The reigning European champions and pre-tournament favourites boasted a squad bursting with talent, but having lost their opening game against Spain 2-1, they emerged for their clash with Scotland with their future in the competition hanging in the balance. And given the nature of their display in their first match, there was no reason for the Scots pups to feel intimidated by their English counterparts. Indeed, they went into the match full of confidence, bidding to emulate their senior colleagues who, just four days earlier, had defeated England 1-0 at Wembley thanks to a John Robertson penalty.

Although there was no repeat of the wonderful football showcased against the Austrians, Scotland duly completed the Double to end England's reign as European champions with a performance based on grit, determination and fighting spirit, traits that have historically been synonymous with the Scottish national team. The only goal of the contest arrived after just eight minutes when McGarvey, the goal-scoring hero against Austria, turned provider, sending in a marvellous cross that McCoist headed into the net. It was the eighteen-year-old's first-ever goal against the Auld Enemy.

With the Spaniards defeating the Austrians 3-0, the outcome of the Spain v Scotland match would decide Group D. Boasting a superior goal difference, Spain only needed to draw the game to progress to the last four; for Scotland, nothing less than a win would do. What unfolded in

22

Duren was a brutal match punctuated by a number of cynical fouls by the savage Spaniards. There were no fewer than eighty-two stoppages during the course of the match, with the French referee, Daniel Lambert, trying manfully to keep a lid on the proceedings. Remarkably in the midst of such malevolent behaviour, he dished out just three bookings to Spanish players and the match had moved into injury-time before one of their players, Sergio Marrera, was ordered off after he kicked out at Scott McGarvey.

Just as had been the case earlier in the season in Monaco, the Scots were eliminated with an unbeaten record. Spain took the lead in the fifty-second minute thanks to a diving header from Real Sociedad's Baquero, but Scotland responded in typically bullish fashion and restored parity within four minutes. Just minutes after McGarvey had had a goal ruled out for offside, McCoist stepped forward to score a superb goal, bending a free-kick from 25 yards round the defensive wall and into the top left-hand corner. It was a wonderful effort from the St Johnstone starlet and it prompted the Scots to flood forward in search of the winner. Alas, it was not forthcoming, although Celtic's David Moyes did strike the post with a header six minutes after McCoist's equaliser.

Although Scotland had fallen at the first hurdle, the trip to West Germany catapulted Ally McCoist to the attention of clubs all over the United Kingdom. Suddenly he was hot property, with his prowess in front of goal reportedly attracting interest from English giants Tottenham Hotspur and Wolverhampton Wanderers, and when St Johnstone were drawn in a tantalising League Cup section alongside Premier Division sides Celtic, Hibernian and St Mirren at the outset of the 1981/82 season, the chase for McCoist's signature really began to hot up.

The Saints began their Section One fixtures with a trip to Easter Road to face newly promoted Hibernian. On their previous visit to Edinburgh in March, the Perth side had won 2-1, and they repeated the scoreline to get their season off to a flying start, with McCoist opening the scoring and then setting up the winning goal, scored by Beedie.

Next up were reigning Premier Division champions Celtic at Muirton Park, but the lofty status of Billy McNeill's side did not frighten the home team. They had after all given Celtic's Old Firm rivals Rangers a run for their money at the same venue only six months previously, so Alex Rennie and his players were confident of causing another shock. And they did exactly that, felling the Glasgow giants in dramatic fashion with a 2-0 win. McCoist broke the deadlock seven minutes before the interval when he latched on to a Joe Pelosi pass, outpaced Willie Garner and rounded Celtic goalkeeper Pat Bonner before slotting the ball into the back of the net. He had a hand in the second goal too, winning the penalty that was converted by substitute Jim Morton.

Claiming the scalp of Celtic was a splendid result for St Johnstone, who now topped the section after the opening two games, and the First Division side looked set to sail into the quarter-finals. However, the chances that their prolific young forward would still be in their ranks should that circumstance arise were looking increasingly unlikely: the journalists in the Scottish media who conducted the match analysis for the Celtic game were purring about the maturity of McCoist's displays. In his match report in the *Evening Times*, Chick Young reckoned that McCoist was 'a snip'[4] at his £400,000 valuation, and that he had taken his goal with 'the arrogance and cool of a natural born striker'[5], while Alex Cameron in the *Daily Record* called the youngster Perth's 'best asset since the advent of Bell's [Bell's Whisky had its origins in Perth in the late 1800s] '.[6]

Despite such lavish praise, McCoist was remaining grounded. 'I'm happy enough to leave everything to the boss,' he said. 'OK, I want to be a full-time player and I would like that chance as soon as possible. But I will be sad to leave St Johnstone. They have been tremendous with me and I'll stay there until they decide that a move is on. I'm willing to be guided by them.'[7]

Press speculation linking McCoist with a move to England was now an almost daily occurrence, but it did not appear to faze the eighteen-year-old and he scored his third goal in as many games when he netted in the Saints' 3-2 home defeat against St Mirren three days after the Celtic triumph. A number of scouts had been in attendance as St Johnstone's unbeaten start to the campaign had drawn to a close and when Alex Rennie took his team to Parkhead to tackle Celtic the following Wednesday, representatives from Wolverhampton Wanderers and Middlesbrough were among the 14,600 crowd. They watched Celtic gain revenge for the shock loss at Muirton Park, with the Hoops hammering the visitors by four goals to one, and they saw McCoist nullified for most of the evening. However, the Celtic defence could not keep him quiet for the whole night, and he maintained his goal-a-game ratio by netting St Johnstone's consolation goal.

Joining Middlesbrough and Wolves in the chase for McCoist's signature were Sunderland, and Rangers were also interested, tabling a £300,000 bid on the eve of St Johnstone's fifth League Cup sectional tie with Hibernian. Following the 2-1 defeat against Hibernian, a match that would be his last in the blue of St Johnstone, McCoist spoke with Rangers manager John Greig before, in the company of his father, Alex Rennie and the St Johnstone chairman Alex Lamond, embarking on a whistle-stop tour of each of the interested English clubs to talk over what was on offer.

By the end of a hectic weekend, reports in the media suggested that Wolves had won the race for McCoist's signature. Their manager, John Barnwell, had acquired the services of the rugged Scotland striker Andy Gray for a record fee of £1.5 million in 1979, and he had designs on creating an all-tartan strikeforce at Molineux. However, despite making a very good offer, McCoist elected to join Sunderland instead. 'Most people thought I would agree to join Wolves,' he told the *Glasgow Herald*, 'but the thing that swayed it for Sunderland in the end was that they are just that little bit nearer home. I'm a bit of a home bird and East Kilbride is only a couple of hours away from Sunderland.'[8]

The decision to join Sunderland also meant that Rangers, McCoist's boyhood heroes, had missed out on snaring the talented striker. Ever since he could remember he had dreamed of pulling that famous royal blue jersey over his head and running out at Ibrox as a Rangers player, but the attraction of the English First Division and the prospect of pitting his wits against centre-halves such as Alan Hansen and Mark Lawrenson at Liverpool and Terry Butcher and Russell Osman at high-flying Ipswich Town tipped the scales in Sunderland's favour. 'The lure of playing in the English First Division was all that stopped me going to Rangers,' he said. 'John Greig impressed me a lot. The set-up was good, too, and I knew that I would have the chance of playing in Europe. But it's been an ambition to play in the top league in England and that's what eventually took me south.'[9]

On Wednesday, 26 August 1981, Ally McCoist put pen to paper and signed for Sunderland in a deal that cost the Wearsiders £400,000, a club record fee and a significant outlay for such a young player. His three-year stay in Perth had yielded twenty-seven goals in sixty-eight appearances and had brought him international recognition in the shape of ten caps for the Scotland Under-18 team. He had developed both physically and mentally during his time at Muirton Park and was now on the verge of opening a new and potentially exciting chapter in his embryonic career. Sadly, his stint south of the border did not turn out quite the way he had planned.

CHAPTER THREE

ROKER DAYS:1981–83

Sunderland Football Club was established in October 1879. Their founder was a Scot, a schoolteacher and graduate of the University of Glasgow by the name of James Allan. Allan, who had been teaching at Hendon Board School, formed the team with some of his colleagues and originally named their side Sunderland and District Teachers' Association Football Club. After a year, however, the doors were opened to people from outside the teaching profession, and the name of the club was changed to Sunderland AFC.

The newly formed club played their first games at the Blue House Field at Hendon and spent two years there before moving to Ashbrooke, and then, after a similar time period, on to Roker and Fulwell. In 1886, they moved to Newcastle Road, a ground that boasted grandstands around its perimeter and which could hold 15,000 patrons.

Two years earlier, in 1884, Sunderland AFC had won their first trophy, the Durham Senior Cup, after an impressive 7-2 victory over Aston Villa, one of the teams who would go on to become one of the founder members of the Football League in 1888. Sunderland were themselves elected to the Football League in 1890 and, in only their second season in the highest echelon of English Football, were crowned champions, a feat they would repeat the following season and again in 1895 and 1902. This was a Football League made up of unfamiliar names such as Newton Heath (who later became Manchester United), Woolwich Arsenal (later Arsenal) and Ardwick (Manchester City). By now, Sunderland had taken up residence at Roker Park, a ground that was officially opened on 10 September 1898 when the home side christened their new abode with a 1-0 win over Liverpool.

The rich vein of success the club enjoyed in the late nineteenth and early twentieth century was to be short-lived, however. After a splendid season under manager Robert Kyle in 1913, when they won their fifth First Division title – amassing a record fifty-four points in the process – and were runners-up to Aston Villa in the FA Cup, it would take another twenty-three years, at the end of the 1935/36 season, before the championship trophy found its way back to Wearside. The following season, Sunderland, now under the guidance of Jimmy Cochrane, added to their roll of honour when they celebrated their maiden FA Cup victory, defeating Preston North End by three goals to one in the 1937 final thanks to goals from Bobby Gurney, Horatio 'Raich' Carter and Eddie Burbanks.

Sunderland never really got close to the top honours again after that triumph, although they were narrowly pipped to the title in the 1949/50 season, finishing third, a mere point behind champions Portsmouth. The club reached the last four of the FA Cup in 1938, 1955 and 1956, but their star was on the wane and, having flirted with relegation in 1956/57, when they finished twentieth, Sunderland were demoted for the first time in their history at the end of the 1957/58 season after they finished second bottom of the league and were relegated on goal difference along with Sheffield Wednesday.

They remained in the wilderness of Division Two for six seasons before gaining promotion back to the top flight under the management of Alan Brown in 1963/64, finishing as runners-up behind Leeds United. But after achieving promotion, Brown left to join Sheffield Wednesday and former Scotland manager Ian McColl took over the reins.

McColl, an excellent wing-half in the fêted Rangers side of the forties and fifties, had taken charge of Scotland in April 1961 and had enjoyed just over four successful years at the helm in what was an excellent era for the Scottish national side. Despite making a less than auspicious start – he lost his first match 9-3 to England at Wembley – he masterminded two revenge victories over the Auld Enemy in 1962 and 1963, with the 2-1 win at Wembley in 1963 still remembered with great fondness north of the border today. His remit at Roker Park was first to keep Sunderland in the top division and then to push them back into contention for the long-overdue silverware. He failed to deliver, though, and despite signing the supremely talented Jim Baxter from Rangers, he could do nothing other than stave off relegation for the three years he was in charge. McColl left the club in 1968, at which point Alan Brown was tempted back for a second spell at the helm. Brown kept Sunderland in the First Division until the end of the 1960s, but they bowed to the inevitable in 1969/70 and suffered the depression of relegation once again.

It was during this second spell as a Second Division club that Sunderland enjoyed arguably their greatest hour-and-a-half. In 1973, they became the first club outside the top division to win the FA Cup since the Second World War. En route to Wembley, the Wearsiders saw off Notts County, Reading, Manchester City, Luton Town and Arsenal to set up a date with Don Revie's Leeds United in the end-of-season showpiece.

Now managed by Bob Stokoe, Sunderland, up against one of the most revered club sides of that era, were massive underdogs. The Yorkshire side, boasting the likes of Peter Lorimer and Billy Bremner in their ranks, were in the midst of a particularly fruitful period in their history, having won the Inter-Cities Fairs Cup – the predecessor to the UEFA Cup – in 1967/68, before going on to collect the First Division title the following season, and they were the current holders of the FA Cup, having defeated Arsenal 1-0 in the 1971/72 final at Wembley. And Revie's side seemed certain to retain the trophy against a Sunderland side that had only managed to finish sixth in Division Two, but in a match that has gone down in the annals as one of the greatest shocks of all time, an inspired display by goalkeeper Jimmy Montgomery plus a goal from Ian Porterfield were enough to take the trophy back to the North East.

The FA Cup win granted Sunderland passage into European football for the first time in the club's history the following season and they acquitted themselves well in the European Cup-Winners' Cup, defeating Hungarian side Vasas Budapest 3-0 on aggregate in the opening round before succumbing to top Portuguese outfit Sporting Lisbon in round two.

This successful period stretched in to the mid-seventies, and Sunderland enjoyed a brief flirtation with the First Division after they won the Second Division title in 1975/76, but their return to the top flight lasted only one season. Their yo-yo like league fortunes continued for the remainder of the seventies, but in 1979/80, under manager Ken Knighton, they were promoted once again after finishing as Division Two runners-up behind Jock Wallace's Leicester City.

Although the Sunderland team that Ally McCoist joined ahead of the 1981/82 season was still resident in the First Division, they were still struggling at the wrong end of the table and battling valiantly to steer clear of relegation. The previous season, 1980/81, the Wearsiders had finished seventeenth in the league, only three points clear of the drop zone, and Knighton had parted company with the club four games from the end of the campaign. Mick Docherty took over in a caretaker capacity and had managed to guide the club to safety, although it took a final-day victory over Liverpool at Anfield to preserve Sunderland's First Division status, with Stan Cummins netting the all important goal in a 1-0 win over the European Cup winners.

Despite his side's last-day heroics, Docherty did not manage to secure the job on a permanent basis. He became reserve-team coach instead, and in that role he would become a great source of support for McCoist when the youngster struggled to adapt to the English game.

The Sunderland board chose to appoint Alan Durban, capped twenty-seven times for Wales and a First Division championship winner with Derby County during his playing days, as manager and he immediately indicated his intent to place more of an accent on youth development. Eighteen-year-old Ally McCoist was one of his first signings and Durban had high hopes for his new acquisition. He told the members of the press corps gathered to witness the unveiling of, in the opinion of *The Times*, 'the most wanted man in Scotland'[1]: 'I am just pleased that he has selected Sunderland not because of the money we have offered him, but because of the future he sees in the club. He is one of the best prospects to come out of Scotland in a long time and I hope he turns out to be another Kenny Dalglish or Steve Archibald.'

Unfortunately, McCoist failed to live up to Durban's billing. Despite his tender age, the large transfer fee shelled out to secure his services – he had just become the most expensive purchase in Sunderland's 102-year history – and the huge expectation of the Roker Park faithful placed a huge burden on the young Scot. And he had next to no time to settle in, either.

Having been signed and paraded in front of the media on Wednesday,

had returned home to Scotland to visit his parents with a view to travelling back to Sunderland on the day of the game in order to catch the team coach bound for Rotherham. However, a double dose of car trouble meant he arrived at Roker Park too late and missed the bus, so as the first team headed to Millmoor, McCoist was ordered to stay behind and turn out for the reserves in a match against Mansfield Town instead.

While two goals from Tam Ritchie helped Sunderland's top team to a 3-3 draw against Rotherham and a 5-3 aggregate win, McCoist racked up all four of Sunderland's goals in his second-string run-out against a hapless Mansfield side. However, any hopes Sunderland may have harboured of an extended cup run to help alleviate their Division One blues were extinguished in the very next round when Crystal Palace, a team who had not registered a win on their travels in the Second Division for almost twenty months, came to Roker Park and won 1-0 thanks to a goal from their Scottish skipper Jim Cannon.

Although McCoist's free-scoring performance for the second team had gone some way to restoring his confidence, goals in the First Division were proving a little harder to come by. In fairness, McCoist was not alone. Goal-scoring was proving a real problem on Wearside in the early months of the 1981/82 season, with Sunderland only managing to score seven times in their opening fourteen league matches, and in that run they had gone eight games without finding the net.

McCoist eventually chalked up his first goal for the Wearside club on his fifteenth league appearance, netting after seventy-eight minutes of a midweek fixture against Brian Clough's Nottingham Forest on 25 November. His goal was an important one, too. Sunderland had been 2-0 down, but goals from Rob Hindmarch and McCoist helped claw them back to level terms although a goal by the visitors in the last five minutes robbed the home side of a much-needed point.

Sunderland had managed to stop the rot in the league four days earlier when they visited Goodison Park and beat Everton 2-1, a result that marked their first league win since the triumph over Villa in September, but Durban's men failed to build on their success, and the defeat at the hands of Forest was the first of three successive losses, all of which plunged them deeper into trouble as Christmas approached. At least they weren't bottom of the heap over the festive period, as a 3-2 win over Manchester City at Maine Road six days before Christmas lifted Sunderland up to twenty-first place in the First Division.

This time the club managed to build on their victory, and they won their first league fixture of 1982, a morale-boosting 1-0 win over fellow strugglers Wolves. They did so without the services of their £400,000 striker, though. Having failed to add to his goal-scoring tally since notching his first goal against Nottingham Forest in November, McCoist paid the price for his profligacy by losing his place in the team. He made only two substitute appearances in Sunderland's next five matches, but buoyed by a goal from the penalty spot against Hull City reserves on 3 February, McCoist was recalled to the first eleven to help engineer a way out of the relegation zone when the club lurched through another rocky spell in February and March.

After defeating Wolverhampton Wanderers on 30 January, Durban's side picked up just two points in their next six league matches, but with the aid of McCoist's second goal in English football, Sunderland managed to arrest the decline in their fortunes when they defeated high-flying Southampton 2-0 at Roker Park on 10 March. It was a spectacular goal, too; a superb curling shot from the edge of the penalty area.

That triumph was Sunderland's first win in six games, but the writing still seemed to be on the wall with regard to relegation, particularly when they lost 2-0 at home to fellow relegation candidates Middlesbrough in early April. The result saw the North East rivals swap places in the league table, with Sunderland replacing the Ayresome Park side at the bottom of the heap with only eleven games of the season remaining.

However, just as the scribes were penning Sunderland's First Division obituary, the listing ship was steadied and Sunderland surged to safety. After the setback against Middlesbrough, Durban freshened up his team, with McCoist once again relegated to the sidelines. After having enjoyed his longest run in the first team since his arrival in the North East, a sequence of seven successive starts, he was replaced in the side by another nineteen-year-old, Colin West, and the change certainly worked, as West found the net six times in those final eleven games as Sunderland embarked on an unbeaten run of six matches, with wins chalked up over Stoke City, Birmingham City, Everton and West Brom, coupled with two draws against Ipswich and Tottenham Hotspur.

They were now sixteenth in the table, and although the sequence was brought to a shuddering halt following a 6-1 defeat by Coventry City at Highfield Road, five points from their final four league games were just enough to keep them in the division, although the club and its supporters faced an anxious wait to confirm their survival. Sunderland completed their fixture list with a 1-0 win over Manchester City at Roker Park, but fellow strugglers Leeds United, lying two points behind, had a game in hand which, if they won, would mean they would stay up and Sunderland would drop into Division Two. The Wearsiders survived, though, when West Brom beat Leeds 2-0 at The Hawthorns, and the Yorkshire side bid adieu to the top flight along with Wolves and Middlesbrough, ironically two of the clubs McCoist had turned down when he had opted to sign for Sunderland nine months previously.

McCoist had undoubtedly failed to live up to expectations in his maiden season in England. His star, one that had shone so brightly and vibrantly only twelve months previously, appeared to be on the wane, a fact borne out by a paltry return of just two goals in twenty-eight league appearances during his debut campaign. This was clearly not the kind of return the Sunderland board had expected when they had signed a cheque for close to half a million pounds the previous August, and it looked likely that McCoist's stay on Wearside was to be a short-lived one.

Matters were not helped when his personal life suffered a setback during the campaign: his parents had decided to separate and the situation merely compounded the misery McCoist was engulfed in at the time. Things were not going to plan on the park, he was homesick and, on top of everything else, this was the last thing he wanted to have to deal with. He would, however, look back in later life with regret that his own plight at that time meant that he was not more supportive and sympathetic towards his parents during what must have been an incredibly difficult period.

On the pitch, however, McCoist knew there was only one way to silence the critics: he had to get back into the team and improve his scoring return. However, it looked, for a while at least, that he would not be given that opportunity when Alan Durban made a bid to lure Gordon Strachan from the northeast of Scotland to the northeast of England. Strachan may not have been direct competition for McCoist, the flame-haired dynamo was, after all, a midfielder, but part of the proposed deal to Strachan's current employers, Aberdeen, was to offer McCoist to the Pittodrie side as a makeweight in the transaction. The Aberdeen hierarchy had no interest in conducting business, though, and issued a hands-off warning to Durban and any other potential suitors. Strachan, who had turned in three fine performances for Scotland during their World Cup campaign in the summer, was an integral part of an Aberdeen side on the up; a side who were scrapping toe-to-toe for the major honours north of the border with the Old Firm of Rangers and Celtic and the emerging Dundee United. So Durban had to look elsewhere for new recruits and McCoist, for the time being at least, was staying put in England.

Undeterred by the pre-season rumblings in the transfer market, McCoist was determined to bounce back from that wretched first season and hand those who were suggesting he could not cut the mustard at the top level of the game a large helping of humble pie. He laid the foundations of his revival back on home soil, scoring three goals in three games against Dunfermline Athletic, Dundee and former club St Johnstone during Sunderland's tour of Scotland.

McCoist carried the confidence he had gathered from his successful pre-season outings into the opening act of the new season, a First Division curtain-raiser against Aston Villa at Villa Park. For the second successive season, Sunderland kicked off their campaign against European champions, as Villa, one of the leading lights in the English game in the early eighties, had won the European Cup by beating Bayern Munich in Rotterdam in May. Their success on foreign soil meant that an English club's name had been etched on Europe's premier club trophy for the sixth year in a row.

The match on 28 August was Villa's first competitive match at Villa Park since their European triumph, but Sunderland and McCoist spoiled their homecoming party. The Wearsiders brought Villa crashing down from their lofty pedestal by winning 3-1 thanks to goals from McCoist, Colin West and Nick Pickering.

Sunderland built on their opening-day success by drawing their next match at home to Notts County and then dumping West Ham United by one goal to nil in their third outing. They were in nosebleed territory. With seven points from a possible nine, perennial strugglers Sunderland found themselves fourth in the First Division.

Alas, it was yet another false dawn, and they were soon sinking to the bottom rather than rising to the top. Coventry were the first team to inflict defeat on Alan Durban's side when they won 1-0 at Highfield Road and, a week later, a trip to the seaside was far from pleasant as Brighton and Hove Albion edged a five-goal thriller. Suddenly, in the space of a fortnight, Sunderland had fallen seven places to eleventh, although

McCoist had at least managed to register his second goal of the season in the latter match. A third defeat on the bounce followed at home to Spurs, but if that result was difficult for the Roker regulars to stomach then it paled into insignificance when Alan Durban took his beleaguered troops to Vicarage Road to take on Watford on the 25 September.

Durban had hoped to use the match against the First Division new boys to stop the rot and bring to an end their winless run, but instead Sunderland turned in a pathetic performance and were hammered 8-0. Luther Blissett scored four times for the home side on a day when the First Division went goal crazy, with fifty goals being netted in the eleven matches played. The drubbing equalled the worst defeat in Sunderland's history, matching the 8-0 reverse they had suffered at the hands of West Ham United in 1968. Speaking after the match, Durban gave an indication of just how poorly Sunderland had performed when he said that his side had been lucky to lose only by eight goals!

Sunderland's players were glad to see the back of September, and their hopes of starting afresh in October were boosted when they put Norwich City to the sword at Roker Park, winning 4-1 courtesy of goals from Gary Rowell (two), McCoist and Cooke. McCoist's goal, a powerful low drive in the sixty-ninth minute, was the start of something of a glut for him; it was the first of five goals he would score in October. He was on the mark again in the next three consecutive league matches, hitting the target in a home match against Southampton (1-1), against Manchester City at Maine Road (2-2) and against Everton at Goodison Park (1-3). He also managed to register his first goal in English Cup competitions when he scored one of Sunderland's five goals in the second leg of the League Cup second-round tie against Wolves. It seemed as though McCoist had now adjusted to life in English football and was about to illustrate to all and sundry why the Sunderland board had paid out such a large fee for him.

Unfortunately, the team did not mirror McCoist's change in fortune. The win over Norwich failed to herald the start of a winning run and Sunderland failed to register a victory in their next ten First Division fixtures. During that run, they lost four matches on the spin and, in the process, plunged to the bottom of the league. They also exited the League Cup when Norwich won a third-round replay by three goals to one at Carrow Road.

In an attempt to arrest the decline, Durban dipped into the transfer market and swelled the striking contingent at Roker Park when he signed one of the most gifted players English football has ever produced, Frank Worthington. Worthington was recruited from Leeds United for whom he had netted fourteen goals in thirty-two league matches. The striker, who was as famous for his off-the-park behaviour as he was for his performances on it, had been one of the cult heroes of the 1970s, scoring a wealth of goals for Huddersfield Town, Leicester City and Bolton Wanderers and winning eight caps for England. He was an excellent goalscorer (he was the top marksman in the English First Division in the 1978/79 season, with twenty-four goals for Bolton), but he had other strings to his bow, such as a superb range of passing and the ability to ghost beyond defenders with the ball at his feet.

His one shot at the big time presented itself in 1972 when Liverpool expressed an interest in signing him to spearhead their attack alongside Kevin Keegan, and a deal with his employers, Huddersfield, was ironed out and a fee of £150,000 agreed. Worthington would be joining a Liverpool side managed by the great Bill Shankly, which stood on the verge of one of the greatest eras in their history, but he was denied the opportunity to exhibit his talents on Merseyside when he failed a medical. His blood pressure was abnormally high and, after taking advice from his medical staff, Shankly pulled out of the deal, unwilling to take any risks on the player given the sum of money involved.

When he arrived at Roker Park, one of the first things Worthington noticed was that Ally McCoist had all the necessary attributes to become a great striker. Reflecting on his first impressions of the young McCoist some years later, Worthington recalled: 'When I arrived at Sunderland I was in the twilight of my career and without a doubt saw a lot of myself as a young man in Coisty. He had this obvious talent, along with a desire and hunger to make something of his career which I had when I first started out in the game. I could see Coisty had all the ingredients to make a great player. He had a brilliant attitude to the game and loved nothing more than kicking a ball around.'[2]

Although he was approaching veteran status, Worthington's skills were showing no signs of eroding and his arrival at Roker Park presented McCoist with a terrific opportunity to train and play alongside such a gifted individual, which undoubtedly helped to nurture and improve his game. In a similar manner to Gary Rowell and John Brogan before him, Frank Worthington played a significant role in shaping McCoist into a well-rounded centre-forward.

Worthington made his debut for Sunderland in a match against Ipswich at Roker Park in early December. And he made a scoring start too, notching Sunderland's second goal during a 3-2 defeat. Although the arrival of Worthington was beneficial for McCoist's development, the presence of another striker in the first-team pool only served to increase the pressure on him to keep delivering the goods on the park, but by the twilight of 1982, the youngster was once again stuck in the middle of a dry spell in front of goal. The October Feast had been followed very quickly by a goal-scoring famine and although he partnered Worthington in attack in the Ipswich match, a run of six games without a goal eventually cost the twenty-year-old his place in the team. He was an unused substitute when Sunderland lost 3-0 against West Bromwich Albion at The Hawthorns and by the time Arsenal visited Roker Park the week before Christmas, McCoist had dropped out of the first-team pool altogether. In his absence, Sunderland sent their followers home after the Arsenal match with a good deal of festive cheer in their hearts, with the players handing their fans an early Christmas present by thrashing the Gunners 3-0 thanks to a Gary Rowell hat-trick.

That emphatic victory brought a run of ten matches without a league win to a halt and signalled the start of a run that saw Sunderland lose only one of their next fourteen First Division matches, shooting themselves up to fifteenth in the table in the process. A defence that had been somewhat porous up until that point – shipping thirty-seven goals in only eighteen league matches – suddenly shored up, and a club record of six consecutive clean sheets was equalled as goalkeeper Chris Turner and his back-line kept the attackers of Arsenal, Manchester United, Liverpool, Nottingham Forest, Notts County and Aston Villa at bay. The only disappointment in the early months of 1983 was an early exit from the FA Cup when Sunderland were eliminated by Manchester City, who won a third-round replay at Maine Road by two goals to one.

With the team settled and performing well, McCoist found it difficult to force his way back into the first-team picture, and in that fine run of results he only made four appearances, all of which came from the substitutes' bench. He did manage to get back on the goal trail in the reserves, though, scoring against Middlesbrough, Barnsley, Bradford City and Derby County, but he was unable to reproduce that kind of goal-scoring form in his sporadic appearances in the first eleven.

However, just when it seemed as though Sunderland would escape from their annual relegation scrap and ease themselves into a mid-table comfort zone, the Wearsiders rumbled off the rails and were sucked back towards the relegation precipice. After defeating David Pleat's Luton Town 3-1 at Kenilworth Road at the end of March, Sunderland went seven matches without a win and, following a 2-1 home loss against Birmingham City in April, Durban's men stood only two points clear of the bottom three. McCoist made four appearances during that dire sequence, his confidence boosted by some prolific scoring in the reserve team – he netted a hat-trick against Nottingham Forest and doubles against Preston North End and Rotherham United – but yet again he failed to replicate that rich vein of goal-scoring form when elevated to the first team.

With only three matches of the season remaining and with Sunderland due to visit Highbury and welcome title-chasing Watford to the North East, many felt they were one of the favourites for relegation, but Durban managed to rally the troops and squeeze one last ounce of effort out of them. They took five points from those last three games, beating Arsenal 1-0, drawing 2-2 with Watford, and holding mid-table West Brom to a 1-1 draw at Roker Park on the final day of the campaign. That was enough to lift Sunderland to a sixteenth-place finish, three points clear of Manchester City, who were demoted to the Second Division along with Swansea City and losing FA Cup finalists Brighton & Hove Albion.

McCoist, who had only started one league game since early December, was recalled to the starting line-up for the last two league games, but he failed to add to his tally of six league goals. Despite the fact that his name had not appeared on the scoresheet since October, that total was sufficient to see McCoist finish the season as third top league goalscorer at the club behind Gary Rowell, who netted sixteen times, and Nick Pickering, who grabbed seven to finish second. All in all, it was a poor goal-scoring season for Sunderland, as they only managed to score forty-eight goals in their forty-two First Division fixtures. Only Brighton (thirty-eight), Birmingham City (forty) and Manchester City (forty-seven) had scored less.

The Sunderland players were rewarded for avoiding the drop when they were given a week-long break in Magaluf. On the vacation, McCoist shared a room with Frank Worthington and was treated to a first-hand insight into Worthington's playboy lifestyle and love of partying. Wherever Frank went, Ally tagged along, and although shattered by the end of the seven-day session, by all accounts the youngster thoroughly enjoyed himself: 'He [Worthington] decided to take me under his wing for the trip,'[3] recalled McCoist. 'Where he went I went, and boy did he know how to enjoy himself. But the next morning, as I tried to recover from the trauma of the night before, my room-mate had my welfare in hand. He brought me my breakfast in bed, ran me a bath and made sure I was ready for the rigours of another day in his company. Honestly, this morning ritual went on for the week we were there.'

The duo would not be teaming up again in Sunderland colours for the 1983/84 season, though. Worthington took the chance to continue his whistle-stop tour of most of the First Division clubs when he left Roker Park in June and signed for Southampton and, a few days later, McCoist was on his way, too.

His long-time admirer John Greig had just endured another wretched season in charge of Rangers. The Glasgow side had ended the campaign without a trophy and Greig was coming under increasing pressure to turn the ailing club around and restore them to what their band of followers perceived to be their rightful place at the summit of the Scottish game. He was given the dreaded vote of confidence by the Ibrox board in the summer when they voted three to one in favour of retaining him as manager, but having sold Jim Bett to Belgian side Lokeren, he had money to spend in order to strengthen his player pool and he immediately pinpointed McCoist as his top target.

Having watched him in action at various stages of the 1982/83 season, Greig approached Alan Durban and the Sunderland board to enquire about McCoist's availability and the possibility of tempting the young, out-of-favour striker back to Scotland. The first McCoist learned of the interest from his boyhood heroes was when he had arrived for pre-season training one morning in June and the prospect of linking up with his favourite team was one that appealed to him greatly.

However, before agreeing to meet with the Rangers representatives, McCoist sought the advice of his manager, and Alan Durban advised the young striker that perhaps a change of scenery was just what he needed to reinvigorate his career. Perhaps sensing that his own time in the hot seat at Roker Park was drawing to a close and that things were about to change on Wearside, Durban urged McCoist to discuss Rangers' proposal, as there was no guarantee his services would be required at Sunderland after the alterations had been made. Durban's prophecy turned out to be accurate: within a year he too was seeking pastures new when, after another poor season, he was relieved of his duties and replaced by Len Ashurst.

Having witnessed such a poor return on his substantial investment, one may have expected Durban to be filled with regret over his extravagance. On the contrary, his only disappointment is that he did not get the opportunity to work with McCoist when he had matured into the fearsome striker he thought he could become many years later. In an interview for the brochure that celebrated McCoist's career in his testimonial season, Durban stated:

> He [McCoist] needs people to keep putting the ball in the box for him and we weren't a team that could do that. Like a lot of strikers of that age, Ally relied mainly on his scoring instinct, and when that could not work for him, he did not have the knowledge of the game to be able to compensate in other ways. It was a great pity that Sunderland were not in a position to be more patient with him. Not for a moment did I regret paying St Johnstone what I did for him; not for one moment did I think that I had over-estimated his potential. At that time he had so much to learn about the game, but because of the money we paid for him, people tended to overlook that.[4]

Ian Bowyer, a two-time European Cup winner with Brian Clough's Nottingham Forest and McCoist's Sunderland team-mate during the 1982/83 season, agrees with Durban's sentiments:

> I do not think Ally would have had the same degree of success in England that he has had in Scotland, but he would still have got his twenty to twenty-five goals a season. There were a number of problems for him at Sunderland. Apart from his inexperience, you could not in all fairness say that he was in a good team. I found it very difficult myself, and I was thirty/thirty-one then with two European Cup-winners' medals under my belt.[5]

Thus, with his manager's blessing, McCoist made the journey north to Carlisle to meet the Rangers management team of John Greig and Tommy McLean. In addition to breathing fresh life into his career, he knew as he journeyed up the motorway that this might well be his last chance to sign for the club he loved. It did not take long for a deal to be thrashed out, and on 8 June 1983, John Greig's persistence ultimately paid off when Ally McCoist signed for Rangers at the second attempt for a fee of £185,000, less than half the sum Sunderland had paid for him a little under two years earlier. The passing of time would show this to be perhaps the biggest bargain buy in the history of football transfers.

Although his time with Sunderland had been blighted by patchy, inconsistent form and had not been as profitable as both parties had hoped at the outset, McCoist left Wearside with only good memories. He may have only scored a mere nine goals in sixty-five appearances, but he had struck up a rapport with the Sunderland supporters and is still thought of fondly in the North East today. Speaking on the first of three video releases chronicling his career, McCoist said: 'I look back on my Sunderland days and people say to me that I couldn't really have enjoyed it, but it's crazy, I did. I met some fantastic people down there, and although I didn't do as well as I would have liked, the Sunderland fans were fantastic with me. I think they appreciated that I was just a young kid down there trying to do my best.'[6]

In the summer of 1983, however, the door was slammed shut on the Sunderland chapter of Ally McCoist's football career. At last he had secured his dream move and he returned to his homeland determined to prove he had the game to cut it as a striker at the top level. After his dry spell in England, McCoist intended to silence the critics by establishing himself in the Rangers team, help bring success and silverware back to Ibrox and, hopefully, in time, to elevate himself to the same legendary status that was afforded to the likes of Derek Johnstone and Colin Stein, two strikers he had worshipped during his time cheering on Rangers from the sloping Ibrox terraces in the 1970s.

Unfortunately for the twenty-year-old, he was to find that the road to the lofty perch to which he aspired would prove long and unforgiving. Indeed, within eighteen months of his arrival at Ibrox, McCoist found himself standing at a career crossroads and staring into the abyss.

CHAPTER FOUR

A DREAM COME TRUE: 1983–84

Rangers Football Club is simply huge, a venerable institution in the eyes of many. Founded in 1872 by a group of rowers on the banks of the River Clyde, they have since gone on to achieve unparalleled success in Scotland, winning a world record fifty-two League Championship titles, the Scottish Cup on thirty-three occasions, while the League Cup has found its way into the majestic Ibrox trophy room a record twenty-five times. In addition to that considerable haul, the club also collected the European Cup-Winners' Cup in 1972.

The club was initially called Argyll until one of the founder members, Moses McNeil, found the name Rangers in a book about English rugby and decided to christen the new team with that identity. The first matches were contested at Fleshers Haugh on Glasgow Green, but the team soon moved to Kinning Park, which lay south of the River Clyde and beat Vale of Leven 2-1 in their first match there on 2 September 1876, thanks to goals from Willie Dunlop and Alex Marshall. The 1876/77 season also saw Rangers reach the Scottish Cup final for the first time. They took on Vale of Leven and three matches were required to decide the winners, with Vale eventually picking up the trophy after winning the second replay by three goals to two.

Rangers were beaten Cup finalists again in 1879, with Vale of Leven once more the victors after Rangers refused to play in the replay due to a contentious refereeing decision in the first game that denied the Light Blues a second goal in a match that ended 1-1. Rangers did, however, gain some revenge a month later when they met Vale of Leven in the final of the Glasgow Merchant's Charity Cup and won 2-1; it was a result that gave the club their first-ever piece of silverware.

In 1886, Rangers competed in the English FA Cup, defeating Everton away from home en route to the semi-finals, at which stage they were clinically despatched from the tournament by an Aston Villa side who they had thumped 7-1 in 1882. Villa won 3-1 at Nantwich Road in Crewe and went on to win the trophy when they defeated West Bromwich Albion in the final. This was Rangers' one and only foray into the English FA Cup.

The following year the club moved to the first Ibrox Park situated in Govan on the south side of the city, although they got off to a somewhat inauspicious start at their new home when the high-flying English outfit of that era, Preston North End, gate-crashed the housewarming party and blitzed the new owners by eight goals to one. Later that season the seeds of the Old Firm rivalry were planted when Rangers and newly formed Celtic, who played their games in the East End of Glasgow, clashed for the first time. Celtic claimed first blood, emerging victorious by five goals to two.

In 1890 the Scottish League was formed. Rangers defeated Hearts 5-2 in their first-ever league fixture and by the end of that inaugural year shared the championship with Dumbarton. Both clubs were tied on twenty-nine points after eighteen matches and a playoff match was ordered to decide the champions. When it ended in a 2-2 draw, the league's governing body declared the pair as joint champions. Under today's rules, however, Dumbarton would actually have won the league outright due to a superior goal difference, but such rules were not yet in place so the trophy was shared.

Over the next eight years, Rangers, managed by William Wilton and captained by Davy Mitchell, enjoyed mixed success in the league, but they did win the Scottish Cup for the first time in 1893/94, beating Celtic 3-1 in the final at Hampden. When Rangers did win the championship again, in 1898/99, they did so in quite spectacular fashion, winning all eighteen of their league matches and scoring a remarkable seventy-nine goals in the process. R.C. Hamilton was the top goalscorer, netting twenty-one goals in eighteen league appearances.

On 30 December 1899, with the game's popularity increasing exponentially, Rangers moved home for what would be the final time, moving to the second Ibrox Stadium which is still their home today. It is a mere stone's throw from the first one.

Rangers quickly adapted to their new surroundings and were the dominant force in Scotland as the world waved goodbye to the nineteenth century and ushered in the twentieth, winning the league title for four successive years between 1899 and 1902. This spate of success was then followed by a barren run in the championship, and the trophy did not return to Govan until 1910/11, although Rangers lost out to rivals Celtic in a playoff in 1905 and won the Scottish Cup in 1903. By now, the league had been expanded, with nineteen teams taking part, and Rangers were never far away from the top of the Scottish game. By the time hostilities commenced in the First World War in 1914, they were among the most successful sides in the country, having claimed the Scottish Cup four times and the League Championship on eight occasions.

In 1920, manager Wilton was tragically killed in a boating accident, and Bill Struth, who had been a trainer at Ibrox since 1914, took his place in the manager's office. Struth was an austere man who lived by the maxim that no player was greater than the club and he proceeded to enjoy a period of unparalleled success at Ibrox. A strict disciplinarian, he insisted that his players showed the highest possible standards wherever they went. He was in the manager's chair for thirty-four years and during that time he oversaw eighteen League Championship victories, ten Scottish Cup wins (including a 4-0 thrashing of Celtic in 1928 that busted a twenty-five year hoodoo in the competition), and two successes in the Scottish League Cup, a competition that was born in 1946. He was the man who brought legendary players such as Alan Morton, Bob McPhail and Willie Waddell to Ibrox, and in the 1948/49 season, he became the first manager to lead Rangers to the domestic Treble of League Championship, Scottish Cup and Scottish League Cup.

When Struth retired in 1954, a former player, James Scotland Symon, took over the reins. After two barren seasons, Symon, known to everyone as Scot, continued where his predecessor had left off, sustaining the wave of glory that was sweeping through Ibrox by winning a further six league titles, the Scottish Cup in 1960, 1962, 1963, 1964, and 1966, and the League Cup on four occasions.

Symon, who managed the club to its second Treble in the 1963/64 season, was the first manager to lead Rangers in European competition when he took charge of the European Champions Cup match against OGC Nice of France in October 1956. The club enjoyed some decent runs in their early continental sojourns, reaching the semi-finals of the Champions Cup, regarded as the premier European club competition, in 1959/60 (they lost heavily to eventual runners-up Eintracht Frankfurt), before becoming the first British club to contest a European final when they met Italian side Fiorentina in the 1960/61 European Cup-Winners' Cup. Symon's men lost out 4-1 on aggregate, but they were finalists again in 1966/67, only to see success elude them when Bayern Munich won 1-0 after extra-time in Nuremberg.

Symon's thirteen-year tenure was not without its trials and tribulations, though. In the League Cup final of 1957, his side were humiliated and humbled 7-1 by rivals Celtic and, in January 1967, he oversaw arguably the most ignominious moment in the club's history when the Light Blues were dumped out of the Scottish Cup in the opening round by lowly namesakes Berwick Rangers of the Second Division. Within months of the latter, Symon was relieved of his duties by club chairman John Lawrence, albeit with Lawrence sending a business associate who had no formal connection with Rangers to inform the deposed manager that he would no longer be in charge.

Symon was replaced at the helm by his assistant, Davie White, as the Rangers hierarchy tried to formulate a plan to wrestle the balance of power back from Celtic, who were emerging as a real force once again under the stewardship of Jock Stein. White was part of a new breed of managers who were beginning to make their mark on the Scottish game. He was what was termed a 'tracksuit manager', someone who was much more heavily involved with training and tactics than previous incumbents had been. He was appointed by the board in a bid to freshen things up at Ibrox, but, at just thirty-four years of age, was arguably too young for such a high-pressure job. Within two years he too had been sacked and, until the ill-fated tenure of Paul Le Guen in 2006, White was the only manager to take charge of Rangers and not win a major trophy.

In December 1969, Willie Waddell, a stalwart of the halcyon days of the forties and fifties, was appointed as the fifth manager in Rangers' history. Latterly Waddell had been a respected journalist, but he also had managerial experience on his CV following a successful spell in charge of Kilmarnock, during which he had led the club to three cup finals (the

Scottish Cup in 1960 and the League Cup in 1960 and 1962) and capped it all by masterminding the Ayrshire side's dramatic victory in the First Division championship in the 1964/65 season.

His return to Ibrox roused Rangers and less than a year after taking charge he led the club to their first trophy since 1966 when a goal from sixteen-year-old Derek Johnstone was sufficient to beat Celtic 1-0 at Hampden in the League Cup final. Among the crowd of 106,263 that October afternoon was a young eight-year-old by the name of Ally McCoist, who was attending one of his first football matches. The match-winner swiftly developed into one of McCoist's heroes – his other idol from that era was Colin Stein – and, some years later, the pair became close friends.

Although Rangers continued to find the recipe for league success elusive, Waddell's team made their mark in Europe in the 1971/72 season when they competed in the European Cup-Winners' Cup. Having overcome Rennes of France, Portuguese side Sporting Lisbon, and Italian cracks Torino in the opening rounds, Rangers faced old foes Bayern Munich in the two-leg semi-final with the prospect of a third European final at stake if they won the tie. After drawing 1-1 in Germany, Waddell's men triumphed 2-0 at Ibrox and went through to face Moscow Dynamo in the final at the Nou Camp in Barcelona. It was to be a case of third time lucky for Rangers, as goals from Colin Stein and a double from Willie Johnston were enough to stave off a late fight back by the Russians and hand Rangers their first, and to date only, piece of European silverware.

Shortly after the triumph in Barcelona, Waddell resigned from his post as manager, moving 'upstairs' to take on the role of general manager, and his first-team coach, Jock Wallace, replaced him in the manager's office. Wallace, a former jungle fighter, had kept goal for Berwick Rangers when they had shocked their more illustrious namesakes 1-0 in the opening round of the 1967 Scottish Cup. And, after securing the Scottish Cup in his first season in charge and enduring a barren season in 1973/74, Wallace guided his troops to the championship the following season and brought arch-rivals Celtic's quest for ten league titles in a row to a shuddering halt. In the three seasons that followed, he sandwiched a bleak, trophy-less season in 1976/77 with two glorious domestic Trebles before departing in the summer of 1978 after a rift with general manager Willie Waddell.

Wallace was replaced at the helm by club captain John Greig, who inherited an ageing squad from his predecessor (and one that was littered with many of his former team-mates), but initially it looked as if he would continue the success of the mid-to-late seventies, securing a Cup double in his first season and coming to within a whisker of an unprecedented back-to-back Treble, only losing out to Celtic in the title race when two goals in the final ten minutes of the final Old Firm game gave the Parkhead side the win they needed to clinch the Premier Division championship.

In the remaining years of his managerial tenure, John Greig never came as close again to leading Rangers to the championship, and over the course of the next three seasons the Light Blues' fortunes declined alarmingly. In 1979/80, they slumped to a fifth-place finish in the league (their lowest final position since 1965) and lost both of the cups they had won the previous season. They fared little better in 1980/81, winning the Scottish Cup but ending up third in the league, and in 1981/82 they won the League Cup but lost heavily to Aberdeen in the Scottish Cup final and once again finished third in the title race.

Thus, it is fair to say that the Rangers squad Ally McCoist joined up with ahead of the 1983/84 season was a group of players desperately short of confidence and struggling to maintain the trophy-enriched history of this great Scottish institution. The season before McCoist's arrival (1982/83), had been a barren one for Rangers and represented the nadir of Greig's tenure as manger. Rangers finished fourth in the league, a massive eighteen points behind champions Dundee United, and lost in both domestic cup finals, falling 2-1 to Celtic in the League Cup and 1-0 to Alex Ferguson's Aberdeen in the Scottish Cup.

United's championship win was further evidence that a new force was emerging in Scotland to challenge the Old Firm of Rangers and Celtic. Along with Aberdeen, who had won the title in 1979/80 and the Scottish Cup in 1981 and 1982, they had finally broken the Old Firm hegemony on the League Championship. Their duel triumphs had been the first by a club other than Rangers or Celtic since 1964/65, when Kilmarnock had won the title on goal average under Willie Waddell. The emergence of this force from the North, dubbed the 'New Firm', was bad news for Rangers manager John Greig.

Greig was (and still is for that matter) a true legend down Govan way. He had spent seventeen glorious years at Ibrox as a player, playing in over 750 games for the club and had been part of three Treble-winning squads in 1963/64, 1975/76 and 1977/78, the latter two as captain. He had skippered the club to their solitary European success in the shape of the 1972 European Cup-Winners' Cup and had also remained resolute as Celtic swept all before them in the mid-sixties and early seventies. He was held in high esteem among the Rangers community, but that lofty status was now being challenged by the increasingly poor displays on the field and lack of trophies in the trophy cabinet.

The nature of the job at Ibrox meant that Greig consistently had to deliver the Holy Grail of the League Championship, as regular success in the two domestic cups was never going to be enough to placate the club's unforgiving supporters. By the time McCoist arrived in Govan, the championship trophy had not rested on the Ibrox sideboard for five long seasons, a lifetime in the eyes of the Rangers faithful. The natives were becoming increasingly restless, with Rangers not just trailing in the wake of bitter rivals Celtic, but also lagging behind Aberdeen and United.

Greig now had to plot to overcome the top trio and, having been given the dreaded vote of confidence by the Rangers board of directors in the close season, was acutely aware that the 1983/84 season would be a colossal campaign for him. It was for that reason he splashed the majority of the cash he had gathered from the sale of midfielder Jim Bett to recruit McCoist, investing his faith in the twenty-year-old striker to score the goals that would propel Rangers back to the top of the Scottish game.

Greig, who had been keeping tabs on McCoist for five months, told the media: 'I am very pleased to get a player who has been full-time with an English club, and has matured both physically and mentally in the process, since I tried to sign him two years ago.'[1] He went on to explain that he felt McCoist would enjoy more success at Ibrox than he had done at Roker Park, as Rangers were 'a more attack-minded team'. In the end, Greig's faith in McCoist would be wholly justified, and he believes the purchase of the striker is one of the biggest legacies he left the club.

The signing of McCoist was not welcomed with open arms by the Rangers fans, though. The Ibrox regulars were a little apprehensive about the new acquisition, as only two years earlier he had turned down the chance to sign for Rangers when he had opted to join Sunderland. This anxiety simply heaped more pressure on the shoulders of McCoist, although he was quick to point out that, despite not having enjoyed as much success in the English First Division as he would have liked, Rangers had now recruited a far better player than the one they would have brought in had they signed him from St Johnstone in the summer of 1981. He told the club newspaper:

> I'm not coming to Rangers now to opt out of English football, or because I feel I have been a failure there or anything like that – far from it. My two years at Sunderland were very happy ones and I feel they were invaluable to me in terms of experience. I am coming back to Scotland a better player. When I took the step up from Scottish First Division football to playing at the highest level in England, I knew it would be hard. That was why I went. It made me a much better all-round player and I was looking forward to next season with the club, as I felt it would have been my best yet.[2]

Things started well for the new recruit. He made his debut on 21 July 1983 in a pre-season friendly against Swedish minnows Arlovs and, sporting the number eight jersey, netted a hat-trick as Rangers got their Scandinavian tour off to an emphatic start with a crushing 11-0 victory. His first goal arrived in the thirty-ninth minute when he stabbed a pass from strike-partner Sandy Clark into the net, and he added two more goals in the second half, netting a Davie Cooper cross a minute after the restart before completing his treble after sixty-six minutes when the ball broke to him after a goalmouth scramble.

More goals followed two days later when Solvesborgs were thrashed 12-0, McCoist grabbing four this time around, although he was upstaged by Clark who notched five. A goal in each of the final two tour matches against Norrstrands and Myresjo IF took McCoist's tally to nine goals in four matches, and although the standard of opposition was poor, the goal-scoring return did wonders for his confidence ahead of the new season. The fact that Clark, a £160,000 buy from West Ham United in March 1983, had also hit nine goals augured well for the new campaign and suggested that Greig had discovered a potent strike-pairing that could chalk up the goals required to shoot Rangers back onto the glory trail.

Rangers completed their pre-season preparations with two matches in Belgium – McCoist failed to score as Rangers lost 2-1 to Beerschot and defeated Berchem Sport 4-0 to finish third in the Metropool Cup – and a 4-2 Ibrox victory over West Bromwich Albion – again the new boy was absent from the scoresheet, but he did create goals for Bobby Russell and Robert Prytz. McCoist then got his hands on his first piece of silverware when Rangers defeated Celtic 1-0 at Hampden on 13 August to lift the Glasgow Cup. Watched by a small crowd by Old Firm standards of just 32,707, Sandy Clark scored Rangers' goal to hand them the trophy for the forty-first time.

Buoyed by his exploits in Sweden and now fully integrated into the Rangers side, McCoist made a good start when the competitive action got under way seven days after the win over Celtic. Although he did not score on his competitive debut, a 1-1 draw with St Mirren in the opening league match, he did find the net for the first time in Rangers colours a week later in a League Cup tie with Queen of the South at Palmerston Park in Dumfries, notching Rangers' fourth goal seven minutes from the end to complete an 8-1 aggregate victory over the Doonhamers.

Better was to follow on the first Saturday in September when McCoist lined up against Old Firm rivals Celtic at Parkhead in his first real taste of one of the world's most famous derby matches. He had encountered the unsavoury, almost tribal, warfare of this head-to-head in the Glasgow Cup final in pre-season, but this was the first 'major' confrontation he was taking part in. He later recalled that he had 'never been more nervous before the start of a game'[3], but his nerves were soon suppressed thanks to his record-breaking first touch of the ball.

With the match barely underway and the majority of the 50,662 supporters still trying to find their vantage point on the terraces and in the stands, Roy Aitken clattered into the back of Sandy Clark and referee David Syme awarded the visitors a free-kick. Swedish midfielder Robert Prytz took the kick quickly and sent right-back Davie MacKinnon scampering down the right flank. He reached the goal-line and pulled the ball back invitingly into the penalty area. Lurking there was McCoist and he rapped the ball through the legs of Celtic goalkeeper Pat Bonner with his right foot to score his first-ever goal against Celtic. A mere twenty-seven seconds had elapsed since the kick-off and McCoist's strike set a new record for the quickest-ever goal in the history of Old Firm conflict. The record stood for almost twenty years before Chris Sutton of Celtic beat it when he scored after only nineteen seconds of the December 2002 clash between these two titans.

A delirious McCoist ran with arms aloft towards his new public who were celebrating wildly at the other end of the ground. If there is one way to ingratiate yourself with the Rangers fans instantly then it is by scoring against Celtic and McCoist had done just that with his first touch of the ball. Their collective joy was to be short lived, though, as Celtic restored parity within eight minutes through Roy Aitken before Frank McGarvey popped up late in the match to net the winning goal.

That defeat at Celtic Park was the first of three straight league losses, which meant that Rangers only had one point on the board after the first four Premier Division matches. Greig's men finally chalked up their first league win when newly promoted St Johnstone came to Ibrox on 24 September and were beaten 6-3. McCoist, on the day of his twenty-first birthday, was on the scoresheet, netting two of the six goals against his former club.

A further two victories against defending champions Dundee United and Hibernian were reeled off, but the results merely papered over the large cracks that were beginning to appear. Greig was now living on borrowed time and when Rangers followed up a 3-2 reverse against Dundee at Dens Park by going down 2-1 at home to Motherwell on 22 October, it was the end of the line for the manager. Amid furious supporters' demonstrations calling for the board to sack him, Greig resigned from his post. He had won four trophies in just over five seasons in charge, but the supporters craved success in the championship and Greig paid the ultimate price for failing to deliver the premier trophy.

McCoist, who had scored from the penalty spot in the defeat against Motherwell, later recalled that Greig's departure saddened many of the first-team squad at Ibrox. He said: 'I can still vividly remember the scene in the dressing room the day he told us. He'd known a lot of the squad for years and quite a few of the players were in tears on his behalf. I must admit I was a bit upset myself.'[4]

Although Greig's assistant Tommy McLean took the job on a caretaker basis, the Rangers board had two names in the frame to take over from Greig on a permanent basis. Top of their list was the manager of Aberdeen, Alex Ferguson.

Ferguson had been on Rangers' books as a player from 1967 until 1969, signing from Dunfermline Athletic for a then Scottish record fee of £65,000. He proceeded to score thirty-five goals in sixty-six appearances in light blue, but was sold to Falkirk in November 1969 for only £20,000. He had fallen out of favour with manager Davie White following the 1969 Scottish Cup final, a match in which Rangers were battered 4-0 by rivals Celtic. Celtic had taken the lead after only two minutes when Billy McNeill rose unchallenged to direct a header beyond Norrie Martin in the Rangers goal, and White placed the blame for conceding the early goal squarely on the shoulders of Ferguson, who was supposed to be picking up Celtic's skipper at set-pieces. Ferguson never pulled on a Rangers shirt again.

Following the end of his playing career, Ferguson took up the managerial reins at East Stirlingshire before winning promotion to the Premier Division as manager of St Mirren in 1977. He was sacked in 1978, but when Aberdeen manager Billy McNeill was tempted to take charge of Celtic a few months later, Ferguson was recruited to replace him in the Granite City. After finishing fourth and reaching the final of the League Cup in his first season, Ferguson guided the Pittodrie outfit to the championship in 1979/80, their first title win since 1955, and followed this with further success in the Scottish Cup in 1982 and 1983 and then triumph in Europe, as Aberdeen beat Alfredo di Stefano's Real Madrid to win the 1983 European Cup-Winners' Cup. With those credentials on his CV, he was a man in demand and when Rangers' vice-chairman John Paton contacted him to sound him out over the possibility of taking over from Greig, he was, initially at least, tempted by the offer. However, after mulling over the pros and cons of the move, Ferguson decided to stick with Aberdeen and Rangers had to turn their attentions towards their second candidate, Jim McLean of Dundee United, the brother of caretaker boss Tommy.

Like Ferguson, McLean had been hugely successful at United, rearing a quality crop of young players and blending them into a side that won the League Cup in 1979/80, the Tayside club's first-ever piece of silverware. They retained the trophy the following season and then, in the 1982/83 season, McLean led United to the Premier Division title. It looked as though this time Rangers would get their man, with McLean informing his assistant Walter Smith that he was on his way to Ibrox and that he was taking him with him. However, McLean had an eleventh-hour change of heart and rejected Rangers' overtures, prompting the Ibrox directors to swallow their pride and invite Jock Wallace back to Ibrox to take charge of team affairs for the second time. Given the success he had brought to the club during his first spell as manager, Wallace's return to the manager's office in 1983 was met with widespread approval within the Rangers community.

Although he would later be regarded as having had a significant impact on the career of Ally McCoist, it initially looked as though the arrival of Wallace was going to signal a premature end to McCoist's stay at Ibrox. He was in the team when Wallace's second stint in the manager's chair got off to a shocking start when Rangers were thumped 3-0 by Aberdeen at Pittodrie, their fifth defeat on the bounce, but despite retaining his place when the rot was stopped with a 0-0 draw at home against Dundee United and a 1-0 victory over St Johnstone at Muirton Park, McCoist was struggling to find his true form. Despite making his first appearance for Scotland at Under-21 level against Belgium in October, he failed to score for five league matches and, although he netted his sixth goal of the League Cup tournament in the 3-0 win against Clydebank at Kilbowie in a sectional tie, his lack of firepower in the league soon cost him his place in the team. He was dropped to the reserves at the end of November and replaced in the first team by new £100,000 signing Bobby Williamson.

While the top team recorded comprehensive back-to-back wins over Hearts and Motherwell – both by three goals to nil – McCoist turned out in three second-string fixtures, scoring against Hearts in a 3-0 win at Tynecastle and netting the winner in a 3-2 victory over Aberdeen at Pittodrie. However, just as he seemed to be rediscovering his scoring touch, he suffered further misery when he broke his right wrist playing for the club in an indoor five-a-side tournament in his hometown of East Kilbride. The injury kept him out of action for four games and during his spell on the sidelines rumours surfaced of a swift return to Sunderland. The Wearsiders made an initial enquiry regarding his availability, but no formal bid was lodged, so McCoist would remain at Ibrox for the time being at least.

In McCoist's absence, Wallace galvanised an ailing Rangers side. The no-score draw at home to Dundee United in late November heralded a dramatic change of fortune, and the two victories over Hearts and Motherwell triggered a golden spell, as Rangers reeled off five straight wins in the title race, the first time they had achieved the feat since January 1978.

McCoist eventually made his return to the first team in January when he came on as a substitute in a challenge match against Feyenoord at Ibrox. The Dutch cracks had one of the finest players of all time, Johan Cruyff, in their ranks and also a talented youngster by the name of Ruud Gullit, but Rangers forced a 3-3 draw before eventually succumbing 7-6 on penalties. Despite not having fully recovered from his broken wrist,

McCoist replaced Bobby Williamson at half-time and scored one of the penalties in the shootout.

With the team in such fine form, it was proving difficult for McCoist to force his way back into the starting eleven, and he was used as a substitute for Rangers' next two matches, a 2-0 victory over St Johnstone in the league and a Scottish Cup third-round triumph over Second Division outfit Dunfermline Athletic. His contribution to the latter match was priceless, though, as he netted the winning goal seven minutes from time to help the Ibrox side scrape into the next round thanks to a 2-1 victory. Rab Stewart had fired Dunfermline into a shock lead, but Colin McAdam equalised after eighty-one minutes before McCoist hit the net to spare the home side's blushes.

McCoist's goal, his first in the top team since November, was enough to convince Wallace that he merited being reinstated to the starting eleven, and he repaid his manager's faith by grabbing a goal in the 2-1 home win over Motherwell and another in the 2-2 draw against Hearts at Tynecastle seven days later. The results helped stretch Rangers' unbeaten run to thirteen matches.

A decisive factor in Rangers' resurgence was the players' improved physical conditioning thanks to the radical change in the way training sessions were now conducted at Ibrox. During his first spell in charge, Wallace had made a name for himself with his gruelling sessions on the sand dunes at Gullane and on the old terracing at Ibrox, often pushing his players beyond their physical limits in order to increase their stamina, which in turn, he believed, would help them outlast opponents in the latter stages of games. This was the kind of training McCoist needed. 'I became stronger and harder and that physical edge helped my game,' he said. 'Under Jock, I developed more than I had done in the previous six years.'[5]

Wallace focused in particular on the upper body and his players would undergo a daily circuit of exercises in the away dressing room at Ibrox that were geared towards building this area of the body. McCoist recalled: 'I can't emphasise strongly enough how important this particular spell was to me. It might be a bit melodramatic to say it, but I think Jock Wallace saved my career at that time. All I am sure of is that the Ally McCoist who emerged midway through the 1983/84 season was a more complete player than the one who'd started it.'[6]

McCoist's resurgence continued in March when he netted Rangers' fourth goal in a 4-1 win over St Johnstone, but he was unable to prevent the Light Blues' unbeaten streak coming to an end on St Patrick's Day 1984 when Dundee won 3-2 at Ibrox in the Scottish Cup quarter-final replay. The run had lasted for twenty matches, but attention was now being focused on securing some silverware, as Wallace's men were gunning for glory in the Scottish League Cup.

In parallel with the good run in the championship and the Scottish Cup, Wallace's troops were also enjoying a fruitful campaign in the League Cup. Under John Greig's leadership, Queen of the South had been beaten in round two, before Rangers recorded six wins out of six to top qualifying section two ahead of St Mirren, Hearts and Clydebank. This granted them passage to the last four, and waiting for Wallace and his players in the semi-finals were defending Premier Division champions Dundee United.

McCoist had shown an early liking for this particular tournament. Back in September, he had turned in a fine performance against Clydebank at Ibrox, with the *Rangers News* rating his display as 'the highlight of the night'.[7] Playing in a more withdrawn role behind strikers Sandy Clark and Davie Mitchell, he had played exceptionally well and topped off a wonderful night by netting his first-ever goals at Ibrox in a Rangers jersey in the twenty-fourth and sixty-eighth minutes. Another brace against St Mirren in a 5-0 win at Ibrox and a strike against Clydebank at Kilbowie took his tally to six goals in just seven League Cup appearances.

The semi-final against United was contested over two legs in February. McCoist started both matches and although he failed to add to his impressive haul of League Cup goals over the course of the two fixtures, a late goal from Australian striker Dave Mitchell earned a 1-1 draw in the first leg at Tannadice, and second-leg strikes from Clark and Redford booked Rangers' place in the final by virtue of a 3-1 aggregate win. The reward for Rangers was a 25 March meeting with Celtic at Hampden, as their rivals had disposed of Aberdeen in the other semi-final. For McCoist, it was only his second visit to the national stadium as a player and it was also the first major national cup final of his career.

Rangers arrived at Hampden with a depleted squad, though. Midfielders Ian Redford and Robert Prytz were both suspended as a consequence of being ordered off in the Scottish Cup defeat against Dundee, leaving Wallace desperately short of options in that area of the team. He therefore had to reorganise his ranks to compensate for their absence and chose a trip to Belfast five days before the final to try out his proposed Cup final line-up. Rangers took on Linfield in a friendly and, instead of spearheading the attack alongside Sandy Clark, McCoist was deployed on the right-hand side of midfield. The deeper role did not seem to faze him, though, as he notched one of Rangers' four goals in a comfortable 4-0 win. He also had another strike ruled out for offside and over the course of the ninety minutes showed his manager that he could help plug the gaps in midfield while also advancing forward to trouble the opposition defence. Clearly Wallace was convinced and he asked McCoist to fulfil the role again on the day of the Cup final. Indeed, the Rangers manager made just one change to the team that had won in Northern Ireland – a fit-again Bobby Russell replaced young Derek Ferguson – and the team he put his faith in on a sunny spring afternoon read: Peter McCloy, Jimmy Nicholl, Alistair Dawson, John McClelland, Craig Paterson, David McPherson, Bobby Russell, Ally McCoist, Sandy Clark, John McDonald and Davie Cooper. The substitutes were Colin McAdam and Hugh Burns.

Despite fielding what the *Glasgow Herald* perceived to be a 'patchwork side',[8] Rangers took command of a keenly fought contest and almost took the lead after just seven minutes when Russell released McCoist on the right. He arrowed a low cross into the danger area, which a well-placed Clark somehow contrived to miss. The ball ran on to John McDonald, who saw his goal-bound shot cleared off the line by Tom McAdam.

It had almost been a dream start for Wallace's side, but they eventually broke the deadlock on the stroke of half-time. The wonderfully gifted Russell, who was orchestrating all of Rangers' good midfield play, worked a 'one-two' with Davie Cooper on the left, but his route to goal was halted illegally when Murdo McLeod brought him crashing to the turf. Referee Bob Valentine awarded Rangers a penalty-kick, and with resident penalty taker Prytz suspended, McCoist took the responsibility and duly despatched the kick with aplomb, sending Pat Bonner to his right as the ball fizzed to his left.

The goal did come against the run of play, as Celtic were enjoying a good spell at the time, but Rangers looked to have cupped one hand around the trophy when they scored for a second time one minute shy of the hour mark. Sandy Clark got his head on to the end of a mammoth clearance from goalkeeper Peter McCloy and flicked the ball into the path of McCoist, who kept his composure to slot a shot behind Bonner before jumping for joy in front of the Rangers masses at the traditional 'Rangers End' of Hampden.

It looked as though Rangers' name was etched on the trophy, but Celtic, fresh from thumping Motherwell 6-0 in the Scottish Cup and still in with a realistic chance of winning the Treble, mounted a stirring fight back. Brian McClair halved the deficit from a cleverly worked free-kick in the sixty-seventh minute, and the Parkhead side forced the match into extra-time by drawing level as the clock ticked beyond the ninety-minute mark and into injury time. It was a case of hero turning to villain for Rangers, as McCoist upended Murdo McLeod as he shaped to shoot inside the penalty area prompting Mr Valentine to point to the penalty spot once again. Although adamant that there had been no infringement ('I've watched the incident umpteen times on television since then and I know it looks like a foul, but I still maintain to this day that I touched the ball first'), McCoist watched in horror as Mark Reid scored from 12 yards to restore parity at 2-2.

Wallace roused his charges ahead of the extra half-hour and made a tactical switch by moving McCoist from midfield to his more familiar striking role. It paid dividends, as with sixty seconds of the first period of extra-time remaining, the ball was played in towards McCoist and, as he attempted to turn towards goal, he was barged over by Roy Aitken inside the penalty area. Penalty number three was swiftly awarded, and McCoist dusted himself down, grabbed the ball, placed it on the spot and chose to shoot to the same corner as he had in the dying minutes of the first half. However, on this occasion, Bonner guessed correctly and swooped to save the striker's effort, but he could only parry the ball out and McCoist, following up his initial shot, gladly devoured the rebound to complete his Cup final hat-trick. In doing so he became only the third Rangers player to net a hat-trick against Celtic in a competitive match since the end of the Second World War. (For the record, the others were both scored in league fixtures on New Year's Day, by Jimmy Duncanson in 1949 and South African Johnny Hubbard in 1955.)

Wallace's men successfully managed to see out the remaining minutes of the match and when referee Valentine blew the final whistle it brought about scenes of mass celebration in the Rangers ranks. Within the space of just four months, Jock Wallace had roused a ragged Rangers side and delivered the club's first piece of domestic silverware since their success in the same competition two years previously.

For match-winner and hat-trick hero McCoist, it was also a memorable moment. He was showered with congratulations and gifts as a result of his performance. On top of his first-ever major winners' medal, he claimed the match ball and a Seiko gold watch for netting the last goal of the final, and he also hoped his achievements would finally bring a halt to the transfer rumours that had been circulating a few months earlier. 'I'm delighted for myself, delighted for Rangers and the fans,' he said at the post-match media conference. 'It's really a dream come true to score a hat-trick in an Old Firm Cup final. I would also like to thank John Greig for giving me my chance by buying me. There seemed to be some doubts about my future as an Ibrox player not so long ago, but hopefully that's all behind me now because this is the club I want to play for.'[10]

Celtic gained a modicum of revenge for the League Cup reverse eight days later when they ended Rangers' four-month unbeaten run in the title race, winning 3-0 at Parkhead. This result, coupled with the poor start to the campaign, meant that McCoist did not add a League Championship medal to his collection. Despite defeating Celtic 1-0 at Ibrox and drawing at Pittodrie in the run-in, Rangers finished fourth in the title race for the second successive year, this time languishing fifteen points adrift of champions Aberdeen.

Aside from the lack of success in the Premier Division, McCoist was justifiably happy with his first campaign in light blue. Despite the mid-season blip when he had been out of sorts, dropped to the reserves and seemingly on his way out of Ibrox, he finished the season with one major medal and a total of twenty goals in forty-seven league and cup appearances. This goal haul was good enough to see McCoist finish as the club's top goalscorer, an achievement that, coupled with the Cup final hat-trick against Celtic, had the striker thinking that he had finally won the seal of approval from the notoriously hard-to-please Rangers fans and Jock Wallace. Indeed, Wallace stated at the end of the season that his first impression of the young striker was incorrect. 'I have to admit the laddie proved me wrong last season,' confessed the Rangers manager:[11]

> I wasn't sure of him. I didn't know if his attitude was right and there was a spell when I might have thought of selling him. But he was dropped and he didn't complain. He just went out on the training ground and worked as hard as he knew how. He did the same in the reserves, worked and played, until he forced his way back into the first team. And before he scored that hat-trick in the final against Celtic he

had convinced me that he was a Rangers man. He grew up a lot last season and became an important player for us, and so he will remain as long as his attitude stays the same.

Troubled times lay ahead, though, and events that were to unfold over the next six months would illustrate that the young striker still had a lot to learn and that he had a long way to go to convince not only those supporters but also his manager that he had what it took to be a goal-scoring success at Ibrox.

CHAPTER FIVE

ALMOST THE END OF THE ROAD: 1984–86

For the first time in many years the dawn of a new season was ushered in with an air of excited expectation around Ibrox Stadium. The League Cup success over Celtic and the mid-season unbeaten run in the league during 1983/84 had lifted the flagging spirits of the Rangers fans, with both going a long way to help banish the memories of what had been a painful final two years under John Greig. With the indomitable Wallace about to embark on the first full season of his second spell in charge, there was a genuine belief that the club's six-year title famine could finally be ended.

Rangers were certainly well travelled as they prepared for the 1984/85 season. Ally McCoist and his team-mates clocked up the air miles and added several stamps to their passports, as the Light Blues embarked on a tour of Australia, New Zealand, Canada and the United States before refining their preparations with a series of matches in Switzerland and West Germany.

The trip to Australia, New Zealand, Canada and the US took place just a few weeks after the conclusion of the 1983/84 season. Jock Wallace arranged the trip in a bid to foster a real team spirit in the first-team player pool. He had implemented the same strategy midway through his previous spell in charge of Rangers when he had taken his players to Australia and New Zealand in the summer of 1975, and the trip laid the foundations for two domestic Trebles. He was clearly hoping this excursion would deliver the same results as it had done nine years earlier.

The trip was by no means a jolly one, though. The team-bonding sessions were interspersed with a number of tough matches, with Rangers taking on the national sides of Australia and New Zealand before crossing swords with Toronto Blizzard, Minnesota Strikers and Bundesliga champions VfB Stuttgart once they arrived Stateside.

The round-the-world trip also afforded some ex-pats the rare opportunity to watch their Rangers heroes at close quarters and the attendances for all the matches were healthy, with the presence of such a large number of Rangers supporters only serving to illustrate to McCoist what a unique association Rangers have with their following. 'Whenever you walk through the imposing front doors at Ibrox and into the marble hall you know that the club is special,' he said. 'But if you ever had any doubts, just one lengthy tour with the team would demonstrate the bond which exists between the club and its supporters. It is honestly quite incredible.'[1]

Rangers played in a total of nine matches on their travels, winning three, drawing three and losing three, with McCoist playing in all the games and scoring four goals. He netted a brace against Australia in a 3-2 defeat in Sydney, once against the Australia 'B' side in a 4-2 victory in Newcastle, and once in a 5-2 defeat against Minnesota that was played on artificial grass at the indoor Metrodome Stadium in Minneapolis.

The tour was not without its troubles, though, with strikers Bobby Williamson and Colin McAdam both sustaining injuries that would effectively sideline them for the whole of the season ahead. Williamson made just one appearance before breaking his leg when he fell awkwardly after trying to jump over a small fence at the team hotel, and McAdam suffered the same injury during the defeat against the Aussies. The loss of Williamson, in particular, was a real blow for Wallace, as he had intended to team him with McCoist in attack for the season ahead.

With the ranks swelled by new additions Iain Ferguson and Cammy Fraser, both of whom were purchased from Dundee, Rangers completed their preparation for the new season with five games in Europe and an Ibrox friendly against Leicester City. Injury kept McCoist out of the first three fixtures in Switzerland and also excused him from a trip to the famous 'Murder Hill' on the beaches of Gullane in East Lothian. In his first stint as manager, Wallace and his players had been regular visitors to the sand dunes for pre-season training, and although the sessions were torturous (many players were physically sick as they ran up and down the unforgiving sandy slopes), they boosted stamina, which meant Rangers often outlasted their opponents when the competitive action got underway. Wallace was clearly keen to apply the tried and tested formula again, and although McCoist missed out this time around, he endured the 'ordeal' the following summer ahead of the 1985/86 season.

It was evident that the harsh training at Gullane was working as, in McCoist's absence, Rangers racked up three straight wins against relatively modest opposition, knocking in eighteen goals in the process. McCoist returned to the ranks for the fourth match of the tour, a 3-0 reverse at the hands of FC Sion, and also took his place for the final contest, a fine 2-1 win over FC Kaiserslautern. He was paired alongside new recruit Ferguson in attack, and the duo showed signs of promise when they both got on the scoresheet in the last friendly before the league programme began, a 2-2 draw against Gary Lineker's Leicester at Ibrox.

Three days after the draw with Leicester, the competitive action kicked off with a drab 0-0 draw at home to St Mirren in the Premier Division, a result that seemed to quell the initial optimism that had reverberated around the corridors of Ibrox Stadium just a few months earlier. However, Rangers soon recovered their stride and lost just two of their opening twenty league fixtures to leave them handily placed in the race for the championship. They recorded several morale-boosting victories in that period, with fellow challengers Dundee United beaten at Ibrox and draws registered home and away against Celtic, which meant that, as 1984 drew to a close, Wallace's side were only six points adrift of league leaders Aberdeen.

For Ally McCoist, however, the opening gambit of the 1984/85 season had not been such a pleasant experience, as he struggled to rediscover the form that had made him top goalscorer at Ibrox during his debut season. He continued his love affair with the League Cup, scoring twice and delivering a Man of the Match display against Raith Rovers in the third round and three times over the course of the two-leg semi-final against Meadowbank Thistle (his tally of five goals made him the tournament's top scorer for the second successive year), but he failed to reproduce that kind of scoring return in the Premier Division. He scored just twice in the opening twenty league matches – against Dumbarton at Boghead in August and Morton at Ibrox in September – and by November had lost his place in the first team following a glaring miss in a UEFA Cup tie against Inter Milan.

In addition to putting up a sustained challenge for the Premier Division title, one of Jock Wallace's objectives for the season was to enjoy a prolonged run in Europe. The League Cup triumph against Celtic had handed Rangers a place in the 1984/85 UEFA Cup and they were drawn to face Bohemians of Dublin in the first round.

The first leg of the tie, played at Dalymount Park, was not McCoist's first experience of competitive continental football, though. He had made his European debut on the holiday island of Malta a year earlier, as Rangers thrashed Valletta 8-0 in the opening round of the European Cup-Winners' Cup. The name 'McCoist' may not have appeared on the scoresheet, but he did create three of the four goals scored by unlikely hero Dave McPherson. A bout of flu kept McCoist out of the return leg, a match Rangers won 10-0 to rack up a Scottish record 18-0 aggregate victory, but he played in both legs of the second-round tie against FC Porto. Rangers won 2-1 at Ibrox, but a 1-0 defeat in Portugal, while under the charge of caretaker manager Tommy McLean, saw them eliminated from the tournament on the away-goals rule.

Unfortunately, the match against Bohemians will always be remembered for events off the field rather than on it. The tie was played against the backdrop of a poisonous atmosphere stimulated by sectarian hatred, with passions stirred further when a Union Jack was torched in the Bohemians end during the first half. Both sets of fans exchanged vitriolic insults throughout the opening forty-five minutes to such an extent that the football match unfolding in front of them seemed coincidental.

By half-time, with the sides level at 2-2, the trouble had escalated, and when a Bohemians supporter entered the field of play in an attempt to attack the Rangers substitutes, the riot that had threatened to erupt at various junctures during the first half finally came to pass. A Rangers fan entered the fray in an attempt to attack the Irish pitch invader and within minutes supporters from both sides had also scaled the fencing that penned them onto the terraces. The police eventually restored some semblance of order, aided by Jock Wallace, who emerged from his half-time team talk to appeal for calm among the Rangers supporters.

Rangers were severely reprimanded by UEFA for the conduct of their supporters, but survived a threatened expulsion from the tournament to scrape through to the next round. McCoist actually broke his European scoring duck in the first leg in Dublin, hooking a cross from Davie Cooper into the net after just seven minutes, but the Dubliners fought back to win by three goals to two, and it took two late goals in the second leg at Ibrox to carry Rangers through 4-3 on aggregate.

Rangers' opponents in the second round were Italian cracks Inter Milan, one of the most distinguished names in the history of European football. This was the second time Rangers had met them in European competition, with the previous contest in the 1964/65 European Cup ending in a narrow 3-2 aggregate victory for the Italians. As had been the case in the earlier meeting, the first leg of the tie with Inter was played in Milan, and took place just four days before Rangers were due at Hampden to face Dundee United in the League Cup final and it was in the cauldron of the San Siro that things began to turn sour for Ally McCoist.

Few gave Rangers much hope of progressing against the star-studded Serie A side. No Scottish club side had ever won a match on Italian soil, and Inter were a side decorated with a multi-national assortment of talent, ranging from Walter Zenga in goal through to Liam Brady in midfield and the dynamic front pairing of Alessandro Altobelli and Karl Heinz Rummenigge. Wallace's men refused to be intimidated, though, and gave an excellent account of themselves throughout the match.

Inter took the lead early in the game but, despite doubling their advantage after sixty-eight minutes, Rangers were always in with a chance of snatching a crucial away goal, and sixty seconds after the veteran Franco Causio had notched Inter's second goal, the golden opportunity presented itself. Midfielder Ian Redford unleashed a shot from the edge of the penalty area, which beat Zenga all ends up, and the Italian goalkeeper could only watch as the ball fizzed towards goal. It rebounded from the crossbar and McCoist, lurking in the six-yard box, followed the trajectory of the ball as it spun towards him, setting up a simple chance to score. With Zenga lying powerless a few yards away, the goal gaped in front of the striker and all he had to do was hit the target to give Rangers that much sought-after goal. McCoist mistimed his jump, though, and his header failed to find the target: the proverbial 'sitter' had been missed. 'It was the kind of opening I should be able to put away every time,' he said, 'but in the circumstances I snatched at the ball, the chance disappeared and you know the rest of the story.'[2]

It was a glaring miss. Had McCoist scored, the whole complexion of the tie would have changed, as the away goal would have presented Rangers with a realistic chance of progressing to the third round. Instead, 'the rest of the story' that McCoist spoke about saw the striker punished for his profligacy when Inter stepped up a gear and chalked up a third goal three minutes from time. Altobelli was the architect, sprinting down the left before crossing for Rummenigge to head into the net from close range.

Although he retained his place in the starting eleven for the League Cup final at Hampden fours days later – Rangers defeated United 1-0 thanks to an Iain Ferguson goal a minute before half-time – McCoist was relegated to the substitutes' bench for the second match against Inter at Ibrox. From his vantage point on the sidelines, he watched along with over 30,000 others as Rangers almost climbed the seemingly unassailable mountain. Wallace, who was unable to field Davie Cooper, after the winger failed to pass a late fitness test, gambled, throwing centre-half and captain John McClelland up front alongside League Cup match-winner Ferguson and the Australian Dave Mitchell, and it almost paid off when a spirited performance produced a 3-1 victory on the night. The result was not enough, though, and Rangers tumbled out 4-3 on aggregate, with many rueing the missed opportunity that had fallen to McCoist in Italy. One of them was Jock Wallace, who said: 'Ally McCoist had the best chance of the game [in Milan] and failed to score. If that had gone in then we would have gone through. I'm convinced of that.'³

McCoist suffered as a result of his misfortune in front of goal in Milan. He was omitted from the squad for the next league match, a 2-2 draw with Hibernian at Easter Road, and was banished to the reserves. During his nine-game stint in the second team, he scored against Hibernian, Aberdeen (twice), Hearts, and St Mirren, but his return to form did not result in instant restoration to the top team. He missed a total of seven fixtures and rumours once again surfaced that his time at Ibrox was at an end. Alan Durban, now in charge of Cardiff City, approached Jock Wallace with an offer to take McCoist on loan, but Wallace rebuffed the proposal, stating that he had 'no intention of letting the player go anywhere on loan or otherwise' before moving to boost McCoist's spirits by saying: 'He has been put in the reserves to find his feet again and I have been pleased by his attitude.'⁴

McCoist's improved attitude and form eventually prompted Wallace to recall him to the first-team squad and he made his return to the top team when he replaced Derek Ferguson after sixty-eight minutes of a 4-2 win over Dumbarton at Boghead four days after Christmas. However, although back in the first-team picture, the New Year kicked off just as the old one had ended for McCoist, as he made just one substitute appearance in the first three matches of 1985. He was left out of the squad that travelled to Parkhead on New Year's Day, a fixture Rangers lost by two goals to one, and he missed out again when Rangers lost by the same scoreline at home to Hibernian eleven days later, turning out for the reserves instead.

Those two defeats, coupled with a 2-2 draw at Dundee, meant that Wallace's men did not enjoy a happy start to the New Year, and when they were thrashed 5-1 by Aberdeen at Pittodrie on 19 January, all the early season promise evaporated. Their league form went into a sharp decline, with Wallace's men winning only four of their last sixteen matches and losing nine of the other twelve. Such form is hardly the hallmark of championship challengers and Rangers once again limped home in fourth place, although this time only goal difference separated the Light Blues and fifth-placed St Mirren. The gulf between Rangers and the rest of the championship contenders was of mammoth proportions: they finished up twenty-one points adrift of champions Aberdeen, fourteen behind runners-up Celtic and nine away from third-placed Dundee United.

McCoist, without a goal for the first team for four months, had made his first start since the San Siro debacle in the 5-1 pummelling at Pittodrie, and he was still in the side when Dundee arrived at Ibrox on Scottish Cup business on 16 February. With the league challenge petering out, the Cup represented the last realistic chance for the Light Blues to add to the League Cup they had won in October, but on a desperate afternoon, their season came to a shuddering conclusion. The ninety minutes played out in front of a crowd of 26,619 represented the nadir of Ally McCoist's Rangers career.

In the early 1980s, Dundee had been something of a bogey team for Rangers. The Light Blues had won just three of the previous eight Premier Division fixtures contested between the pair, and it was the Dens Park men who had extinguished Rangers' hopes of an eighth successive Scottish Cup final appearance the previous campaign when they eliminated Wallace's men at the quarter-final stage. Dundee arrived in Govan imbued by the confidence garnered from a 2-0 league victory over title-chasing Celtic seven days earlier and, with only ten minutes of the match gone, they set themselves on course for an Old Firm double when John Brown, who would later become a Rangers legend himself, put the visitors ahead when he flicked a corner-kick beyond Peter McCloy.

Rangers recovered from the early blow, though, and began to take control of the match, creating goal-scoring opportunities and dominating possession. Chance after chance fell to McCoist, but he contrived to spurn all the scoring opportunities that came his way, either putting the ball beyond the post, over the bar or seeing it stopped by the goalkeeper. No matter how hard he tried, he simply could not get his name on the scoresheet. His fortune on the day was summed up when he eventually did find the net only to have his 'goal' ruled out for offside. 'I'd give up twenty of the other goals I've scored in my time at Ibrox just to have got one in the net that day,' he recalled some years later. [5]

The match ended 1-0 in Dundee's favour and another opportunity to bring silverware to Ibrox had vanished. As the despondent players trooped off the Ibrox turf, the home support howled and booed, baying for blood, with McCoist their number one target, the scapegoat for another afternoon of total frustration. Ibrox rose in unison to berate the striker and launched into a tirade of abuse that culminated in a song that told McCoist, in no uncertain terms, where he could go.

Once back inside the dressing room, the young striker was overcome with emotion and he burst into tears. 'The months of abuse and controlling my feelings took their toll,' he said, 'and I howled like a baby.'[6] Experienced pros like Derek Johnstone and Colin McAdam intervened in a bid to diffuse the situation and reassure their heartbroken team-mate, and they eventually helped McCoist compose himself.

Outside the main entrance at Ibrox, Edmiston Drive was alive with a throng of supporters angrily demonstrating against the inept performances of their team, with one disgruntled fan even hurling the remainder of his season ticket book through the front door. Wallace and his players were pilloried, with McCoist berated more than most. It seemed harsh on the young striker, as no one in a blue jersey had performed well on the day, but in situations such as this a scapegoat is often sought and his wastefulness in front of goal saw McCoist cast in that role on this occasion.

Taking the advice of his team-mates to keep his head down and not inflame the situation by engaging in any sort of discussion with the dissatisfied fans, McCoist simply gathered his belongings and headed for the exit. He did not stop until he reached the sanctuary of his car, but en route his ears were bombarded with vitriolic comments, ones that hurt to his very core. It was all the more upsetting, as McCoist's girlfriend Allison and her aunt and uncle had made the trip to Scotland to see McCoist in action for the first time.

Rangers were torn to shreds the next day, as their supporters and the media sifted through the wreckage of another 'car crash' season at Ibrox. The focus of the fury of a clutch of supporters was the profligate Ally McCoist, and although Wallace leapt to his defence – 'Nobody works harder than him and let's not forget that it was the same McCoist who won us the League Cup last season'[7] – it failed to prevent the beleaguered striker receiving a sack load of hate mail from a minority of supporters in the Rangers community. The criticism was stinging and upsetting, but the nasty correspondence was offset by a letter McCoist received from a gentleman by the name of Willie Woodburn.

Nicknamed 'Big Ben', Woodburn had made over 300 appearances for Rangers between 1946 and 1955 and had been a linchpin at the heart of the club's celebrated 'Iron Curtain' defence of that era. He was a tough customer and a passionate man who hated to lose, but above all he had been a very gifted centre-half. Unfortunately, he is best remembered for receiving a *sine dine* suspension in September 1954, a punishment dished out after he had been ordered off in the final minute of a League Cup tie against Stirling Albion. It was the fifth time Woodburn had been sent from the field in his fourteen-year career and the beaks at the SFA decided to make an example of him. The ludicrous ban was eventually lifted in April 1957, but Woodburn had long since quit the game. In his letter to McCoist, Woodburn instructed the young striker to forget about his woes from the Dundee game. 'He thought that I'd all the makings of a great player and that one day I'd prove all these fans wrong,' McCoist recalls. 'Getting a letter like that from a real Rangers legend was a tremendous lift – at a time when I really needed it. I can't thank him enough for that.'[8]

McCoist was dropped for Rangers' next match after the Cup exit, a 2-0 league defeat at the hands of Hearts at Tynecastle, but he played for the reserves and scored twice as the second string beat their Edinburgh counterparts by five goals to one at Ibrox. Another brace three days later in a 2-2 draw against Forfar Athletic in Stewart Kennedy's testimonial staked his claim for a swift return to the top team, and Wallace, who had demoted McCoist in a bid to rebuild his shattered confidence, was clearly impressed with his striker's performances, for he was immediately reinstated to the first eleven for the next league match against Dumbarton at Ibrox. It proved a seminal moment in Ally McCoist's Rangers career, as it marked the beginning of one of the most successful goal-scoring stories in the history of Scottish Football.

Only 8,424 patrons graced the Ibrox stands that March afternoon, but the sparse attendance witnessed an emphatic return to form for McCoist. Eric Ferguson, making his first Premier Division appearance since August, opened the scoring after sixteen minutes, grabbing Rangers' first competitive goal for a month in the process, and McCoist doubled the home side's advantage in the twenty-seventh minute when he fired home a pass from Cooper. He then proceeded to complete his third double of the week two minutes into the second half, and only the athleticism of the Dumbarton goalkeeper Gordon Arthur denied him a hat-trick, the Sons' stopper diving to tip away McCoist's goal-bound header. Rangers eventually won the match by three goals to one to pick up only their second league victory of 1985 and, although it may sound a little melodramatic, it could be argued that the goals scored by McCoist that day were among the most important he ever struck in a Rangers jersey.

A goal-scoring contribution that had slowed to little more than a trickle was now back in full flow, and a spate of goals followed as McCoist became a mainstay in the side for the remainder of the campaign. Feeding on the confidence successful strikers thrive upon, he scored ten goals in the last nine league fixtures, a real purple patch for the striker. He only failed to score in two of those games, and included in his scoring haul was a late equaliser from the penalty spot in the last Old Firm match of the season at Parkhead and a superb hat-trick in a 3-0 win over Morton at Cappielow. One of McCoist's goals in the latter match was created by debutant Ian Durrant, who was rewarded for a stellar display with the Man of the Match trophy. In those days, eighteen-year-old Durrant was McCoist's boot boy, and the duo forged a brotherly bond from that moment. 'I have made many friends in this football life,' McCoist penned in the foreword to Durrant's autobiography *Blue and White Dynamite*, 'but in Ian Durrant I found the little brother I never had.'[9]

Given that McCoist had been staring into the abyss only three months earlier, his late-season goal glut represented a remarkable turnaround in both form and fortune. He was now back in favour with both the manager and the discerning supporters (his late penalty goal against Celtic had been greeted with a less than melodic rendition of 'Super Ally'), and the ten goals scored in that period gave him a total of eighteen for the season. For the second successive campaign, he finished as the club's top goalscorer, with a breakdown of twelve league goals, five in the League Cup and one in the UEFA Cup. He also scored one of Rangers' goals when they defeated Kuwait 2-1 in a friendly match in Jordan – Rangers played three matches in the Gulf in March to complete a whirlwind year of travel for the club – and he had the distinction of becoming the first player to score a hat-trick in the annual Tennents Sixes tournament. McCoist's treble helped Rangers to a 4-0 win over Hibernian, but his goals were not enough to keep the trophy at Ibrox. Despite beating Morton 4-3, holders Rangers lost 3-1 to both St Mirren and Dundee to exit the tournament at the group stages.

As the season drew to a close, McCoist was looking to the future with renewed vigour. His thirst for goals had finally been quenched and the twenty-two-year-old was now riding on the crest of a wave. He was refusing to rest on his laurels, though, saying: 'I want to do better next season and keep my form all the way through the year. If I can work at that then maybe I can help the team challenge for the Premier League title – which is what we all want to win at Ibrox.'[10]

As the new campaign dawned, though, the pressure was mounting on Jock Wallace. He had been reappointed as manager in the hope that he could return Rangers to their former glories, but instead of closing the gap that had developed between themselves and the top trio of Aberdeen, Celtic and Dundee United, his Rangers side were being cast further adrift. Wallace was wise enough to know that neither the board nor the fans would tolerate another abysmal campaign.

He intended to prepare for the 1985/86 season in West Germany, but the Heysel tragedy in Brussels prompted a change of plan and Rangers toured the Highlands instead. McCoist found the net in both of Rangers' games, scoring twice in a 5-1 win over Ross County and netting once in a 6-0 thrashing of Inverness Caledonian. The pre-season schedule was completed with victories over Ayr United and FC Twente Enschede, with the match against the Dutch side delivering McCoist's fourth goal of the pre-season.

Despite the dreadful end to the previous campaign, Jock Wallace made only one new signing for 1985/86, recruiting midfielder Dougie Bell from Aberdeen. The fact that he did not attempt to shore up a leaky defence that had conceded forty-one goals in twenty-seven games in the wake of the departure of club captain John McClelland surprised many in the Rangers community. The big Northern Irishman had quit the club to join Watford in the English First Division in November 1984 having been at loggerheads with both Wallace and the Rangers board for some months over his wage demands. Failure to plug the gap he left ultimately proved to be Wallace's downfall.

Initially, at least, things looked good for Rangers. The team got off to a good start and were unbeaten in their first six league games, with victories over Dundee United, Hibernian, Hearts, St Mirren and Clydebank and a 1-1 draw with Celtic at Parkhead taking the side to the summit of the Premier Division table. McCoist started the season in fine form too, netting in each of the opening two Premier Division fixtures against Dundee United and Hibernian and also making the breakthrough after thirty-four minutes of the Old Firm match when he knocked the ball into the net following some excellent wing play from full-back Hugh Burns.

However, Rangers' good fortune did not last long and the wheels came off their championship bandwagon spectacularly in late September when the club suffered back-to-back home defeats against Dundee (0-1) and Aberdeen (0-3). Further defeats against Hibernian (1-2), St Mirren (1-2), Hearts (0-3) and Dundee (2-3) threatened to leave Rangers marooned in the bottom half of the table.

Throughout this calamitous spell, McCoist managed to maintain his free-scoring form, finding the net against Motherwell (a double in a 3-0 win at Fir Park in October and the only goal of the game at Ibrox two months later), Dundee United (solitary strikes in 1-1 draws at Tannadice and Ibrox), St Mirren (Rangers' only goal in the 2-1 defeat at Love Street in October), Celtic (the third goal in a surprise 3-0 win at Ibrox on 9 November) and Dundee (a brace in a 3-2 defeat at Dens Park in which John Brown stole the show with a hat-trick for the home side). However, despite boasting an abundant goal-scoring return, McCoist was still powerless to prevent the club's slide into mediocrity.

The team fared little better in the New Year. They lost 2-0 at Parkhead on New Year's Day, and although they offered hope by stringing together a run of three successive victories that included a 5-0 home victory against Dundee, Rangers won only two of their last twelve league games. In total, Wallace's men lost fourteen of their thirty-six matches in the

Premier Division and eventually finished fifth in the table. They failed to average a point per game for the first time in their illustrious history and fifth place and passage to European football for 1986/87 was only granted on the last day of the season by virtue of a 2-0 home win over Motherwell. Salt was poured into the already gaping wounds when arch-rivals Celtic won the championship, their first since 1982, on the last Saturday of the season, winning 5-0 at Love Street against St Mirren to pinch the title from Hearts on goal difference.

No solace could be derived from the cup competitions either and the season ended without domestic silverware. Hibernian extinguished hopes of a third successive League Cup triumph with a 2-1 aggregate win in a two-leg semi-final. Alan Rough saved a McCoist penalty in the first leg at Easter Road as Rangers went down 2-0 and, despite halving the deficit courtesy of a trademark Davie Cooper free-kick at Ibrox a fortnight later, Rangers tumbled out of the competition. It was another side from the nation's capital that halted any charge in the Scottish Cup too, with Hearts defeating the Light Blues 3-2 at Tynecastle in their third-round encounter. Any hope that a decent run in the UEFA Cup could bring some much needed cheer to Govan also ended in the opening round. In fact, the 2-1 aggregate defeat from Spanish minnows and European debutants Osasuna only served to deepen the depression that had enshrouded Ibrox. The 1985/86 season had been without doubt the worst in the club's history. Rangers had hit rock bottom.

The one shining light through all the gloom, however, was the prolific form of McCoist, with 1985/86 being the most productive of his first three seasons in a blue jersey. He played in thirty-three of the thirty-six Premier Division games and scored twenty-five goals to finish the season not only as the club's top goalscorer, but also as the leading marksman in the Premier Division. His haul included hat-tricks against Dundee (in January) and Hibernian (in March) and three Old Firm goals. He also netted a vital penalty-kick on the final day of the season, as Rangers defeated Motherwell 2-0 to clinch a place in Europe. Goals against Hearts in the Scottish Cup and Clyde in the League Cup took his final tally for the season to twenty-seven.

The last of his three strikes against Celtic came in a quite splendid clash of the titans in March. The compelling match, played out in lashing rain at Ibrox, developed into a real seesaw affair, with Rangers clawing their way back from 3-1 down at one point to lead 4-3 only to be pegged back to 4-4 in the dying moments of the contest. McCoist scored Rangers' second goal, a sizzling 25-yard 'daisy cutter', and played a pivotal role in their first goal of the match too, as he provided an inch-perfect cross for Cammy Fraser to net the first of his two goals. 'It finished 4-4 and it was one of those games, the only game, where both sets of Old Firm fans went home happy,' McCoist recalled when reflecting on the contest in 1991.[11]

The one blemish on the McCoist report card for the season was a red card, the first of his senior career, dished out during a league match against Hearts at Ibrox in August. He was dismissed for his part in a skirmish that ensued following an incident involving Dougie Bell and Walter Kidd eighteen minutes from the end of the game. McCoist was one of a number of players from both sides to have got involved, and when he threw a punch at Hearts striker Sandy Clark, he was sent for an early bath. Clark, who had been a team-mate at Ibrox less than eighteen months previously, was also ordered off, along with the initial perpetrator, Walter Kidd.

McCoist was heavily censured for his conduct. On top of a hefty fine from Rangers and the automatic one-match ban that accompanies a dismissal, he was suspended for a further three games by the SFA. He did attempt to have the additional ban quashed by lodging an appeal, but his plea fell on deaf ears at Park Gardens in spite of the fact that he boasted an exemplary disciplinary record up until that point. He had accrued just five bookings since he had signed for Rangers, but the ban stood and he missed Rangers' league matches against St Mirren, Clydebank and Dundee and a League Cup tie against Forfar Athletic as a result.

The red card aside, the 1985/86 season was a personal triumph for McCoist. He had now expunged the memories of that horrific spell in the latter part of 1984 and the early months of 1985, and was now becoming a firm favourite with the Rangers crowd. This was borne out by the countless 'Player of the Year' awards he received from Supporters' Clubs throughout the country, and McCoist also became an icon for the club's young supporters, becoming the first recipient of the Young Rangers Club 'Player of the Year' award. He was an overwhelming winner too, polling seventy percent of the votes cast. However, although delighted to pick up these awards, McCoist was acutely aware that football was a team game and that personal accolades and praise in the media meant nothing if they did not bring with them success in the shape of silverware for Rangers.

ALMOST THE END OF THE ROAD: 1984–86

The return of Jock Wallace to the helm at Ibrox had clearly failed, and his second spell in charge came to an end when he was sacked on the 7 April 1986, the day after a dismal 2-0 home defeat to Tottenham Hotspur in a friendly that only attracted a meagre 12,665 patrons through the Ibrox turnstiles. McCoist recalled that Rangers 'were disgraceful that day'[12], but even victory over the London side would not have earned Wallace a reprieve. Performances throughout the previous campaign had been unacceptable on all fronts and, in the end, it turned out to be a somewhat ignominious departure for the colossal figure of Wallace, with the memories of his successful first stint in charge now fading into the distance.

Alarm bells were now tolling around Ibrox, with fans disillusioned and fearful of what lay ahead for their beloved club. David Holmes, the newly installed chief executive, knew he had to do something to stop the listing Rangers ship from crashing into the rocks, and the salvage plan he drew up and implemented not only reinvigorated the fortunes of the Ibrox club, it also shook up Scottish football and dragged it kicking and screaming into the twenty-first century.

CHAPTER SIX

THE AWAKENING: 1986–87

The winds of change that would eventually sweep through Ibrox Stadium like a hurricane started out as little more than a breeze in November 1985 when Lawrence Marlborough, a successful businessman and the grandson of former Rangers chairman John Lawrence, purchased a sufficient number of shares to gain a controlling interest in Rangers Football Club. With much of his business interests lying in the United States, Marlborough knew he would be unable to take the usual hands-on role that goes with running a football club, so he moved quickly to install David Holmes, a native of Falkirk and chief executive of one of Marlborough's UK-based firms, as chairman and chief executive at Ibrox.

On the day of his appointment, Holmes was eager to stress to the restless supporters that there would be no quick-fix solution. He intended to take six months to assess the lie of the land at Ibrox and then make moves to rectify what was now a dire situation. True to his word, almost half a year after his appointment, David Holmes stood proudly in the Blue Room at Ibrox and announced to the expectant media that he had finally snared the man he felt would lead Rangers out of the mire. On the 8 April 1986, twenty-four hours after Jock Wallace had emptied his desk in the manager's office, Graeme Souness was unveiled as Rangers Football Club's eighth manager.

Souness first registered his interest in the Rangers manager's job in a television interview shortly before the start of the World Cup in Mexico in 1986. At that time he was plying his trade with Sampdoria in Italy, having moved to Genoa in 1984 after enjoying a trophy-laden seven years with Liverpool in the English First Division. In his time at Anfield, he had captained the Merseysiders to their third European Cup success in 1984 and had collected an array of medals and baubles that included a further two European Cup-winners' medals, five League Championship badges and four consecutive English League Cup medals. He was also captain of the Scottish national team and had fifty-two international caps to his name. The interviewer asked if Souness, by now at the age of thirty-three and approaching the veteran stages of his career, whether he would ever consider gracing the Scottish game with his considerable talents. Souness was quick to point out that while fiercely patriotic, the financial rewards of playing football outside his native land were far more enticing, but he did say that, one day, he wouldn't mind coming back to be player-manager at Rangers. As luck would have it, Holmes saw the interview and immediately pinpointed Souness as the man he wanted at the Ibrox helm.

Ally McCoist was deeply saddened by the departure of Jock Wallace. He was in Sunderland when his mother telephoned him to inform him that Wallace had been sacked and replaced by Souness. After a difficult start, their relationship had blossomed, with Wallace acting as a footballing father figure to McCoist, often taking the striker into his confidence and discussing his plans for the future at Ibrox with him. 'My first reaction was to feel absolutely gutted for big Jock,' said McCoist upon hearing the news of Souness' appointment. 'We had become very close and although I never got the chance to hear his farewell at Ibrox, I went round to his house in Bothwell as soon as I came back north to see him and his wife Daphne and to wish them both all the best.'[1]

The arrival of Souness had Ibrox buzzing again and the day after he had been appointed there was a real air of excitement around the stadium as he was introduced to his new charges for the first time. 'My first impression was of the immediate presence of the man,' recalls McCoist. 'He was dressed immaculately, he looked fit and tanned and he spoke with firm authority. He said that he was used to success and he wanted to bring success to Rangers. Everyone on the staff would have the chance to show what they could do and he was looking forward to working with us as a team. Straight to the point – short and sweet.'[2]

However, although he had vast experience in football, Souness had little or no knowledge of the Scottish game. To help him on this score, Walter Smith was appointed as his assistant manager. Smith, a lifelong Rangers supporter, had an impressive coaching CV that included involvement with the Scotland Youth team (during which time he had encountered Ally McCoist for the first time), and latterly as a hugely successful assistant to Jim McLean at Dundee United. He had also assisted Alex Ferguson during Scotland's World Cup campaign in Mexico '86.

A fresh and exciting era beckoned for Rangers, but for one of their main protagonists in the 1985/86 season there remained a degree of uncertainty. The three-year contract McCoist had penned when he joined up at Ibrox in the summer of 1983 had now expired, and although talks over an extension had begun under Jock Wallace, Rangers' principal marksman was unsure whether the new management team would still require his services.

On the face of it he need not have worried. He had just enjoyed his most consistent and productive season with Rangers and had become the 946th player to represent his country as a full international when he had won his first cap for Scotland at the end of April 1986, pulling on the dark blue jersey for a 0-0 draw with Holland in a World Cup warm-up friendly in Eindhoven. His international debut earned him a new nickname in the dressing room, with team-mate Derek Johnstone christening him 'Ally Two-Caps', as he felt, somewhat tongue-in-cheek, that McCoist had earned two caps on the one night, his first and his last!

With reported interest from clubs in Spain, Belgium and England, Graeme Souness was keen to tie up the services of the club's top goalscorer, and contract talks were arranged to take place prior to Souness' first significant match in charge, the Glasgow Cup final against Celtic at Ibrox on 9 May. However, the arrival of the new manager had aroused more interest in the match than normal – an extraordinary crowd of 40,741 came through the Ibrox turnstiles, over ten times the audience that had witnessed the previous year's final between Rangers and Queen's Park at Hampden Park – and McCoist, never famed for impeccable time keeping at the best of times, found himself stuck in the heart of the heavy matchday traffic, resulting in a late arrival at the stadium and prompting a postponement to the contract discussion until after the match. Souness was not exactly pleased with the delay, but McCoist was soon back in his good books thanks to a typical storybook performance.

Celtic arrived on the south side of Glasgow still basking in the glory of their last-gasp triumph in the Premier Division just six days earlier, but Rangers and McCoist took them down a peg or two with the kind of display that had been sadly lacking for much of the 1985/86 season. Only nine minutes had elapsed when Rangers hit the front. In the midst of a heavy downpour, Hugh Burns scampered down the right flank and his ball into the box picked out McCoist who, despite not connecting properly with his shot, beat Peter Latchford in the Celtic goal. Celtic drew level just before the interval through Brian McClair, but Rangers assumed control once more fourteen minutes from time when McCoist again got the better of Latchford. Cammy Fraser provided the supply on this occasion, and although the Celtic goalkeeper took the sting out of McCoist's effort, he could not prevent the ball from dribbling over the line. A Maurice Johnston goal in the eighty-third minute forced a thrilling match into extra-time, but McCoist completed his hat-trick to claim a third successive Glasgow Cup triumph for Rangers with a stunning 20-yard effort seven minutes into the first period of extra-time. Added to the two goals he had netted in the semi-final against Queen's Park, the treble took McCoist's Glasgow Cup tally to seven goals in six appearances – he had also scored in the semi-final and final of the 1984/85 competition – and gave Souness a piece of silverware in just his second match in charge.

After the match, McCoist, still on a high after his match-winning display, climbed the marble staircase to the manager's office to discuss his new deal. Even when offers for his services from other clubs had been flooding in earlier in the season, McCoist had reiterated his desire to extend his stay at Rangers and the arrival of the ambitious Souness had done nothing to dampen his desire. He had very little problem agreeing personal terms and promptly signed a new four-year contract. 'Rangers and Graeme Souness were going places,' he said. 'No way was I going to miss out.'[3]

In truth, Rangers were in a shocking state when Souness breezed in through the Ibrox doors. Aside from their woes on the pitch, the club was also in dire need of an overhaul off it. Both Souness and Smith were astounded at the mess the place was in. For years it had been commonplace for the players to return from training, leave their muddy kit in a pile on the dressing-room floor and then return the next day and simply extract their kit from the same pile, unwashed, and wear it for that day's session. This practice was quickly changed and each player was issued with a fresh set of training gear every day. Souness also noted that many of the players entered and left the shower room barefoot, which left them susceptible to injury should there be any sharp objects or debris on the floor. To combat this, the new manager made the wearing of flip-flops in and around the dressing room compulsory and any player caught without them soon found himself issued with a reprimand and a fine. The players' diets were also revolutionised. From the time he had spent in Italy, Souness had observed how well the Italians looked after themselves, with fatty foods and red meat replaced on the menu by pasta, chicken and other foodstuffs high in carbohydrates and protein. Souness was quick to point out that, for a footballer, your body was your bank and that it needed to be looked after in the best way possible. Training was different too, with the accent not just on improving fitness but also suppleness, and most sessions were preceded with a spell of stretching exercises.

As if that wasn't enough, Souness set about moulding Rangers into a top-class side once again. At that time, the tendency was that players moved from Scottish clubs to English clubs and it was almost unheard of for players to move from the First Division in England to what was perceived to be the inferior Premier League in Scotland. Souness elected to challenge that paradigm, though, by attempting to coax top players from the English First Division north of the border, and he succeeded, going about his business quietly at first before rounding off his dealings with a resounding bang.

First to join was Colin West, a striker and former team-mate of McCoist at Sunderland, at a cost £170,000. During his time at Roker Park, West had developed into an accomplished striker. He made his debut at the age of eighteen and went on to form a decent partnership with Gary Rowell, particularly in the season after McCoist had departed

Wearside, when he scored thirteen goals in forty-four appearances. The following season, West scored three of Sunderland's five goals as they defeated Chelsea in the Milk Cup semi-final, but he missed the final after being dropped by manager Len Ashurst. A few days later he was transferred to Watford, where he enjoyed two seasons under the guidance of Graham Taylor and continued his fine goal-scoring form with a return of twenty-three goals from fifty-five appearances.

The arrival of West, though, was low-key when compared to Souness' next two acquisitions. Firstly, the new Ibrox chief shattered the record transfer fee paid out for a goalkeeper when he brought in Chris Woods, England's second-choice goalkeeper, from Norwich for £600,000. But his *pièce de résistance* was the signing of Terry Butcher.

Having recognised that the Rangers defence had had something of a sieve-like quality about it and had been haemorrhaging goals in the last few years, Souness was looking for a commanding presence to play at the heart of his defence and, standing at 6ft 4in tall, Butcher certainly fitted the bill. At that time, he was regarded as one of the best centre-backs in the game. He was vice-captain of England and had enjoyed an excellent spell with Ipswich Town, during which time he had won a UEFA Cup-winners' medal.

In the summer of 1986, having excelled during the World Cup in Mexico, Butcher was attracting interest from a number of top clubs, including Manchester United. In truth, United was Butcher's preferred option and initially he did not entertain the idea of coming to play his football in Scotland, but Souness persuaded him to come to Ibrox, have a look around and listen to his plans for the future. Once he had toured Ibrox and listened to what Souness had to say he was hooked, and in August 1986, Terry Butcher snubbed Manchester United and signed for Rangers for a fee of £725,000, a deal which broke the club's transfer record. He was immediately installed as club captain and represented the cornerstone of Souness' rebuilding programme. Souness now had in place a solid spine for his new team (Woods, Butcher, himself and McCoist), and his transactions underlined his desire to reinstate Rangers at the forefront of the Scottish game and reinstall the club into what many believed to be their rightful place in the upper echelons of the game on the continent, too.

It was not all one-way traffic, though, and there were inevitably some casualties, with free transfers handed to Derek Johnstone, Eric Ferguson,

David MacKinnon, Andy Bruce, Billy Davies and John MacDonald. Bobby Williamson joined West Bromwich Albion in exchange for Jimmy Nicholl, and although Craig Paterson, club captain when Souness arrived, survived the initial cull, he was transferred to Motherwell shortly before Christmas.

After a relatively successful four-match pre-season tour of West Germany that yielded two wins, one draw, one defeat, and two goals for McCoist in the opening match against Union Solingen, Souness put the finishing touches to his preparations with two high-profile friendlies. The first was a visit to White Hart Lane to take on Tottenham Hotspur in Paul Miller's testimonial match, where a goal from Cammy Fraser earned Rangers a 1-1 draw, and the second was a 2-0 home defeat from top Bundesliga side Bayern Munich, a match that marked Butcher's first appearance in a Rangers jersey.

The new era for the club kicked off in earnest on Saturday, 9 August, when Souness led his new charges to Easter Road to take on Hibernian in the opening league fixture of the 1986/87 season. It turned out to be an explosive afternoon in the sultry summer sunshine.

Rangers, with their proud tradition and trophy-laden history, were always the team others in the Scottish League wanted to beat, and the arrival of the flashy Souness and his expensive imports from England only served to stoke this desire. Hibernian were the first team given the opportunity to take the big shots down a peg or two, and the hype ahead of the match was incredible. Indeed, it can be argued that this publicity went some way to contributing to the poisonous atmosphere that greeted Rangers on their arrival in the capital. 'It certainly was one of the nastiest games I've ever played in,' recalled McCoist a few years later.[4]

As Rangers, led by new skipper Butcher, emerged from the tunnel that day, they were greeted with a chorus of booing and jeering that cascaded down from the Easter Road terraces. From the kick-off it was clear that Souness was being singled out for some 'special' treatment from the home support, and the Hibernian players were not exactly slow at doling out their own brand of physical and verbal abuse. Tackles were flying in thick and fast from all angles, raising hackles and fraying tempers to the extent that the unsavoury scenes that came to pass seven minutes shy of the half-time interval were almost inevitable.

The blue touch paper was lit when Souness, booked fourteen minutes earlier for a foul on Billy Kirkwood, launched into a physical challenge with Hibernian striker George McCluskey in the middle of the park. The resulting collision detonated the bomb that had threatened to explode since the start of the match, and soon twenty of the twenty-two players were brawling in the centre-circle. It was mayhem, with fists and feet flailing. Colin West was fortunate to escape a heavier censure after he landed a punch on Mark Fulton, and McCoist, who boasted a fine disciplinary record, was also fortunate to stay on the field. Having been on the receiving end of some hard challenges from West's victim, Fulton, he used the clash as a means to exact some retribution and had a pop at the Hibernian centre-half. His actions may have been missed by the referee, Mike Delaney, but were captured by the television cameras: McCoist was lucky to escape further punishment, as this was still an era where television evidence was not scrutinised; he would not have been so fortunate today. 'It was sneaky and devious,' he recalled ashamedly. 'I cringe at the memory.'[5]

When calm was restored, Souness was given his marching orders and to cap a shameful Scottish Football baptism for the new player-manager, the Light Blues contrived to lose the match 2-1. Stuart Beedie gave Hibernian the lead in the sixteenth minute, but McCoist restored parity two minutes later when he scored from the penalty spot. The penalty incident actually proved the warm-up for the main event involving Souness and McCluskey. McCoist went to ground after becoming the meat in a Gordon Chisholm-Mark Fulton sandwich, and the Hibernian players were incensed when Delaney awarded Rangers a penalty-kick. They felt McCoist had been guilty of embellishing his fall, and Alan Rough and Billy Kirkwood's protests were so vehement that their names found their way into the referee's notebook. McCoist dusted himself down to score from twelve yards, but the home side won the match when Steve Cowan netted what proved to be the winning goal three minutes before the interval.

It had hardly been the most auspicious of starts to the Souness era. The *Sunday Mail* commented that 'this was a damning indictment on Rangers, who tossed aside credibility and control in a match which bordered on a street brawl'[6], and the Scottish Football Association also took a dim view of events. Souness was fined and handed a three-match ban, while Rangers were heavily censured to the tune of £5,000.

The media in Scotland were having a field day, gorging themselves on

Souness' on-field behaviour and Rangers' erratic start to the season. The club followed up the opening-day defeat with a narrow home win over Falkirk – another McCoist penalty handing Souness' men a 1-0 victory – but then contrived to toss away a two-goal lead against Dundee United to lose 3-2 at Ibrox.

The latter match was particularly alarming and really set the cat among the pigeons. For the first hour Rangers were in splendid form, racing into a 2-0 lead courtesy of a brace from McCoist, and they played some quite outstanding football into the bargain. However, a dramatic late capitulation allowed United to score three times in the final half-hour to make the trip back up the A9 with the points in the bag. To make matters worse for the men from Ibrox, there was a further stumble eleven days later in the League Cup when lowly East Fife were only taken care of by virtue of a 5-4 penalty shootout win after a 0-0 stalemate at Bayview. The formula for success was thus proving hard to find, but the opening gambit of the United match had at least indicated that the solution was not too far away from being discovered.

McCoist's potent early-season form was also encouraging. In addition to his four league goals, he also netted in a 4-1 win over Stenhousemuir in the opening round of the League Cup, a match that also yielded Colin West's first goal in a Light Blue jersey.

McCoist and West had kicked off the season spearheading the Rangers attack, and their partnership was ideal for Souness as he craved a forward line comprising a penalty-box striker (McCoist) and a tall, robust target man (West). The pair had played together in a handful of matches at Sunderland, but their time together at Ibrox was blighted after West picked up an injury in the League Cup fright at East Fife. Robert Fleck took West's place in the team and by the time the Englishman was fit again, young Fleck was regularly appearing on the scoresheet, which meant that West was unable to force his way back into the reckoning. After a season or so on the periphery of the first team and languishing in the reserves, West moved back to England when he signed for Sheffield Wednesday.

The promotion of Fleck, a product of the Rangers youth policy, to the first eleven proved a significant moment in Souness' opening season at Ibrox, as he and McCoist forged a lethal combination up front that shot Rangers back into contention for the principal prizes. The youngster had been on the fringes of the Rangers first team for the past two seasons, but despite being a prolific scorer with the reserve team (he had found the net twenty-nine times as the Rangers second string won the Premier Reserve League title in 1985/86), it looked likely that the arrival of the likes of West would see the diminutive forward plying his trade elsewhere. A move to Dundee was touted during the early months of Souness' reign (the club actually accepted a bid of £25,000), but West's setback in Fife presented the twenty-one-year-old with the opportunity to stake a claim for a regular slot in the first team. And he grabbed the opportunity with both hands, scoring two hat-tricks in his first two starts of the season, the first in a 4-0 win over Clydebank in the Premier Division and the second in the opening round of the UEFA Cup against Ilves Tampere of Finland.

McCoist, however, was no mere sideshow to Fleck's Ibrox super show. After his initial flood of four goals in the opening three league matches, he endured five Premier Division matches without a goal before ending the drought with a fine breakaway goal in a 2-0 win over Aberdeen at Ibrox at the end of September. He scored again in a 5-1 away win over Falkirk – a match that witnessed another Fleck hat-trick – and netted the equaliser three minutes into the second half of the season's second Old Firm league match to take his tally to seven in fifteen league fixtures. Brian McClair had handed the Hoops the lead in the twenty-fifth minute of the Old Firm clash when he exploited some indecisive Rangers defending to beat Woods, but McCoist earned the visitors a deserved share of the spoils when he shot home a pass from Fleck three minutes into the second half.

The combination play that fashioned the equalising goal at Parkhead, and the fact that both Fleck and McCoist were snaffling up the majority of goal-scoring opportunities to come their way, only served to illustrate that Souness had unearthed a lethal spearhead. The pair dovetailed perfectly, with their ceaseless movement unnerving defenders, and that quality, allied with their ability to apply the finishing touch to much of the good football Rangers were playing, suggested they could supply the amount of goals necessary to propel the Light Blues towards the title.

By the time that second instalment of the Old Firm conflict came to pass, Souness had already secured his first domestic trophy, less than five months after taking control at Ibrox. For the third time in four years, the League Cup was bound for Govan after Souness guided the club to a 2-1 win over Celtic in a tempestuous final at Hampden on 26 October. Goals from Ian Durrant and a late penalty from Davie Cooper gave Rangers the trophy, and maintained Souness' 100 percent winning record over the club's greatest rivals, as his new charges had won the opening league clash at Ibrox by one goal to nil in August. McCoist, who had scored in the 2-1 victory over Dundee United in the semi-final, missed a good opportunity to get on the scoresheet in the opening ten minutes of the match and was one of ten players cautioned by referee David Syme when he fouled Derek Whyte in the closing stages. The contest actually boiled over in the final minutes, with Maurice Johnston ordered off by Syme, who also appeared to dismiss Tony Shepherd before allowing the Celtic midfield man to remain on the field.

Consistency in the title race was still a problem, though, and Rangers lost a further three matches in the League Championship before the start of December, a run of results that saw Souness' men slip nine points behind Celtic in the race for the flag. One has to remember this was still in the days when a win yielded only two points, so at this pivotal juncture of the season, hopes of bringing the nine-year title famine to an end were looking increasingly forlorn.

One thing that was consistent during that spell of inconsistency, however, was the fact that McCoist and Fleck were maintaining their fine goal-scoring form. By Christmas, the pair had claimed twenty-two goals between them, twelve from McCoist and ten from Fleck, and all Rangers needed now was to track down the ingredient needed to halt the irregular form that was holding them back in the title race. In early December, Souness found it in the shape of Graham Roberts, who proved to be the final piece in the Rangers manager's championship jigsaw.

The arrival of Roberts, a centre-back from Spurs, added some solidity in the back-line alongside Butcher. He had picked up two FA Cup-winners' medals and a UEFA Cup-winners' badge during his time at White Hart Lane, and had fallen in love with Rangers when he had attended the League Cup final against Celtic back in October. He was tempted north of the border at a cost of £450,000 and made an impressive debut in a 2-0 home win over Dundee United, showing grit and determination to win the ball in a fifty-fifty challenge with the United goalkeeper, Billy Thomson, to set up McCoist for the opening goal of the game.

The turning point in the season came when Rangers first-footed Celtic at Ibrox in January. David Hay's side had dropped three points in the three league matches they played prior to their trip to Govan, but still led the table by five points, which made this a must-win match for Rangers, even although they had played a game less than their Old Firm rivals. With so much at stake, Rangers were not about to disappoint the capacity crowd and with Souness now free from injury and suspension and imperious in midfield, and Roberts immense at centre-back alongside Terry Butcher, they swept their rivals aside, emerging as convincing 2-0 winners following a fine footballing display. Typically, the goals came from Fleck and McCoist, with the latter the type of predatory strike with which Rangers' resident number nine was fast becoming synonymous. Cooper swung in a cross from the left and when the ball squirmed out of Pat Bonner's grasp, McCoist pounced in the six-yard box and lashed the ball into the net with his left foot.

Rangers never looked back. By the end of January they had eaten into and consumed the pre-Christmas points differential, reaching the summit of the table when goals from Durrant and McCoist handed Rangers their seventh straight league victory, a 2-0 win over Hamilton at Ibrox. It was a tousy affair, with Durrant and Roberts dismissed in the closing fifteen minutes of the match, but that was of little consequence, all the players and supporters were concerned about was the fact that Rangers had hit the front, and Souness and his troops were in no mood to be toppled.

Their resolute attitude was typified during a home game against Motherwell at the end of March. The visitors had won at Ibrox earlier in the season, and put on a typically stoic defensive display to shut out Rangers again on this their second visit to Govan. It looked like a precious point was about to be dropped when, as the clocked ticked into the ninetieth minute, McCoist finally penetrated Motherwell's defensive cocoon when he prodded the ball over the line after a goalmouth scramble to give the leaders the two points they craved. 'It wasn't the prettiest goal I ever scored,' recalled the goalscorer. 'It certainly wasn't the hardest, but it was one of the most important.'[7]

The goal against Motherwell was just one of a string of vital strikes from McCoist, who was proving an indispensable asset in the title run-in. Thriving on the service that came his way from the cast of top-drawer talent around him, his name was seldom missing from the scoresheet, and in the seventeen league matches Rangers contested from their Ne'erday win over Celtic until the visit of Hearts to Ibrox on 25 April, McCoist found the net on twenty-one occasions. In that run, he grabbed two hat-tricks (against St Mirren at Love Street and Hearts at Ibrox) and when he notched a double against Clydebank at Kilbowie on 18 April, his sixth brace of the season, he became the first Rangers player since Jim Forrest in the 1964/65 season to net thirty league goals in one season. When he scored the first goal against Hearts seven days later, he eclipsed Forrest's post-war record for league goals in one season by a Rangers player.

It was not all plain sailing, though, and there were some hiccups along the way, most notably in the Scottish Cup. Most observers expected Rangers to dispose of the Premier Division's basement club, Hamilton Academical, comfortably when they visited Ibrox on 31 January in the third round, but clearly Hamilton striker Adrian Sprott had not read the script, as he scored the only goal of the game in the seventieth minute to present the Accies with a place in the fourth round. The goal, the first Chris Woods had conceded in 1,196 minutes of football, was conceded cheaply, with Sprott taking advantage of an awful error from Dave McPherson, and although the home side held territorial advantage for the majority of the match, they could not breach the Hamilton rearguard, with McCoist and Fleck superbly policed throughout. In contrast to the defeat against Dundee two years earlier, when he had spurned numerous good chances, McCoist had little in the way of goal-scoring opportunities, save an effort in the first half that drew an excellent stop from Hamilton's hero, Dave McKellar.

'HUMILIATION!' chanted the headline in the *Evening Times*, and the result was rated as being equally as shocking as the humbling Rangers had suffered back in 1967 at the hands of Berwick Rangers. The two forwards who turned out for Rangers in that infamous match against Berwick, Jim Forrest and George McLean, were harshly jettisoned for their profligacy and never played for the club again, and speculation was rife that the same fate would befall the attacking duo who had played in the Hamilton debacle, Ally McCoist and Robert Fleck. Lightning did not strike twice, though, and in Rangers' next match after their Cup exit – a Premier Division match with Hearts at Tynecastle – both McCoist and Fleck were in the starting line-up and the duo contributed three of Rangers' five goals, with Fleck netting a double and McCoist knocking in a solitary strike. As if to prove the Cup match had been nothing more than a blip, Souness selected exactly the same eleven that had lost to Hamilton for the Hearts match, and the players repaid their manager's faith by bouncing back from their setback in the best possible way, thrashing the home side by five goals to two.

With two games in the title race remaining it was still neck and neck between Rangers and Celtic. The Hoops had reinvigorated their title challenge in April with a 3-1 win over Rangers at Parkhead, a defeat that marked Souness' first reverse in an Old Firm fixture and which had also ended Rangers' nineteen-match unbeaten run in the league. Two penalties from Brian McClair gave Celtic a 2-0 lead at the interval, and although McCoist turned in a Cooper cross in the fifty-third minute, an Owen Archdeacon goal five minutes from time completed the scoring and slashed the gap at the summit of the table to just two points.

McCoist helped quell any jangling nerves that may have been induced in the Rangers camp following the Old Firm defeat by grabbing six goals in the next three matches, convincing victories over Dundee (2-0), Clydebank (3-0) and Hearts (3-0), and when Celtic dropped a vital point at home to Dundee United on the same afternoon the Light Blues defeated Clydebank, Souness' men held the edge with two matches remaining, leading the table by three points. The penultimate Saturday of the season would provide the campaign's defining moment.

Rangers travelled north to face Aberdeen at Pittodrie – a ground where they had only been victorious once (in 1982) since the inception of the Premier League in 1975 – while, in Glasgow, Celtic were at home to a Falkirk side struggling to stave off relegation to the First Division. The odds were firmly stacked against Rangers and their cause was further handicapped when Souness was red-carded in the thirty-first minute, but five minutes before the interval the ten men of Rangers took the lead. The Light Blues won a free-kick on the left-hand side of the penalty area, and Davie Cooper's left-footed delivery was as immaculate as usual allowing Butcher to meet the ball flush on the forehead and guide it into the far corner beyond a statuesque Jim Leighton. Rangers had taken the lead and with it a giant stride towards the title.

A matter of minutes later, however, Aberdeen drew level when Brian Irvine scored deep into first-half stoppage time, but Rangers held on for a priceless point, shutting out the Dons throughout a second half that called for resolute and dogged defending by the ten players in blue. They formed an impenetrable line the red tide simply could not breach, with Butcher and Roberts immense at the heart of the defence.

Attention now turned to matters at Parkhead. Would the point gained in the Granite City actually turn out to be a point lost and force the title race to go down to the wire, or would lowly Falkirk record a priceless victory in the east end of Glasgow to hand Rangers their first championship crown for nine years? Remarkably, the latter proved to be true, as news filtered through that Celtic had been reduced to tears by the Bairns, crashing to a 2-1 defeat, a result that meant Rangers had been crowned champions of Scotland for the thirty-eighth time in their history. The fallow period had ended.

The celebrations were wild and manic, with supporters flooding on to the pitch to congratulate their heroes. When McCoist, who had been substituted with thirteen minutes of the match remaining, finally reached the sanctuary of the visitors' dressing room, he did so only in his underpants, as the supporters had relieved him of all other items of his kit and a gold neck chain (which was later returned), souvenirs of a momentous day in the club's history.

The bus trip back to Glasgow was unforgettable. After remedying the lack of champagne on the team bus by making a pit-stop at an Aberdeen hotel, countless bottles of France's finest were swilled by the squad as they toasted the club's first title triumph in almost a decade. 'I heard some people say that they wished we'd clinched the title at Ibrox,' said McCoist, 'I disagree. I wouldn't have swapped that bus journey back for anything. No one could sit still in their seat for any length of time. We all wanted to be up and about, talking to one another – laughing and joking. League Champions – what a feeling!'[8]

McCoist savoured the experience more than most, though, for he knew just how fortunate he was to still be a Rangers player that day. Earlier in the season he had been involved in an incident in a chip shop in East Kilbride that led to him having a criminal record and a threat from his irate manager that he would never play for the club again. Following a night out, McCoist and team-mates Ian Durrant and Ted McMinn were targeted for some unwarranted abuse as they queued for some food. One of the aggressors turned on Durrant and seeing his friend in trouble – Durrant was on crutches and in plaster from ankle to knee at the time – McCoist went to his aid, but the ensuing scuffle led to all three players being arrested. The consequences for McCoist were dire: a £150 fine and a conviction for minor assault. He was humiliated.

When news of the incident made its way to the manager's office at Ibrox, it was not well received. Souness tore into each of the perpetrators and informed them that their days at the club were numbered. He spelt out his message very clearly: they would be sold as a result of their behaviour, at a cut price if necessary. Souness deemed that conduct such as this besmirched the good name of the club, and he preached that as members of the playing staff at Ibrox, each individual had a responsibility to behave, no matter the provocation. Eventually Souness calmed down, withdrew his transfer threat and administered fines of £1,500 to each player instead. For McCoist the incident was another painful step on the learning curve of professional football in the goldfish-bowl existence that comes with playing for one of the Old Firm.

The final fixture of the season – a Robert Fleck goal gave Rangers a 1-0 home win over St Mirren seven days after they had secured the title at Pittodrie – marked Ally McCoist's forty-fourth league appearance of the campaign. He was the only member of the first-team squad to have started in every match in the league race, a remarkable achievement for a man who two years previously had stared the Ibrox exit door firmly in the face. He had also found the net on thirty-eight occasions in all competitions, his best single-season tally since signing for the club. It was hardly surprising, therefore, that he was the top goalscorer at Ibrox for the fourth successive season, but Brian McClair denied him the chance to retain his title as the hotshot of the Premier Division, as the Celtic striker found the net on thirty-five occasions in the league, once more than McCoist, to pip his Old Firm rival in the race for leading scorer in the Premier Division.

There would be precious little time for McCoist and his fellow Rangers players to rest on their laurels, though, or to reflect on the achievements of what had been a successful first season for Souness. Aside from the embarrassing Scottish Cup defeat against Hamilton and elimination at the third-round stage of the UEFA Cup on away goals at the hands of the West German side Borussia Monchengladbach, Souness had achieved what he had set out to do in his first season in charge: to win the championship. That would do for now, but he knew the Ibrox board and the Rangers fans would demand continued success.

THE AWAKENING: 1986–87

The target for the season ahead would be to retain the title and make a successful fist of the club's first sojourn in to the European Cup since 1978. It was clear that Rangers Football Club were going places under the guidance of Graeme Souness and it was also clear that the journey was only just beginning.

CHAPTER SEVEN

GOALS, GOALS, GOALS: 1987–89

With the Premier Division championship trophy and the League Cup draped in red, white and blue ribbons and sitting proudly in the Ibrox trophy room, Graeme Souness and his players set about the task of proving they were no one-season wonders. The Rangers manager was fully aware that the main threat to his ambitions of retaining the Premier Division title would be posed once again by Old Firm rivals Celtic, and the Parkhead side kicked off the 1987/88 season under new management, with their legendary former captain Billy McNeill replacing David Hay at the helm. They were also entering their centenary season intent on celebrating it with some tangible success on the field, so the Rangers contingent knew that the reply from their great rivals would be fierce.

In an attempt to combat this challenge, the Rangers board loosened the purse strings and released more transfer funds to allow Souness to strengthen his player pool. He spent just under £500,000 acquiring, among others, Avi Cohen (an Israeli international full-back who had been at Liverpool when Souness played there), Trevor Francis (Britain's first million-pound footballer when he had joined Nottingham Forest in 1979) and Mark Falco, a striker who boasted an excellent pedigree, having been a regular scorer for both Tottenham Hotspur and Watford in the English First Division.

However, despite the arrival of competition for the centre-forward role in the shape of Francis and Falco, Ally McCoist was in no mood to relinquish his position as the club's number one goal-grabber. In fact he viewed the increased competition for the striking berths in the team as a positive for the club. 'Guys like Mark and Trevor joining doesn't worry me,' McCoist told the *Rangers News*. 'They are both great players and they will act as an extra spur to me. I know they'll be after my place and it just shows the new standards at Rangers that Robert Fleck and myself, who scored sixty-four goals between us last season, aren't guaranteed a place in the team. But that's how it should be.'[1]

In order to prepare his troops for their assault on the Premier Division title, Souness took his squad to Switzerland and West Germany for a series of warm-up matches before concluding preparations by participating in the four-team Glasgow International Football tournament. McCoist staked his claim for a place in the team when the competitive action kicked off by netting twice against SR Delemont and FC Wettingen and once against Solothurn in the six matches played in Europe, before adding another in the final of the Glasgow International Football tournament. Having missed the semi-final win over Real Sociedad with flu, he was back in action when Rangers took on Brazilian side Porto Allegre twenty-four hours later, but although his thirty-third-minute goal gave Rangers the lead, the South Americans fought back to level the game before taking the trophy by winning the penalty shootout.

Six days later, the curtain was raised on the new season and the defence of the championship when Betty Holmes, wife of club chairman David, unfurled the League Championship flag ahead of the home match with Dundee United. Although United took the lead in the twelfth minute, Rangers snatched a point when McCoist restored parity from the penalty spot in the sixty-eighth minute. He won the award himself when he was felled by United goalkeeper Billy Thomson and made an expert job of converting the spot-kick, firing it low into the bottom left-hand corner. Thus, McCoist opened Rangers' goals account in the Premier Division for the third successive season, and he was unfortunate not to secure full points for the defending champions three minutes after converting his penalty, but on this occasion he was denied by the post.

The penalty goal against United was the precursor for a devastating burst of goal-scoring form from Rangers' number nine. Although he drew a blank in the next two league matches – defeats at the hands of Hibernian and Aberdeen – he scored against Stirling Albion in the League Cup and followed that with a staggering fifteen goals in his next eight matches. McCoist's impressive haul included hat-tricks against Falkirk, Dunfermline (twice) and Morton, and he also grabbed his first two goals in the Dark Blue of Scotland. Despite suffering a painful toe injury in the opening minute of the friendly match against Hungary at Hampden, McCoist broke his duck at international level when he scored in the thirty-fourth minute with a right-foot shot that slipped under the diving body of Peter Disztl, and he added a second in the sixty-first minute when he took a pass from debutant Ian Durrant, rounded Disztl and rolled the ball into the empty net. He was justly rewarded for his scoring exploits when he picked up the Tartan Special Player of the Month award for September.

It soon became apparent, though, that the Rangers championship bandwagon that had purred so beautifully the previous season was now spluttering its way through the early stages of the new campaign. Souness' men lost three of their first five league matches, and although they recovered to inflict heavy defeats on Falkirk (4-0), Dunfermline (4-0) and Morton (7-0), another loss at the hands of Dundee United at Tannadice in October left Souness' side six points adrift of early leaders Hearts after just twelve matches.

One of that trio of early season reverses had come at Parkhead in the season's first Old Firm clash. Rangers lost 1-0, but the match had no shortage of contentious incidents, with McCoist having a goal controversially ruled out for offside eight minutes before the interval (television pictures indicated the striker had in fact been onside) and Graeme Souness was dismissed in the second half for a foul on Celtic's goalscorer Billy Stark. The ninety minutes were littered with debatable decisions, but they were mere child's play in comparison with the events that unfolded when the two giants collided again on 17 October.

In a volatile encounter, the Rangers goalkeeper Chris Woods and captain Terry Butcher received their marching orders along with Celtic's Frank McAvennie. Woods and McAvennie were sent for an early bath following a flare-up in the sixteenth minute, and Butcher joined them when he received his second booking from referee Jim Duncan after sixty-two minutes. By then Rangers were trailing 2-0, but three minutes after Butcher's dismissal, McCoist, fresh from scoring for Scotland in a 2-0 win over Belgium in a European Championships qualifier, pulled one back with a left-foot strike, and parity was restored right at the death when new £1.1 million signing Richard Gough, a player Souness had been chasing for some time, scored a dramatic equaliser.

That Ibrox draw was part of a run of twelve league matches that included eight wins and only one defeat for Souness' men, and by early November they had hauled themselves back into the title race. That sequence of results was boosted by a glut of goals from McCoist, with the marksman finding the net twelve times in that period. In addition to hat-tricks against Dunfermline and Morton, as well as his priceless goal against Celtic at Ibrox, he netted a brace against St Mirren at Love Street and single goals in victories over Dundee (2-1), Dunfermline (4-0) and Motherwell (1-0). He could have added to his tally too had Andy Goram not saved his penalty in a 1-0 home victory over Hibernian on 7 November.

However, although McCoist sustained his scoring rate over the remainder of the season, the championship challenge ultimately foundered on a fateful midweek night in November when, in a home fixture against Aberdeen, Terry Butcher broke his leg. The match was lost 1-0, but the result bore little consequence in the grand scheme of things. Now the old adage that one player doesn't make a team could be applied here, but Butcher wasn't just any player, he was a colossus, a leader of men, and his presence on the field would be sorely missed for the rest of the season.

He would be missed primarily in defence, but the injury also blunted one of Rangers' most potent attacking weapons. Butcher had a fantastic range of passing, and McCoist would often refer to his left leg as 'The Winchester'; so accurate were the passes that the Englishman would distribute when turning defence into attack. In the absence of Butcher, Graham Roberts took over the captaincy and did a sterling job, shoring up the defence alongside Richard Gough and cajoling his team into action when necessary, but Butcher's absence left a huge void that simply could not be filled.

Celtic emerged from the shadows and won the title, with Hearts ten points adrift in second, and Rangers a further two points back in third. There would be no solace for Souness in the Scottish Cup either, as the bogey was still not laid to rest, with Dunfermline dumping Rangers out of the competition in the fourth round with a 2-0 win in an ill-tempered match at East End Park that saw Rangers' new £350,000 signing John Brown ordered off. This meant that, for the second successive season, Rangers had been eliminated from the Cup by a team that would ultimately be relegated from the Premier League.

The only consolation, however scant, was that Rangers did not end the season empty-handed: they retained the League Cup after a quite splendid final against Aberdeen in October. Rangers won a pulsating match 5-3 on penalty-kicks after an epic 3-3 draw that had included a breathtaking free-kick goal from Davie Cooper, a left-foot rocket that was struck with such venom that it almost tore the goal net from its rigging. Ian Durrant and Robert Fleck scored Rangers' other goals, with the latter strike coming in the dying moments of the match to force the tie into extra-time. Although McCoist did not score in the final, he had netted six goals in the earlier rounds and, in the final itself, he was involved in Durrant's goal when his perceptive flick sent his midfield buddy clear on goal. He also scored the first penalty in the nerve-shredding shootout, with Man of the Match Durrant converting the clinching penalty after Aberdeen's Peter Nicholas had blazed his spot-kick against the bar.

The elaborately named Dubai Gold Challenge Cup also decorated the Ibrox trophy room. In December, Rangers faced English champions Everton at the Al Maktoum Stadium in a match that was immediately billed as an unofficial 'British Championship' decider. With just ten minutes remaining, the Scots appeared to be in a 'sticky' situation, as goals from Kevin Sheedy and Dave Watson had handed the Toffeemen a 2-0 lead, but Robert Fleck struck to haul the Light Blues back into contention before a fine finish from McCoist in the eighty-eighth minute forced a penalty decider. McCoist scored the opening spot-kick in what proved to be a marathon shootout and a total of sixteen penalties were taken before Rangers edged home by eight goals to seven.

Although disappointed at his side's performance in the championship, Souness was delighted with the progress Rangers made in the 1987/88 European Cup, with the team's performances going a considerable way towards re-establishing the club as a force to be reckoned with on the European stage. This was Rangers' first taste of the continent's premier competition for nine years, and they produced a series of fine displays in their run to the quarter-finals.

The first-round draw looked ominous, with a trip to the USSR to take on the highly fancied Dynamo Kiev. Kiev had won the European Cup-Winners' Cup the previous season, and boasted internationals from the USSR such as Oleg Blokhin and Alexei Michailitchenko on their roster, but a stout defensive display from Rangers in the first leg in Kiev in front of a crowd of 100,000 restricted the home side to a solitary goal, a penalty from Michailitchenko. Rangers could even have snatched a draw had McCoist, the subject of some heavy treatment throughout the match from his marker Oleg Kuznetsov, scored in the twenty-eighth minute. A stunning run down the left wing took him beyond two Kiev defenders, but a heavy touch gave the Kiev goalkeeper, Victor Chanov, the opportunity to stop his shot. 'I was furious with myself that I didn't score,' McCoist told the *Rangers News*. 'Having done all the hard work in beating the two players on the left, I just pushed the ball a wee bit too far ahead of myself inside the box and Chanov was able to block my shot.'[2]

Two weeks later, Kiev arrived in Glasgow for the second leg, a night on which the Rangers supporters created what McCoist later reckoned to be one of the best atmospheres he had ever experienced at Ibrox Stadium. It was an evening when the home crowd really did act as the valuable twelfth man, and the wall of sound they created, coupled with a stroke of genius from Graeme Souness, saw Rangers through to a famous victory.

Noticing that Kiev posed a significant threat from wide areas, the Rangers manager attempted to curb the danger presented by their speedy wingers by instructing the ground staff at Ibrox to narrow the playing field by bringing in the touchlines. Souness' cunning plan had the desired effect. The previous locations of the touchlines were still clearly visible, and that unnerved the Russian visitors and prompted their officials to complain to UEFA after the match. Their appeals fell on deaf ears, though, as Souness had ensured that the Ibrox pitch remained within the boundary of the governing body's regulations.

Watched by England manager Bobby Robson, Rangers restored parity on aggregate when they opened the scoring after twenty-four minutes courtesy of a dreadful error from Kiev's international goalkeeper, Chanov. A Rangers attack petered out and the ball ran through to Chanov, and he tried to spring a counter-attack by quickly fielding the ball. However, his throw-out struck the back of Bessanov and, as the Kiev defenders froze, McCoist pounced to prod a pass through to his strike-partner Mark Falco and the Englishman gleefully rammed the ball into the empty net.

Rangers still led by a single goal at half-time, but five minutes after the interval, the home crowd almost raised the roof when their heroes grabbed their second goal of the night. Again there was a degree of fortune about it. Trevor Francis slung in a cross from the right and Falco rose above his marker to head the ball back across the face of the goal where McCoist deceived Chanov with a mistimed header. Initially, he claimed (somewhat tongue-in-cheek) that he had intentionally tried to catch the goalkeeper out with his attempt on goal, but he later admitted that his poor connection on the ball had deceived the hapless Chanov.

Whether the contact on the header was clean or not mattered little to a raucous home support that cranked up the volume for the remainder of the game as Rangers staved off a late onslaught to move into the next round at the expense of one of the pre-tournament favourites. Some years later McCoist recalled:

> I can't remember how long there was to go when I scored, but the atmosphere for the last fifteen or twenty minutes was something I have never experienced before or since at Ibrox or anywhere else. Even at the likes of the European Cup tie against Leeds United when we had the first leg here [at Ibrox] and everybody in the crowd supported us because there was a ban on visiting fans at both grounds, even when we have played Celtic in cup finals or when we beat them 5-1 at Ibrox, none of these games – and they were all occasions when the ground was actually shaking with the sound – none of them quite reached the level we heard against Kiev.[3]

Buoyed by this excellent result, Rangers eagerly awaited the draw for round two. The Scottish champions were paired with Polish cracks, Klub Sportowy Gornik Zabrze, which meant another trip to the Eastern Bloc. Memories were rekindled of the two European Cup-Winners' Cup ties between the sides in the 1969/70 season when Gornik had triumphed 6-2 on aggregate, with the 3-1 home defeat arguably costing the then Rangers manager Davie White his job. There was to be no such joy for the Poles this time round, though.

In the first leg at Ibrox, Rangers produced a breathtaking performance in the opening forty-five minutes that yielded three goals. McCoist netted the first of them after just six minutes, shooting home a Jimmy Nicholl cross from ten yards, and further goals from Ian Durrant and

Mark Falco placed Rangers in a commanding position. A Jan Urban goal in the second half gave the Poles a glimmer of hope for the return leg, but any designs they had on overturning the two-goal deficit were extinguished five minutes before the interval in Poland. Davie Cooper released McCoist with a terrific pass, but as the striker attempted to round Gornik's goalkeeper, Josef Wanzik, he was brought crashing to the turf. The Greek referee awarded Rangers a penalty, which McCoist duly despatched to chalk up his twenty-ninth goal of the season. The Poles equalised in the second half, but Rangers progressed to the quarter-finals 4-2 on aggregate, thus emulating the achievements of the last Rangers team to have played in the European Champions Cup back in 1979.

With the competition now down to the last eight, there was a real sense of belief around Ibrox that Rangers could match the achievement of rivals Celtic in 1967 and bring the continent's premier trophy back to Glasgow. Rangers, now installed as joint second favourites with the bookmakers to win the competition, were joined in the hat for the last eight by Steaua Bucharest, Real Madrid, Bayern Munich, Benfica, Anderlecht, Bordeaux and PSV Eindhoven, and it was the Romanian champions Steaua with whom the Scottish champions were paired.

The first leg of the tie took place in the Romanian capital on 2 March 1988, but Rangers' preparations for this crucial encounter were far from ideal. Captain Terry Butcher, who had played in all the European matches thus far, had of course broken his leg in November and was ruled out of both ties, and the Light Blues were woefully short of strikers since both Mark Falco and Robert Fleck had been sold shortly before Christmas. Falco and his family had failed to settle in Glasgow and he moved back to London to join Queens Park Rangers, while Fleck, who was reportedly growing tired of living in the Old Firm 'goldfish bowl', left to join Norwich City for a fee of £560,000. He departed despite the best efforts of Graeme Souness who, with the potential of success in Europe's premier tournament at the forefront of his mind, tried manfully to convince Fleck to remain at the club.

The departures of Falco and Fleck meant that McCoist was the only recognised first-team striker on the books, but the club's top goalscorer was struggling ahead of the match and looked to be a dead cert to miss out. He had missed Rangers' previous three matches with a knee injury (his absence broke a remarkable run of 131 successive appearances in Light Blue), and exactly one week before the game in

Romania, he was on the operating table undergoing surgery on the cartilage in his knee.

There looked to be no chance of him taking his place in the side. Despite the operation being much more straightforward than had been first feared – instead of having the cartilage removed, surgeons used modern microsurgery to trim away the pieces that were troubling McCoist – it looked likely that the striker would face up to three weeks out of action. He managed to confound medical opinion, though, showing astonishing powers of recovery to pass a fitness test one hour before kick-off to take his place in the starting eleven in Bucharest.

Although his return to action came as a timely boost for Rangers, the talismanic striker could do nothing to prevent them from going down 2-0 to the classy Romanians. Victor Piturca opened the scoring after just two minutes and only a series of excellent saves from Chris Woods kept Rangers' hopes alive, as the Romanians swarmed forward in the opening exchanges. Rangers regained their composure, however, and enjoyed a good spell in the match shortly before half-time, carving out a couple of good goal-scoring chances, with McCoist slipping at the vital moment when played in by Souness before the player-manager tested the home goalkeeper, Dumitru Stingaciu, when he flashed in an effort from the edge of the penalty area on the stroke of half-time.

With the Romanians becoming increasingly frustrated as they pressed forward in search of a second goal, Rangers looked to be in command of the tie until a dose of ill-fortune tilted the balance back in Steaua's favour. In the sixty-sixth minute, Richard Gough was harshly penalised for fouling Iosif Rotariu, and from the resulting free-kick, Stefan Iovan beat Woods with the aid of a wicked deflection.

Although a 2-0 deficit left Rangers with a mountain to climb, the tie was far from over, with McCoist looking to the earlier victory over Dynamo Kiev as inspiration. 'We took two goals off Dynamo Kiev at Ibrox and they were a better side than Steaua in my opinion,' he said. 'I really believe that we can still win this tie.'[4]

Despite their advantage, the Steaua players were also wary of counting their chickens, particularly now that a fully-fit McCoist was back in the Rangers ranks. Their star playmaker and midfield fulcrum Gheorghe Hagi, nicknamed 'The Maradona of the Carpathians', stated that the tie was far from over, as he and his team-mates, 'knew of McCoist's reputation as a scorer of so many goals.'[5] However, although

McCoist did get on the scoresheet in Glasgow, it was too late to keep Rangers in the competition.

The last thing the home side wanted was lose an away goal, but that's exactly what they did after only two minutes when Steaua exploited confusion in the Rangers defence to extend their aggregate lead to 3-0. Stoica's long pass eluded both Gough and Roberts and allowed Marius Lacatus to advance and lob the ball over Chris Woods. It was disappointing to lose the goal so early, particularly as it could have been prevented, and it left Rangers with an even steeper mountain to climb, as they required four goals to make it through to the semi-finals.

Rather than be deflated by the early blow, Rangers struck back and pounded the Steaua goal in search of a quick equaliser. The Steaua goalkeeper, Stingaciu, looked uncomfortable for much of the night when dealing with cross balls, and it was this type of supply that got the home side back on track after sixteen minutes. Davie Cooper flighted in a corner, and when Roberts flicked the ball to the back post, Gough was on hand to nod it into the net.

The goal seemed to revive Rangers' hopes of clawing back the deficit, and when they edged ahead on the night after half an hour, a great many of the 44,000 patrons inside Ibrox started to believe that the seemingly impossible was going to become possible. The goal came from the penalty spot. Durrant won the award when Miodrag Belodedici's challenge brought him crashing to the turf, and McCoist took the responsibility, confidently rapping the ball into the net with his right foot.

Souness' troops were now halfway towards their target, and they launched an all-out attacking strategy after the interval, as they manfully searched for a chink in the Romanians' armoury. The home side had to ensure that the back door remained closed, though, and they were almost punished when Hagi burst clear, but the little Romanian wasted his opportunity. At the other end, Gough had another opportunity with a header, but his attempt failed to find the target, and then McCoist was presented with the best chance to score with eighteen minutes remaining. Everyone inside the stadium rose in expectation as Durrant's back-heel fell into McCoist's hitting zone, but the striker, who had been so clinical all season, was uncharacteristically wasteful, blasting his effort over the bar. Had he scored, it would undoubtedly have set up a grandstand finish, but instead the game petered out and the European dream died for another year.

It was difficult to find fault with the effervescent McCoist, though, as without his goal-scoring contribution it is doubtful that Rangers would have made it into the last eight in the first place, and despite being a largely disappointing campaign for the club in terms of silverware, the goal-scoring exploits of their number nine had once again provided a huge positive. In the calendar year of 1987, he had found the net a phenomenal sixty times in a Light Blue jersey and his goal-scoring form at both club and international level was rewarded when he picked up the BBC TV *Sportscene* 'Personality of the Year' award in December.

By the end of the 1987/88 campaign, McCoist had registered forty-two goals in fifty-three appearances, the first time in his career that he had scored over forty goals in one season. His haul included five hat-tricks, and he finished as the club's top goalscorer for the fifth successive season. McCoist also made his mark in the European arena, finishing as joint top goalscorer in the European Cup, with his four goals against Dynamo Kiev, Gornik and Steaua Bucharest sufficient to share the title with Rabah Madjer (Porto), Jean-Marc Ferreri (Bordeaux), Michel (Real Madrid), Rui Aguas (Benfica) and Gheorghe Hagi (Steaua Bucharest).

The 1987/88 season also brought about a major career milestone for McCoist, as he chalked up his 100th league goal for Rangers when he found the net with a nineteenth-minute penalty-kick in a 2-0 win over Dundee at Ibrox on Boxing Day 1987. He had amassed the total in only 158 league appearances, and it was ironic that he should reach such a milestone against the same opponents and at the same venue where he had plummeted to the nadir of his Rangers career just short of three years previously.

With the goals flowing, it was no surprise that McCoist had now become hot property in the football transfer market. He was much sought after, and during the latter part of the season was linked with a £1 million move to Italy's top league, Serie A, with Pisa rumoured to be the interested club. Everton were also reported to be keen to lure McCoist back to the English First Division, but the striker moved quickly to diffuse the speculation. 'There's no way I'll be leaving Rangers for Italian football, or anywhere else for that matter,' he told the *Rangers News*. 'I've got two-and-a-half years of my current contract to run at Ibrox and I'd like to think I'll be with the club after that has been completed.'[6] His manager was also keen to play down the rumours, with Souness stating that he was 'in the process of building a team, not dismantling one. To suggest I would think of selling Ally McCoist is ridiculous.'[7]

The 1988/89 season dawned with the now-customary flurry of transfer activity at Ibrox, with many joking that a revolving entrance should have replaced the huge oak door at the front of the stadium in order to cope with the almost daily comings and goings. Again a striker was at the top of the shopping list, with a move for Ian Rush mooted. However, Rush, a prolific goalscorer and a former team-mate of Souness' at Liverpool, decided to end an unhappy year with Juventus in Italy by returning to Merseyside, so Souness swooped to capture Kevin Drinkell for £500,000 from Norwich City instead. Drinkell was once again cast in the mould of striker that Souness craved, big and bustling with a keen eye for goal, and he certainly proved both a worthwhile investment and an effective foil for McCoist, scoring nineteen goals in his one and only full season at the club.

Souness also attracted Gary Stevens north of the border. Stevens, an established England international signed from Everton for £1.5 million, was an exceptionally gifted and energetic right-back who balanced foraging forward runs with perceptive defending. Rarely injured in the early part of his Rangers career, he would go on to become a consistent and prominent member of the squad for the next six seasons.

The 1988/89 season would also be the first full season at Ibrox for three players who had been signed during the previous campaign. Veteran midfielder Ray Wilkins had arrived from Paris St Germain for £250,000 in November, bringing with him a wealth of experience, having plied his trade with Chelsea, Manchester United and AC Milan in addition to winning eighty-four caps for England, while Mark Walters, a mercurial winger, had arrived in January from Aston Villa, and in his twenty-one appearances he had shown the Rangers fans that he could be a very important player for the side. The last of the trio was Ian Ferguson, a young Scottish midfielder who cost £1 million when he joined up from St Mirren in February. He, too, would be a mainstay in the side that evolved over the next few seasons into one of the most celebrated teams in Rangers' illustrious history.

One player who would not be on board for the new season, though, was Graham Roberts. The man who had deputised so ably as club captain in Terry Butcher's absence had a heated dressing-room bust-up with Graeme Souness after an end-of-season match with Aberdeen at Ibrox, with the pair quarrelling when Souness blamed Roberts for the concession of Aberdeen's winning goal. Roberts disagreed with his manager's assessment of the situation and a fiery exchange ensued, the upshot of which was Souness vowing that Roberts would never play for the first team again. The Englishman was despatched to play with the third team in the Highlands before being sold to Chelsea for a fee of £475,000 prior to the start of the 1988/89 season.

After completing a rigorous pre-season programme at the Il Ciocco training camp in Tuscany, Rangers warmed up for the forthcoming season with friendly matches against Raith Rovers (a match that marked the return of Terry Butcher, now fully recovered from his broken leg) and Ayr United, and testimonial matches against Kilmarnock, Clydebank and Bordeaux, the latter being for Davie Cooper, in recognition of the winger's ten years' service on the Ibrox playing staff. McCoist, who had signed a new contract in August that would tie him to the club for a further five years, polished off any close-season rustiness by netting six goals in the five matches, and he received the perfect boost for the new campaign when his manager commented that he was 'worth forty goals a season to us and he must be worth over £2 million – it would certainly cost us that in today's market to replace him adequately.'[8]

The Premier Division had undergone some reconstruction during the close season, and there were now ten teams in the top flight rather than twelve, with the league programme reduced from forty-four games to thirty-six accordingly. The opening Saturday of the new season took Rangers on a trip to Douglas Park to take on newly promoted Hamilton Academical, and they recorded a comfortable 2-0 win, with Stevens netting on his competitive debut and McCoist adding the other with a fine diving header from a Walters cross. This was followed by a goal-less draw at home to Hibernian before reigning champions Celtic visited Ibrox on 27 August. Today, almost twenty years later, it remains a date that will be forever etched in the minds of Rangers followers everywhere.

Having snatched the championship trophy from Rangers' grasp the previous season, Celtic arrived at the home of their arch-rivals in a confident frame of mind, and their self-assurance did not seem to be misplaced when they took the lead after just five minutes through Frank McAvennie. Their joy, however, was short-lived as, from that moment on, Rangers simply destroyed their great rivals, marching into football's equivalent of Valhalla thanks to a resounding 5-1 victory.

The home side were only behind for five minutes. Ray Wilkins chipped a free-kick into the danger area that broke to John Brown, and when his shot was charged down by Mick McCarthy, McCoist pounced to level matters when he swept a left-foot shot beyond Old Firm debutant Ian Andrews. The Rangers number nine almost edged his side ahead when he struck the base of the post shortly afterwards, but the throbbing Ibrox stands did not have long to wait before their heroes went in front with a strike that is quite rightly regarded as one of the greatest goals ever witnessed in the long history of Old Firm matches. Nine minutes before the half-time interval, Gary Stevens took a long throw from the right touchline, Butcher headed the ball on, and when it was only half cleared, Ray Wilkins met the ball on the full volley and smote his shot from the edge of the penalty area into the top corner. Andrews hardly moved as the ball whistled past him.

Sixty seconds into the second half, McCoist, who was developing an uncanny knack of netting against the men in green-and-white hoops, put Rangers 3-1 ahead when he back-headed Ian Durrant's cross into the net before Drinkell, on his Old Firm debut, and Walters completed the rout. With some twenty-five minutes still to play and Celtic punch drunk and lolling around on the ropes, the home support smelt blood and urged their heroes to prolong the pummelling in an attempt to exorcise the ghosts of Celtic's 7-1 League Cup final victory in 1957. It was not to be, though. Souness, perhaps still a little naïve in just how much this fixture means to the Rangers public, brought himself on as a substitute and slowed the tempo of the game down to the extent that the last period of the match was played out in what was little more than an exercise of 'keep ball' for Rangers. To this day, McCoist admits that while he was utterly euphoric when celebrating the victory – Rangers' biggest home win in an Old Firm fixture since the Second World War – his memories are tinged with regret that the triumph was not an even more emphatic one.

The club's good fortune in the League Cup continued, with victories over Clyde, Clydebank (McCoist's opening goal in the 6-0 win was his 200th in a Rangers shirt), Dundee and a 3-1 win over Hearts in the semi-final setting up another titanic final against Aberdeen at Hampden Park on 23 October. It was Rangers' third successive final and their seventh in eight years, and McCoist, who had added to his strike against Clydebank by netting against Dundee in the quarter-finals, maintained his fine League Cup scoring record when he put Rangers ahead from the penalty spot in the first half after Aberdeen goalkeeper Theo Snelders had fouled Drinkell.

The match then evolved into a classic joust, much the same as the one that the teams had acted out twelve months earlier. Davie Dodds equalised for Aberdeen before the half-time interval, but Ian Ferguson restored Rangers' one-goal advantage early in the second half with a spectacular bicycle kick. However, Dodds equalised again to level the match at 2-2, and both teams had chances to win the match in the latter stages, with former Rangers man Jim Bett perhaps passing up the most gilt-edged opportunity when clean through on goal with only Woods to beat ten minutes from the end.

The final looked to be heading for extra-time for the second successive season, but Rangers pushed until the end and reaped the reward in the dying moments of the match. They won a corner on the right-hand side and when Walters floated the ball into the danger area, it broke loose in the six-yard box, where McCoist was inevitably sniffing around on the lookout for an opportunity to score. As the ball dropped in his vicinity, he eluded his marker and swept a right-foot shot underneath the diving Snelders to win the trophy for Rangers. It was yet another priceless contribution from the club's principal marksman, and the victory took his medal tally in the League Cup to five.

The game of football, however, has a habit of ebbing and flowing, moving very swiftly from marvellous highs to equally depressing lows, and McCoist experienced a double dose of this phenomenon in the six days that followed the Hampden showdown.

Having disposed of Polish side GKS Katowice 5-3 on aggregate in the opening round of the UEFA Cup, Rangers were drawn to face 1FC Cologne in the second round, with the first leg scheduled to take place in West Germany on Wednesday, 26 October, three days after the League Cup final. Having taken great confidence from their run to the last eight of the European Cup the previous season, Rangers and their fans had high hopes of embarking on another good run in the European arena, but Cologne, one of the form sides in the Bundesliga, had other ideas.

The team that hailed from the German Federal state of North Rhine-Westphalia were no strangers to Rangers. The two sides had crossed swords three times in European conflict before this tie, once in the European Cup, once in the UEFA Cup and once in the Inter-Cities Fairs Cup, the predecessor to the UEFA Cup. The last of those meetings, a UEFA Cup-tie in 1982/83, had been a particularly painful experience for the Light Blues, as the West Germans hammered the Scottish giants 6-2 on aggregate in the second round, rounding off the tie with a resounding 5-0 victory in their own Mungersdoffer Stadium.

The likelihood of a repeat of that scoreline on this occasion was extinguished, though, as Rangers played superbly in the first leg. For seventy-seven minutes, they successfully contained the home side, and repelled everything that was thrown at them. Indeed, as the game entered its closing stages, Rangers should have been two goals in front, as they had twice passed up gilt-edged goal-scoring opportunities. The first fell to Terry Butcher after seventeen minutes. Gary Stevens meandered forward, and his cross into the penalty area found its way through to Butcher, but the skipper failed to punish the home defence's slack marking, as he tugged his left-foot shot wide of the target. Thirteen minutes into the second half, Rangers carved out their second excellent chance, but once again they were denied the coveted away goal, with the prolific McCoist the offender this time. Released by Walters, he tried to chip the ball over the advancing Bodo Illgner, but he failed to get sufficient purchase on his shot and Jann Jensen managed to retreat and hook the ball to safety.

Souness' men were duly punished for their profligacy. Late goals from Olaf Janssen and Thomas Allofs handed the West Germans a comfortable lead to defend at Ibrox in the second leg, and the miserable end to the match was completed when the visitors were reduced to ten men in the final minute.

McCoist had had a lean night in front of goal. Aside from the one decent opportunity that fell to him in the second half, he struggled to escape the clutches of his marker, Paul Steiner. The Cologne centre-half spent the entire evening winding the striker up with a dose of dirty tricks like nipping, pushing, jersey pulling, all of which were very cleverly administered out of sight of the referee. McCoist became increasingly agitated at the German's antics, and eventually his frustration boiled over. Shortly after the home side netted their second goal, three minutes from full-time, and with the abuse from Steiner now verbal as well as physical, both players challenged for a high ball, and McCoist lashed out at his opponent. It was a stupid thing to do, and although Steiner made the most of the challenge, the Hungarian referee brandished the red card in front of the Rangers striker.

McCoist was duly punished for his indiscretion. Not only did he miss the next leg of the tie – Rangers drew 1-1 and tumbled out of the competition 3-1 on aggregate – but UEFA added another two matches to his suspension which, should Rangers qualify, meant he would also miss the first two European matches of the following season. He was also heavily criticised for his actions by Graeme Souness, who was far from impressed with the conduct of his centre-forward stating: 'Ally has not only let himself down, he has let his team-mates and Rangers Football Club down. He broke the golden rule and allowed himself to be provoked and the consequences make life difficult for both Ally and the team.'[9]

In the next league match at Love Street against St Mirren three days later, McCoist's midweek agony was compounded when he suffered a torn hamstring in the first half. Hamstring problems earlier in the season had caused him to miss five matches, but this time the injury was much more of a concern, with the lay-off estimated to be in the region of two months. He was helped from the field by the Rangers medical staff, and replaced by new signing Andy Gray, a striker who was now entering the latter stages of his playing career, but who had finally realised a lifelong ambition of playing for Rangers when Souness had signed him from West Bromwich Albion for £25,000 to act as experienced cover for McCoist and Drinkell. After Rangers fell behind early in the second half, Gray repaid some of his transfer fee when he rescued a point for the visitors with a late header.

In the weeks that followed the match, McCoist spent some time in the rehabilitation centre at Lilleshall in England but, after seeking advice from a specialist in Holland, it soon became apparent that an early return to the action would be unlikely. Indeed, McCoist would not see action in the first team until the following January, but although frustrated at the prospect of spending a period of time out of the first-team picture, McCoist knew his predicament paled into insignificance when compared to that of his close friend and team-mate Ian Durrant.

John Greig had signed the precociously talented Durrant from youth side Glasgow United in 1983. It was the realisation of a dream for Durrant, a local boy brought up only a few miles from Ibrox in Kinning Park, who had, in his younger days, sneaked into Ibrox to watch his heroes, squeezing himself through a hole in the fence at the back of the old Centenary Stand. As an apprentice, one of his responsibilities had been to clean the boots of the first-team players, and one of the top team players on Durrant's roster had been Ally McCoist. What proved to be an enduring friendship and a deadly double act on and off the field was born.

Having performed at a consistently high standard in the reserve team, it was not long before the eighteen-year-old Durrant was elevated to first-team status, and he made his debut in the latter stages of the 1984/85 season in a league match against Morton at Cappielow. Rangers won 3-0, and although McCoist scored a hat-trick, his new team-mate claimed the Man of the Match award after turning in a virtuoso performance.

It was a portent of things to come and by the early part of the 1988/89 season, Durrant had become one of the most talked about players in the Scottish game. A goal-scoring midfielder (he netted sixteen times in all competitions in 1987/88), he had the eye for the killer pass and had developed uncanny understandings with both Davie Cooper and McCoist. Both players knew that if they made a run into a goal-scoring position, Durrant would find them. A high percentage of McCoist's goal tally from the previous three seasons had come about as a result of assists from Durrant, and his performances had the media labelling him as world-class and touting him for a megabucks move abroad, with the Italian Serie A widely regarded as the perfect arena in which he could showcase his talents. All hopes of such a dream becoming a reality, though, were cruelly obliterated at eight minutes past three on Saturday, 8 October 1988.

Rangers were at Pittodrie on league business. New signing Neale Cooper, a former Aberdeen player, made his debut for Rangers and opened the scoring with a raking 20-yard drive, but Aberdeen came back to win the match 2-1 thanks to a Jim Bett penalty and a late Charlie Nicholas header. There was a venomous atmosphere at Pittodrie that day, stimulated by the appearance of one of the Dons' former heroes, Cooper, in a Light Blue jersey, and there had been a few tasty challenges in the opening minutes, but with less than ten minutes on the clock, the worst of them all was administered by Neil Simpson.

The ball broke loose in the middle of the field, with Durrant and Simpson on a collision course to challenge for possession. However, referee Louis Thow blew his whistle to award a free-kick so, hearing the whistle, Durrant withdrew from his challenge. Simpson, on the other hand, did not hold back, and the studs on his right boot were driven deep into Durrant's right knee. The extent of the damage was three ruptured ligaments and another being badly stretched, a very serious diagnosis that left Durrant's future as a footballer hanging in the balance. It would be over two-and-a-half years and seven operations before Durrant played for the first team again, so McCoist knew that, in the grand scheme of things, a paltry three months on the sidelines was nothing more than a mere blip.

During McCoist's absence from the first team, there was a radical shake-up in the Ibrox hierarchy. In November 1988, Lawrence Marlborough ended the Lawrence group's thirty-four year association with Rangers when he sold his controlling interest in the club to a thirty-six-year-old Scottish businessman named David Murray, with Marlborough's reasons for the sale driven by the fact that it was becoming increasingly difficult to fulfil the responsibilities associated with being the club's majority shareholder when he lived and worked thousands of miles away in the United States.

Murray, a man who had lost both his legs in a car accident in the late 1970s, was a very successful businessman, with his involvement in the steel stockholding industry making him a multi-millionaire, and he acquired just under seventy percent of the club's share capital at a reported cost of around £6 million. In addition to being the major shareholder, Murray would eventually replace David Holmes as Rangers' chairman. Graeme Souness' role at the club changed, too. The Rangers manager was a close companion of Murray, and he bought a ten percent share in the club and gained a place on the board of directors, a move that made him the first man in the history of the game to hold the role of player-manager-director at a football club.

On the field, Rangers kept up their relentless pursuit of the championship despite a pre-Christmas stumble that brought back-to-back defeats at the hands of Dundee United and Hearts. The team responded, though, by hammering Celtic at Ibrox again in early January – this time by four goals to one – although they did falter momentarily the following week when Motherwell won 2-1 at Fir Park.

After several aborted attempts at a comeback, McCoist finally returned to the first team on 21 January 1989, replacing Stuart Munro for the last twenty-two minutes of a 3-1 home win over Dundee. He had attempted to return to the top team just before Christmas but, despite making scoring return in a specially arranged friendly against Queens Park, had been forced to cool his heels on the sidelines for another few weeks when it emerged that his injury required further treatment. Two more trips to Lilleshall followed early in the New Year before the rehabilitation process was completed with his return against Dundee.

The 43,202-strong crowd afforded him a terrific ovation when he stepped onto the field and he gave the Rangers fans more to shout about four minutes from the end of the match when he grabbed his first goal since the League Cup final back in October. Ian Ferguson, scorer of Rangers' first goal, made headway down the right flank, and when he pulled the ball back into the centre, McCoist was perfectly placed to knock it into the net. The fans were then treated to his version of 'The Ickey Shuffle', as McCoist mimicked the celebration that had been made famous by Elbert L. Woods, a running back who had helped the Cincinnati Bengals reach that year's Super Bowl.

McCoist's rehabilitation continued with two appearances for the reserve team – the latter against Hamilton yielding two goals – and a substitute appearance as Rangers opened their Scottish Cup campaign with a 1-1 draw against Raith Rovers at Starks Park. He made his first start for the top team since October in the replay against Raith, a match Rangers won comfortably, 3-0, and showed no ill-effects from the injury for the remainder of the season, appearing in all but one of the remaining eleven league games, scoring four times, as Rangers secured their thirty-ninth championship with an emphatic 4-0 thrashing of Hearts at Ibrox. He also returned to the Scotland set-up, playing in a stirring 2-0 victory over France at a rain-soaked Hampden and scoring in a 2-1 win over Cyprus that edged the Scots closer to a place at the World Cup finals.

With the League Cup and League Championship trophy safely under lock and key in the Ibrox trophy room, Rangers stood on the verge of the club's first domestic Treble since 1977/78. Celtic presented the last remaining obstacle to be cleared in order to complete a clean sweep, with Billy McNeill's side providing the opposition in the Scottish Cup final. It was the first time Rangers had appeared in the end-of-season showpiece since 1983, and they were looking to break a hoodoo in that particular competition by bringing the Cup back to Ibrox for the first time since 1981.

Rangers' road to the final had been rocky to say the least. Souness' team had almost fallen at the first hurdle against Raith Rovers, needing an Ibrox replay to cure the hiccup of a 1-1 draw in Kirkcaldy. In the fourth round, they walloped Stranraer 8-0 – McCoist scored twice, but squandered the chance to grab his first-ever Scottish Cup hat-trick when he missed a late penalty – and Dundee United were dismissed in the last eight, with McCoist on the scoresheet again, netting in the 2-2 draw at

Ibrox and then grabbing the only goal in the Tannadice replay when he fired home the rebound after Billy Thomson had parried a fierce Mark Walters effort onto the woodwork. First Division St Johnstone were then disposed of at the second attempt in the semi-finals, with Rangers winning 4-0 at Parkhead after the first match had ended goalless. Once again McCoist was among the goals, scoring Rangers' fourth goal in the sixty-third minute.

Celtic had finished third in the title race, ten points adrift of Rangers, and were still smarting from the emphatic drubbings they had suffered on league business at Ibrox during the season. The Hoops had also lost out in the final league meeting between the clubs on April Fool's Day – Rangers won 2-1 to chalk up their first Old Firm victory in the East End of Glasgow since August 1980 – and they were thus out to exact revenge and add a silver lining to what had otherwise been a poor campaign by their standards.

Celtic enjoyed the better of the first-half exchanges in front of the 72,069 fans who were basking in the afternoon sunshine that bathed the Hampden Park arena. McCoist and Drinkell, with five goals each in the competition, formed Rangers' attacking spearhead, but with Ray Wilkins absent through injury, the Light Blues struggled to dominate the midfield and create chances for the front two and any openings that were created were spurned, with McCoist guilty of a bad miss from eight yards when he got himself on the end of a header from Butcher. 'It should have been a goal,' said Graeme Souness afterwards. 'Earlier in the season, when he [McCoist] was scoring so regularly, it would have been a goal.'[10]

In the end, a poor final was won by Celtic when, shortly before half-time, Joe Miller scored the only goal of the game, capitalising on a woefully short backpass from Gary Stevens to slide a shot behind Chris Woods. Rangers battled manfully after the interval in an attempt to restore parity and Butcher had a goal disallowed in the dying embers of the match – Cooper was alleged to have impeded Pat Bonner as he came off his line to field a corner-kick – but it was clearly not to be Rangers' day.

The season may have ended on a negative note, but the overall report card was positive, with two pieces of silverware won – the most important of which being the reclamation of the League Championship – and the club also enjoyed another creditable run in Europe. Despite his two-month injury absence, McCoist still managed to find the net on eighteen occasions but, for the first time since signing for the club, had not finished as top goalscorer. That accolade went to his striking partner Kevin Drinkell, who netted nineteen times in forty-seven appearances.

What would subsequently prove to be the most successful era in the club's history was well underway, but around the next corner was a sensation that would rock not only Rangers Football Club but also Scottish football to its very core.

CHAPTER EIGHT

MO JOHNSTON AND ITALIA '90: 1989–90

Maurice Johnston was a very good friend of Ally McCoist. The pair had first crossed paths in the early eighties when McCoist had travelled to Scarborough to watch ex-team-mate John Brogan in action for the Scotland semi-professional side. Johnston, who was emerging as a talented striker with Partick Thistle, had also been part of the Scottish set-up, and he and McCoist immediately struck up a rapport, with their off-field relationship eventually developing into a very productive partnership in the international arena with Scotland. However, any thoughts of them continuing that relationship at club level were never entertained, and anyone suggesting otherwise would have either been laughed out of Glasgow or advised to check themselves into the nearest psychiatric facility for fear he had taken leave of his senses. At that time, such a notion was simply 'pie in the sky'. For a start, Johnston had once played for Celtic and, although performing for both clubs had not been uncommon in the late nineteenth century, in the modern era it was actively discouraged, simply because of the ramifications for the player concerned. Then there was the fact that Maurice was a Roman Catholic.

Throughout their history, Rangers had achieved notoriety as a result of an aged policy they adopted when it came to signing players. This went along the lines of if you were brought up as a Roman Catholic you would not be signed for the club, irrespective of how good a footballer you were. The board of directors often denied this was the guiding principle when recruiting fresh talent, but there are several cases that suggest otherwise. Perhaps the most famous are those of Danny McGrain and Kenny Dalglish, two of the finest footballers Scotland has produced in the past forty years. Both were ardent Rangers followers from Protestant backgrounds, but they both slipped through the net purely based on the assumption that they were Catholics. Indeed, McGrain's situation is arguably the most damning indictment of this parochial policy, as he was reportedly overlooked based on the supposition that having a name like Daniel Fergus McGrain must have meant that he hailed from a Roman Catholic background. In the long run, Rangers' loss was Celtic's gain, with both players eventually signing up at Parkhead before progressing to win countless honours and international caps over the course of their respective careers.

This sectarian sore was in dire need of lancing and Graeme Souness was about to become the man who would administer the definitive blow. From the day and hour he had taken his seat in the manager's office at Ibrox, Souness, who was married to a Catholic, had vowed to rid the club of this millstone-like policy. Before attempting to lure Johnston to Ibrox, he had tried to sign Ray Houghton, a Glasgow-born Republic of Ireland international, and John Collins, a Scottish midfielder who played for Hibernian, but both players had turned down his overtures simply because of the hullabaloo that would inevitably be associated with the fact that they would be the first high-profile Roman Catholic signing. Maurice Johnston, however, was an altogether different proposition.

Towards the end of the 1988/89 season, he made it clear that he wished to leave his current employers, Nantes, in France and return to Scotland. During his two-year stint in France, Johnston had improved as a player to the extent that he was widely regarded as one of the best British centre-forwards at that time. For a while it looked like a return to Celtic, with whom he had enjoyed a prolific three years between 1984 and 1987 – winning a League Championship medal and a Scottish Cup-winners' badge – was his preferred destination. Representatives of Nantes and Celtic agreed a fee for the striker and the deal to take him back to Glasgow's East End looked to all intents and purposes to have been signed and sealed. Johnston was even paraded in front of the

Above: The journey begins: a young Ally McCoist pictured in the early days of his playing career at St Johnstone.　　　　　*© SNSPIX*

Below: A rare sight from a two-year stay at Sunderland: McCoist celebrates scoring against Southampton in October 1982.　　　　　*© Sunderland Echo*

Above: Holding aloft the League Cup with Peter McCloy in 1984. McCoist's hat-trick secured a 3-2 win over Celtic – the first of a number of trophies that he would pick up during his illustrious career.   © *PA Photos*

Below left: On the receiving end of one of Jock Wallace's infamous bear hugs after the Scottish League Cup final in 1984. Despite a rocky start, Wallace played a pivotal role in moulding McCoist into a top-quality striker.

© *PA Photos*

Below right: With the Glasgow Cup in May 1986. McCoist's hat-trick handed Rangers a 3-2 win over Celtic and the first piece of silverware of the Graeme Souness era.   © *SNSPIX*

Above: Sliding in to score Rangers' second goal in the 1987 New Year victory over Celtic at Ibrox. © *SNSPIX*

Below: Celebrating winning the Premier Division Championship in 1986/7 with 'The English Connection' – Chris Woods, Terry Butcher and Graham Roberts.

© *PA Photos*

Above: Happier times with Graeme Souness after the League Cup final in 1988. The relationship would eventually sour, culminating with the Cheltenham fiasco in March 1991. © *Mirrorpix*

Below: With close friend Maurice Johnston, whose transfer to Rangers in July 1989 rocked Scottish football. © *PA Photos*

Above: Scoring for Scotland against Norway at Hampden. The goal booked
Scotland's place at the World Cup finals in Italy in 1990. © *Mirrorpix*

Below: With Mark Hateley after the Scottish Cup final in 1992. The pair forged
arguably the most potent goalscoring partnership in Rangers' history. © *SNSPIX*

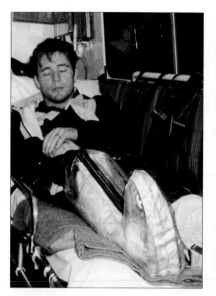

Above left: Returning to Edinburgh Airport after sustaining a broken leg while playing for Scotland against Portugal in April 1993. © *Mirrorpix*

Above right: Pictured with the second of his *Soulier d'Or* (Golden Boot) awards in 1993. McCoist became the first person in history to successfully retain the award. © *SNSPIX*

Below: Celebrating a goal with the late, great Davie Cooper. Cooper's untimely death in 1995 shocked Scottish football. © *Chris Cole/Allsport/Getty Images*

Posing with former World Boxing Champion Barry McGuigan after receiving
an MBE from Prince Charles at Buckingham Palace.   © *PA Photos*

Above: Curling a shot into the net from the edge of the penalty area against Raith Rovers to beat Bob McPhail's long-standing record of 230 league goals for Rangers.

© *SNSPIX*

Below: Lashing the ball into the back of the net during Scotland's 1-0 win over Switzerland at Euro '96. It was one of the 19 goals that McCoist scored during his international career.

© *PA Photos*

media bedecked in green and white hoops alongside a clearly delighted Celtic manager Billy McNeil. It seemed that the prodigal son had indeed returned.

Behind the smiles at that hastily arranged press conference, though, lay the fact that any deal was far from complete. There was still a dispute over the player's personal terms and, when the talks stalled, Souness stepped into the equation. Rangers' interest in the player was stimulated when Souness had a chance encounter with Johnston's agent, Bill McMurdo, in the Ibrox foyer after a match at the end of the 1988/89 season. Souness is said to have remarked that if he'd known Johnston was available for transfer he'd have been interested in making a bid to bring him to Rangers. When McMurdo informed the Rangers manager that the deal with Celtic was far from complete and that the press conference held at Parkhead had been a little premature, Souness needed no second invitation to join the race for Johnston's signature. After a discussion with chairman David Murray over the logistics of such a transfer, meetings were convened with Johnston and his agent, and the most controversial deal in the club's history was hammered out. The fact that religion is no longer a barrier when Rangers attempt to sign new players today is perhaps the most outstanding legacy of Graeme Souness' time in charge at the club.

On 10 July 1989, Maurice Johnston turned his back on the move to Celtic and signed on the dotted line at Ibrox for a fee of £1.5 million. The news of the signing sent shockwaves reverberating throughout the Scottish game. For once the Old Firm supporters were united, with elements from both sides of the divide condemning the deal. The Celtic fans branded their former icon 'Judas' for his eleventh-hour u-turn, while a knot of Rangers followers were left seething that an ex-Celt and a Catholic would be turning out in their beloved red, white and blue for the forthcoming season. They were further repulsed by the fact that it was Johnston, a player who had openly discussed his dislike for Rangers in his autobiography and who had blessed himself in front of them following his dismissal in the 1986 League Cup final.

However, the fact of the matter was that Rangers had secured the services of one of the most accomplished strikers in the game; his religious background should have had no bearing whatsoever on the deal. The Light Blues were now looking to build on the success of the previous season in a bid to retain the League Championship – a feat the club had not achieved since 1976 – and to forge ahead in Europe. To achieve this goal they would need the best possible players at their disposal, irrespective of their religion, creed or colour, and Johnston most definitely fitted the bill in that respect. He was a seasoned international who had scored a hatful of goals for all the clubs he had turned out for – Partick Thistle, Celtic, Nantes and Watford – in addition to boasting a respectable scoring ratio at international level with Scotland.

An illustration of the bond that existed between McCoist and Johnston emerged some years later when McCoist admitted that he had known about the move for some time. He said 'When wee Mo came to the club, I was very privileged and proud because he told me he was actually coming to the club about three weeks before it happened in the strictest of confidence, which shows the relationship we have got, on and off the park. It wasn't easy to keep because it was probably the biggest secret in Scottish soccer, but I did manage to keep it.'[1]

However, if rumours in the media were to be believed, then McCoist and Johnston were not destined to team up together in a Rangers jersey. During the close season, McCoist was once again being touted for a move away from Ibrox, with Arsenal, Everton and Italian outfit Bologna rumoured to be chasing his signature but, as he had done twelve months earlier, the striker moved quickly to distance himself from talk of a transfer. He told the *Rangers News*: 'I've got four years of my contract at Ibrox left and I'll see out every single one of them. I'll be thirty then and I would hope to be a Rangers player beyond that, too. In fact, I'd like to see out my career with the club.'[2] Walter Smith also added that: 'Ally is the last player we would want to sell. You don't find goalscorers like him very easily.'[3]

With rumours over an impending departure from Ibrox firmly denied, McCoist joined his team-mates in the opulent surroundings of Il Ciocco in the Tuscan hills to prepare for the new season. On their return, Rangers played a number of friendly matches, with Johnston making an encouraging start to his career in a Light Blue jersey. He found the net in a couple of closed-door matches before knocking in his first Rangers goal in front of the paying public in a 3-0 win over Kilmarnock at Rugby Park in Allan McCulloch's testimonial, and he and McCoist then shared four goals in a 4-2 win over Partick Thistle at Firhill. The home side burst out of the blocks to take the lead after just ten seconds of play, but Johnston drew Rangers level with a close-range finish nine minutes later, and restored parity again in the eighteenth minute, equalising a goal from Gerry McCoy to make it 2-2. Victory was clinched in the second half when McCoist opened his account for the season with a header in the fifty-ninth minute before completing the scoring from the penalty spot twelve minutes from full-time.

Johnston took a bow in front of the Ibrox legions for the first time four days later when Rangers welcomed a Tottenham Hotspur side boasting the mercurial talents of one Paul Gascoigne to Glasgow, but although the spotlight was trained on Johnston, it was Souness' other close-season signing who stole the show. Trevor Steven, who had quietly signed for the club from Everton for £1.5 million while the furore surrounding the Johnston deal was at its height, scored ten minutes into the second half to give the home side a 1-0 victory. Although both McCoist and Johnston failed to add to their respective pre-season goal tallies, they continued to show signs of striking up a formidable partnership. They combined on several occasions to create a number of chances, but were thwarted by an excellent display from Erik Thorsvedt in the Tottenham goal, with the Norwegian producing a number of excellent saves, particularly in the final minute when he kept out an effort from McCoist.

Both McCoist and Johnston knew, though, that they would ultimately be judged when the serious business got underway and on the opening Saturday of the new season the gaze of the media and the world of Scottish football was firmly focused on Ibrox Stadium when Johnston made his competitive debut in the opening league match against St Mirren at Ibrox. However, Rangers and their new charge stumbled in the limelight, going down 1-0 and losing goalkeeper Chris Woods into the bargain. The big Englishman dislocated a shoulder as he attempted to prevent Kenny McDowall from netting the only goal of the game. It was an injury that would keep him out of action for four games.

Israeli international goalkeeper Bonni Ginzburg, recruited from Maccabi Tel Aviv for £200,000, replaced the stricken Woods between the posts, and he enjoyed a relatively easy start to his Ibrox career, as Rangers chalked up their first win of the season when they disposed of Arbroath in the second round of the League Cup at Ibrox. The home side cruised to a 4-0 victory, with McCoist the hero of the hour. He opened the scoring after five minutes with a close-range finish and doubled his tally fourteen minutes later with a header. He was denied a first-half treble when the Arbroath goalkeeper saved his twenty-sixth-minute penalty, but he made the net billow again in the sixty-eighth minute when he turned in a pass from Johnston to claim his third goal of the evening. McCoist's performance certainly impressed Terry Butcher, as the Ibrox skipper voted him Most Valuable Player and credited him with Goal of the Week in his weekly column in the *Rangers News*.

However, when Souness' men contrived to lose their second league match of the season, going down 2-0 to Hibernian at Easter Road, the vultures were beginning to circle Ibrox, ready to move in for the kill, as both Rangers and Johnston struggled to reproduce the form everyone knew they were capable of, and a sluggish 2-1 win over Morton in the League Cup did little to suggest that the corner was about to be turned.

Three days later, Rangers travelled to Parkhead for their third league match and, given that Celtic had won their opening two games, it was imperative that the Light Blues emerged from the clash with at least a point, as defeat would have meant falling six points behind their great rivals, leaving a mountain to climb even at this early stage of the championship marathon.

McCoist, who had been an unused substitute for the League Cup tie against Morton, was again given a watching brief at Parkhead, with Souness pairing Johnston and Kevin Drinkell in attack, but it was Terry Butcher who got Rangers off the mark for the season when he chalked up their first league goal with a thumping header in the fifth minute. Celtic restored parity eight minutes later to secure a share of the spoils but, despite emerging with their first point of the season, Rangers perhaps should have won the match, with Johnston passing up a couple of routine chances later in the game. Unsurprisingly, he was subjected to a torrent of abuse from the home support and was harangued every time he touched the ball, with jeers and catcalls raining down from the Parkhead terraces. Had he taken one of the opportunities that came his way, then he would have undoubtedly dampened the ardour of the home support, but not even the introduction of McCoist in the fifty-seventh minute could aid him in his quest.

It was argued that Johnston had perhaps been trying too hard when he returned to his former abode, but the following week the moment he and those close to Rangers had been waiting for, that elusive first competitive goal, finally arrived. One could almost feel the sense of relief wash over Johnston as he got on the end of a right-wing cross from Trevor Steven to head the ball beyond Theo Snelders to hand Rangers a 1-0 win over

Aberdeen at Ibrox. It was an important goal too, as it gave Rangers their first league victory of the season.

McCoist, who replaced the match-winner after sixty-two minutes after being rested following a physically exhausting appearance for Scotland in a World Cup qualifying match against Yugoslavia in Zagreb three days earlier, was in the midst of a dry spell, too. Following his treble against Arbroath, the marksman had failed to hit the target for four matches, but he eventually broke his league duck for the season when Dundee visited Ibrox in mid-September. After twice being denied by Bobby Geddes, McCoist fired Rangers into the lead in the twentieth minute with a close-range finish, and he looked to have secured full points for the home side when he nodded the ball into the net six minutes from time to make it 2-1. However, a late lapse allowed Keith Wright to equalise for the Dark Blues in the final minute, and when Souness' men drew 1-1 against Dunfermline seven days later (McCoist was again on the mark, expertly controlling a pass from Trevor Steven before cutting inside his marker and rifling a shot into the net with his left foot), they chalked up only their fifth league point of the season. And defeat at Motherwell in only their eighth league outing of the season left Rangers just two points clear of the foot of the Premier Division table.

However, goals from Johnston and McCoist – the first time the duo had appeared on the scoresheet together since the pre-season friendly against Partick in August – secured a narrow 2-1 victory over Dundee United, and sparked a fine run of form that drove Rangers to the top of the table. It also signalled the gelling of the McCoist-Johnston combination, with the pair finally finding the formula that had reaped numerous rewards at international level. They had borne the brunt of some criticism earlier in the campaign when things did not seem to be clicking, but their respective strikes against United finally burst the dam. A spate of goals duly followed, with one apiece securing a 2-0 win over St Mirren at Love Street eleven days later before a brace from McCoist sandwiched a Johnston penalty in a 3-0 victory over Hibernian at Ibrox.

Remarkably, the duo had contributed seven goals within the space of three matches and their input helped Rangers recover their poise in the title race. Souness' men were now within touching distance of the top of the table, and going into the campaign's second instalment of the Old Firm at Ibrox on 4 November, they were just two points adrift of their greatest rivals. By the time referee George Smith sounded his final whistle at the end of a dramatic ninety minutes, that advantage had been consumed by a ravenous Rangers side courtesy of the boot of Maurice Johnston.

Although the new boy had now got off the mark in a Rangers jersey, there were still dissenting voices that doubted whether or not he would ever score against Celtic. He had been wasteful in front of goal at Parkhead earlier in the season, but he expunged memories of those missed opportunities by netting a stunning winner at Ibrox that propelled Rangers to the top of the table. With the sides tied at 0-0 as the November twilight descended, Johnston pounced on a poor clearance from Chris Morris to sweep the ball beyond Bonner in the Celtic goal to win the match for the home side in the dying seconds. Ibrox exploded with joy as the ball ruffled the rigging, and Johnston milked the applause, running arms aloft towards the Copland Road Stand. Indeed, Johnston had been so energised by finally shedding this particular monkey from his back that McCoist later joked that he finally caught up with his buddy at Cessnock underground, a tube station half a mile from Ibrox! The much sought after seal of approval from the Rangers community had finally been achieved, and Johnston's strike earned two points that would ultimately prove pivotal in the outcome of the championship flag.

The Old Firm victory was one of five successive league wins for Rangers. Although they lost 1-0 at Pittodrie on 22 November to break their successful sequence, triumphs over Dunfermline Athletic, Hearts and Motherwell got Souness' men back on track, with the 3-0 victory over Motherwell at Ibrox providing a significant moment in Ally McCoist's career.

When he scored Rangers' third goal in the 3-0 win over Dunfermline (a match that saw Ray Wilkins make an emotional final appearance in a Rangers jersey), McCoist moved on to 127 Premier League goals, equalling the record set by Frank McGarvey during his time with St Mirren and Celtic. Therefore, McCoist now stood on the verge of a place in the history books, and although an upset stomach hampered his efforts to break McGarvey's record in Rangers' next league outing against Hearts at Tynecastle, he duly carved his name into the annals of Scottish football when Motherwell visited the south side of Glasgow on 9 December 1989.

As the game entered the closing stages, Terry Butcher's forty-third-minute header was all that separated the two sides, as a typically stubborn Motherwell defence had frustrated Rangers for much of the match. However, with eight minutes remaining, McCoist scored a goal fit to break the record he was chasing. Butcher's long ball forward was cushioned into McCoist's path by Johnston, and the record-chaser took a touch to beat his marker before lifting an exquisite chip shot with his right foot over the advancing Ally Maxwell in the Motherwell goal. It was a special moment for the Rangers hitman, who had written himself into the record books in the space of just 208 league appearances, a splendid goals-to-game ratio, and his goal also represented a landmark moment in Rangers' history: it was the club's 7,000th goal in the Scottish League Championship. Clearly proud of his achievement, McCoist said: 'Records mean a lot to me. It's nice to set new standards and beat old records, and now I'm chasing Derek's [Derek Johnstone's] post-war scoring record [of 131 league goals for Rangers], and the best of it is he's promised me a bottle of champagne if I get it.'[4]

Record-breaking was a habit McCoist was to get used to over the next few seasons, and he began reeling in Derek Johnstone's goals tally by scoring against Aberdeen and Dundee at Ibrox early in the New Year. Another thrust from his rapier-like right foot pulled McCoist level with Johnstone when he grabbed league goal number 131 in a 3-1 win against Dundee United at Ibrox in February, but a run of four games without a goal, and a groin strain that kept him out of two matches, delayed his attempts to eclipse his former team-mate's milestone. However, the record eventually fell on April Fool's Day, and it was perhaps fitting that Celtic, a team against whom McCoist had enjoyed great success during his time at Ibrox, provided the opposition on the day in question.

When Celtic arrived at Ibrox for the campaign's final Old Firm encounter, they were drinking in the last-chance saloon in terms of their quest to wrestle the championship title away from their rivals. Since winning 1-0 against Celtic at Ibrox in November, Rangers had won ten of the eighteen matches they had played in the league, losing only twice in that spell. They had also beaten their rivals in the New Year Old Firm derby, with new signing Nigel Spackman netting the only goal at Parkhead when he turned a McCoist cutback into the net. Spackman, a midfielder signed from Queens Park Rangers for a fee of £500,000, was soon bearing the brunt of the banter in the Ibrox dressing room, with McCoist and Durrant quickly renaming him 'Rab', as they reasoned that his chances of survival in Glasgow with a name like Nigel were remote! Irrespective of what he was called, 'Spackers' was a good player and he did an excellent job of filling the void left by the departing Ray Wilkins, who had headed back to London shortly before Christmas to sign for QPR.

With Rangers nine points clear, it was vital that Celtic left Ibrox with the two points, and they arrived on the south side in good heart having dumped their rivals out of the Scottish Cup thanks to a 1-0 win at Parkhead in February. They were also buoyed by Rangers' recent dip in form, with Souness' men seemingly a little off-colour: they were in the midst of a sticky spell that had failed to yield a victory in any of their previous five league matches. Four matches had been drawn, while Hibernian had won 1-0 at Ibrox the weekend prior to Celtic's visit.

The home support had no need to worry, though, as Rangers shook themselves out of their lethargy to dominate the match. They drew first blood after twenty-eight minutes when Terry Butcher swung in an inviting cross from the left flank towards his central defensive partner Richard Gough. Gough rose to meet the ball, but was denied the chance to head the ball towards goal by Celtic full-back Anton Rogan, who inexplicably elected to punch the ball out of the danger area. It was a clear penalty and Mark Walters stepped up to score the spot-kick, squeezing the ball inside the right-hand post despite the best efforts of Bonner, who got a hand to the winger's shot but could not prevent it from crossing the line.

Rangers, playing some of their best football of the season, pinned their rivals against the ropes and delivered another hammer blow six minutes before half-time. Johnston, who along with McCoist gave Celtic's backline a torrid afternoon, was the marksman this time, expertly volleying the ball beyond Bonner after he had chested down a cute pass from McCoist. It was his second goal against his old side and his fourteenth league goal of the season.

In the second half, the home side continued to pummel their rivals and were rewarded with a third goal ten minutes from the end when referee Jim McCluskey awarded them their second penalty of the afternoon. On this occasion, Peter Grant fouled Johnston and McCoist stepped up to the mark with the chance to carve yet another niche in the history books.

After failing to score from the twelve-yard mark against St Mirren in October, his third successive penalty miss, McCoist had been relieved of the penalty-taking duties, with Mo Johnston initially assuming the role before Mark Walters took over when Johnston failed to find the net against Dunfermline in November. However, his lack of recent success from twelve yards did not deter McCoist from taking this one, especially as the kick gave him the chance to break Derek Johnstone's goal-scoring record. He did just that, emphatically sending Bonner the wrong way and thundering the ball into the top left-hand corner of the net.

Johnstone, now a media pundit with *Radio Clyde* having quit playing in 1986, was on the radio gantry commentating on the game, and he was one of the first to offer his congratulations to McCoist at the end of the game. Quick-witted in much the same way as the man who had just made him Rangers' second top league goalscorer in the post-war era, the jovial Johnstone was quick to remind the record-breaker that his total would have been nigh on impossible to beat had he taken penalties and not spent some of his career playing centre-half!

Rangers duly delivered their second successive championship with two games to spare when Trevor Steven scored with a header to secure a 1-0 win against Dundee United at Tannadice. Their winning margin over second-placed Aberdeen was seven points, with Celtic languishing a further ten points behind in fifth place. The championship was the only piece of silverware to remain in the Ibrox trophy cabinet at the end of 1989/90, though. Celtic had, of course, ended interest in the Scottish Cup and Aberdeen gained a modicum of revenge for losing the previous two League Cup finals when they emerged victorious by two goals to one in Part III of the Rangers v Aberdeen League Cup final trilogy.

McCoist ended the campaign with eighteen goals from forty appearances. Fourteen of his strikes came in the league, with another four added in the League Cup, and for the sixth time in seven seasons he topped the Rangers goal-scoring charts, finishing one goal better off than his striking partner, Mo Johnston. Neither Johnston nor McCoist were the top man in the Premier Division, though. That accolade went to John Robertson of Hearts, with the diminutive forward's seventeen goals helping the men from Gorgie to finish in third place in the Premier Division.

With another excellent and consistent season under his belt, McCoist was understandably in fine fettle when he left Glasgow in early June along with the rest of the Scotland squad bound for the World Cup finals in Italy. Although he had represented his country at the European Youth Championships in 1981, this was McCoist's first crack at an international tournament with the senior team, as Scotland had failed to qualify for the

1988 European Championships in West Germany and he had missed out on a place in the Scotland squad for the 1986 World Cup in Mexico after being overlooked by Alex Ferguson.

Despite having only earned his first cap a month before the squad was decided, McCoist felt that, given his excellent form in the 1985/86 season, he had an outside chance of making the flight to Mexico. It was not to be, though. Initially, Ferguson, who had taken over as national team manager following the death of Jock Stein, offered him some hope when he said that he would be first reserve should any strikers drop out through injury, but when Kenny Dalglish of Liverpool pulled out from the squad prior to departure to the USA for altitude training, Ferguson opted to bring Barcelona's Steve Archibald into the squad instead. 'I really felt very hurt and let down,' recalled McCoist, 'and I think to this day I would have done as well as any one of the front men who did make the trip.'[5] He has a point. Scotland scored just once in their three group matches, and none of the strikers in the party got off the mark, with the Scots' only goal coming from the boot of a midfielder, Gordon Strachan, during the 2-1 defeat against West Germany.

By 1990, however, it was a different matter. McCoist was no longer a reserve; he was now a regular in the international fold and a first pick if he was free from injury. In Scotland's qualifying campaign for Italy, he missed only two of the nation's eight group matches and both of the games – a 2-1 win over Norway in Oslo and a last-gasp 3-2 victory over Cyprus in Limassol – had been missed through injury.

Alongside the Norwegians and the Cypriots in Scotland's section were France and Yugoslavia. The unbeaten Yugoslavs, who drew 1-1 at Hampden and beat the Scots 3-1 in Zagreb, won the group, which left France and Scotland vying for the second qualifying berth. Both nations won their respective home matches against each other, the Scots by two goals to nil in March 1989 and the French by three goals to nil seven months later, but going into the final round of fixtures it was advantage Scotland, as Andy Roxburgh's men held a two-point advantage. Thus, the Scots only needed to register a point from their final group match at home to Norway to ensure progress to their fifth successive World Cup finals, while the French, who boasted a superior goal difference, had to defeat Cyprus in Toulouse and hope that the Norwegians did them a favour at Hampden.

Rather than sit back and play for the draw, Roxburgh adopted a bold approach and elected to go for the win, partnering McCoist and Johnston in attack and selecting Davie Cooper, who was in terrific form following his move from Rangers to Motherwell, to play on the wing. Roxburgh's positive approach reaped its reward one minute before the half-time interval when McCoist, who had found the net just once in his five previous qualifying matches, got on the end of a Maurice Malpas clearance and steered a beautiful lob over the out-rushing Erik Thorstvedt and into the back of the net. The Scots clung to their slender lead and made it to Italy despite suffering a late scare when Jim Leighton allowed a speculative 40-yard strike from Erland Johnsen to slip through his hands to give the visitors a share of the points.

When Andy Roxburgh named his squad for the finals early in the New Year, it came as no great surprise that Ally McCoist's name was in the party of twenty-two, with many observers fully expecting that he and Ibrox striking buddy Mo Johnston would spearhead Scotland's assault in Italy, as the nation pushed for qualification into the knockout stages for the first time ever. Both had been prominent in the series of warm-up matches arranged ahead of the departure to Italy, with Johnston netting in a 1-1 draw with Poland at Hampden and McCoist scoring in the 3-1 defeat by Egypt at Pittodrie. Ominously, though, McCoist failed to start the last of the five matches against Malta, only appearing as a late substitute for Johnston. Alan McInally of Bayern Munich took McCoist's place in the forward line, and 'Rambo' helped himself to both of Scotland's goals in the 2-1 win.

When the draw was made for the fourteenth World Cup, Scotland were grouped alongside three-time winners Brazil, Sweden and minnows Costa Rica in Group C, with their games taking place in Genoa and Turin. First up for Roxburgh and Scotland would be the Costa Ricans followed by the Swedes, with the third game bringing the Scots face to face with the formidable Brazilians.

On the day of the opening game, Andy Roxburgh took McCoist and his fellow strikers (Johnston, McInally, Gordon Durie of Chelsea, and McCoist's ex-team-mate Robert Fleck, now with Norwich) to one side and announced that he would be playing just two of them in the match against Costa Rica. McCoist had good reason to believe that he would be one half of the double act. The defenders in the squad had complimented him on his sharpness in training, he felt he was mentally and physically at his peak, and initially it looked as if he had made the team. Roxburgh continually referred to McInally as 'Nally', so when he announced that his strike-pairing would be 'Mo and Nally', McCoist thought that Roxburgh had said, 'Ally'. However, the awful realisation soon began to sink in, and McCoist had to come to terms with the fact that he would not start for Scotland against Costa Rica. He recalled:

> *I was absolutely gutted and very disappointed in Andy Roxburgh, firstly that he didn't pick me, and secondly that there was no word of explanation as to why I was dropped, no hint of a warning. Now I wasn't looking for special privileges, but Andy is a great squad man. He must have known that I would be totally devastated by his decision. Even if he had pulled me aside before the meeting and given me a ten-second explanation of what was about to happen, it would still have hurt, but maybe not as much. I felt, rightly or wrongly, that I was owed that much.*[6]

McCoist took his seat among the substitutes at the Stadio Luigi Ferraris, home to Sampdoria and Genoa, on 11 June, but could only watch in horror as the name of Costa Rica was added to the long list of countries that have humiliated Scotland over the years. Their striker, Juan Cayaso, scored the only goal of the game shortly after half-time, and by the time McCoist took to the field, replacing Jim Bett with sixteen minutes remaining, it was too late to help mount a salvage mission. 'I was glad to get on,' he told the *Rangers News*, 'but really upset to finish on the losing side. Coming off the bench with just over a quarter of an hour to go didn't give me much of a chance. It's impossible really to find your feet and settle in, especially in the World Cup, in such a short time.'[7]

With McInally performing poorly against the Costa Ricans, McCoist had good reason to believe that he would get more game time in the now make-or-break second fixture with Sweden. Yet again, however, he was overlooked. McInally was indeed dropped from the line-up, but instead of picking McCoist to partner Johnston (a partnership that had contributed thirty-five goals for Rangers in the season just past), Roxburgh opted for a three-pronged attack, with Durie and Fleck installed alongside Johnston. 'I was pulverised, totally gutted,' said McCoist. 'From joint first-choice striker out of five, I had gone to fifth choice – without kicking a ball.'[8]

In order to gain some sort of explanation for his omission, McCoist sought a private meeting with Roxburgh at the conclusion of the final training session. The result was an angry exchange in the middle of the training field – 'the most heated argument I ever had with a football manager,'[9] according to McCoist – as the rest of the squad looked on. Roxburgh told McCoist he felt he had looked tired, 'not 100 per cent McCoist'[10], and although this opinion contradicted those of the team-mates, McCoist simply had to grin and bear it, as Roxburgh was the manager and picked the team that he saw fit.

As always, McCoist managed to find some humour in what was a deeply disheartening situation. He was sharing a room with Alan McInally and ahead of the Costa Rica game, 'Rambo' had returned to their room to find McCoist engrossed in a crossword book. He had jocularly instructed McCoist to put the light out in order to allow him to get some sleep ahead of the big game, but when McInally also found himself dropped ahead of the Sweden game, McCoist pitched the crossword book at his room-mate and said: 'I guess you can help me with them today.' It was a typical piece of McCoist humour and one that helped lift the gloom that had threatened to enshroud the two forwards in the wake of their exclusion from the starting eleven.

At least this time the viewing from the sidelines was more pleasant. Scotland turned in a polished and efficient performance to win 2-1, with Everton's Stuart McCall on the scoresheet along with Johnston, who netted a penalty. In doing so, Johnston had thus become the first Rangers player to score for his country in the World Cup finals since Sammy Baird had netted for Scotland in a 2-1 defeat against France in 1958.

The victory over the Swedes now put the Scots firmly back in contention in their quest for qualification for the second phase of the World Cup for the first time ever. All they required from their final group match with Brazil, who having beaten both the Swedes and the Costa Ricans were already through to the next round, was a draw. Amazingly McCoist, who had replaced Fleck for the final thirteen minutes of the Sweden match, was included in the starting line-up alongside Johnston, despite having been considered too tired to face either Costa Rica or Sweden.

It turned out to be a painful night for Scotland. Over the course of the ninety minutes in the Stadio Delle Alpe in Turin, they huffed and puffed but could not blow the Brazilian house down. McCoist and Johnston were starved of the service upon which their respective games thrived, and the inevitable happened when Muller scored the only goal of the game with nine minutes left. Johnston almost snatched the coveted equalising goal in the dying moments of the contest, but he was thwarted by a miraculous save from Claudio Tafferel that preserved Brazil's slender advantage and ultimately eliminated the Scots from the tournament.

Ally McCoist's World Cup had also ended early when he was replaced by Robert Fleck after seventy-seven minutes. 'The World Cup finals in 1990 in Italy should have been the pinnacle of my football career – the extra special moment I would always treasure when it came to looking back over my playing days,' recalled McCoist. 'Instead it left me bitter and disillusioned with an empty feeling of disappointment that I can still recall to this day.'[11]

If McCoist had learned anything from his troubles in Italy, though, it was that, in football, nothing could be taken for granted, no matter how good your form was. This lesson may have been learned the hard way, but it was one that would stand him in good stead for the season ahead with Rangers, for he was about to embark on a rollercoaster campaign during which he seemed destined for the Ibrox exit door.

CHAPTER NINE

THE JUDGE: 1990–91

It could be argued that the events that unfolded over the course of Graeme Souness' fifth season in charge at Ibrox had been brewing for some time, with the foundations of the eventual fallout between the Rangers manager and Ally McCoist perhaps being laid as early as the beginning of his Ibrox tenure.

When Souness was appointed to the Ibrox hot seat in the summer of 1986, the dark cloud that had hung around McCoist and which had been a constant companion for a great many of his early days at Rangers career had finally lifted. The striker was now benefiting from a new lease of life having finally discovered his goal-scoring touch, and was enjoying universal popularity among both the Rangers supporters and his team-mates, having established himself as one of the characters in the home dressing room in his role as the joker in the pack alongside Ian Durrant. This iconic status and popularity is something that is said to have grated Souness, with the Rangers manager thinking that McCoist often played on his image a little too much and coasted through games at times. He often felt that the striker was more interested in number one than in the team ethic and this was against the image of the consummate professional that Souness was looking to create at Ibrox. Falling foul of the law in 1987, as we have seen in an earlier chapter, also did little to ingratiate McCoist with his manager.

There were seemingly issues with McCoist's quick wit and sharp humour, too. While Souness enjoyed having a happy and bubbly working environment, there were times when his team-talks would be punctuated with a series of wisecracks and one-liners delivered by McCoist, which would generally result in the dressing room descending into uproarious laughter and any hope Souness had of making a serious point would be gone.

On one occasion, the court jester had the dressing room in stitches when Souness recounted a story from his time in Italy during an important discussion about the spiking of food or drink with banned substances. Trevor Francis had suffered food poisoning the night before a big game after someone had interfered with the chicken he had eaten in a restaurant, and Souness was eager to warn his charges to be on their guard when eating out in case a similar fate befell them. McCoist, who had further raised the ire of his manager by typically turning up late for the meeting, is then said to have retorted that the Italians were famous for this, and when Souness enquired what he meant, McCoist simply said 'fowl play', a response that sent the assembled masses into fits of laughter. It is fair to say that Mr Souness was less than impressed, and the icy stare that he fixed on McCoist suggested that the impish humour had not been well received.

Further evidence hinting at the inevitable collision course between the two also stemmed from the fact that on the few occasions when Rangers had played badly since the summer of 1986 and lost matches it had become increasingly likely that McCoist would be apportioned most of the blame for the team's poor display. Although each member of the first-team squad had been subjected to the 'hair dryer' treatment at some point during Souness' four-year reign, the rollickings doled out to McCoist were often regarded as being the most severe. Arguably the most famous was the one meted out after a match against Dundee United at Tannadice when Souness lambasted his number nine and told him that he had been a 'dud' at each of the clubs he had played for and was still 'a f*****g dud'. The bollocking promptly earned McCoist a new nickname, 'Dudley'; a moniker that stuck for a few weeks afterwards.

McCoist also had another theory as to why he seemed to bear the brunt of Souness' criticism. At the start of the 1990/91 season, he was part of a unique trio in the first-team dressing room at Ibrox. The other members of the triumvirate were Stuart Munro and Ian Durrant, and the common link between them was that they were the last remaining remnants of the first-team squad from the previous regimes under Jock Wallace and John Greig. From the amount of transfer activity that had buzzed around Edmiston Drive in the past half decade, it was clear that Souness had one vision in his mind: to create his very own Rangers team, a squad made up of players he himself had acquired. As the only three remaining ghosts from eras past, this left the respective coats of Messrs McCoist, Durrant and Munro on the proverbial 'shoogily' nail, with McCoist's the most precariously balanced of all. He recalled: 'Durranty was so exceptional that I don't think even Graeme Souness would ever have seriously considered selling him, but I always felt Stuart Munro and I had to keep battling away under far more of a threat than some of the others.'[1]

Over the course of the 1990/91 season, McCoist's theory began to come true. Munro, a quiet and unassuming left-back signed for the princely sum of £25,000 from Alloa Athletic in 1984, had played to a consistently high level during the previous season, a campaign in which a miserly Rangers defence had only leaked nineteen goals in thirty-six Premier League matches. He had picked up the *Rangers News* Player of the Year accolade and had been a valuable member of the squad throughout the Souness era, but he became more marginalised in the new season, making only twenty-one appearances, as Souness introduced youngsters Chris Vinnicombe and Tom Cowan on the left side of his back four. He was eventually sold to Blackburn Rovers for £350,000 in the summer of 1991.

As for McCoist, despite consistently outscoring the other forwards at the club, notching 116 goals in four seasons, rumours always seemed to be circulating Glasgow that he was about to move away from Ibrox. Although Souness had been quick to quash the speculation when it had appeared in the press, it was no secret that he was still seeking his dream striker and, in the summer of 1990, he finally got the man he was looking for.

Mark Hateley, a striker of some repute with thirty-one England caps to his name, finally put pen to paper and agreed a move that would take him to Ibrox from the principality of Monaco in a £1 million deal. Hateley, who had enjoyed successful spells at Coventry City, Portsmouth, AC Milan and latterly Monaco, was the stereotypical target man Souness had craved since he took over the managerial reins at Ibrox in 1986.

Indeed, the Rangers manager was so convinced that the Englishman was the man he wanted that he had tried to lure him to Govan on two separate occasions before finally nailing him while the World Cup finals were taking place in Italy. Christened 'Attila' by the Milan fans, Hateley was strong, robust, excellent in the air and also handy on the ground; attributes enough to convince Souness that he was tailor-made for Scottish football and would thus prove a success at his new club.

While Souness was delighted to have snared the big Englishman, it was the last thing McCoist needed to hear after his negative experiences during the World Cup. Having stuck rigidly to playing a 4-4-2 system deploying two strikers, Souness now had three international-class forwards at his disposal, so it was clear that unless the successful tactics of the previous years were to be changed, one of the trio would be disappointed. Given the extent of his endeavours to lure Hateley to Ibrox, it seemed unlikely that Souness would overlook his latest acquisition, leaving McCoist and Johnston to fight it out for the right to partner the Englishman in attack, a contest that, in the eyes of Ally McCoist, was weighted firmly in the favour of the latter. 'There was obviously no doubt in his [Souness'] mind which of his two strikers – McCoist or Johnston – was under threat,' he noted. 'It was yours truly. Mo Johnston had had a fantastic first season as a Rangers player. I had scored more goals, but Mo had been quite sensational. There was no way Souness was going to drop him.'[2]

Sure enough when the time came for pre-season friendlies, McCoist found himself relegated to either the substitutes' bench or to an unfamiliar role in midfield, with Johnston – who had been sent home early from the pre-season training camp in Italy following a drunken incident – and Hateley the preferred partnership up front. McCoist scored just once in a series of warm-up games, the opening goal in Rangers' 3-1 victory over Kilmarnock in Walter McCrae's testimonial, and although he was in the starting line-up for the 3-1 defeat at the hands of Dynamo Kiev at Ibrox, he was listed among the substitutes for the final pre-season friendly against Manchester United four days later.

And when the serious business started in August, nothing changed. Despite being barracked, somewhat unfairly, by a section of the Rangers support, Hateley retained his place alongside Johnston for the opening gambit of the League Championship race against Dunfermline at Ibrox, and both strikers scored in a 3-1 win. McCoist took in most of the match from the substitutes' bench before replacing Rangers' other goalscorer, Mark Walters, with ten minutes remaining.

The striker refused to be beaten by this latest setback, though. He redoubled his efforts on the training pitch and regained his place in the starting line-up, sending out a clear message to his manager that he still had the ability to produce the goods by netting a hat-trick in a 6-2 League Cup thrashing of Raith Rovers and a brace of goals from midfield in a 3-1 win over Hearts at Tynecastle in the Premier League.

With Johnston ruled out for three games with a hamstring injury and Hateley's form indifferent, McCoist retained his place in the team for the next fourteen matches, a spell that yielded a further six goals for the striker. He netted twice in a 5-0 league win over St Mirren, once in a 2-1 home defeat by Dundee United (a match in which he also saw a penalty saved by Alan Main in the United goal), and added three goals to his European tally, with home and away strikes against Valletta of Malta and the consolation goal as Rangers' pursuit of glory in the European Cup was abruptly halted by eventual winners Red Star Belgrade in the second round. McCoist claimed his sixth League Cup-winners' medal in that spell too, as goals from Walters and Gough were sufficient to secure a 2-1 victory over Celtic in the final. His excellent club form also carried over into the international arena, with McCoist scoring Scotland's winner in their 2-1 home win over Romania, although he did blot his copybook by missing a penalty in the next international against Switzerland at Hampden.

October also saw dramatic changes at Ibrox, with Rangers appointing a new leader on the field, Richard Gough. Gough had taken the captain's armband from Terry Butcher when the Englishman had been dropped for the semi-final of the League Cup against Aberdeen. Souness had elected to leave the big defender out of his plans for the crucial game after Butcher had had a poor game against Dundee United at Tannadice the previous weekend. Not only had he scored a spectacular own-goal, he had also missed a tackle in the lead-up to United's winner, so Souness, who felt his captain had returned from the World Cup in Italy nursing the effects of a knee injury, decided to remove him from the squad. 'I saw the big fellow moments after Souness told him he was dropped for the 1990 League Cup semi-final against Aberdeen,' recalls McCoist. 'The big man was in tears – and it was like a slap in the face to see that colossus crying.'[3]

The match at Tannadice turned out to be Butcher's last in a Rangers jersey. After four trophy-enriched seasons, the man who had been the cornerstone of much of that success was literally sent to Coventry, signing up at Highfield Road for a fee of around £500,000. His departure saddened McCoist, who held Butcher in high regard, not only as a footballer but also as a friend both on and off the pitch.

Away from the football field, McCoist had cause to celebrate when, on Sunday, 7 October 1990, he married his fiancée, Allison Mitchell, at Whitburn Parish Church near Sunderland. The couple had been together for almost ten years, having met during McCoist's time with Sunderland in the early eighties. Allison, a local model who had won Miss Tyne and Wear, had little or no interest in football, but her mother, Marjorie, was an avid Sunderland fan (she had been a season-ticket holder at Roker Park for twenty-five years) and it was she who got her daughter interested in her local club and in one of their players in particular. After McCoist left Sunderland in 1983 to return to Scotland, the relationship had continued, with each taking their turn to travel to Scotland or England to see the other.

However, domestic bliss soon gave way to a winter of discontent, as by mid-November things were starting to turn sour on the field for McCoist. Maurice Johnston had by then regained full fitness and, with Mark Hateley now settled and scoring goals, it was inevitably McCoist who stepped aside to accommodate the return of his international team-mate. After scoring against Dundee United, McCoist started only one of the next twelve matches in the league, but in that spell he still succeeded in netting a number of crucial goals, notably on 25 November when he came off the bench to grab the winning goal against Celtic at Parkhead, a result that thrust Rangers back to the top of the Premier Division table.

Despite suffering from gastroenteritis, Johnston fired Rangers in front after eight minutes, but Paul Elliot equalised in the thirty-ninth minute to take the teams in level at the interval. With Johnston struggling through illness, McCoist was introduced to the fray for the second half, and in the fifty-third minute he scored to maintain his astonishing record of netting against the men in green and white hoops at least once in each season since he had arrived at the club. Terry Hurlock, a close-season signing from Millwall, created the goal, robbing Stevie Fulton of the ball in the heart of the pitch with a crunching challenge before splitting the defence open with a wonderful pass that sent McCoist in on goal. The striker did the rest, rounding Bonner and rolling the ball into the gaping goal with his right foot.

Despite his goal against Celtic, though, this was an exasperating time for the striker. Every professional footballer wants to play on a regular basis, and the fact that McCoist was unable to command a regular starting berth in the Rangers team marked this spell out as one of the most miserable of his Rangers career. He attempted to lighten the mood by christening himself 'The Judge' (an allusion to the fact that he was spending so much time on the bench), but despite this self-deprecating humour, McCoist was at a loss when it came to understanding his constant exclusion from the team and matters came to a head in December when Rangers welcomed a resurgent Aberdeen to Ibrox for a crucial Premier Division fixture.

Not since Alex Ferguson had been in charge of the North East side in the early- to mid-eighties had the Dons been genuine championship challengers, and they arrived in Glasgow only three points behind leaders Rangers in second place. Despite having netted two goals in his last four appearances as substitute, including the winning goal at Parkhead, McCoist was again listed among the replacements for the match, but when Trevor Steven was injured after only ten minutes, he was called into action.

With the scoresheet still blank midway through the second half and in conditions more akin to a monsoon than a football match, Gary Stevens picked out McCoist with a throw-in from the right-hand side. The ball reared up awkwardly as it reached him, but McCoist, with his back to goal, skilfully tamed the spinning orb with one touch on his chest and spun round to unleash a fantastic volley towards goal with his left foot. The ball roared beyond the statuesque figure of Aberdeen keeper Theo Snelders and into the top left-hand corner of the net to give the home side the lead. 'Well I went berserk,' recalled the ecstatic goalscorer. 'I gave it the robotic dance routine, the punters went wild as every Rangers man in the place celebrated. Well, nearly everyone. Graeme Souness, watching in the stand, didn't move a muscle.'[4]

The reason behind the Rangers manager's nonplussed reaction came to light two days later. Not content with one goal, McCoist doubled his and Rangers' tally ten minutes later, and the home side looked to be coasting to a crucial victory and a five-point advantage at the top of the table until Aberdeen pulled a goal back from the penalty spot and then, in the dying minutes, levelled matters at 2-2 when Jim Bett scrambled a corner into the net.

The inevitable post-match inquest took place the following Monday after training and Souness was incandescent with rage. He berated the performance of each and every one of his players, branding the display 'shocking', and he told McCoist that he struggled to celebrate his wonder goal as he felt so downcast at the way the team was playing. 'I could hardly believe what I was hearing,' said McCoist. 'That was a good goal, a vital goal, and although we let Aberdeen off the hook later on, that shouldn't have stopped him enjoying the moment of the strike. What did I have to do to please the man? I was really down, and convinced now that whatever defect Souness found in my personality was affecting his assessment of me as a player.'[5]

The following week, despite his heroic two-goal contribution against the men from the Granite City, McCoist was back cooling his heels on the bench, as Rangers defeated Dundee United 2-1 thanks to goals from Johnston and Walters. The New Year (1991) began as the old one had ended, with McCoist resident on the substitutes' bench, and he finally cracked when Souness sanctioned a team-bonding trip to St Andrews towards the end of January. Sitting in the pub one evening, the normally bubbly personality felt strangely detached and out of place in the jovial atmosphere, and decided to pack his bags and head for home. 'Suddenly I couldn't keep up the pretence any more,' McCoist recalled. 'I had nothing to contribute.'[6] He returned home and played forty-five minutes for the reserves in a 6-0 win over Albion Rovers at Cliftonhill the following evening, and turned out for the second team again the following week, scoring the opening goal in a 3-0 win over Kilmarnock.

The release of tension that resulted from his premature departure from St Andrews seemed to have the desired effect. Although he was on the bench for the tie against Dunfermline Athletic in the third round of the Scottish Cup, McCoist enjoyed a run of four consecutive starts in February, scoring in three of the four matches. He scored the only goal in a 1-0 home win over St Mirren with a spectacular scissors kick, the opener against Motherwell in a 2-0 win at Ibrox and Rangers' fourth goal in a 5-0 Scottish Cup hammering of lowly Cowdenbeath. The goal against Motherwell was the highlight: a sublime chip with his left foot that was reminiscent of the goal he had netted against the Fir Park side two years earlier which had made him the top scorer in Premier Division history.

The string of appearances in the starting line-up proved a false dawn, though, and McCoist was back on the bench for the top-of-the-table clash with Aberdeen at Pittodrie in March. Rangers travelled to the Granite City defending an unbeaten run of seventeen matches, but a last-gasp goal from Hans Gillhaus handed Aberdeen the points and trimmed Rangers' lead in the title race to six points. But if the defeat at Pittodrie and his exclusion from the starting eleven had been a bitter pill to swallow, then the situation was about to get a lot uglier for McCoist: his relationship with Souness was about to plumb new depths.

It was widely known that Ally McCoist loved horse racing, a fondness he had inherited from his father. He enjoyed nothing more than to relax away from the stresses of football at the racetrack and, for the previous two years in March, he and his entourage had descended on Cheltenham for the National Hunt racing festival, three days of racing that culminates with the running of the Cheltenham Gold Cup, one of the major events in the racing calendar.

March of 1991 was no different. Having enjoyed a brief return to the team when he replaced the injured Mo Johnston in a league win over Hearts at Ibrox, McCoist and his team-mates were gearing themselves up for an Old Firm double header with Celtic. When the first of the ties, the Scottish Cup quarter-final, was moved to Sunday, 17 March for the purposes of live television, Souness granted his players two days off early in the week prior to the tie with the instruction to relax before returning to training on the Friday to focus on the weekend match. McCoist decided that his method of relaxation would be a couple of days at the races in England. He travelled down on the Tuesday after training and attended the race meets on the Wednesday and Thursday, managing to catch the feature race, the Gold Cup, before flying back north in order to make training on the Friday.

When he arrived at the stadium on the Friday morning, McCoist was given little indication of what was about to happen. Souness enquired as to whether he had attended the racing at Cheltenham, and when McCoist confirmed his attendance, Souness smiled, nodded and gave the striker no hint whatsoever that he was upset with him. If he had committed a breach of discipline, then surely this would have been the time to censure him.

On the day of the game against Celtic, it soon became apparent that all was not well. When Souness read out the team there was no place for McCoist in the starting eleven. This came as no great surprise, but the hammer blow was administered when the manager revealed that he was not even listed among the substitutes. Given the fact he was fully fit and had shown decent form in the weeks leading up to the match, the news left McCoist seething with rage and he stormed off to the players' lounge at Parkhead, ready to finally throw in the towel in his personal war of attrition with Souness.

In the lounge McCoist met up with Bobby Lennox, a Celtic legend and a member of the team that had won the European Cup in 1967. Lennox could see McCoist was upset at his exclusion, and when McCoist told him that he was ready to walk out of Ibrox he advised him not to be so hasty. He told McCoist that walking away now would mean his manager would have won their battle, and instead of turning his back on Rangers, Lennox advised McCoist to get his head down and prove his worth to the team. 'Looking back, it is one of the best pieces of advice I've ever been given,' recalls McCoist. 'If I stormed out then, it would have been public knowledge, words would have been said and my Rangers career might have ended that afternoon.'[7]

Instead of departing Parkhead in a rage, McCoist took his seat among the Rangers party in the dugout for what proved to be a painful ninety minutes of viewing for the blue half of Glasgow. Goals from Gerry Creaney and a Terry Hurlock own-goal consigned Rangers to a 2-0 defeat, but the match was overshadowed by the dismissals of four players, with referee Andrew Waddell brandishing the red card in front of Peter Grant of Celtic and Hurlock, Hateley and Walters of Rangers. Remarkably, Rangers were perceived to be the cleanest team in the league before kick-off, boasting the best disciplinary record in the country, but they lost their cool in a tempestuous second half as any hopes of lifting the Scottish Cup withered.

As the dust settled after the defeat, it soon became apparent that McCoist's trip to Cheltenham had been the catalyst that drove Souness to exclude him from his final thirteen. Two days after the Parkhead debacle, his suspicions were confirmed when Souness announced after training that he wished his striker to attend a press conference, during which he would apologise to the Rangers supporters for attending the race meeting at Cheltenham and, in the view of Souness, breaching club discipline. A dumbstruck McCoist initially refused to attend the meeting with the press, but eventually decided it was better to go along, although he still could not fathom what he had done wrong. At no time prior to this had the manager indicated that attending the races was a source of indiscipline. Indeed, some players in the Ibrox dressing room had played golf during their time off, a pastime Souness frowned upon, but unlike McCoist, the golfers had escaped any form of punishment.

Throughout the charade of a press conference, McCoist tried to remain composed as he informed the assembled media personnel of his alleged indiscretion. Looking nervous, he said: 'The reason I was left out of the thirteen [at Parkhead] was because, in the manager's view, there was a breach of club discipline. I fully accept that and as far as I'm concerned that's the matter finished. I think the manager has the same view.'[8]

McCoist was now convinced that although he had had no involvement in the shambolic Parkhead defeat, he was being made the scapegoat for Rangers' Cup exit. He was neither fined nor disciplined by the club for his alleged indiscretion at any juncture, but by putting him up in front of the media, he believed Souness ensured that any heat directed at Rangers in the wake of the 2-0 defeat would now have been cleverly re-directed to focus on the miscreant McCoist.

The following day, Souness pulled the shell-shocked striker aside to inform him that the slate had been wiped clean. What had happened was in the past and he was now to concentrate on the forthcoming league match, Part II of the Old Firm double header, in the knowledge that he would be playing from the start in that match. McCoist knew why he had suddenly gained an instant recall, though: Mark Hateley had been suspended following his dismissal the previous week.

McCoist, by now struggling for match fitness due to a niggling groin muscle problem, played in the league match, but Rangers again lost heavily, by three goals to nil, with Scott Nisbet adding to the club's recent indiscipline by receiving his marching orders in the fifty-seventh minute. News of the result was well received in the North East, as it meant Aberdeen had now slashed the gap at the top of the table to just three points.

Despite his well-documented problems at Ibrox, McCoist was still a regular in the Scotland squad. He had put his World Cup woes behind him and had started all five of the national side's matches that had followed the return from Italy, scoring against Romania and Bulgaria as Scotland made an impressive start to their qualifying campaign for the European Championships due to be held in Sweden in the summer of 1992. Three days after losing to Celtic in the league, he won his thirty-first cap in a European Championship qualifier against Bulgaria at

Hampden, but it turned out to be a painful night for the front man as, during the match, he aggravated his groin problem. Scotland were left disappointed too, as a late goal from Emil Kostadinov snatched a vital point for the visitors.

A few days later, McCoist's groin complaint was diagnosed as being a hernia, and he was promptly whisked into hospital for an operation. As a result, he missed six matches for Rangers during the title run-in and did not feature again until the dramatic last game of the season.

Less than a month after the back-to-back defeats from Celtic, though, Graeme Souness was gone. In the wake of the dreadful Hillsborough disaster, Liverpool manager Kenny Dalglish had found it impossible to cope with the demands of football management and had resigned from his post. The bookmakers and pundits immediately installed Graeme Souness as the number one candidate to succeed his former team-mate, but Souness was quick to pour cold water on the speculation, reassuring the Rangers supporters in the pages of the club's newspaper that he had no plans to leave Ibrox. 'Right now I'm speaking to the chairman about a new contract,' he said. 'I've no intention of ever leaving this place. I see my short-term and long-term future here.'[9]

In the end, however, the offer of a return to Anfield, the scene of a great many of his triumphs as a player, proved too difficult to resist and, on 16 April 1991, Souness resigned as Rangers manager to take charge at Anfield. He had been hugely successful during his near-five-season stay in Govan, winning three league titles and four League Cups in addition to helping revolutionise a football club that had been in a state of disrepair when he arrived.

Many observers expected McCoist to have been elated when news of Souness' departure reached the dressing room, but he had mixed emotions. While he and Souness had had their differences (ones that led McCoist to reflect some years later that if Souness had remained in charge at Ibrox for much longer he would have had to consider leaving Rangers, as the gulf between player and manager was now massive and unworkable), he was quick to recognise the significant role Souness had played in not only changing the face of Rangers and Scottish football, but also in refining his own game. Jock Wallace may well have restored his confidence and got him back on his feet again when he was teetering on the brink of falling into a career abyss, but it was Souness who had oiled the goal-scoring machine McCoist had now become. Despite the fractious nature of their relationship in the early 1990s, there is no simmering animosity between the pair today, and they have met up on several occasions to reflect on the time they spent together at Ibrox, sharing a few laughs along the way.

In the wake of Souness' sudden departure, chairman David Murray had to act fast. Souness had wanted to remain in charge at Ibrox until the end of the season, but Murray felt it would be best if he left immediately. In order to minimise the disruption in the dressing room, Murray resisted the temptation to install a caretaker manager and assistant manager Walter Smith was immediately promoted to the manager's chair as Souness' successor. With the destination of the championship still hanging in the balance, Smith took charge of the team he had supported since boyhood for the first time against St Mirren at Love Street on 20 April, a match his new charges won 1-0 thanks to a late strike from young midfielder Sandy Robertson.

Try as they might, though, Rangers could not shake Aberdeen from their coat-tails and, as the league programme reached its penultimate weekend, the Light Blues led Alex Smith's side by just two points, although the Glasgow side did hold a superior goal difference. Both of those advantages were relinquished, however, by the time the clock struck quarter to five on Saturday, 4 May, as Rangers collapsed dramatically at Fir Park, hammered 3-0 by Motherwell, and Aberdeen won their match. The upshot of all the drama meant that Aberdeen, who had spent so much of the season in Rangers' rear-view mirror, had now overtaken the Glasgow giants and edged ahead of them in the race for the title. Although they were level on both points and goal difference with Rangers, the Dons had scored more goals and were now top of the heap with only one game to go. And what a game it promised to be.

For the first time since 1965, the two teams in contention for the championship were due to face each other on the final day of the season, with Aberdeen visiting Ibrox. To take the title back to the North East for the first time since 1985, the visitors only required a draw; for the home side to clinch their third consecutive championship, only a victory would do. For Smith, although essentially nursing Souness' team through the remainder of the campaign, this was a mammoth match so early in his tenure. Whether he liked it or not, he knew the Rangers public would form their opinions of him based on his ability to prise the championship trophy out of Aberdeen's grasp.

Smith's cause was not helped in the lead-up to the title showdown when inspirational skipper Richard Gough was ruled out was after being admitted to hospital suffering from Hepatitis A. John Brown was also struggling with an Achilles problem, but Smith was at least heartened by the news that McCoist was fit enough to occupy his usual station on the substitutes' bench, although he had still not fully recovered from his hernia operation.

With a capacity crowd of 37,652 shoe-horned into Ibrox, one of the most memorable days in the club's history kicked off in a cagey fashion, with the visitors managing to carve out the best of the early scoring opportunities. Former Rangers midfielder Jim Bett blazed a half-volley over the bar, Hans Gillhaus headed over when well placed at the back post, and Peter van de Ven shot straight at Chris Woods when released in behind the Rangers back-line. On the stroke of half-time, though, Rangers bounced off the ropes and secured the crucial breakthrough when Mark Walters floated a cross into the penalty area from the left flank and Mark Hateley leapt imperiously above Alex McLeish to flash a rocket-like header beyond Michael Watt in the Aberdeen goal. With the stands of Ibrox throbbing with passion and noise, Hateley added a second shortly after the interval, capitalising when Watt fumbled a shot by Mo Johnston, and from then on there was only going to be one winner.

McCoist was called into action for the last eighteen minutes of the game when John Brown ruptured his Achilles tendon and, although barely fit, the striker ploughed a lone furrow up front and played his part in a truly historic day. When he entered the fray, he joined a real patchwork Rangers team, with Hateley retreating to centre-half to replace Brown and Mo Johnston dropping back into midfield to replace Terry Hurlock, who was filling in at left-back for young Tom Cowan, who had left the field earlier with a broken leg.

When referee Brian McGinley blew his whistle to signal the end of the match, and with it confirm Rangers as champions of Scotland, the emotions of a traumatic campaign got the better of McCoist and during the lap of honour, he wept. Despite his trials and tribulations, however, he could be justifiably proud of his achievements over the course of what had been a rollercoaster season, with a return of eleven league goals from twenty-six appearances, eleven of which were as substitute. Three League Cup goals, one strike in the Scottish Cup and three in Europe took his tally to eighteen in all competitions, and he also gained recognition for his efforts from his own supporters when his goal against Motherwell in February was voted Goal of the Season.

Although he was now rid of his nemesis, McCoist knew he would still have to work hard to regain his place in a new-look Rangers side about to embrace a new era under the stewardship of Walter Smith. The 1990/91 season was now consigned to the history books, and McCoist was determined to kick-start his career and become a regular fixture once again in the Rangers first team.

Although he did not know it at the time, this would prove a watershed moment in Ally McCoist's career, as he was about to embark on arguably the most successful period of his footballing life, with goals, medals and awards raining in thick and fast, both at home and on the European stage.

CHAPTER TEN

A PAIR OF GOLDEN BOOTS: 1991–93

It was Walter Smith's grandfather who had first introduced him to Rangers Football Club. With his father taking more of an interest in junior football, Smith would often accompany his grandfather to games at Ibrox, travelling aboard the bus that left from the Rangers Supporters' Club located in his hometown of Carmyle. He was eight years old when he went to see Rangers play at Ibrox for the first time, and his inaugural visit was certainly a memorable one, as the home side hammered visitors Queen of the South by six goals to nil in a sectional tie in the Scottish League Cup. Norman Arnison made what turned out to be the first of just two first-team appearances in place of the injured Max Murray and scored twice, and another brace from Alex Scott and goals from Johnny Hubbard and Billy Simpson completed the rout and secured Rangers' place in the last eight of the competition. Young Smith had been captivated by the sheer majesty of Ibrox Stadium, the vast crowds and, of course, the fantastic players who the masses gathered to acclaim every other Saturday, and from those early days, the youngster harboured real ambitions of playing a part in the history of Rangers.

It was not to be in a playing capacity, though. Smith himself is the first to concede that he was never destined to be one of Scotland's better footballers ('As a professional footballer, I was ordinary, very ordinary,' he admitted[1]), but he still enjoyed a decent career before it was curtailed by injury. He began his footballing life with Glasgow junior side Ashfield, and it was from there that Jerry Kerr, the manager of Dundee United, signed him in 1967. He was just eighteen years old when he joined up at Tannadice, but he did not become a full-time player straight away. Instead, he followed instructions from his father and completed his apprenticeship as an electrician and, in the early days of his career, Smith trained in the evenings while completing the final two years of his apprenticeship with a company called Loudon Brothers in Dundee during the day.

Smith found his early experiences in the City of Discovery very pleasant. Kerr had a policy of maintaining a backbone of senior professionals at the club and, for a young player like Smith, the experience garnered from training and playing alongside those players was invaluable. Players such as Jimmy Millar and Davie Wilson, both legends during their time at Smith's boyhood heroes Rangers, were plying their trade in tangerine back then alongside some Scandinavian imports such as Lennart Wing and Mogens Berg. Smith enjoyed playing alongside Millar in particular, as the big centre-forward had been his favourite player when he was starring in the great Rangers side of the early 1960s.

Although never destined for greatness as a player, Smith was a solid professional and during his two stints at Tannadice (his stays on Tayside were bisected by a spell on the books of Dumbarton between 1975 and 1977), he enjoyed a modicum of success, scoring the winner in a Dundee derby and playing in the 1974 Scottish Cup final when United lost out to Jock Stein's Celtic.

A persistent pelvic injury brought his playing days to a premature conclusion at the age of twenty-nine, but it did not end his involvement in the game. Jim McLean, assistant to Jerry Kerr when Smith had arrived at Tannadice, was now in charge of the club and noticing that Smith had a flair for coaching, encouraged him to help out with the training and tuition of players the club had signed on schoolboy forms in the latter days of his playing career. Indeed, it was the arrival of McLean as assistant manager at Tannadice that had first alerted Smith to the possibility of moving into coaching and management, and the career-ending injury had merely served to accelerate the process. Smith was soon taking charge of the United reserves, overseeing the development of players such as Maurice Malpas, Davie Dodds and John Clark, players who would mature and make a name for themselves in the successful United side of the early and mid-eighties.

Promotion to the position of first-team coach followed in 1979 and, a couple of years later, Smith was installed as United's assistant manager, a job he would retain until he left to take up a similar position at Ibrox as part of the Souness Revolution in 1986. During his time in the assistant's position at Tannadice, Smith played a significant role as United won the Premier Division championship in 1983 and reached the semi-finals of the European Cup the following season, where they lost out narrowly to eventual runners-up AS Roma.

Smith's coaching credits were not just confined to club level. In the early eighties, he had been part of the Scotland youth team's backroom staff and, shortly after joining up at Ibrox, was asked to assist Alex Ferguson when he was in charge of the Scottish national team at the 1986 World Cup in Mexico.

However, despite this success and his achievements during his time at United, the lure of Rangers, his boyhood idols, was too much to resist, and when David Holmes called in May 1986 to offer Smith the role of assistant manager to Graeme Souness, he needed little time to mull over his decision. While recognising he was never good enough to represent the club in a playing capacity, Smith knew he had the ability to be a success in a coaching role, and relished the opportunity to become part of a thrilling new era in the club's distinguished history alongside Souness and David Holmes.

He could, in fact, have been Ibrox bound some three years earlier. When John Greig resigned as Rangers manager in October 1983, Jim McLean had been approached to take over in the managerial hot seat, and as McLean carefully considered the offer, he made no secret of the fact that were he to take up the position he intended to take Smith with him as his assistant. In the end, however, McLean rejected the overtures of the Rangers board and stayed at Tannadice, which meant Smith would have to wait another few years to fulfil his dream of moving to Ibrox.

Having been a key figure in the management team that helped guide Rangers through a successful first three seasons following Graeme Souness' arrival in Govan, it came as no surprise that Smith took the step up to the post of Rangers manager when Liverpool tempted Souness out of the Ibrox manager's chair in April 1991. Despite the media touting many of the leading lights in the world game as replacements for the departing Souness, in the mind of chairman David Murray there was only one man suitable for the job. He had always said his policy would be one of promotion from within and, in April 1991, Walter Smith was appointed as the ninth manager in Rangers' history.

It was a fantastic appointment as far as Ally McCoist was concerned. He had already worked under the tutelage of Smith in his younger days at Under-18 level with Scotland, and he knew the man well enough to know that he would be given an opportunity to prove his worth and illustrate that he still had the ability to cut it as a regular goalscorer in the Rangers first team. Had Souness remained in the Ibrox hot seat, it is questionable whether McCoist would have remained at the club, as at the age of twenty-nine, another year on the periphery of the first team would have been of no great benefit to him. Under Smith, though, he felt things would be different, and his optimism was certainly not dampened when the manager poured scorn on rumours linking McCoist with a move to Aberdeen in the close season. The striker was believed to be heading to the Granite City as a makeweight in the deal being struck to tempt young Scotland left-back David Robertson to Ibrox, but Smith said tersely: 'Ally McCoist will remain a Rangers player as long as I am the manager and as long as he is happy to play for Rangers … which I can assure you he is.'[2]

One of Smith's first tasks as Rangers manager was to bring a more tartan look to his cosmopolitan squad of players. The effects of UEFA's new law limiting club sides to three foreign players in European matches was beginning to bite hard, and Smith realised from the outset that he would have to add a more Scottish flavour to his player pool, while releasing a number of the overseas players who had been prominent, not to mention hugely successful, during the Souness era.

In a similar fashion to Souness' first campaign as Rangers manager, the revolving door reappeared at Ibrox, with four players leaving for pastures new and five coming in to claim the pegs the departees had vacated in the dressing room. In came Scottish international goalkeeper Andy Goram from Hibernian for £1 million, with established number one Chris Woods heading south to join up with Sheffield Wednesday. Joining Goram in the home dressing room were David Robertson and Stuart McCall along with token foreigners Alexei Michailitchenko and Dale Gordon. Mark Walters, Terry Hurlock and Trevor Steven all moved on, although the latter might well have stayed had French side Olympique Marseille not tendered a bid of £5 million for his services.

The new recruits linked up with McCoist and the rest of their new buddies in July when the squad headed off once again for their customary pre-season retreat in the Tuscan hills. The players were subjected to gruelling double training sessions in the Italian sunshine and on their return the first team played a series of friendly matches in a bid to hone their match sharpness.

Still battling back to full fitness after his hernia operation at the end of the previous campaign, McCoist missed the first two matches, an 8-2 stroll against Queen's Park and a 1-0 win over Morton, but he made it into the starting line-up for a 3-1 defeat at the hands of Dundee United in Maurice Malpas' testimonial match on 31 July. He marked his return by opening his scoring account for the season with a consolation goal nine minutes from the end, and was on the scoresheet again when he netted twice for the reserves in the opening game of their three-match Highland tour against Deveronvale two days later.

Thereafter, McCoist returned to duty with the first team ahead of the Forum Cup, a four-team tournament hosted by Kilmarnock. He was an unused substitute when Rangers defeated Coventry City 4-3 on penalties in their opening match, but he returned to the starting eleven when Rangers faced the hosts twenty-four hours later in the final. Killie, who included former Old Firm stars Bobby Williamson and Tommy Burns in their line-up, took the lead five minutes before half-time through Calum Campbell, but Mark Hateley equalised a minute before the break, and McCoist shot Rangers into the lead after fifty-nine minutes when he pounced on an errant backpass from Paul Flexney to lob Paul Geddes in the home goal. Trevor Steven, playing in one of his final games for the club before his move to Marseille, added a third Rangers goal six minutes later to give Smith his first piece of silverware of the season before a competitive ball had been kicked in earnest.

Thus, with four goals in three games, McCoist looked to be in razor-sharp goal-scoring form, but hopes of a berth in the team for the first league fixture of the season against St Johnstone were dashed when he picked up a thigh strain in the final warm-up game against St Mirren at Love Street. As a result, he had to watch the opening-day action from the stands, and his chances of an immediate reinstatement to the team were dealt a blow as Rangers opened the campaign in rampant form, thrashing visitors St Johnstone 6-0, with the strike-pairing of Johnston and Hateley contributing five of the goals.

McCoist continued to work hard in training, though, and after playing for fifty-three minutes for the reserves in a 3-2 defeat against Partick Thistle, he made his first appearance of the season for the first team when he replaced Pieter Huistra in the fifty-ninth minute of a League Cup second-round tie against Queen's Park at Ibrox. Maurice Johnston stole the show on the night, notching up four goals in a 6-0 hammering, and he scored again four days later when Rangers welcomed Dunfermline to Ibrox in the Premier Division. As had been the case in midweek, McCoist was utilised from the substitutes' bench, but this time he got himself among the goals, grabbing Rangers' fourth goal in a 4-0 victory. The strike rang up a significant milestone in McCoist's Rangers career: it was his 200th competitive goal for the club.

Although he was back among the substitutes for the next two matches – back-to-back 2-0 wins over Celtic in the league at Parkhead and Partick Thistle in the League Cup – the opportunity McCoist had been waiting for finally presented itself when Rangers travelled to Tynecastle on Wednesday, 4 September 1991 to tackle Hearts in a League Cup quarter-final tie. He was included in the starting eleven for the first time since 24 March and that wretched 3-0 reverse at Celtic Park the previous season, and in true McCoist fashion, vindicated Smith's decision to play him.

This was, in fact, Rangers' second visit of the season to Tynecastle, and the League Cup duel had added spice since, on that previous visit, the home side had inflicted Rangers' only defeat of the new campaign up until that point, winning 1-0 thanks to a Scott Crabbe goal. Lightning was not about to strike twice, though, and the scoreline was reversed, with the reinstated McCoist netting the only goal of the game when he latched on to an intelligent headed knockdown from Mark Hateley and thumped the ball into the net with a superbly executed right-foot half-volley in the twenty-fifth minute. It was McCoist's first top-team goal for over six months, and his match-winning contribution caught the eye of the public and drew praise from his manager, with Walter Smith commenting: 'It was a good finish from Alistair. People are always asking me why he can't get a game. In Mo Johnston and Mark Hateley we have two players who are hitting a terrific spell of form, but Ally is a proven goalscorer. He's been a great asset for Rangers and I hope he will continue to be so.'[3]

McCoist's goal and overall performance were of sufficient quality to convince his manager that he warranted an extended run in the first team. He took his place again for the following weekend's league match, a 2-0 success over Falkirk at Brockville, and although he drew a blank in that match, he was back among the goals in the next league encounter against Dundee United at Ibrox, controlling a long pass out of defence from Scott Nisbet before rifling a shot into the United goal with his right foot.

An ankle injury sustained against Sparta Prague in the opening round of the European Cup disrupted his comeback, however, and he missed the next two matches – a 2-1 win at St Mirren and a 2-0 home defeat at the hands of Aberdeen – but he reclaimed his favourite number nine jersey for the visit to Broomfield to meet Airdrie, and promptly scored twice in a 4-0 romp. He repeated the feat in the next two league matches too, netting braces against Hibernian at Ibrox – one of his goals was a rasping 25-yard free-kick – and St Johnstone at McDiarmid Park. Despite suffering a temporary setback in the wake of the game in Perth when his ankle injury flared up and denied him the chance to play for Scotland in a vital European Championship qualifier against Romania in Bucharest, McCoist's consistent scoring form had supporters, media and the Rangers management singing his praises. It was a stark contrast to the situation he had found himself in post-Cheltenham just a few months earlier.

Hibernian ended Rangers' interest in the League Cup at the semi-final stage in late September, but Smith's men were performing exceptionally well in the title race, and McCoist, with ten league goals in only nine appearances to add to the crucial strike against Hearts in the League Cup, was riding on the crest of a wave. He returned from injury to net Rangers' opening goal in a 2-0 win over Hearts at Ibrox – he also missed a penalty five minutes from the end of that match – and grabbed another double in a 3-2 defeat against Dundee United at Tannadice at the end of October. McCoist's phenomenal goal-scoring form continued into November too, when his near-post diving header from a Gary Stevens cross helped secure a vital 1-1 draw with Celtic, although the loss of a point cost Rangers the leadership of the Premier Division.

The goal against Celtic took McCoist to the top of the Premier Division scoring charts and his purple patch continued, with further goals against Dunfermline and Airdrie and a brace against Hibernian in a 3-0 win at Easter Road. With the striker in such a rich vein of form, it was no surprise that his fine displays were recognised when he was named as the B&Q Superskills Award winner for November.

By now the McCoist–Hateley front-line partnership was in full swing, and one match in particular where they really seemed to gel was a 3-2 victory over Aberdeen at Pittodrie in early December. The Dons, still smarting from the previous season's dramatic championship finale, were always a tough proposition on their own patch, but two excellent goals from Hateley and an exquisite chip from McCoist following an equally delightful Hateley assist secured a crucial two points. However, a pre-Christmas defeat at home to St Mirren knocked Rangers out of their stride in the title race, and the year ended with Smith's men in second place in the table behind pacesetters Hearts.

Shortly before the Christmas festivities kicked off, Rangers opened the new Club Deck stand at Ibrox, taking the capacity of the arena beyond the 50,000-mark. Dundee United were the visitors on the day the new seating area was opened, and McCoist ensured that the new patrons went home happy with yet another brace – his sixth of the season – in a 2-0 win. The striker was celebrating off the field too when it emerged that his video, *Super Ally – The McCoist Phenomenon*, which charted his eight years at Ibrox, had reached the top twenty in the video sales chart.

The emergence of the formidable McCoist–Hateley double act unfortunately resulted in the demise of Maurice Johnston's Rangers career. Johnston had been in terrific form during his first two seasons at Ibrox, silencing the cynics and scoring many crucial goals, but that form and sharpness had now shaded. Unlike his international team-mate, Johnston was not willing to cool his heels on the substitutes' bench for any length of time and wait patiently for a recall, to the extent that by the time Celtic visited for that early November league match, Johnston had left the club, moving to Everton, with the Goodison Park outfit paying £1.5 million to take his services to Merseyside.

The traditional Ne'erday derby between Rangers and Celtic opened 1992, but it was a case of 'same old story' for Rangers and the irrepressible McCoist, as he scored the opening goal at Parkhead, sliding in at the back post to convert yet another assist from Hateley, shortly before the interval. He was involved in the second goal too, when he won a penalty-kick soon after the restart when he was hauled to the ground by the Celtic goalkeeper, Gordon Marshall. The Celtic players vehemently complained about the award (they felt the Rangers man had gone to ground too easily), but referee George Smith dismissed their protests and Hateley converted from twelve yards. In what would become a time-honoured tradition, Andy Goram shattered any hopes of a Celtic comeback when he produced an inspired save to keep out a fierce drive from Paul McStay before a John Brown goal late on secured a convincing 3-1 victory for Walter Smith's side.

The following week, McCoist had even more reason to smile, as his recent abundance of goals was rewarded with a new three-year contract. Although he still had some two years to run on his existing deal, the news of the extension was welcome, not only to McCoist but also to the Rangers supporters, who held their number nine in high esteem. He was now contracted to the club until the end of the 1995-96 season, by which time he would be approaching thirty-four years of age.

The new deal completed a total turnaround in fortunes for the striker: less than a year earlier, following the Cheltenham saga and his constant exclusion from the starting eleven, McCoist had been contemplating an Ibrox exit. The appointment of Walter Smith, however, had revitalised his flagging Rangers career, and the team were now reaping the rewards. 'It's the best Christmas present I've ever had,' a delighted McCoist told the *Rangers News*. 'I'm glad this ends all the speculation about my future. There are always rumours going about about me moving on, especially last season when I wasn't in the team regularly. But I always knew that, given the chance, I could continue to score goals here and I always wanted to stay. I've spoken to many players who have left and they all genuinely say there's not another club like it.'[4]

Rangers returned to the summit of the Premier Division on 11 January thanks to a 2-0 home win over Hibernian, with McCoist netting his twenty-second league goal of the season two minutes from the end of the game. The position was then consolidated with a second successive 2-0 victory, Motherwell were the victims this time, and McCoist once again got his name on to the scoresheet. He had now scored twenty-three league goals in just twenty-four appearances, and he carried his red-hot league form into the Scottish Cup when he struck a left-foot shot beyond Theo Snelders to send Aberdeen spinning out of the competition at the first hurdle.

Having regained top spot in the league, Smith's men had no intention of relinquishing it, and when February opened with a top-of-the-table clash with Hearts at Tynecastle, Rangers were intent on putting some daylight between themselves and their nearest rivals. It was a crucial match, with the home side only two points adrift of their opponents, but

McCoist, who had just been named Player of the Month for January, was once again the difference between the two sides, netting his fifth goal in as many games with a rasping volley from twelve yards. He could have added a second in stoppage time too, but contrived to spoon the ball wide of a gaping goal when it seemed easier to score. That bizarre miss failed to dilute his joy or dent his soaring confidence, though. 'I can honestly say that I am enjoying my football now more than at any time in my career,' he said afterwards. 'It's always easy when you're scoring goals and the team is winning, and that is probably the reason why I am enjoying myself so much. At the moment I'm very happy with my goal-scoring. I've got a good ratio – nearly a goal a game and that's good by any standards.'[5]

There seemed to be no way to stop the Rangers juggernaut as it powered its way towards a fourth league title in a row. Smith's men were on an unbeaten run of sixteen league matches – a sequence that delivered fourteen victories and two draws – and with McCoist in such scintillating goal-scoring form and Andy Goram and his defence forming an almost impregnable barrier at the back, Rangers welcomed Celtic to Ibrox in March for the final Old Firm match of the season in the knowledge that a victory would not only fortify their position at the top of the league but also kill off any hopes Celtic harboured of bridging the eleven-point gap that existed between the two sides at the start of the match. However, the visitors succeeded where others had failed, temporarily derailing the title charge of the Light Blue brigade with a comprehensive 2-0 success. In addition to reducing Rangers' lead at the top over Hearts to just five points, the result also afforded the Hoops a massive psychological boost ahead of the Scottish Cup semi-final meeting due to take place between the two sides at Hampden Park ten days later.

Rangers' route to the last four of the competition had been arduous to say the least, with two ties away from home at difficult venues sandwiching a home draw against the Cup-holders. A trip to Pittodrie was first up in the third round, but despite being without the injured Mark Hateley, Rangers progressed thanks to a solitary McCoist strike, and followed that with a come-from-behind 2-1 home win against Motherwell in round four. McCoist's former club, St Johnstone, were then brushed aside 3-0 in Perth in the last eight, with the striker returning to haunt his former employers by netting the first of Rangers' three goals when he turned a Pieter Huistra cross into the net in the fourteenth minute. With Rangers, Celtic, Airdrie and Hearts in the hat for the semi-final draw, many were salivating at the prospect of the first Old Firm Scottish Cup final since 1989, but they were left disappointed when the balls came out of the hat. They had to settle instead for the first Old Firm Scottish Cup semi-final since 1960, as the Glasgow giants were paired together, while Airdrie and Hearts went into battle for the right to face one of the 'Big Two' in the final.

Having emerged victorious in the recent league match, Celtic were installed as the pre-match favourites among the bookmakers, and a brief look at Rangers' injury list added further credence to this status. The most notable absentee from the Rangers party was Mark Hateley, who had injured his back during the weekend league victory against St Johnstone, and McCoist was also struggling with a groin injury. However, on a night when the weather at Hampden Park – still in the dilapidated and exposed pre-reconstruction state – was atrocious with swirling winds and torrential rain greeting the players as they emerged from the tunnel, McCoist managed to shake off his ailment to take his place in the forward line.

As if the climatic conditions and the non-appearance of the talismanic Hateley were not enough of an inconvenience, Rangers were further handicapped shortly after the match kicked off. Barely six minutes had passed when referee Andrew Waddell brandished a red card in the face of David Robertson when he deemed that the left-back's robust body check on Celtic winger Joe Miller was worthy of an instant dismissal. Miller had given Robertson an uncomfortable afternoon in the recent league match, so the Rangers man was obviously keen to put a marker down in the early stages, but his conduct did not find favour with the match official, and Rangers were now really up against it.

Smith's men weathered the initial storm, though, and as the half-time interval approached they were enjoying the better of the exchanges, albeit with no goals to show for their territorial advantage. That statistic changed, however, when Rangers were rewarded for their endeavours in the forty-fourth minute. Stuart McCall, tigerish as ever with his tackling, won the ball in the centre of the field, and released a perfectly weighted pass into the path of the on-rushing McCoist. The quality of McCall's delivery was so good that McCoist did not even need to check his stride or take a touch to control the ball: he simply took it on the run and flashed a low, right-footed drive beyond Celtic goalkeeper Gordon

Marshall from eighteen yards. It was McCoist's thirtieth goal of the season. It was also significant for being the first Rangers goal against their arch-rivals in a Scottish Cup tie since Tom Forsyth's famous strike in the Centenary Final of 1973, ending a barren spell that lasted for over 550 minutes.

The latter stages of the first half had belonged to Rangers, and they richly deserved their interval lead, but the second half was simply a procession, as Celtic emerged from the dressing room in the hunt for the goal they needed to restore parity. Wave after wave of green and white rained down on Andy Goram's goal, but Rangers, superbly marshalled by captain Richard Gough and the redoubtable John Brown defended doggedly, and in the end held out for victory, albeit carrying a large slice of luck on more than one occasion, particularly when Paul McStay made the crossbar shudder with a ferociously struck shot from twenty yards.

The Rangers performance that evening epitomised the never-say-die attitude and 'all for one, one for all' spirit that prevailed in this squad of players; an indomitable spirit that would carry the squad through many battles in the years ahead. This was indeed the night a team was born, and it would mature into one of the finest ever in Rangers' history as it reigned supreme in Scotland over the course of the next six years.

The following day, McCoist got his hands on the first silverware of the season when he collected the annual *Daily Record* award for becoming the first player in Scottish Football to net thirty goals over the course of the season, and he carried his good form into the next league match, netting his first hat-trick of the campaign in a 4-1 win over Falkirk, a result that inched Rangers to within four points of the title.

The championship was eventually clinched on 18 April. St Mirren were the visitors to Ibrox, but the Paisley side were merely a support act as the home side romped home by four goals to nil, with McCoist, by now the leading goalscorer across all the European leagues, scoring his thirtieth and thirty-first league goals of the season. His second goal, which put Rangers 3-0 ahead, was particularly special. Receiving a pass from Ian Durrant just inside the penalty area, McCoist cleverly used his pal's forward run as a decoy and spun away from his marker before arrowing a right-foot shot into the far corner of the net. Victory presented Rangers with their fourth League Championship in succession, and handed McCoist the fifth championship medal of his career. It was the first time the Govan side had won four titles on the trot since Bill Struth's great Rangers team of the late twenties and early thirties (who won five consecutive titles between 1927 and 1931).

With the serious business of securing the championship now out of the way, all eyes now turned towards the prospect of a domestic Double. Airdrie, who had finished seventh in the Premier League and who had beaten Hearts in the semi-final of the Scottish Cup, stood in the way of that achievement, but before the showpiece event at Hampden, McCoist was keen to add to his tally of league goals in the three remaining fixtures, especially now that the award of the prestigious *Soulier d'Or* (Golden Boot) for the top goalscorer in European league football had become a distinct possibility. No Scotsman had ever won the award, instituted by the French magazine *France Football* in the 1967/68 season, and the last player from the British Isles to do so had been the great Ian Rush of Liverpool in 1983/84. There was also the potential that Rangers could complete the season having scored a century of goals in the league, a feat yet to be achieved by any other team since the inception of the Premier Division in 1975.

McCoist added a further three goals in the remaining fixtures, following up a tap-in against Hearts with two awesome strikes that were right out of the top drawer on the last day of the season in a 2-0 win over Aberdeen at Pittodrie. His first arrived in the thirty-eighth minute when he took possession of a quickly taken free-kick, nutmegged Stephen Wright and curled a terrific shot into the net from the edge of the penalty area; his second, scored in the fifty-fifth minute, was a searing drive from 25 yards that left Snelders motionless.

The goals at Pittodrie took McCoist's final goal count for the league season to an impressive thirty-four goals from thirty-eight appearances, and it was fitting that the first at Pittodrie was also Rangers' 100th league goal of the season. The McCoist–Hateley partnership had contributed fifty-five of those goals, and McCoist's own total eventually proved sufficient to secure the Golden Boot. His phenomenal performances over the course of the season were also recognised by the Football Writers and his fellow professionals: he was voted Player of the Year for the 1991/92 season by both parties. He drew praise too from his captain, Richard Gough. The skipper told the *Rangers News*: 'I have known Ally for ten years or so and he is really at the top of his game and playing the best football I've ever seen from him. He is so confident and, at twenty-nine, he looks like a player who has really hit his peak. He is showing that just now in everything he is doing, especially his touch and sharpness.'[6]

Still missing from the glittering array of baubles and badges that he had collected during his career, though, was a Scottish cup-winner's badge. Since McCoist had signed up at Ibrox in the summer of 1983, Scotland's national cup competition had not been kind to Rangers, with the club reaching the final on just one occasion in that timeframe. Indeed, the old trophy had only resided in the Ibrox trophy room once in the previous eleven years, and McCoist and his team-mates set about putting an end to the hoodoo when Rangers faced Airdrie at Hampden on 9 May.

Most observers thought the final would be a mismatch, as Rangers had rattled thirteen goals past the Diamonds in the four league encounters that season, but on the day, Airdrie, managed by former Rangers midfielder Alex MacDonald, put on a spirited display only to be undone by the season's golden couple. Hateley opened the scoring after half an hour with his twenty-third goal of the season after Robertson had profited from an error by David Kirkwood to tee him up, and McCoist added a second, his thirty-ninth of the campaign, shortly before the interval when he expertly volleyed home a pass from McCall with his left foot. Rangers eventually ran out 2-1 winners, but as he cavorted around the National Stadium celebrating the success with his fellow players and the Rangers supporters, McCoist was unaware that this would prove the first and last Scottish Cup-winners' medal of his playing career.

Buoyed by a quite exceptional campaign at club level, McCoist joined up with the Scotland squad less than a week after the Cup final for two warm-up friendly matches in the United States against the USA and Canada. The two clashes, followed by a duel with Norway in Oslo, would be the Scots' last matches before they travelled to Sweden for the European Championships.

Although drawn in a difficult qualifying group alongside Switzerland, Romania, Bulgaria and minnows San Marino, Scotland had emerged to qualify for the finals after losing only once – a 1-0 defeat against Romania in Bucharest – in their eight group matches. McCoist had been an integral part of the squad, and the role he played in getting the nation to the finals for the first time cannot be underestimated. With his negative experiences at Italia '90 now firmly behind him, he was now fully established as first choice in the striker's role, and he played in six of the eight qualifying matches, scoring four goals in the process. The goals he netted had been crucial ones too, none more so than his seventy-fifth-minute strike in the 2-1 win over Romania at Hampden, and his late equalising goal against the Swiss in Berne that had rescued a 2-2 draw from a match in which the Scots had been trailing 2-0 at one stage.

With thirty-eight caps to his name, McCoist was one of the senior members of the squad that travelled to Scandinavia for the finals, ranking fifth behind goalkeeper Jim Leighton, club-mate Richard Gough, Celtic's Paul McStay and Maurice Malpas of Dundee United in terms of appearances made for his country. In addition to his goal-scoring contribution, McCoist's effervescent personality also shone through in a group of players who had formed a really strong camaraderie.

Not surprisingly, the Ibrox court jester was at the centre of most of the fun to have taken place during the pre-tournament trip to the United States. On one particular afternoon, the players had intended to enjoy a liquid refreshment or two in Sears Tower – the tallest building in the world at the time – but hopes were dashed when it was discovered that there was no bar on the premises. Instead, McCoist led an expedition up to the ninety-sixth floor of the Johns Hopkins Tower in Chicago, the fourth largest building in the world at the time, and when they reached the bar, McCoist and his cohorts ordered a selection of all the cocktails the establishment had to offer. Names were placed in a hat and each player had to consume the beverage with which he was paired, with Gary McAllister drawing the short straw when he received his concoction. 'It was a tequila-based drink,' recalls McCoist, 'and was actually giving off smoke when it arrived. I'm sure his [McAllister's] brilliant performances in Sweden were down to that drink.'[7]

Soon, however, it was down to the serious business. Scotland were bracketed with Holland, Germany and the Commonwealth of Independent States (CIS for short) in a tough first-round group stage, but they arrived in Sweden in fine fettle on the back of two wins in America (McCoist scored in the match against the Canadians), and a 0-0 draw in Oslo. The Scots' opening group match was against the formidable Dutch, the reigning European champions, in the Ullevi Stadion in Gothenburg on 12 June. This was a Holland side that boasted a host of supremely talented individuals such as Marco van Basten, Ruud Gullit, Dennis Bergkamp and Frank Rijkaard, and they were considered to be among the pre-tournament favourites.

After all that had gone on in Italy two years previously, McCoist was certainly not taking a place in the starting line-up for granted but, despite suffering a scare on the eve of the game, when he suffered a bout of hayfever induced by a training session on freshly cut grass, he was relieved when Andy Roxburgh announced the team and revealed he was in it. He was to partner Gordon Durie of Tottenham Hotspur in attack, but he was aware that he would be in for a tough night, as he would be up against the fearsome Ronald Koeman, who less than a month previously had delivered a flawless performance, topped off with the winning goal, when his club side, Barcelona, had won the European Cup final against Sampdoria at Wembley.

With such an array of talent to call upon, it was no surprise that the Dutch were overwhelming favourites to sweep Scotland's challenge aside. However, as is often the case with the Scots, they thrived upon the underdog tag, and the team delivered a disciplined and dogged performance that took them to within thirteen minutes of securing a remarkable result. With the finish line in sight, though, Dennis Bergkamp popped up to shoot past Andy Goram and grant the Dutch a win they scarcely deserved.

It was cruel luck on Scotland, and McCoist, who had had very little in the way of goal-scoring opportunities throughout the match and was substituted after suffering a head injury shortly before Bergkamp's goal, was gutted along with the rest of the squad at the end of the match. 'The atmosphere in the Scottish dressing room was understandably gloomy,' he recalled. 'Andy Goram was furious – he hates losing goals. The rest of the lads were more depressed than angry. We had deserved something for our efforts.'[8]

Next up were the Germans in Norrkoping and in order to keep their hopes of advancing to the knockout stages alive, the Scots had to take something from the match. Confidence in the camp was still high after the performance in the opening fixture against the Dutch; the players genuinely believed they could get a victory from the match. But what followed was a game that typified Scottish performances at major competitions: it was yet another glorious failure.

McCoist was selected from the start of the match alongside Durie once again, and for large portions of the match, the Scottish midfield was the dominant force against the well-organised Germans. However, they could not translate that superiority into the hard currency of scoring goals, although this was more down to the stoic defending of the overworked Germans – particularly Guido Buchwald and Jurgen Kohler – than any wastefulness shown by the Scots forwards in front of goal.

With Richard Gough again imperious in the heart of the defence, it is hard to fathom how the Germans, who had drawn 1-1 with the CIS in their opening fixture, managed to win 2-0, and it has to be said there was an element of fortune about each of their goals. For the first, Jurgen Klinsmann was guilty of backing into Gough in order to cushion a pass for Karlheinz Reidle to fire the Germans ahead on the half-hour, and then, barely two minutes into the second half, Stefan Effenberg's harmless cross looped over the head of Andy Goram following a wicked deflection from the outstretched leg of Maurice Malpas. The Scots were sick, and out of the tournament, but praise was forthcoming for the second match in succession, as the scribes waxed lyrical about the team's display.

McCoist, however, was the subject of some heavy criticism in the wake of the match. Following his golden season at Ibrox, the expectation was that he would be the main source of goals for Scotland in Sweden, but now with the nation out of the competition with no goals from two matches, irrespective of the two performances, the media directed their disappointment at McCoist. Despite finding himself in illustrious company alongside Gary Lineker, Klinsmann and van Basten, who had also failed to open their scoring accounts during their respective nations' opening two fixtures, the Football Writers' Player of the Year had gone from hero to zero in the space of 180 minutes. The callous comments were somewhat harsh to say the least, as one fails to recall any genuine goal-scoring opportunities falling McCoist's way over the course of the opening two matches.

Even McCoist's team-mates got in on the act, playfully dubbing him 'The Golden Slipper', but Andy Roxburgh refused to bow to public pressure and omit his striker from the final match of the tournament against the CIS and McCoist was selected for his forty-first cap alongside Coventry City's Kevin Gallacher, the player who had replaced him from the substitutes' bench in the previous matches.

The Scots rewarded the Tartan Army with a tremendous display in their final fixture in Norrkoping, winning 3-0 thanks to goals from Paul McStay, Brian McClair (his first for his country in this his twenty-sixth cap) and a penalty from Gary McAllister. Yet again there were no goals for McCoist, but this time he had played better than he had done against the Dutch and the Germans, and it was his pass that had created McClair's goal. He may well have scored later in the match when the

Scots were awarded a penalty with seven minutes remaining, but he had since been substituted, so McAllister took the responsibility to net the Scots' third goal from twelve yards.

Although publicly laughing off the criticism he had received in some quarters of the media for his performances during the championships, privately McCoist was stung by some of the headlines written about him. The haranguing he received only served to fill him with a renewed vigour and resolve for the new season, and he set about proving to the media hacks that they were wrong to sound the death knell on his top-flight career just yet.

Given their successful partnership during the previous season, it was no surprise when McCoist and Hateley started the new campaign as the spearhead of Rangers' challenge for a fifth successive league title. The groundwork for the new campaign was once again conducted at Il Ciocco in Tuscany and when the squad returned home, they completed their preparations with a number of friendly matches. McCoist, who had told his team-mates in Italy that he was so sharp 'you could open a tin of peas with my feet the way they're working just now'[9], hit the ground running, netting in the bounce games against Queen of the South, Queen's Park and Morton, although he failed to find the net in the glamour friendly against French champions Marseille at Ibrox, a match that Rangers lost by two goals to one.

The Ibrox ranks had been bolstered with the return of Trevor Steven from Marseille and centre-half David McPherson, who returned for his second spell at Ibrox after a successful five-year stint with Hearts, during which time he had become a Scotland international. As the new arrivals fitted back into familiar surroundings, Nigel Spackman, Paul Rideout and John Spencer left, with the latter two seeking out regular first-team football having failed to dislodge either Hateley or McCoist from the first-choice striking berths in the team.

The 'Dynamic Duo' and Rangers started the season as they meant to go on, with McCoist scoring the only goal of the game as the Light Blues ground out an opening-day win over St Johnstone, while Hateley opened his account with a strike in a victory over Airdrie at Ibrox three days later. A goal-less draw at Hibernian followed before McCoist was on the mark again, this time netting a brace at Dens Park against Dundee. His goals could not prevent Rangers falling to a 4-3 defeat but, remarkably, the result in Dundee would be Rangers' last reverse for seven months, during which time Walter Smith's side strung together a mammoth unbeaten sequence of forty-four matches in all competitions at home and abroad.

That defeat in Dundee was the only blemish on an otherwise steady start to the season. The first three rounds of the League Cup were successfully negotiated, with McCoist helping himself to five goals in the wins over Dumbarton (5-0), Stranraer (a hat-trick this time in another 5-0 win) and Dundee United (3-2), all of which set up a semi-final clash with St Johnstone at Hampden Park in September. By then Rangers were top of the Premier Division with six wins from nine matches, with McCoist transferring his League Cup-scoring form into the league campaign, chalking up eight goals in those opening nine matches. His haul included strikes against Aberdeen and Hearts and a hat-trick against Motherwell in a 4-1 win at Fir Park, and his goal feast continued in the League Cup semi-final at the National Stadium, as he put old club St Johnstone to the sword with another treble (his third of the season) in a comfortable 3-1 win that booked Rangers a berth in the final where they would face Aberdeen.

McCoist was rewarded for his stunning start to the season in the league match that followed four days after the semi-final victory. Team captain Richard Gough had played at Hampden, but had picked up an injury, so in his absence McCoist was handed the captain's armband for the match with Dundee United at Tannadice. It was the first time he had been given the honour of skippering Rangers in a competitive fixture, and at the time McCoist rated it as 'the proudest moment of my footballing career'. He recalled: 'We were up at United and big Goughie wasn't playing and the gaffer came into my hotel room and asked me if I'd stand in for big Goughie. It was just an amazing feeling ... to skipper the Rangers was just a phenomenal feeling. It was magic.'[10]

The result of the match was a comprehensive 4-0 win, with the new captain inevitably getting his name on to the scoresheet. He netted Rangers' third goal in the seventieth minute, taking a pass from Ian Ferguson and despatching the ball into the net with alacrity from a narrow angle after his initial effort had been blocked.

With Gough still absent for the next league match, McCoist retained the armband, and he played a captain's part, scoring four times in the same match for the first time in his Rangers career as Falkirk were beaten 4-0 at Ibrox. He opened the scoring after twenty-five minutes, nudging the ball over the line from a yard out after John Brown had turned a Pieter Huistra corner towards goal, and he doubled his tally just sixty seconds later with a fine goal, controlling a superb pass from Hateley before rifling a shot beyond Ian Westwater in the Falkirk goal. Completion of his fourth hat-trick of the season duly arrived three minutes after the interval when he shot home a cross from Dave McPherson, and he completed his one-man show by starting and finishing a move that involved Dale Gordon and Ian Ferguson eleven minutes from full-time. His quartet took his tally for the season to twenty-one in just seventeen matches, fourteen more than he had notched at the corresponding stage of 1991/92, and his display drew praise from team-mate Stuart McCall, who commented that: 'Everyone takes Coisty's goals for granted, but he has led the team well as skipper and his four goals against Falkirk and all-round performances have been good.'[11]

The goals were now overflowing, as Rangers relentlessly powered their way through the first quarter of the league programme in swashbuckling fashion. St Johnstone, still wounded from their semi-final exit from the League Cup, were vanquished by five goals to one at McDiarmid Park, with McCoist and Hateley both netting doubles, and the following weekend a solitary McCoist strike, his ninth goal in his last five league matches, was sufficient to secure a 1-0 Ibrox victory over Hibernian. McCoist was rested and listed among the substitutes for the latter match (the first time he had failed to appear in the starting eleven since September 1991), but he replaced Pieter Huistra in the sixty-seventh minute and grabbed the winning goal with just nine minutes remaining, pouncing inside the six-yard box when John Burridge failed to hold a Mark Hateley header.

What followed the Hibernian match was a monumental period in the season for Rangers. Having defeated Danish champions Lyngby 3-0 on aggregate in the first round of the European Cup, the Scottish champions were drawn to face their English counterparts, Leeds United, complete with mercurial Frenchman Eric Cantona in their squad, in the next round, with a place in the recently formed European Champions League at stake for the winners. Sandwiched in between the two legs of the Leeds tie was the League Cup final against Aberdeen at Hampden Park, and Rangers were due to visit Parkhead for the second Old Firm clash of the season the weekend after the second leg.

The first leg of the European Cup tie, dubbed 'The Battle of Britain', was played at Ibrox on 21 October. For security reasons it had been decreed that there would be no tickets sold to Leeds supporters for the match at Ibrox, with the same rules applying to the Rangers followers for the return leg a fortnight later. This made for a quite unique but nonetheless noisy atmosphere as the teams emerged from the tunnel on a still autumn evening. But the wall of noise that reverberated around the stands was dramatically silenced when the visitors sensationally took the lead within sixty seconds of the kick-off.

Gordon Strachan took a corner-kick from the right-hand side at the Copland Road End of the ground. Gough met the delivery at the near post, and his headed clearance made it to the eighteen-yard line, where it was returned with considerable interest by Gary McAllister, who lashed a volley out of the reach of Andy Goram and into the top corner of the net. Ibrox was stunned, and a deafening hush descended over the stadium. It was a surreal experience for the Rangers players. They had never experienced anything like this before, as teams who had visited Ibrox in the past and scored always had a small knot of their supporters present to create some sort of din. The voices of the 43,251 supporters were stilled for a matter of seconds, though, and soon the chants of the home crowd rose in a crescendo once again, as Rangers bounced back from the ropes to stun Leeds with two goals of their own.

The first was a bizarre own-goal scored by the Leeds goalkeeper John Lukic in the twenty-first minute. He chose to leave his line in order to field an Ian Durrant corner, but he misjudged the flight of the ball as it spun under the Ibrox floodlights and, instead of punching the ball to safety, it skidded off his gloves and fell behind him into the goal, despite a last-gasp attempt to clear by the defender stationed on the goal-line.

The equalising goal gave Rangers added impetus, and although Durrant deflected a Gary Speed effort on to the post, the home side carved out the best chances and it took a superb save from Lukic to keep out a thundering shot from David Robertson in the thirty-fifth minute. However, the Leeds custodian was stooping to pick the ball out of the net two minutes later when Rangers grabbed the goal that gave them the lead on the night. The goal was once again crafted from a corner, this time delivered from the right by Trevor Steven. The English midfielder pinged the ball towards David McPherson who was loitering with intent around the penalty spot, and although Lukic did well to parry the big centre-half's header, the rebound fell to McCoist, lurking six yards from goal, and he gleefully slammed the ball home to send the 43,251 Bluenoses into ecstasy.

After such a tumultuous first period, it was inevitable that the pace would slacken after the interval, and there were few genuine goal-scoring opportunities in the second half. The best of the chances came the way of Rangers, and McCoist should done better than head the ball straight at Lukic after he had been set up by a cute chip from Durrant, while Hateley could well have made it 3-1 in the eighty-sixth minute when he was played through one-on-one with Lukic by McCall, but his final effort was weak, and the Leeds keeper gathered it easily.

The following Sunday, Rangers travelled to Hampden to take on Aberdeen, with the first leg of the domestic Treble, the League Cup, the prize for the winners. Rangers started in determined fashion and dominated the opening exchanges, with Ian Ferguson only a matter of inches away from breaking the deadlock when his blistering 25-yard drive rattled Theo Snelders' left-hand post. Aberdeen's reprieve was short, though, as Rangers took the lead after fourteen minutes and, for the second time in four days, a goalkeeping error gifted them their goal.

The new backpass rule had come into play during the close season, which meant that if the ball was intentionally played back to the goalkeeper from the foot of one of his own players he could not use his hands to collect the loose ball. Instead, he had to field it with another part of his body, or else an indirect free-kick would be awarded to the opposition. There seemed to be little danger to the Aberdeen rearguard when Ian Durrant's through-ball was cut out by the boot of Gary Smith, but the ball spun towards Snelders at an awkward height and, with the new ruling fresh in his mind, the Dutchman decided against using his hands, electing instead to control the ball on his chest before clearing. However, his control let him down and his heavy touch fell kindly to the in-rushing Stuart McCall, who stroked the ball into the back of the net.

Aberdeen battled back in the second half and, just after the hour, they pulled themselves level when Duncan Shearer's sharp turn and shot beat Goram. The score remained at 1-1 at the end of the ninety minutes, necessitating an extra half-hour in an attempt to separate the sides. Given their heavy schedule, another thirty minutes of action was the last thing Rangers needed, but they dug deep into their reserves of energy and emerged victorious thanks to Aberdeen centre-half Gary Smith. David Robertson played a hopeful cross into the box, and Smith, under pressure from Hateley, stretched out a leg and turned the ball behind his own goalkeeper to hand the cup to Rangers. It was the Light Blues' fifth League Cup success in the past seven seasons, and it signified a record-equalling moment for McCoist, as he picked up his seventh winners' badge from the competition, matching the achievement of his great friend Davie Cooper. Despite failing to score in the final, the eight goals he had chalked up on the road to Hampden were sufficient to secure McCoist the prize of the tournament's top goalscorer.

McCoist's goal drought did not last long, though. In Rangers' next match, a home league encounter with Motherwell on Halloween, he haunted the visitors for the second time that season, netting another hat-trick as Smith's men maintained their momentum in the title race courtesy of a 4-2 win. After Ian Angus had fired the visitors into a shock lead, McCoist restored parity from the penalty spot after Ian Ferguson had been fouled, and he handed Rangers a half-time lead when he forced the ball into the net at the second attempt three minutes shy of the interval. John Brown made it 3-1 in the fiftieth minute before McCoist chalked up hat-trick number five of the season in the sixty-second minute when he applied the perfect finish to a wonderful passing move inspired by the enigmatic Alexei Mikhailitchenko. The Ukrainian winger fashioned the opportunity with an excellent reverse pass, and he lauded the hat-trick hero afterwards saying: 'Sometimes I feel the ball is tied to his feet because he gets into the most incredible positions to score an impossible amount of goals. In fact, I get the feeling that if Ally were to stand in the centre circle and close his eyes the ball would hit off his head and still end up in the back of the net! But there is no luck attached to his skill. Any striker who gets into those positions must have an incredible sense for goals and Ally has shown he has great speed of mind and thought.'[12]

Thus, with the first piece of domestic silverware safely under lock and key at Ibrox, their four-point lead at the head of the race for the Premier Division title consolidated, and their principal marksman in razor-sharp form, Rangers made the trip across the Pennines to face Leeds in a buoyant mood. However, given the negative press Rangers had received in the English media since their 2-1 first-leg win at Ibrox, one had to question whether or not it was worth them turning up for the return match.

Leeds admittedly had a formidable home record, and had the advantage of the away goal that meant that a 1-0 win would see them through, but the outlandish predictions printed in the English papers were staggering. As far as they were concerned, Rangers would be lambs to the slaughter, with scores of 3-0 and 4-0 to Leeds being predicted. In the end, however, their ramblings worked in the favour of the Scottish champions, as assistant manager Archie Knox used the newspaper cuttings as motivation in the weeks leading up to the game, challenging the squad to make the English media eat their words by putting on a performance that would see Rangers, and not the much-fancied Leeds, become the first British club to compete in the money-laden riches of the Champions League.

Hateley, Gough and Durrant had all missed the Motherwell match, but were restored to the starting line-up at Elland Road, with Kuznetsov, Michailitchenko and Huistra making way for them. As expected, Leeds went for the jugular from the kick-off, and almost scored in the opening sixty seconds when Cantona burst clear only to be denied by a fine stop by Goram. It was to be the first of many on a night when Goram illustrated just how good a goalkeeper he really was. In a similar manner to McCoist, Goram had struggled in the early stages of his Rangers career, but he had since matured into one of the world's foremost shot-stoppers, and he used the Elland Road stage to showcase his considerable talents.

Goram's next involvement in proceedings was not to repel another Leeds attack, though. Instead, he played a significant role as Rangers set about extending their advantage and nullifying the away goal Leeds had scored at Ibrox. His long clearance was aimed in the direction of Durrant and although not renowned for his aerial prowess ('He's probably the only player at Ibrox who's worse in the air than me,' remarked McCoist[13]), the midfielder won the ball and flicked a header into the path of Hateley. What followed is now part of Rangers folklore. Spotting that Lukic had strayed a little from his line, Hateley unleashed a wicked, dipping volley with his left foot, and although he arched backwards, the Leeds goalkeeper could not reach the ball as it looped over his head and into the net. For the second time in the tie, the huge home support was silenced.

Although Rangers had redressed the balance with regard to the away goal and rocked the home side in the process, Leeds were still very much in the tie, and for much of the remainder of the game, the Yorkshire outfit unloaded a barrage of attacks on the Rangers goal as they strove to find the two goals they needed to force the match into extra-time. Their approach forced Rangers onto the ropes, but the Scottish champions absorbed everything that was thrown at them, and at the half-time interval, the score still read 1-0 in the favour of the Scottish champions. The team had defended solidly as a unit in the midst of the Leeds onslaught, with Goram, Gough and Brown at the heart of the Rangers defence particularly resolute as they repelled all the blows the Leeds forwards could throw at them.

It was a case of more of the same in the early stages of the second half too, with Goram denying Cantona, Rod Wallace and Lee Chapman before Rangers and McCoist delivered the knockout blow in the fifty-eighth minute. As another wave of white rolled towards Goram's goal, John Brown met Cantona with a hard but fair challenge to win the ball. He fed Durrant, who in turn linked with Hateley, sending the Englishman scampering down the left wing with a cute pass played with the outside of his right foot. Hateley had no need to look up; he instinctively knew where his partner would be. His understanding with McCoist was now at its peak, so he simply swept a majestic cross with his left foot to the back post where McCoist swooped to send a diving header back across the bows of Lukic and into the far corner. There were 25,118 people in the stadium, but as the ball kissed the back of the net, one could have heard a pin drop. The silence was only pierced by the whoops of delight emanating from the Rangers players and backroom staff.

Rangers were now 4-1 ahead in the tie, leaving the English side with a little over half an hour to find the four goals they needed to go through. It was a mountain they could not climb, and although Cantona eventually got the better of Goram to net a consolation goal in the last five minutes, the match ended with Rangers in possession. A place in the lucrative Champions League was theirs.

Qualification for the mini-league meant Rangers would be the first British club to compete at a stage of the competition that had been the brainchild of their own secretary/director Campbell Ogilvie, and that night, despite the fact the league match with Celtic was less than seventy-two hours away, the Rangers squad partied into the small hours of Thursday morning, savouring a famous victory over England's finest that tasted even sweeter given the extent to which Rangers had been written off in the English press prior to the second leg.

As far as Leeds United were concerned, the Scottish champions had devastatingly penetrated their impregnable Elland Road fortress, and they never fully recovered from the psychological beating they took that night. From winning the championship the previous season, they ended up in a relegation battle for the remainder of 1992/93, a fight they eventually survived, although they still finished the season languishing in seventeenth place in the Premier League.

. For Rangers, the big-match bandwagon just continued to roll, with rivals Celtic next up at Parkhead on the Saturday. With their arch-rivals riding the crest of a wave, Celtic looked to bring them crashing back down to earth by snatching a victory and, in the process, narrow the four-point gap between the two sides at the top of the table.

Despite being involved in so many epic tussles over the previous fortnight, Walter Smith resisted the temptation to rest some of his key personnel and selected the eleven players that had started the match at Elland Road. As had been the case in midweek, Rangers were on the back foot for most of the match, but once again they absorbed everything the opposition had to throw at them, typifying the resolution and fighting spirit that flowed freely through the side. Andy Goram and his defence were once again exceptional, with Goram in particular producing another outstanding goalkeeping display. He revelled in these conflicts, and over the course of the ninety minutes, Goram, now Scotland's first-choice goalkeeper ahead of Jim Leighton, made three outstanding saves, one from a blistering Darius Wdowczyk free-kick, another from a Stuart Slater volley and the third a fine block to deny Gary Gillespie.

Even when Rangers lost the services of Brown and Gough through injury, Celtic could not breach their defences, and with Goram defying the home side at one end, Rangers converted one of the rare chances that came their way at the other. Thirty-two minutes of the first half had elapsed when Dale Gordon profited from a Mike Galloway error to float a cross to the back post from where McCoist unselfishly cushioned a header into the path of Ian Durrant, who volleyed the ball behind Pat Bonner to give Rangers the breakthrough. Despite relentless Celtic pressure, Rangers held on to their narrow advantage after the interval to stretch their lead over their Old Firm rivals to six points.

In the space of fourteen remarkable days, Rangers had not only triumphed in the face of adversity in Europe, they had also collected the first silverware of the season and swept aside the challenges placed before them in the championship to cement their position at the head of the race. The fact that Smith's men had emerged from this epic series of fixtures unscathed sent out an ominous warning to any of the pretenders to their Premier Division crown. Even taking into account the exertions that go hand in hand with an extended run in European competition, Rangers were going to take some stopping.

Naturally, McCoist was prominent in that sequence of matches, racking up five goals to take his tally for the season to an astonishing twenty-nine, and more joy was to follow for McCoist in the next two league matches, with another three goals added to his total. The defences of Dundee and Hearts were on the receiving end this time, with his goal at Tynecastle, a diving header from 10 yards, chalking up another landmark in his Rangers career; it was his 200th league goal for the club. It was also his thirtieth in domestic football in the 1992/93 season, earning him a second successive *Daily Record* Golden Shot award. He entered the record books by reaching that mark in only twenty-two appearances, thus becoming the fastest player to hit a total of thirty goals in a season for almost twenty years.

The joy of those achievements was tempered, though, when McCoist picked up a calf injury in training, which meant he missed the visit of Partick Thistle to Ibrox in the Premier Division and also the opening fixture in the Champions League against Marseille. The match against the French champions in Glasgow on 25 November 1992 marked the first time McCoist had not appeared in either the Rangers starting line-up or among the substitutes in the league since he had missed out on Aberdeen's visit to Ibrox on 28 September 1991, a run of sixty-six consecutive appearances. The blow of spending some time on the treatment table was softened, though, when McCoist had another personal accolade bestowed upon him; he was named as BBC *Sportscene*'s Personality of the Year for 1992, the second time he had won that particular award.

The draw for the group stages of the Champions League had bracketed Rangers in Group A alongside the champions of France, Belgium and Russia in the shape of Olympique Marseille, Club Bruges KV and CSKA Moscow. For the first round of fixtures, Rangers welcomed the Gallic flair of Marseille to Ibrox on a typically wet Scottish evening, and McCoist watched from the stand alongside 41,623 supporters as his team-mates mounted one of the most rousing comebacks in the club's 120-year history.

Outplayed for the opening seventy minutes by a gifted Marseille side that boasted talent such as Rudi Voeller, Franck Sauzee, Didier Deschamps, Alen Boksic and a young Fabien Barthez, Rangers were fortunate to enter the closing stages of the match only 2-0 down. In an attempt to rescue something from the tie, Smith shuffled the pack, replacing Trevor Steven with young reserve striker Gary McSwegan, a move that restored Durrant back into a midfield role, while McSwegan joined Hateley in attack. The impact was immediate, as within sixty seconds Rangers pulled a goal back to reduce the deficit. Durrant sprayed a wonderful ball from the heart of the pitch to Mikhailitchenko on the left touchline from where the enigmatic winger looped a cross into the penalty area with his left foot. As the ball dropped out of the night sky, McSwegan met it and directed a header out of the reach of Barthez to throw Rangers a lifeline. For the first time in the match, the seemingly imperturbable French were rattled and, five minutes later, the match was all-square at 2-2 when Hateley stooped at the near post to divert a McCall cross into the net. With Durrant revelling in his more favoured midfield role, the home side pummelled the flagging French champions in search of a dramatic late winner, but the match ended with honours even.

Next up were CSKA Moscow away from home, although the tie was switched to Bochum in Germany because of the bitterly cold winter in Russia. With McCoist fit again and restored to the forward line alongside Hateley, Rangers survived a first-minute scare when David Robertson had to hack the ball off his own goal-line, but took the lead shortly afterwards when Ian Ferguson's twenty-five-yard shot looped over the CSKA goalkeeper, aided by a deflection from the leg of a CSKA defender.

Thereafter, Rangers proceeded to produce a textbook away performance in Europe, one that showed maturity and class, while sending out a message that this was a side more than capable of making it through to the final of the competition. Try as they might, CSKA simply could not break down the Rangers defence, as Smith's men fended off everything their opponents threw at them. John Brown, in particular, proved to be an unyielding barrier, and it was his timely intervention in the eighty-ninth minute that thwarted Serguei Sergueev as CSKA looked to rescue a point. At the other end, Rangers should have perhaps made the whole evening a little more comfortable, but a combination of loose finishing and fine goalkeeping denied McCoist and Durrant. In the end, the 1-0 victory, coupled with Marseille's 3-0 victory over Bruges in France, saw the Scots and the French share the lead in Group A as European football went on sabbatical until March.

Although they were enjoying their European adventure, Rangers had not taken their eye off the ball in the title race. The 1-1 draw with Hearts at Tynecastle in November was the first time Rangers had spilled points in the championship since the 1-1 draw with Celtic in August, a run of eleven straight wins, but it merely proved a momentary lapse, as victories over Partick Thistle, Falkirk, Dundee and St Johnstone fortified their position at the top of the Premier League table. In that domestic sequence, McCoist added another two goals to his tally for the season, netting against Falkirk and Dundee to take him to Christmas with a grand total of thirty-four goals in all competitions. That total, coupled with the goals he had scored in the second half of the 1991/92 season meant that, in the calendar year of 1992, McCoist had netted a phenomenal fifty-two goals in just fifty-three appearances, proof if any was needed that this was indeed a striker in his prime.

It proved to be a Happy New Year for Rangers too, as Trevor Steven heralded the start of 1993 by heading the winning goal in the New Year Old Firm match at Ibrox, a result that catapulted Rangers ten points ahead of their great rivals and effectively consigned Celtic to the role of title-chasing also-rans with twenty matches still to play.

The Old Firm match-winner, Steven, had been filling the attacking void left by the injured McCoist, who was absent from duty after injuring his calf nine minutes from the end of the Boxing Day victory over Dundee. However, by the time Dundee United came calling to Ibrox three days after the win over Celtic, Rangers' top goalscorer had shaken off his injury ailment to return to the side, and the home support was grateful for his presence: he netted the decisive third goal, his first of 1993, in a 3-2 win. United had rallied from 2-0 down to draw level, but McCoist denied The Tangerines a point twenty minutes from time when he latched on to a Trevor Steven pass, evaded Alan Main and stroked the ball into the empty net.

McCoist's golden boots continued to sparkle for the rest of the month too, as January was rounded off with a further two victories for Rangers. The Scottish Cup campaign kicked off with a trip to Fir Park to take on a Motherwell side that were anchored to the foot of the Premier Division, and Rangers duly ended the Lanarkshire side's interest in the competition with a comfortable 2-0 win, with both goals coming from McCoist. Remarkably, the brace took McCoist's tally to eight in his last three appearances against Motherwell, and he chalked up another crucial strike the following weekend in an enthralling 4-3 win over Hibernian at Easter Road.

Also on the scoresheet in Edinburgh was Mark Hateley, and the Englishman's brace took his tally to seventeen for the season. Added to McCoist's thirty-eight, the potent pairing had contributed a staggering fifty-five of the eighty-two goals Rangers had registered in all competitions, and were well on course to eclipse the joint total of sixty-two they had supplied in the 1991/92 season.

The duo were now laying claim to be the club's most potent and effective strike-pairing since the fabled Jimmy Millar-Ralph Brand alliance that had terrorised defences throughout the country in the silverware-enriched days of the early 1960s. And there were striking similarities between the two pairings. Like McCoist, Brand was the penalty-box predator, while Millar assumed the same role as Hateley, doing the majority of the foraging in a bid to create the space and opportunities on which his cohort's game thrived. With Millar and Hateley also capable of weighing in with their quota of goals, the resulting fusion cultivated a handsome harvest of goals for Rangers and propelled the Light Blues through two of the most celebrated spells in their history.

The victory over Hibernian set Rangers up nicely for the trip to Pittodrie in early February to face nearest challengers Aberdeen in an eagerly anticipated championship shootout. It turned out to be a night that saw Andy Goram in quite breathtaking form. Aberdeen, looking on this match as an opportunity to derail Rangers' relentless charge towards their fifth successive title triumph, threw everything at a Rangers rearguard missing the presence of their influential captain Richard Gough, but time and time again, Goram repelled their attempts with a stunning array of reflex saves. In a rare attack midway through the second half, Mark Hateley got his head to a David Robertson cross and directed the ball into the Aberdeen net to give the visitors the lead against the run of play and it was an advantage they managed to cling on to until the final whistle. It was yet another heroic display from Rangers and their goalkeeper, in particular, and after the match McCoist took the opportunity to pay tribute to Goram's contribution to what was fast becoming a phenomenal season. He said: 'The whole team is taking so much confidence from Andy's displays. He has been outstanding this season and his performances are inspiring the rest of the team as we know it will take a good one or a lucky one to beat him when he's playing out of his skin as he is at present. And we reckon if he keeps a clean sheet we'll always have a fair chance of winning, because we'll get a goal somewhere along the line.'[14]

The victory over Aberdeen handed Rangers a seven-point lead at the summit of the Premier Division, but far from resting on their laurels and moving into cruise control, the Light Blues continued pushing the pedal to the metal. The other six matches contested in February – five in the league and one in the Scottish Cup at Ayr United – yielded four wins and two draws, with McCoist netting five goals, a haul that included a brace in the surprise 2-2 draw with struggling Airdrie at Ibrox, single strikes against Hearts and Motherwell (again!), and a goal in the cup-tie with Ayr at Somerset Park.

The strike against the Ayrshire side was McCoist's thirty-ninth of the season, matching his total for the previous campaign and leaving him only three short of his best-ever season's total in a Rangers jersey. He had thus steered himself on course to become the first Rangers player since Jim Forrest back in the 1964/65 season to net a half-century of goals in one season, and with sixteen league games still remaining and with McCoist having claimed thirty league goals already, Sam English's record total of forty-four league goals, that had stood since 1931/32, also looked to be in jeopardy.

McCoist's last goal of the month, the first in a 4-0 midweek league win at Motherwell, was also significant, as it was his 207th league goal for Rangers, which meant that he had now overtaken legendary Hearts striker Jimmy Wardhaugh's total of 206 league goals, and had thus supplemented his record collection by surpassing another milestone. He now had the distinction of having scored the highest number of league goals for one club since the cessation of hostilities at the end of the Second World War. Wardhaugh's landmark was one of the many McCoist outstripped during his career, and the benchmark of 251 league goals that the Rangers man eventually set is one that is unlikely to be beaten in today's 'Bosman' era where a player seldom remains with one club long enough to challenge such a magnificent milestone.

March opened with the third instalment of the Champions League matches, a trip to Belgium to take on Bruges, and Rangers once again came from behind to eke out a draw. Dutch winger Pieter Huistra's right-foot strike in the seventy-third minute restored parity in the match after the Belgians had gone ahead in the opening half, and only a terrific goalkeeping display from the home side's Danny Verlinden prevented

Smith's men from taking full points. Rangers registered no fewer than ten attempts on goal in the opening thirty minutes of the second half, but the balding Belgian goalkeeper pulled off two magnificent saves to keep out headers from Hateley and McPherson, and was also on hand to thwart attempts from McCoist and McCall. Nonetheless, the 1-1 draw still left Rangers on top of the group, level on points with Marseille, who had surprisingly stumbled to a draw against the Russians in Moscow.

Two weeks later, the Belgians visited Ibrox for the return match and Ian Durrant, who was beginning to rediscover some of the magic that had been a hallmark of his game before his horrific injury almost five years earlier, handed Rangers the lead late in the first half, latching on to a magnificent through-ball from Trevor Steven before driving the ball right-footed behind the Belgian goalkeeper, Verlinden. The home side were handicapped on the stroke of half-time, though, when Hateley was harshly dismissed by the referee for raising his hands in an attempt to shake off his marker Rudi Cossey. Remarkably, Cossey escaped without punishment, despite the fact he had been holding Hateley in a headlock at the time.

After the interval, Bruges took advantage of the extra man to find an equaliser when Lorenzo Staelens netted after fifty minutes, but Rangers gritted their teeth and, with twenty minutes left, Scott Nisbet scored the winner in bizarre fashion. Attempting to win a fifty-fifty challenge on the right wing, Nisbet's cross spun high into the box after it flew off the toe of the player he was challenging. Verlinden looked to have it covered, but the ball bounced awkwardly in front of him, changed its trajectory and, instead of ending up in the safety of his arms, ended up in the back of the net. Ibrox was sent into raptures and Rangers finished the game with two priceless points.

With Marseille thumping the Muscovites 6-0 at the Stade Velodrome, it was now a two-horse race to determine the group winner and, ultimately, the team who would progress to the European Cup final. With a trip to the South of France next on the agenda for Rangers, the mouth-watering prospect of a winner-takes-all shootout had been fashioned. The two teams were tied at the top of the section on six points, with the French side ahead by virtue of the two away goals they had netted at Ibrox. However, if the Scottish champions won the match at the Stade Velodrome, they would be in the final, with an unassailable two-point advantage and a better head-to-head record against Marseille.

The Bruges match had marked Rangers' forty-fourth match unbeaten in all competitions, and the following Saturday they travelled to Parkhead to take on third-placed Celtic intent on making it forty-five. McCoist had been struck down by a bout of food poisoning in the days leading up to the game, and was only fit enough for a place on the bench, but he was pitched into action after only half an hour when midweek hero Scott Nisbet sustained a pelvic injury that would ultimately end his career. However, the introduction of the talismanic McCoist could not prevent Rangers from sliding to a 2-1 defeat, a reverse that brought the unbeaten run to an abrupt end. However, while undoubtedly smarting as a result of the defeat, Smith's side at least had the consolation of knowing that they were still seven points clear at the top of the table.

Before the visit to Marseille that would determine their European destiny, Rangers had two important domestic matches to take care of, with Aberdeen due at Ibrox in the Premier Division and Hearts lying in wait in the Scottish Cup semi-final, with the latter fixture taking place at Parkhead four days before the clash in France.

The Dons arrived in Glasgow knowing this would be their last chance to wrestle the championship out of Rangers' grasp. Before kick-off, Aberdeen lay seven points adrift of Rangers, and with only eight games and sixteen points to play for after this, only a win would do for Willie Miller's side.

Hopes that Aberdeen might catch Rangers on a downer after the Celtic result ten days earlier were extinguished three days before the midweek clash when Rangers got back to winning ways in the league, comfortably defeating Dundee 3-0 at Ibrox. McCoist notched his thirty-third league goal of the season against the Dens Park side, nudging a Hateley header over the line with his midriff, and he added number thirty-four as Rangers snuffed out any of Aberdeen's lingering title aspirations with a fine display in front of a packed house.

After an even contest in the opening half, Rangers struck the first blow of the evening after sixty-five minutes when Ian Ferguson sent a rasping 20-yard drive into the net from the edge of the penalty area, and McCoist sealed the victory in the final minute, guiding a header beyond Theo Snelders from six yards after yet another assist from Hateley. His league goal count of thirty-four was sufficient to collect a second successive *Soulier d'Or* (Golden Boot), with McCoist becoming the first player to achieve the elite honour of being Europe's top league goalscorer in successive seasons.

The following Saturday, it was more of the same, as Hearts were put to the sword in the last four of the Scottish Cup. Rangers came from behind to win by two goals to one, with McCoist on target for the third successive match. Allan Preston fired Hearts ahead in the fifty-eighth minute, but Dave McPherson equalised with twenty minutes remaining before McCoist grabbed the winner five minutes later. John Brown's headed clearance bisected the Hearts defence, and McCoist beat the out-rushing Nicky Walker in the chase for the ball and lobbed a shot into the net, thus maintaining his record of having scored in every round of the cup that season.

The goal against Hearts was McCoist's forty-ninth strike of the season for Rangers, a remarkable tally that took him to within touching distance of the cherished landmark of fifty goals for the campaign. However, unbeknown to anyone at the time, he would be robbed of the opportunity to achieve that goal. Indeed, the goal scored at Parkhead that day would be the last of the most fruitful goal-scoring period of Ally McCoist's career, and over six months would pass before he would find the net again in a Rangers jersey.

CHAPTER ELEVEN

INJURY HELL: 1993–95

Given that the Scottish national team had performed so admirably at the European Championships in Sweden, the Tartan Army were looking forward to the qualifying matches for the World Cup due to be held in the USA in the summer of 1994 with great anticipation. The displays against the might of the Netherlands, Germany and the CIS had filled the nation with renewed confidence, and the fans and players hoped that a succession of similar performances would be enough to secure a berth at football's version of 'The Greatest Show on Earth'. The Scots were looking to extend a very proud qualification record too, as they had been the only home nation to have taken part in each of the previous five World Cup finals. They were intent on making it six in a row, but the draw for the qualifying stages had not been kind to them, placing them in a tough section with Italy, Portugal, Switzerland, Malta and the minnows from Estonia.

First up was a trip to Berne on 9 September 1992 to take on the Swiss, but although McCoist, winning his forty-second cap, equalised Adrian Knup's opener after thirteen minutes, the Scots stumbled to a 3-1 defeat and had Rangers captain Richard Gough sent off for deliberate handball. Another strike from Knup and a goal from Georges Bregy nine minutes from time proved Scotland's undoing, as the quest for the US got off to a less than favourable beginning. With home fixtures against the might of the Portuguese and the Italians next on the fixture list, it was therefore imperative that the Scots got their campaign back on track, as they did not want to fall too far off the pace in the early stages.

The matches against Portugal and Italy were both played at Ibrox, since Hampden was in the throes of reconstruction at the time, and each ended in 0-0 draws. McCoist, who was named as vice-captain for both fixtures, failed to pierce the unyielding defences of each of the visiting nations, but he notched up a double in the next qualifier, as the Scots returned to winning ways by registering a comfortable 3-0 win over Malta. Thus, with four points on the board, Andy Roxburgh's side were in a good position with the return match against Portugal, widely regarded at the outset as the main rivals for second place behind the Italians, due to take place in Lisbon at the end of April 1993.

By the time McCoist and his international team-mates boarded the flight to the Portuguese capital, Rangers' interest in the European Cup had come to an end. The mission to Marseille had resulted in a 1-1 draw, with the visitors, handicapped by the absence of Mark Hateley, who had been slapped with a three-match European ban following his red card against Bruges, fighting back valiantly to keep their hopes of progression alive. Having fallen behind in the opening twenty minutes, when Franck Sauzee thumped a shot beyond Goram following an error from David Robertson, Ian Durrant hauled Rangers back on to level terms when he scored the crucial equalising goal early in the second half with an exquisitely executed volley. Although McCoist and McSwegan had chances to win the match in the last ten minutes, the contest ended with honours even.

Rangers' fate was now out of their own hands. They had to rely on Marseille dropping at least a point in Belgium, while Walter Smith's men had to take care of CSKA who visited Ibrox for the sixth and final match in Group A on 21 April. It turned out to be an emotionally charged night in Glasgow, but try as they might, Rangers could not break down the Russian defensive wall. McCoist, so prolific throughout the season but still seeking his first goal in the Champions League group matches, had a few good opportunities to score, but uncharacteristically spurned them. In the second half, Trevor Steven volleyed against the crossbar and John Brown was denied in the closing stages when the visiting goalkeeper

Yevgeny Plotnikov clawed away his volleyed effort as the home side probed for that ultimately elusive first goal. It was not forthcoming, though, and a gallant campaign ended with a 0-0 stalemate.

In the end, the result was academic, as Marseille won 1-0 in Bruges to advance to the final where they defeated AC Milan, although their success was later tainted amid shameful allegations of match fixing. The news of the result in Belgium did little to soothe the disconsolate Rangers players, though, and many of them were tear-stained as they left the field, with McCoist, in particular, inconsolable.

With no league matches scheduled for the Saturday after the CSKA match, the next time McCoist took to the field was for the World Cup qualifying tie in Lisbon, his forty-sixth outing for his country. It turned out to be an awful night for both Scotland and their prolific centre-forward. The Scots were torn apart by a rampant Portuguese eleven for whom both Rui Barros and Jorge Cadete scored twice in a 5-0 hammering, a result that effectively signalled the end of Scotland's quest for World Cup qualification. It also concluded the reign of Andy Roxburgh as national coach.

Of more concern to the watching Rangers fans and management team, though, was an incident that occurred midway through the second half. McCoist and his front-line partner, Blackburn Rovers' Kevin Gallacher, had not so much of a sniff in front of goal all night, but in a rare foray forward, the ball was crossed in towards McCoist who was stationed just inside the penalty area. He drew back his right leg in anticipation of a scoring opportunity, but his marker, Oceano Cruz, moved in to challenge him and won the ball. McCoist followed through with his attempted shot at goal, though, and his shin met with the knee of the big Portuguese defender. He knew something was seriously wrong straight away. McCoist recalled: 'Hughie Allan [the national team physiotherapist] came on and said, "How are you doing?" I said: "Just a bit sore, get me up," so as he lifts me up my next statement was, "That's good, that's the first step, now get me aff!"'[1]

When McCoist had applied his weight to his injured leg, the pain had been excruciating and X-rays taken after the match revealed that he had broken his leg. With the pain increasing, he was advised by the medical staff to take some sort of pain relief, but an aversion to taking pills meant that another means of dulling the ache would be required. The team doctor, Dr Stewart Hillis, duly provided a somewhat unorthodox solution, pulling two bottles of red wine from his bag and, after a few glasses of Portugal's finest, the injured party soon found his pain suitably soothed!

Despite the fact that Rangers were only one match away from clinching the title and booked to play against Aberdeen in the Scottish Cup final with the chance to secure the domestic Treble, McCoist refused to be downcast when he heard the diagnosis. Aside from breaking his nose twice, the cartilage trouble that had dogged him in 1988 and the hamstring tear that had sidelined him for two months during the 1988/89 season, this was the first serious ailment of his playing career, and the positive news that he had sustained a clean break meant there would be no need for a plate to be inserted to aid the healing process. It appeared that, if all went well, he would be fit to spearhead Rangers' attack at the beginning of the following campaign.

The Saturday after the nightmare in Portugal, Rangers clinched their fifth successive League Championship title when they defeated Airdrie 1-0 at Broomfield. Young reserve striker Gary McSwegan, drafted in to fill the number nine jersey vacated by McCoist, scored the only goal of the game on the stroke of half-time to give Rangers the two points they needed to claim the title. McCoist was not present during the after-match lap of honour as he was under strict orders from the club doctor not to attend the match, as any cavorting around during the celebrations may have exacerbated his injury. Instead, he tuned in to the match on his radio at home, but he still managed to feature in the celebrations, with Ian Ferguson managing to acquire a life-size cardboard cut-out of Rangers' top goalscorer from two supporters, which was duly passed from pillar to post, making its way into countless photographs that appeared in the Sunday newspapers the next day.

The championship trophy was presented to captain Richard Gough after the next home match, a 1-0 win over Dundee United, with McCoist, complete with crutches, appearing in the flesh this time to join in the party. The cardboard cut-out was also back, strapped to McCoist's back this time, with the face of Hollywood's renowned boozer, actor Oliver Reed, superimposed onto it with the message 'Right Boys Let's Party!' emblazoned below. Clearly the leg break had not diluted McCoist's sense of humour!

Three weeks later, McCoist was joining his team-mates for another celebratory lap of honour, as Rangers successfully completed the third leg of the domestic Treble. Goals from Neil Murray and Mark Hateley were sufficient to overcome the challenge of Aberdeen and bring the Scottish Cup back to Ibrox for the twenty-sixth time. On this occasion, McCoist had dashed or, more accurately, hobbled on his crutches, from the BBC studio where he had taken on the role of match summariser in order to take part in the party.

Although his campaign ended prematurely, Ally McCoist rated the 1992/93 season as his best in Light Blue. In addition to his thirty-four league goals, he had added five in the Scottish Cup, eight in the League Cup and two in the European Cup, giving a grand total of forty-nine strikes in only fifty-two appearances. His deluge of goals included one quadruple, four hat-tricks and five doubles, and the rich striking partnership he had struck up with Mark Hateley flourished and blossomed throughout the season. Hateley was also on fire, contributing twenty-nine goals in a season in which Rangers were completely dominant, bringing all three domestic trophies back to Ibrox, while remaining unbeaten for forty-four consecutive matches – comprising an amazing thirty-four wins and ten draws – and coming so close to making the club's first-ever appearance in the European Champions Cup final.

As the events of a remarkable season took their rightful place in the history books, McCoist began to focus his attention on the road to recovery, with one diary date in particular pencilled in to make his playing comeback. In April, Rangers announced that they would reward McCoist for ten years of sterling service with a testimonial match against English Premiership new boys Newcastle United at Ibrox on 3 August. It was a fitting gesture for a player who had served the club with such distinction, but while he was desperate to be involved in this prestigious match, McCoist was acutely aware that rushing himself through his rehabilitation could be counter-productive, as it could lead to him breaking down with other injuries which would then further hamper his comeback.

After holidaying in New York and Mexico, McCoist travelled with the rest of the first-team squad to their traditional pre-season base in Il Ciocco in Italy. Although unable to take part in the full training sessions, the inclusion of McCoist in the party was a clever move by Smith and his management team, as it kept the ebullient striker involved with the dressing-room banter; banter that he was usually at the hub of.

It wasn't all fun and frolics for McCoist, though, as club physio Bill Collins put him through his paces with morning sessions in the gym and then afternoon stints in the swimming pool as the fight for fitness began in earnest. McCoist's sessions in the pool were the cause of great amusement, with his thrashing and splashing prompting Ian Durrant to liken him to a famous ocean-going paddle steamer. Durrant took great delight in yelling 'Here comes the *Waverley*' as his friend fought to find a suitable swimming style in the early days of his rehabilitation!

Despite his best efforts in the gym and the pool, the visit of Newcastle arrived just too early for McCoist to play an active part in his testimonial match. He still took to the field to acknowledge the cheers of his adoring public, though, with 42,623 of them turning out to pay homage and watch Kevin Keegan's side triumph 2-1. McCoist did play some part in the evening's entertainment, taking a penalty in the celebrity shootout at half-time. However, it was clear that the rediscovery of his old sharpness was still some way off, as McCoist blazed his left-footed effort into the stands behind the goal! The match with Newcastle officially kicked off a series of gala events that would take place during McCoist's testimonial year, including golf, racing and a gala ball, culminating with 'The Ally McCoist Burns Supper' in January 1994.

McCoist continued his journey down the road to recovery by spending two weeks at the FA Rehabilitation Centre in Lilleshall at the end of August. While his team-mates were kicking off the defence of their Premier Division title, McCoist was working on building up the muscle tissue on his right leg by undergoing an intensive programme of exercise routines in the gym, in addition to yet more swimming. The gruelling regime continued on his return to Ibrox, with no fewer than three training sessions per day, two in the morning and one in the afternoon.

The toil eventually paid off when McCoist made his return to action on Saturday, 25 September 1993, the day after his thirty-first birthday. He turned out for the reserve team in a 3-2 win over Hibernian at Easter Road and, although he did not score, his ninety-minute workout was enough to earn him a place among the substitutes for the crucial midweek European Champions Cup tie in Sofia against Levski. It was the end of almost four months of rigorous rehabilitation, but throughout his journey, McCoist had retained his role as 'King of the Quips' within the walls of Ibrox, constantly winding up his fellow team-mates and always carrying around that infectious smile.

Rangers had missed his presence on the field too, as they had endured a somewhat indifferent start to the season. Never one to rest on his laurels, Walter Smith had bolstered his squad in the close season, adding the talents of Fraser Wishart and Dundee United's Duncan Ferguson to the ranks. Wishart, a dependable full-back who counted Motherwell, St Mirren and Falkirk among his former employers, was recruited on a free transfer, while Ferguson, who, at the age of twenty-one, was widely regarded as the hottest property in Scottish football at the time, cost a cool £4 million.

In the mould of Mark Hateley, a target-man-type centre-forward, many expected Ferguson to be groomed as the long-term successor to the Englishman, but his stay at Ibrox would not last long, with his eighteen-month stint in Govan dogged with persistent injuries and indiscipline – he served time in jail after head-butting Raith Rovers' Jock McStay during a league match at Ibrox. He was loaned out to Everton early in the 1994/95 season before moving to Merseyside on a permanent basis, with Rangers recouping most of their outlay when they sold him on. Rather than oust Hateley from the team, the arrival of the young pretender merely forced Rangers' resident number ten to raise his game to another level. By the end of Ferguson's one and only full season in Rangers' colours, Hateley had racked up thirty goals and emulated McCoist's feat of scooping both the Football Writers' and Player's Player of the Year awards.

Despite missing the presence of Ferguson, who was absent from the opening league fixtures through injury, the champions enjoyed a smooth start to the defence of their title, chalking up successive 2-1 victories over Hearts and St Johnstone before marking Ferguson's full debut with a no-score draw against Celtic at Celtic Park. Turbulence was soon encountered, though, notably when newly promoted Kilmarnock plundered maximum points from their visit to Ibrox, winning 2-1 at the end of August thanks to ex-Rangers striker Bobby Williamson, who scored the winner deep into injury-time. It was the first time Rangers had lost a competitive match on their home ground since March 1992.

The defeat precipitated an alarming dip in form, with Rangers winning only one of their next six league matches. Admittedly the labours of the previous season had started to take their toll on the squad, with mainstays such as Goram, Robertson and Brown joining McCoist in the treatment room and missing large chunks of the early season action. At least the erratic league form had not been carried over into the League Cup, with Rangers making it to the final for the seventh time in eight seasons, disposing of Dumbarton, Dunfermline, Aberdeen and Celtic along the way.

September witnessed the commencement of the European Cup campaign, with Rangers pitched against Bulgarian champions Levski Sofia in the first qualifying round. Given the superb run the club had enjoyed only a year previously, there were high hopes of progress to the latter stages once again, and most observers expected that Rangers would easily brush aside the challenge of the Bulgarians and sail through to the next round. However, things did not turn out that way, and despite leading 2-0 and then 3-1, Smith's men contrived to concede a cheap goal in the closing minutes of the first leg at Ibrox, which meant that they arrived in the Bulgarian capital for the second leg clinging to a precarious 3-2 lead.

However, with McCoist looking on from the bench, Rangers looked to have safely booked their passage through to the second round when a disciplined performance in Sofia saw them enter injury-time in the match level at 1-1 on the night and ahead 4-3 on aggregate. Ian Durrant had grabbed the crucial away goal a minute shy of the interval and that seemed to be sufficient to see Rangers through, until they were dealt a devastating knockout blow when Nikolai Todorov rocketed a thirty-yard shot into the net to level the tie and edge the home side through on the away goals rule.

It was a shattering experience for the Rangers players and management, and McCoist, who did not make an appearance on the evening, described it as 'the worst feeling in my football career'. He said: 'I've been in one or two losing cup final teams, broken my leg, had low points during my time in the game, but none of those moments came close to the feelings I had when Todorov scored that winner. Sitting on the bench with the rest of the lads I felt sick, along with everyone else connected with the club.'[2]

The premature European exit left Rangers to concentrate on retaining the three domestic trophies they had picked up during the previous campaign, but the oscillatory league form continued as they stuttered again the following Saturday, with a lingering European hangover no doubt contributing to the tepid performance at Starks Park that resulted in a 1-1 draw with Raith Rovers. The match marked McCoist's first appearance for the first team since the Champions League tie with CSKA Moscow on 21 April, and he completed the full ninety minutes, although a fine defensive display from Jimmy Nicholl's side meant that the type of goal-scoring opportunities he was able to feast on were kept at a premium.

Still some way short of full match fitness, McCoist missed out the following midweek as Rangers slumped to a 2-1 home defeat at the hands of Motherwell, but he made a brief appearance at Tannadice on the Saturday, replacing Mark Hateley in the dying moments of a game Rangers won 3-1. He was then back in the starting eleven when his old club St Johnstone came visiting, playing for seventy-six minutes before being replaced by Ian Durrant. Although he once again drew a blank in the 2-0 win that helped steady a listing ship and lift Rangers to fourth in the table, it took a fine early save from Andy Rhodes in the Saints' goal to deny him his elusive comeback strike.

The match against St Johnstone was Rangers' last before they were due to face Hibernian at Parkhead in the League Cup final, and the showpiece game presented another record-breaking opportunity for McCoist. If selected, he had the opportunity to win his eighth League Cup-winners' medal, thus surpassing the total of his great friend and Rangers legend Davie Cooper, who shared the record of seven winners' medals with McCoist and Celtic's Billy McNeill.

Having made three appearances in the previous four matches and played for sixty-three minutes for the reserves in a 6-2 hammering at the hands of Ayr United four days before the match, McCoist was more than a little disappointed when he found out he had been omitted from the starting line-up and was forced to settle instead for a place on the bench, as Smith deemed he was not quite fit enough to stand up to the rigours of a Cup final that, with the prospect of extra-time and even penalties, could last for over two hours.

With Ian Durrant partnering Mark Hateley in attack, Rangers dominated their Edinburgh opponents in the early stages of the match, but they had to wait until ten minutes after the half-time interval to take the lead. Durrant, who delivered yet another Man of the Match display, played an exquisite one-two with Hateley on the edge of the penalty area before delicately lobbing the ball over the advancing Leighton and into the net. However, Smith's men only held the lead for a mere four minutes, as Keith Wright capitalised on a slack backpass from Gary Stevens to round Ally Maxwell and flash the ball across the face of the goal, where it was despatched into the net by Rangers' Dave McPherson for an own-goal.

Enter McCoist.

After sixty-seven minutes the striker was given the nod, replacing

Pieter Huistra and joining Hateley in attack as Rangers went all out to retain the trophy. As soon as McCoist arrived on the scene one could almost hear the fairytale writers sharpening their pencils in expectation, and the scribes were not disappointed, as the evergreen striker contrived to conjure up a spectacular winning goal nine minutes from time.

David Robertson took a long throw from the left-hand side and aimed it towards the head of Hateley. The ball skidded off the head of Hibernian centre-back Steven Tweed and bounced up in front of McCoist, who had his back to the goal. His initial reaction was to hook the ball towards goal with his left foot but, as it reared up, McCoist elected to take a touch on his chest before sending a magnificent overhead kick beyond Leighton and into the bottom corner. The goal-scoring grin, absent since he had scored at the same venue against Hearts six months earlier, was back, and an ecstatic and emotional McCoist took the acclaim of the Rangers supporters and his team-mates in front of the famous Parkhead 'Jungle'.

Thus, for the umpteenth occasion, Ally McCoist had woven his name into the fabric that makes up the rich tapestry of this wonderful football club. His stunning goal meant that the League Cup was again bedecked in red, white and blue ribbons, and the successful retention of the trophy reaffirmed Rangers' status as the dominant force in Scottish football. Walter Smith's blue and white army had now marched triumphantly to their sixth successive domestic trophy success, equalling the record set by Scot Symon's celebrated side of the early 1960s, and it was all thanks to their most reliable foot soldier, who once again provided prolific and outstanding service when called to the front line.

The goal-scoring hero, not famed for being the shy and retiring type, was for once at a loss for words as he tried to drink in his match-winning contribution. 'The whole thing was a bit of a dream for me,' said McCoist. 'I was disappointed, but the manager was probably right to leave me on the bench for the game due to a lack of match fitness. I always felt we'd get a chance if I came off the bench, but the way things worked out was just incredible for me. That feeling will be with me for a long time, that's for sure.'[3]

Walter Smith was in no mood to take any credit for the substitution, preferring instead to lavish praise in the direction of the darling of the Rangers community. He commented: 'When you make a substitution and he comes on to score the goal that he did score, the credit goes to the player, because I don't think there's many players could have scored in the situation that Alistair was in, back to goal, overhead kick. A lot of people say that it is typical of Coisty just coming on and getting the goal, but I think he has proved his worth and will continue to prove his worth over a period of seasons.'[4]

Smith hoped the return of his golden striker would effect a change in Rangers' fortunes in the title race. They had tottered through their early bouts in the Premier Division, and when rivals Celtic visited Ibrox the weekend after the final, the Light Blues lay fourth in the table, two points and two places above the visitors, but two points behind the early leaders, their vanquished League Cup final opponents Hibernian.

Celtic, who had also been a little off-colour in their opening twelve league matches, arrived in Govan led by a former hero, Lou Macari, who had replaced Liam Brady at the helm after the Irishman had been relieved of his duties in the week leading up to the clash. The Celtic players seemed to be energised by the new appointment, and their midfield controlled an uninspiring first half without ever fashioning an opportunity to test Ally Maxwell in the Rangers goal. However, the introduction of the enigmatic Ukrainian Alexei Mikhailitchencko at the interval seemed to stir Rangers, and McCall and Hateley both went close before the deadlock was eventually broken midway through the second half. Following his heroics at Parkhead, McCoist was back in the starting eleven, but he had had a rather lean afternoon until he was picked out by a low cross from McCall in the sixty-seventh minute, and he demonstrated that his sharpness was returning by firing the ball beyond Pat Bonner at the second attempt. The Celtic goalkeeper did extremely well to block the striker's first effort, but he was powerless as McCoist pounced to hoover up the rebound.

However, on this occasion McCoist's goal did not turn out to be a winning one. Three minutes later, Maxwell fumbled a cross from Pat McGinlay to allow John Collins to equalise and, in the dying minutes, questionable marking at a corner allowed Brian O'Neill to ghost in and head the winning goal for the visitors and consign Rangers to their fourth defeat of the season.

Remarkably, three of those losses had come at Ibrox, a venue that had been such an impenetrable fortress over the previous three years. It appeared as though the fear factor that had paralysed so many visiting teams in the past was no more, as opponents sensed a potential chink in the Rangers armoury. 'We're going to have to battle even harder now than we have done in the previous five seasons,' said McCoist in the wake of the Celtic defeat, 'because it looks as if this is going to be the toughest campaign yet.'[5]

The home defeat by Celtic seemed to cajole Rangers into action, and by early December the Light Blues had managed to recover their form and climb to the summit of the Premier Division table for the first time. An unbeaten sequence of eight matches – that culminated with successive 2-0 victories over challengers Aberdeen and Motherwell – saw Rangers take a two-point lead at the top, but they had achieved much of their success without the help of their eponymous hero.

A calf injury sustained in a 3-1 midweek victory over Dundee (a match in which McCoist scored twice – a penalty after thirty-three minutes and a close-range header eleven minutes later), sidelined him for three matches before his lay-off was extended when he injured his groin while making a scoring comeback in a Reserve League Cup match against St Johnstone. A simple operation was required to cure the groin complaint, but another period in recovery meant McCoist did not return to the field of play until he came on as a substitute against Dumbarton in the opening round of the Scottish Cup in late January.

In his absence, his number nine jersey was filled by Scotland striker Gordon Durie, who had come on board in November. Signed from Tottenham Hotspur for £1 million, Durie made a fine start to his Rangers career, marking his second match for the club with a brace in the 2-0 win over Motherwell at Fir Park that took Rangers to the top of the league table. His arrival and subsequent performances meant that competition for the striking berths would be hotter than ever when McCoist and fellow injury victim Duncan Ferguson were deemed fit enough to return to the fold.

Prior to making his first-team return against Dumbarton, McCoist had joined fellow injury-plagued team-mates Andy Goram, Duncan Ferguson and Dave McPherson in the reserve team for a Reserve League West match against Morton. The presence of the big guns clearly tipped the scales in Rangers' favour, with Ferguson scoring four times as Rangers blasted their way to an 8-0 victory. McCoist, who was replaced after seventy-three minutes by Derek Rae, was also on the scoresheet, and he was back in action for the reserves the following week when he played the full ninety minutes in a friendly against Clydebank.

The game time with the second string earned McCoist a recall to the first eleven, and he followed a substitute appearance against Hibernian in the league with a starting berth against Alloa Athletic in the fourth round of the Scottish Cup. Typically, he marked his return with a goal-scoring contribution, stinging the Second Division side by netting three of Rangers' goals in a 6-0 demolition. His first arrived three minutes after the interval, his second was a rasping volley in the seventy-first minute, and he completed his hat-trick from the penalty spot eight minutes from the end. It was McCoist's first treble for eighteen months and he could have added more goals had it not been for an inspired display by Jim Butter in the Alloa goal. 'I had a couple of chances in the first half, but you've got to give their keeper credit because he was magnificent, Man of the Match,' McCoist said afterwards. [6]

The match represented a significant step along what was proving to be an unforgiving road to recovery, and the goals went a long way to lifting his spirits. He told the *Rangers News*: 'I was delighted to score three goals and I felt as good on Saturday as I have done since I broke my leg. However, I'm not going to kid myself I've turned the corner. There's still a lot of hard work ahead of me, but to get a game like the Alloa one under my belt was really pleasing.' [7]

McCoist retained his slot in the first team for the next four matches, starting against Raith Rovers, Hearts and St Johnstone and replacing Mikhailitchenko for the last half-hour of a last-gasp 2-1 league win over Motherwell at Ibrox, and he added to his tally of goals when he scored with a fine diving header in a 2-1 away win at Tynecastle as Rangers maintained their pursuit of a sixth successive championship. The win in Edinburgh was Rangers' sixth in succession in the league and stretched their advantage at the top of the table over nearest challengers Motherwell to four points. Incidentally, Mark Hateley also scored at Tynecastle to take his total for the season to twenty-eight and bring to an end a year-long spell since the dynamic duo had last appeared on the scoresheet in the same match.

Three days after the win in Edinburgh, McCoist was on the goal trail yet again. Rangers travelled across Glasgow to meet Partick Thistle at a sodden Firhill, and it seemed that a vital championship point was about to be spilled when Isaac English equalised an earlier Richard Gough goal in the fifty-fifth minute. The Glasgow adversaries were still tied at 1-1 in the ninetieth minute when Stuart McCall moved forward into enemy territory. Sniffing out the chance of a last-gasp winning goal, McCoist made a tremendous run in behind the Thistle defence, McCall spotted his run, and the flame-haired midfielder's threaded pass was thumped into the net by McCoist from a tight angle. It proved a crucial goal, as it allowed Rangers to take advantage of a slip by Aberdeen, who lost at home to Hibernian on the same evening. The Light Blues now led the title chase by five points with eight games remaining.

Rangers eventually secured their sixth successive championship in May, limping home three points ahead of runners-up Aberdeen. Smith's men registered just two wins in their last nine Premier Division matches, and their lacklustre league form manifested itself into the Scottish Cup, with Kilmarnock forcing a replay in the semi-final before Ivan Golac's Dundee United extinguished hopes of an unprecedented back-to-back Treble when Craig Brewster profited from a defensive mix-up between McPherson and Maxwell to score the only goal of the final.

McCoist scored twice in that miserable spell, against Raith Rovers at Ibrox – a match now infamous for the altercation between Duncan Ferguson and Jock McStay that earned the big striker his jail sentence – and in a 2-1 defeat at the hands of Motherwell, to take his goal tally, in what had been a stop-start season, to eleven. His campaign had been blighted by injury, with the recovery from the broken leg and subsequent calf and groin complaints restricting him to just twenty-eight appearances, eight of which were from the substitutes' bench. Clearly the recovery process had stretched out longer than expected, but the affable striker was sure that a solid pre-season workout would see him regain the match sharpness he had lacked for much of the season.

Despite his lack of regular match action, McCoist's involvement still managed to hog the headlines at various junctures over the course of the campaign. Although his goals return only managed to earn him third position on the Ibrox scoring chart (Hateley [with thirty] and Durie [thirteen] finished above him), he had made a number of notable contributions, particularly with his stunning winning goal in the League Cup final and his decisive strike against Partick at Firhill, a goal that gave Rangers some breathing space as the chase for the title crown entered the final furlong.

Before returning to action ahead of the 1994/95 season, one of the most decorated players in Scottish football history had yet another honour bestowed upon him. On Friday, 10 June, it was announced that

Ally McCoist would be rewarded for his services to Association Football in the Queen's birthday honours list. He was awarded an MBE (Member of the Order of the British Empire), following in the esteemed footsteps of Rangers legend John Greig who, at that point, was the only other Ranger to have been decorated with this momentous honour. After establishing that he was not in fact the victim of a mischievous wind-up from his Ibrox colleagues, McCoist was flabbergasted to have received what he called the greatest honour of his career. 'It's an unbelievable honour for the club and my family as well,'[8] he told the *Rangers News*.

However, hard on the heels of such glad tidings was the heartbreaking news that McCoist's father Neil would not be present at his investiture, as he sadly passed away at the age of sixty-seven. Eighteen months earlier he had received treatment for a liver problem and had been convalescing at the McCoist family home in Bridge of Weir. He died in Hairmyres Hospital in East Kilbride and McCoist, who had been on holiday in Bermuda at the time of his passing, was left devastated by the news. Some years later, McCoist, who also had to mourn the passing of his Uncle George around the same time, reflected: 'When you have a privileged and lucky life like mine then you never think bad things can happen to you. I was floored by their deaths, devastated.'[9]

After mourning the deaths of his father and uncle, McCoist, with the letters 'MBE' emblazoned on his training gear, arrived back for pre-season training a week in advance of his other team-mates, clearly eager to avoid a repeat of the injury problems that had dogged him for over a year. However, his early return counted for little, as he sustained a calf injury during a 1-0 defeat against German side Kaiserslautern that forced him to return to Scotland. This meant a few days on the sidelines and bouts of double training sessions in order to make up for the time lost at the training camp at Il Ciocco.

The squad that travelled to the salubrious Tuscan base was swelled with the arrival of two 'blue-chip' signings, Basile Boli and Brian Laudrup. Laudrup was part of a footballing dynasty that included his father Finn, who had scored the winner for Denmark against Scotland in a European Championships qualifying match in Copenhagen in 1971, and his older brother Michael, who had starred for Barcelona, Real Madrid and Juventus. Laudrup, a prominent member of the Denmark side that had stormed to a surprise success in the 1992 European Championships, had spent time in the German Bundesliga and the top flight in Italy, Serie A, but his time in Italy had been troublesome, with his considerable talents stifled at both Fiorentina and during a loan spell at AC Milan. It took a cheque for £2.5 million to bring Laudrup to Glasgow, and over the next four years he would demonstrate just what a fine piece of business it had been.

With Spanish giants Barcelona also chasing his signature, many, his brother Michael included, doubted the wisdom of moving to the more physical Scottish league, but Laudrup, captivated by his first visit to Ibrox when he had been swept off his feet by the reception afforded to him and his wife by David Murray and Walter Smith, had no qualms about the move and the considerable ability he possessed would come to the fore during a sparkling four-year career in Scotland. By granting him a free role within the team, Smith gave Laudrup a platform upon which he could fully exhibit his vast repertoire of skills. He was such an unqualified success that he is regarded, alongside Henrik Larsson, as arguably the greatest foreign import to grace the Scottish shores. Unfortunately for Ally McCoist it would be over a year before he would begin to profit from the sterling service that the Danish wizard would provide for the front men at Ibrox.

The signing of Boli, on the other hand, proved to be something of a disaster. Signed from Marseille for a reported fee of £2.7 million, Boli was no stranger to the Rangers fans, having played against the Light Blues for Marseille in the Champions League campaign in 1992/93. He had also netted the winning goal in the final of that season's competition as the disgraced French side defeated AC Milan 1-0. He arrived with a reputation of being a tough, no-nonsense defender and it was expected that that, allied to his wealth of European experience, would stand Rangers in good stead in the season ahead. Alas, he found it difficult to adjust to the Scottish game and, early in the season, he vented his spleen to a French newspaper, criticising, among other things, Walter Smith's tactics. A typical Gallic shrug and claim of innocence – apparently the article had not been translated properly – followed, but within a year he was back in France, with Rangers recouping some of their outlay when they sold him on to Monaco for just under £2 million.

Also joining the group in Tuscany was Andy Goram. Having been dogged by injury and weight problems for almost the whole of 1993/94 (he had only managed ten appearances for the first team), the Scottish international goalkeeper had been sensationally transfer-listed by Walter

Smith in the close-season, but since then he had knuckled down and sweated off the excess pounds to such an extent that Smith removed him from the list and promptly reinstated him as Rangers' number one goalkeeper for the forthcoming season.

With the qualification round for the Champions League scheduled to take place before the Premier League season kicked off, Rangers were anxious to hit the ground running, so a mini-tournament was arranged to take place at Ibrox after the squad's return from Italy, with invitations extended to Newcastle United, Manchester United and Sampdoria. McCoist, fully recovered from his calf strain, was the only player who started both matches, playing the full ninety minutes of the curtain-raiser against Sampdoria, and eighty-six minutes of the third-place playoff against Manchester United twenty-four hours later. In the first match, he created the opening goal for Mark Hateley after just three minutes (despite that excellent start, Rangers contrived to blow a 2-0 lead and lost 4-2), and in the 1-0 win over United, he went agonisingly close to opening his account for the season when he cannoned a shot off the post eleven minutes from the end of the match.

However, despite his fine performances in the friendly matches, McCoist was listed among the substitutes when Rangers took to the field in Greece the following Wednesday to take on AEK Athens in the first leg of their Champions League qualifier. In strength-sapping heat, it made sense for the striker, still not quite fully match-fit, to sit things out, and Smith paired Gordon Durie with Mark Hateley in attack on what proved to be a frustrating night for the Scottish champions. They succumbed 2-0 in the hostile Nikos Goumas Stadium and it took an inspirational display from Andy Goram to maintain some sort of respectability in the final scoreline. The defeat left Rangers with a mountain to climb in the return leg at Ibrox if their dreams of Champions League qualification were to be realised.

Back on home soil, McCoist was included in the starting eleven for the opening Premier League fixture of 1994/95, with Motherwell, who had finished third in the Premier League the previous season, providing the opposition. This was to be the season when Scotland followed the example of their English League cousins and awarded three points for a win as opposed to the normal two in a bid to encourage more open and attacking football, and it took an inspired run from Brian Laudrup in the last minute to secure Rangers their first three points. With the scores tied at 1-1, the Dane picked up the ball on the edge of his own penalty area and embarked on a mazy dribble that culminated with a perfect pass to tee up the winning goal for substitute Duncan Ferguson.

Ferguson's goal gave Rangers the perfect start to their defence of the title, but the opening gambit of the season was anything but inspiring for Ally McCoist, who lasted barely half an hour of the match before he suffered a recurrence of the calf injury that had dogged him at the pre-season training camp. After the match his leg was encased in plaster, with an initial diagnosis of three weeks on the sidelines delivered which, given the ups and downs of the previous season, was the last thing McCoist needed to hear. It was, however, to be the start of another season-long injury nightmare for the thirty-two-year-old.

In his absence, Rangers were dumped out of the Champions League when AEK won the second leg 1-0 at Ibrox to secure a fine 3-0 aggregate success, and the European exit was the forerunner to a cataclysmic run of three successive home defeats, the first time this had happened for twenty-three years. Within the next seven days, Celtic (2-0 in the Premier Division) and Falkirk (2-1 in the League Cup) won at Ibrox to heap more pressure on to the shoulders of Walter Smith. It was perhaps the first time during his managerial rein that he had come in for such fierce criticism from his own public, prompting the inevitable 'crisis' headlines to be bandied around by the Scottish media. The manager was under pressure, so the last thing he needed to hear was that his perennial goal-scoring saviour, McCoist, was going to be sidelined for longer than expected. The initial diagnosis of a three-week lay-off was wide of the mark, and it would be early October before McCoist returned to the ranks when he appeared as a substitute in the 2-0 home win over Dundee United.

By the time he returned, Rangers had steadied the ship, with three wins and a draw propelling them back to the top of the league, and after his twenty-one-minute appearance against United, McCoist continued his rehabilitation the following weekend when he replaced the injured Dave McPherson for the second half of the 2-1 defeat by Hibernian at Easter Road. However, he was soon back on the treatment table when he injured his other calf, although this time it was not as severe as the injury he had sustained on the opening day of the season.

This latest period of inactivity prompted one newspaper to place question marks over McCoist's future in the game, but both he and his manager were quick to refute such conjecture. A clearly irritated Smith said: 'It's very worrying when people start putting question marks over a player's career because of a calf strain. That's the only problem Ally has – pure and simple.'[10] As if to prove the point, McCoist was back in Light Blue within a fortnight, replacing Brian Laudrup late in the second Old Firm clash of the season, a match Rangers won by three goals to one to cement their position firmly at the head of the title race.

The following midweek McCoist registered his first goals of the season. He was part of a strong Rangers line-up that travelled north to take on Huntly in a match that marked the inauguration of the new floodlights at Christie Park. The likes of Goram, Boli, Robertson and Huistra also turned out in front of a crowd of 3,500, but it was McCoist who stole the show with a fine seventeen-minute hat-trick in the second half of a match that Rangers won by five goals to two. Two appearances for the reserves followed, with the latter against Clyde yielding another hat-trick to provide further evidence that he was nearing full fitness and that he had rediscovered his golden goal-scoring touch.

Walter Smith clearly agreed, and when Falkirk visited Ibrox on 19 November, the name of Ally McCoist appeared in the Rangers starting eleven for the first time since the opening match of the campaign against Motherwell. Only the woodwork denied him the opportunity to mark his return with a goal, but he duly registered his first league goal of the season on his next outing, a 1-0 win over Aberdeen at Ibrox. The match was played on a Friday evening, the first time Rangers had ever contested a league fixture on that particular day, and McCoist ensured that the majority of the 45,072 patrons went home happy when he slotted home a Brian Laudrup pass ten minutes into the second half. The strike was his 299th goal for Rangers, leaving him on the threshold of becoming only the third player in the history of the club to score 300 goals, and it crowned a momentous time for McCoist as, just eight days earlier, he had visited Buckingham Palace to receive his MBE.

Resplendent in a Rangers tartan kilt, McCoist accepted the award from Prince Charles, who had appeared very knowledgeable about football and had been particularly interested in the Rangers striker's attire. 'I wore it [the kilt] because playing for them [Rangers] has led me to receive the honour and it was very suitable and I am always proud to wear it,' said the newest Member of the Order of the British Empire before adding, 'It has been a great day and it was a wonderful ceremony but I was so nervous. It was worse than taking a penalty in any Cup final.'[11] His proud mum Jessie, who accompanied Ally to the investiture with his wife Allison and mother-in-law Margaret, noticed her son's anxiety, but said: 'I've seen him nervous, I've seen him excited, but I've never seen him like he was this morning. I am very proud of him.'[12]

However, just when it looked like he had turned the corner and was about to embark on a successful run in the first team, McCoist was struck down with injury yet again, this time picking up a hamstring strain after thirty-seven minutes of a league match against Dundee United at Tannadice. He was back in action two weeks later, playing a full ninety minutes for the reserves in a 1-0 defeat against Celtic in the Reserve League Cup, but the calf muscle niggles that had marred the early part of the season flared up again and counted the striker out of action until into the New Year.

The latest injury setback was tempered, though, when McCoist became a father for the first time when Allison gave birth to a baby boy on 24 January. The new arrival, named Alexander Neil after McCoist's grandfather and father, weighed in at a healthy 8lb 7oz. 'I was there for the whole birth,' said a delighted daddy afterwards. 'I'd been looking forward to it so much, but when it came I was a bag of nerves. I'm looking forward to everything involved with being a dad – being with him, watching him grow up and spending hours playing with him.'[13]

Good news off the park was coupled with positive noises on it when McCoist made yet another comeback from his injury hell. Having finally shaken off the persistent calf problem, McCoist lined up for the reserves at Easter Road at the end of January and netted a brace of goals in a 3-0 win. This was enough to convince Smith that he was ready for another crack in the first team, and he played for twelve minutes as a substitute in the 1-1 draw with Dundee United. However, it turned out to be his ninth and last appearance of the 1994/95 season as, shortly after coming on, he damaged his ankle and X-rays taken a few days later showed ligament damage. Initially, he was expected to be out for six weeks, but it turned out to be significantly longer.

He eventually had to go under the knife to remove a piece of loose cartilage, but before he did, he managed to make a cameo appearance in Scott Nisbet's testimonial against a Rangers International Select side in May. Nisbet, who had been forced to retire from the game after sustaining a pelvic injury, was honoured in a match that pitched the current crop of Rangers players against a team boasting star players from the past, like

Terry Butcher, Ray Wilkins, and Chris Woods. The current squad edged out the former heroes by three goals to two, with McCoist heading home the winning goal with twenty minutes of the game remaining.

Despite the loss of McCoist and the long-term absences of Mark Hateley, Stuart McCall, Ian Ferguson and John Brown, Rangers still managed to maintain their quest for the championship, and by late March 1995 they had opened up a twelve-point lead over Motherwell at the top of the table. With McCoist and Hateley missing for long spells, much of the onus for scoring goals had been placed on the shoulders of Brian Laudrup, and the Great Dane responded to the task brilliantly, finishing the season with thirteen goals from thirty-eight appearances.

As March 1995 drew to a close, though, football was to be firmly placed in perspective. Tragedy was about to engulf not just Ibrox Stadium but Scottish football as a whole, as a nation mourned the untimely passing of one of its true legends.

CHAPTER TWELVE

COOP: 1956–95

The term 'legend' is frequently overused within the footballing fraternity. Too often players are decorated with the title after one act of brilliance rather than earning the tag by sustaining a high level of performance over a number of years. However, when it comes to describing the late, great Davie Cooper, the label has been well earned and there are few who would argue that the winger is, without a shadow of a doubt, a Scottish football legend. His death from a brain haemorrhage on 23 March 1995 sent shockwaves reverberating around the whole of the country. He was only thirty-nine years of age and had been winding down his successful twenty-year professional career with his first club, Clydebank, a matter of months before his untimely passing. In addition to his two spells at Kilbowie, Cooper had also enjoyed success with Motherwell in the early 1990s, but it is for his twelve-year stint with Rangers that he is best remembered.

Cooper's Rangers adventure began in late September 1976. Jock Wallace and his Treble-winning squad were delighted when the draw for the last eight of the 1976/77 League Cup pitched them against First Division side Clydebank, with the first leg to be played at Ibrox on 22 September and the return leg scheduled for Kilbowie two weeks later.

The Premier League champions were confident ahead of the tie and were made overwhelming favourites to reach the semi-finals of the tournament, with no one reckoning that the Kilbowie outfit, who were top of the First Division at the time of the tie, could prevent Rangers from forging on towards another trophy success. However, thanks to the elusive talents of their young outside-left, the Bankies gave John Greig et al an almighty fright in what developed into a marathon cup-tie.

Davie Cooper, a shy and quiet twenty-year-old from Hamilton, was initially reluctant to enter the footballing profession, preferring to remain in his job as a printer in his hometown, but Clydebank supremo Jack Steedman used his powers of persuasion and the takings from the Clydebank Social Club to convince him to join up at Kilbowie in 1975. In his first season, 1975/76, Clydebank won the Second Division title, and they were riding high at the summit of the First Division when they travelled to Ibrox for the League Cup tie. With confidence high in the Bankies' ranks, the first-leg 'formality' everyone had predicted did not come to pass. Clydebank had the temerity to lead 2-1 at half-time thanks to goals from Larnach and McColl, and although Rangers rallied to lead 3-2 after the interval, a late equaliser from Cooper earned the plucky First Division visitors a 3-3 draw. They stunned Rangers in the second leg too, with Cooper again grabbing an equalising goal to cancel out the goal scored by Rangers captain John Greig. Cooper was a constant thorn in the side of the Rangers defence throughout the tie, teasing and tormenting luminaries such as Sandy Jardine, Greig, Colin Jackson and Tom Forsyth, and his guile earned Clydebank another crack at the Scottish champions.

After extra-time failed to eke out a winner at Kilbowie, a third match was staged at Ibrox twelve days later. Rangers won the coin toss that decided the venue of the replay, but home advantage was no great aid to the Premier League giants, as they stumbled to a no-score draw, with Clydebank goalkeeper Jim Gallacher saving a penalty from Alex Miller. The saga was finally concluded in the fourth game at the neutral venue of Firhill, the home of Partick Thistle. Cooper scored again, equalising an early strike from Derek Parlane, but this time the gallant Bankies could not hold out and winger Bobby McKean scored the winning goal to take a relieved Rangers side into the semi-final. Incidentally, the Light Blues were walloped 5-1 by Aberdeen in the last four, a defeat that meant they had to relinquish one of the trophies they had won the previous season.

Indeed, they would go on to follow the feast of that Treble in 1975/76 by enduring the famine of a barren, trophy-less 1976/77. Clydebank, meanwhile, spurred on in no small part by their performances over the course of the tie, ended the campaign by winning promotion to the Premier Division.

Over the course of those four matches, Cooper had made an indelible impression on not only Rangers manager Jock Wallace but also on the Rangers board, to such an extent that when Wallace approached the directorate the following summer with a request for funds to lure this prodigious genius to Ibrox, they were not slow in coughing up the £100,000 asking price. Cooper, by now part of the Scotland international set-up, had little difficulty in agreeing personal terms and he signed for the 1977/78 season alongside fellow new acquisitions, midfield playmaker Robert Russell from Shettleston Juniors and striker-cum-midfielder Gordon Smith.

This triumvirate were the new blood that Wallace reckoned was needed to reinvigorate and refresh a Rangers squad that had stagnated and failed so miserably in their quest for success during the 1976/77 season. The pressure on such young shoulders was immense, but Cooper revelled in it, and he set about repaying the faith his manager had shown in him by making a success of matters on the field of play. He immediately struck up various fruitful partnerships with his new team-mates, with his relationship with Russell verging on the telepathic.

Cooper's most potent weapon, though, was his quite splendid left foot. With it he could either thread precise passes through the most tight-knit rearguards, or send in tantalising crosses from the left wing, both of which created countless goal-scoring opportunities for strikers Smith, Parlane and Johnstone, who gorged themselves on such a plentiful and accurate supply. At the end of the season, Johnstone had netted thirty-eight goals from forty-seven matches; Smith had twenty goals from fifty-two appearances; with Parlane adding eight from thirty-one games. Cooper was also a magician from a dead-ball situation, capable of either imparting some subtle, cunning swerve and spin on the ball or equally hitting the ball with incredible venom, the latter of which would be illustrated to devastating effect ten years later in Rangers' League Cup final success over Aberdeen at Hampden.

Having scored his first goal in Light Blue at Love Street in September – a thunderous volley with his left foot – Cooper ended his first season at

Ibrox with eight goals to his name and numerous assists for others. One of his octet was the opening goal in the League Cup final success over Celtic when he swept Gordon Smith's low cutback high into the net with that wand of a left foot. Smith later went on to score the winner in extra-time as Rangers took the first step towards reclaiming their Treble with a 2-1 victory. The club proceeded to complete legs two and three, winning the championship by two points from Aberdeen and then vanquishing the same Aberdeen side by two goals to one in the Scottish Cup final. Alex MacDonald and Derek Johnstone were the goal-grabbing heroes.

Cooper was fast becoming a darling of the Ibrox faithful and he was making his mark on the international stage, too. Having won six caps at Under-21 level – four as a Clydebank player and two after he had joined up at Ibrox – he made the step up to the senior squad and won his first full cap in a friendly against Peru at Hampden in September 1979. He won his second cap as a substitute in the European Championships qualifier against Austria the following month, but it would be another four years before he pulled on the Dark Blue jersey again.

In the meantime, the winds of change were blowing through the corridors of Ibrox. Jock Wallace, having just led Rangers to their second Treble in three years, sensationally resigned from his post at the end of the campaign, and John Greig, the club captain, was promoted from the dressing room to the manager's office. Initially, the considerable presence of Wallace was not missed, with Greig coming within nine minutes of securing an unprecedented back-to-back Treble in his first season in charge. His team secured the League Cup with a 2-1 victory over Aberdeen and retained the Scottish Cup, courtesy of a 3-2 second replay win over Hibernian, but the championship was prised from their grasp in dramatic fashion by Celtic.

Rangers travelled to Parkhead for their third last league fixture lying three points adrift of their arch-rivals. Celtic, who were playing in their final match of the season, required a victory in order to extinguish Rangers' title dreams, but Greig's side could afford to draw and still win the championship provided that they picked up points in their final two matches against Partick Thistle and Hibernian.

Rangers drew first blood after nine minutes when Cooper beat two men on the left and crossed for Alex MacDonald to head home. Celtic's Johnny Doyle was then sent off ten minutes after the interval, and although the home side equalised through Roy Aitken and then took the lead courtesy of a goal from George McCluskey, Russell restored parity and put Rangers back into the championship driving seat when he drove the ball into the net after a Cooper corner had broken in his direction. However, an own-goal from Colin Jackson and a strike from Murdo MacLeod right on the stroke of full-time broke Rangers' hearts and handed Celtic the title. It was the nearest Greig would come to lifting Scotland's premier honour in his time in the Ibrox managerial hot seat.

Cooper missed just twelve of the sixty-one competitive matches Rangers played that season and scored ten goals, but by 1980/81 he was starting to find himself increasingly out of favour with Greig. He made a total of forty-six appearances in what turned out to be an abysmal 1979/80 season – Rangers won nothing and finished fifth in the Premier Division – but in 1980/81 he appeared just thirty-six times, with a third of those appearances coming from the substitutes' bench. His form became patchy and inconsistent as he found himself regularly consigned to a place on the sidelines, but when called upon he still had the ability to contribute the odd bit of magic.

Rangers had the opportunity to win some silverware in 1980/81 when they came up against Dundee United in the Scottish Cup final. The match was a dour affair and ended scoreless, with United goalkeeper Hamish McAlpine saving a last-minute Ian Redford penalty with his legs. On the day of the game, Greig had elected to leave Cooper, Derek Johnstone and young striker John MacDonald, the club's second top goalscorer, out of his starting eleven, but the dropped trio were restored when Greig announced his side for the midweek replay. The direct result of their reinstatement was an emphatic 4-1 win for Rangers, with Cooper producing a breathtaking display, one that many observers regard as his finest in a Rangers jersey. He opened the scoring himself and created the other three goals on the night, two of which were scored by MacDonald, with the other netted by Bobby Russell.

Cooper was more of a regular feature in the next two campaigns and was now the shining beacon in a Rangers team that was being sucked into a downward spiral towards a painful spell in the doldrums. He scored another Cup final goal in 1981 when he netted the equaliser with a stunning free-kick in the 1981/82 League Cup final in which Rangers defeated Dundee United 2-1 and, in 1982/83, he found the net eleven times in what turned out to be another trophy-less season for Rangers.

The pressure on John Greig was mounting and he eventually resigned in October 1983. He was replaced by the man who had signed Cooper, Jock Wallace, and the winger enjoyed a successful and almost uninterrupted run in the team after Wallace retook the reins, missing only thirteen matches over the course of the next three seasons. He picked up two League Cup-winners' medals in that timeframe, but Rangers still struggled in the Premier Division and, after a diabolical season in 1985/86, Wallace was sacked and replaced by the club's first-ever player-manager, Graeme Souness.

Souness' arrival finally gave Cooper a platform upon which he could fully exhibit his considerable array of talents. The new manager believed that Cooper was more naturally gifted than Kenny Dalglish and, under his guidance, the winger prospered and discovered the consistent form that had eluded him for so long under both Greig and Wallace.

In Souness' first season, Cooper played in all but two of Rangers' fifty-four matches, scoring eleven times, a goal-scoring haul that included the winner from the penalty spot in the League Cup final against Celtic. He also laid on the title-clinching goal for Terry Butcher at Pittodrie, but Cooper's undoubted highlight of the season was his mesmerising run in a UEFA Cup tie against Ilves Tampere of Finland at Ibrox that took him slaloming past seven defenders before setting up Robert Fleck for a simple tap-in.

Cooper was now in his element. In the four years that preceded the Souness Revolution, he had been part of an extremely mediocre Rangers side, one that was arguably among the worst in the club's history. However, he was now playing alongside players of exceptional quality, and their presence helped coax out the best of the winger's abilities.

One player who profited more than most from Cooper's renaissance was Ally McCoist. When McCoist signed for Rangers in 1983, he immediately struck up a rapport with Cooper both on and off the pitch. On the park, they developed an almost telepathic understanding, with Cooper instinctively knowing where McCoist would make his forward runs, and invariably finding him with the perfect pass or a pinpoint cross, carving open the opposition defence in the process. This weapon, which later became three-pronged as Ian Durrant shot to prominence, would be responsible for numerous Rangers goals over the next few years as the club re-established itself at the summit of the Scottish game. Off the field, both Cooper and McCoist shared a mutual love of horse racing, and they would often be seen either at the races together or chewing over the form guide in the racing press before placing a few bets on that day's card.

Many regarded McCoist and Cooper as something of an odd couple. McCoist was far more outgoing and bubbly in public than the shyer and quieter Cooper, with the latter earning the moniker 'Moody Blue' in sections of the media in his early playing days because of his reluctance to give interviews. Behind closed doors at Ibrox, though, he was an altogether different character. He was much more relaxed and loved nothing more than joining in with the dressing-room wind-ups normally instigated by McCoist or his 'partner in crime' Ian Durrant. Cooper possessed a very dry sense of humour and this was an aspect of his character that few outside the confines of the Rangers dressing room ever saw. In that home dressing room, he was nicknamed 'Albert', with the tag stemming from a television character at the time, Albert Tatlock in *Coronation Street*. Tatlock was the Street's resident moaner and since this was a role that Cooper also assumed in and around Ibrox, either at training or on match days, he was immediately dubbed with the moniker.

Cooper was never the most eager trainer – when one possesses a talent as natural as his, there was little need to work on striving to improve one's game – but he used to revel in bounce matches between the Scottish players in the Rangers squad and those that Souness had imported from England. These games were introduced by Souness and normally took place on a Friday and were designed to hone the players' sharpness ahead of the weekend game. The games were taken very seriously and both teams used to adopt a no-holds-barred approach, and Cooper loved it, using the contests to showcase all the skills he possessed in his armoury. The Scottish side were victorious more often than not, and McCoist, Durrant and Cooper loved getting one over their English team-mates.

It was probably these training games that went a long way towards developing the intuitive relationship the trio managed to transfer so successfully on to the park. 'He used to be ecstatic when we scored another famous victory over the Auld Enemy and although it happened all the time he never got bored with it,' recalled McCoist. 'The games often had a little edge to them as you would expect, but that suited Davie down to the ground and he danced past the English as if they weren't there... I'm sure they [the English contingent] knew a fair bit about Coop before they came north, but they saw him in a different light when they played alongside him. He was a genius.'[1]

Cooper won a third League Championship badge in 1988/89 and another League Cup medal in 1987/88, with his ferociously struck free-kick in the final almost tearing the goal net out of its rigging, but the arrival of Mark Walters in January 1988 effectively relegated him to a supporting role at Ibrox and, in the summer of 1989, at the age of thirty-three, he joined former team-mates Tommy McLean and Bobby Russell at Motherwell.

Cooper made a sum total of 540 appearances in a Light Blue jersey and scored seventy-five goals. In his time at Ibrox, he won three league titles, three Scottish Cups and seven League Cups. He also collected twenty caps for Scotland, and it was his penalty-kick against Wales that earned the Scots a place in the playoff for the 1986 World Cup finals in Mexico. He was on the scoresheet again when Scotland defeated Australia 2-0 in the first-leg of their playoff, and Cooper was the only Rangers player picked for the squad that travelled to the World Cup. He made just two appearances at the finals, though, replacing Eamonn Bannon for the final sixteen minutes of the 2-1 defeat at the hands of West Germany and Steve Nicol after seventy minutes of the final group match against the cynical Uruguayans. Unfortunately, Cooper was unable to create the goal Scotland needed to qualify for the knockout stages, and Alex Ferguson's side were eliminated in the first round.

Although some expected his star to wane after he left Ibrox, Cooper proceeded to enjoy an Indian summer when he joined up at Fir Park. He won a further two Scotland caps to take his total to twenty-two – such a paltry return for one of the most talented Scots of his generation – and was instrumental in Motherwell's victorious Scottish Cup campaign in 1991. He left Motherwell at the end of the 1993/94 season to wind down his career at his first club, Clydebank, and he announced that the new campaign, 1994/95, would be his last as a professional footballer. After retiring he was looking to concentrate on coaching promising youngsters who were coming up through the ranks.

Cooper was actually coaching kids as part of the *Shoot* television series when he collapsed. The show was screened on Saturday lunchtimes and appealed to all ages. Cooper, along with former Arsenal and Celtic star Charlie Nicholas and Celtic coach Tommy Craig, took the enthusiastic youngsters through a series of drills and taught them skills such as dribbling, shooting and taking set-pieces, all of which Cooper was a master of.

The show also illustrated a different side to Cooper, the one he had shown in the Rangers dressing room but very rarely in front of the cameras. He enjoyed sharing a laugh and a joke, and the kids were so used to his clowning around that when he did collapse on that fateful day in March, they thought it was some kind of joke. It soon became apparent, however, that something was seriously wrong. Cooper had suffered a brain haemorrhage and was immediately rushed to the Southern General Hospital in Glasgow where surgeons were soon fighting to save his life. McCoist, who was battling back to fitness at Ibrox when he heard the terrible news, immediately rushed to the hospital to maintain a vigil at his friend's bedside along with Derek Johnstone and Cooper's close family.

Davie battled through the night, but the next morning he lost his fight for life and the neurosurgeon who had tried desperately to revive him broke the news that no one wanted to hear: Cooper was gone. The news sent the football world reeling.

Shortly after the announcement, McCoist, grief stricken, visibly shaken and face tear-stained, conducted a short press conference at Ibrox. The passing of Cooper had clearly devastated the Rangers striker, but he was determined to face the cameras in order to pay tribute to his close friend. 'This is a very distressing time and I'm sure you can all appreciate how we are feeling,' he said. 'It is as though we have lost a brother, someone who was with us and a part of our lives. As a person he was one of the best and he meant so much to myself and the players in the dressing room, and although he was away from the club, I think it is safe to say that he never really left. Our thoughts are with his family.'[2]

McCoist also felt cheated that Cooper had been snatched away from the world at a time when he was on the cusp of giving something back to the game he loved. It was no secret that he was looking to start coaching youngsters and who better to learn from than a man who had been blessed with a unique and special talent.

Ibrox, Fir Park and Kilbowie became Davie Cooper shrines in the days that followed his death. Scarves, football shirts, flowers and messages were placed on the gates at the corner of the Main Stand at Ibrox and the playing surface at Fir Park gave way to a sea of floral tributes. McCoist visited both venues several times. He was joined by hundreds of other mourners. It is something of a sad indictment on the Scottish game that it took such a tragic event to unite all the clubs and their supporters, as tributes poured in not only from Rangers, Motherwell and Clydebank fans, but also from punters the length and breadth of the country. 'The floral tributes, the scarves, the jerseys, the flags were testimony to his popularity,' said McCoist. 'And, surely, the fact that there were so many items put at those gates by fans of other clubs says it all.'[3]

When his funeral was held at Hillhouse Parish Church in Hamilton on 27 March 1995, the streets of the town were mobbed, as an estimated 10,000 fans stood to watch this icon make his final journey. Each of Scotland's forty senior clubs were represented at the service, and luminaries of the Scottish game, past and present, were among the 350 mourners to pack into the church.

During the service, McCoist delivered an emotional tribute to his great friend. He had initially been nervous and apprehensive about delivering the eulogy, fearing he would break down in tears as he recalled the memories Davie had left him and many others with, but he showed great courage and maintained his composure as he bid a final farewell. He told the congregation and those that stood in silence outside – the service was relayed to the crowd that had gathered via a tannoy system – that on the morning of the funeral he had cradled his eight-week-old son in his arms and told him all about Cooper, and he spoke of the sadness he felt that young Alexander would only be able to marvel at Cooper's consummate talents on video. He also recalled a magical Cooper moment from a match against Hearts, when the winger had danced his way beyond five defenders before playing a perfect pass to McCoist, who was left with a simple chance to score. 'I went off on my usual celebrations – a few somersaults and waves to the crowd,' recalled McCoist. 'Then I felt a tap on my shoulder and looked round. It was Davie and he said, "Was the Mitre the right way up for you Coisty!"'[4]

McCoist also remembered how he had looked up to Cooper when he had initially joined up at Ibrox. 'When I arrived in 1983, Davie Cooper was already an established superstar and I was the youngster,' he said. 'I watched and learned from him. I would have liked to have copied him, but that was mission impossible. Davie also taught me the importance of strength of character.'[5] He then concluded what many called 'the most moving tribute of the day'[6] by saying that Cooper was: 'a remarkable talent and a fine, fine man. God bless you, Davie.'[7]

The memories of Davie Cooper will never fade. He was a Brazilian genius in a Scotsman's body. When Rangers announced their Greatest

Ever XI in 1999, as voted for by their supporters, it came as no surprise that Cooper was in it. On the same evening he came third in a poll to ascertain who was the greatest Rangers player of all time, and his unforgettable goal against Celtic in the 1979 Dryborough Cup final – a piece of individual brilliance that saw him juggle the ball through the Celtic defence before despatching a shot behind Peter Latchford – was bestowed with the honour of being the club's greatest-ever goal.

Aside from the multitude of memories Cooper showcased to football fans, there is a lasting memorial to Davie Cooper in his hometown of Hamilton. It is a bronze statue which has Cooper, dressed in his Scotland kit, in a typical pose, head up, seeking out that killer pass with the ball naturally tied to that mesmerising left foot. It overlooks the Palace Sports Grounds and was unveiled in March 1999, four years after his untimely passing, by McCoist and the Lord Provost of North Lanarkshire Council. 'I swear to God, I don't think I have ever been so proud in my life than to be asked to unveil that statue,' said McCoist after the unveiling.[8]

The statue is a fitting tribute to the wizard of the wing, Davie Cooper, a true Scottish legend.

CHAPTER THIRTEEN

THE LAST CHANCE SALOON: 1995–96

For Ally McCoist, the 1995/96 season was arguably his most significant in a Rangers jersey. With only one year left on his existing contract and having only appeared a meagre nine times during the previous campaign, he knew he would have to put his injury troubles behind him, win his place back in the starting line-up and get among the goals if he was going to secure a new deal that would keep him at Ibrox for the rest of his career. There was also the small matter of his notching up his 300th goal for the club. His only strike of the previous campaign, against Aberdeen, had been his 299th competitive goal for Rangers, so he was desperate to rack up another strike to join Jimmy Smith in the select band of players who had scored over 300 goals for the Light Blues.

Unfortunately his preparations for the new campaign did not get off to the best of starts. After recovering from the surgery on his ankle, McCoist looked set to join up with his team-mates for the start of pre-season training until he picked up a knee injury that ruled him out of the three-match tour of Denmark. It was a bitter blow and yet another impediment in his quest for the match fitness that had deserted him since his leg break in 1993. His absence also meant he would have to wait before getting the opportunity to team up with Rangers' latest recruit, one Paul John Gascoigne.

Despite cantering to the 1994/95 Premier Division championship – Rangers won their seventh successive title by a distance, fifteen points in advance of second-placed Motherwell – Walter Smith bolstered his squad yet again in an attempt to sustain the momentum that was building towards equalling old foes Celtic's record of nine League Championships in a row. Although the playing pool at Ibrox was already overflowing with an abundance of quality, Smith made four new signings. Gordan Petric, an experienced centre-half with a good pedigree, signed from Dundee United at a cost of £1.5 million, while Russian international Oleg Salenko, who had shot to prominence the previous summer by scoring five goals in a World Cup finals match against Cameroon, cost £2.5 million from Valencia. Stephen Wright, a fine young full-back, also came on board from Aberdeen, but there was no doubt that the most significant purchase of the summer had been that of Gascoigne. ·

The mercurial midfielder joined the Light Blues in a £4.3 million deal after having endured an injury-ravaged spell in Italy with Lazio. The move was something of a coup for Rangers as many of the English Premiership's leading lights had also sought his signature, but Gascoigne had struck up something of a rapport with Walter Smith following a chance meeting in Florida in 1993 and elected to snub a return to the Premiership, opting instead to ply his trade in Scotland and open what ultimately proved a thrilling chapter in his turbulent career.

While McCoist was back in Scotland, Gascoigne and Rangers got their season off to a fine start, winning two and drawing one of the three matches they played in Brian Laudrup's homeland. The Geordie genius netted on his debut, a 2-1 victory over Brondby, and scored again with a sumptuous free-kick in the final match of the tour, a 2-1 win over Hvidovre. Meanwhile, in the slightly less salubrious surroundings of Paisley's Kibble training ground, McCoist was back in action, playing ninety minutes for the reserves during their 4-1 defeat to St Mirren. James McGuire stole the limelight with four goals for the Buddies, but McCoist boosted his confidence by grabbing a consolation goal twenty minutes from time.

Two days later, he was back in the first-team frame, as Rangers once again hosted the Ibrox International Tournament, with holders Sampdoria joining the hosts, Steaua Bucharest and Tottenham Hotspur for the two-day event. McCoist was listed among the substitutes for the opening match against Romanian cracks Steaua, and by the time he was introduced to the action, with nineteen minutes remaining, Rangers were already strolling in the sunshine, leading by three goals to nil following goals from Ian Ferguson, Paul Gascoigne and Mark Hateley. And McCoist joined them on the scoresheet in the eighty-third minute when he pounced on a defensive error to head the ball into the net. Rangers place in the final was sealed, and in some style.

There they faced Sampdoria – the Italians had defeated Spurs 2-0 to qualify – and Rangers claimed the silverware with a fine 2-0 win. Gordon Durie handed them the lead six minutes before half-time and McCoist, who replaced Laudrup at the interval, completed the scoring ten minutes from the end, taking a pass from Durie and beating Walter Zenga with a good right-foot finish. There were no ill-effects from his time on the pitch, and the goals breathed new life into his flagging spirits. 'With run-outs against Bucharest and Sampdoria I'm feeling good and I know there's a few goals left in me,' he said. 'Within myself I'm feeling pretty confident and optimistic about the season ahead.'[1]

McCoist completed his pre-season training with another forty-five-minute appearance in a 4-0 victory over Clyde, and he was on the bench again when the competitive action started with the visit of Cypriot champions Anorthosis Famagusta for the first leg of the European Champions League qualifier. Rangers, unbeaten in the seven friendlies they had played during pre-season, struggled to break down their opponents' stubborn defensive resistance, but a second-half strike from substitute Gordon Durie handed the home side a slender 1-0 lead to take to the holiday island a fortnight later.

Although he was yet to play a competitive match for Rangers, McCoist's good pre-season form had not gone unnoticed, and national coach Craig Brown gave him a call-up to the Scotland squad for the crucial European Championships qualifier with Greece at Hampden on 16 August. McCoist started the match on the bench but, deep into the second half, with the Scots struggling to break down a resolute Greek rearguard, he was pitched into action, replacing Aberdeen's Duncan Shearer after seventy-one minutes to win his forty-seventh cap.

It was his first appearance in Scotland colours since that fateful night when he had broken his leg in Lisbon over two years previously and, within seconds of his arrival, he marked his return by getting his name on the scoresheet, glancing a header beyond the Greek goalkeeper Ilias Atmatzidis to give the Scots a priceless 1-0 victory. It was his sixteenth goal for his country and took him past the record of the distinguished former Rangers forward R.C. Hamilton, who had netted fifteen goals in Dark Blue in the late nineteenth and early twentieth century. McCoist was now Rangers' top goalscorer for his country, and he told the *Rangers News*: 'I had no idea I was anywhere near becoming Rangers' top Scotland goalscorer, but I'm thrilled to bits with the news. It's another milestone for me and I always enjoy reaching new targets.'[2]

After two years of torment brought on by numerous injuries, the goal came as a huge boost for McCoist and it provided yet another defiant riposte to all those who had written off his chances of returning to top-flight football. 'People didn't realise the feelings they hurt when they were saying that was my career over,' said McCoist. 'It was very cruel but, really, I loved it. I can't describe the feeling when I saw the ball sail into the net against Greece. It really was the release of two years' worth of tension.'[3]

However, McCoist was adamant that his goal against Greece did not automatically signal an end to the dark days induced by his injury nightmares. He knew there was still a long way to go before he attained full fitness, but at least the shaft of light at the end of the tunnel was growing larger with each passing day.

His international exploits were rewarded at club level when Walter Smith included him in the starting line-up the following Saturday when lowly Morton came to Ibrox in the second round of the League Cup. It was the first time since 4 December that Ally had tugged his favourite number nine jersey over his head, and he wasted no time in resuming normal service, taking just nine minutes to vindicate his manager's decision to select him. He maintained his rich vein of scoring form when he picked up a pass from Charlie Miller, spun round and drove the ball beyond David Wyllie in the Morton goal to hit the net for the 300th time in a Rangers jersey.

Mark Hateley and Paul Gascoigne completed a comfortable 3-0 victory for Rangers and, after the match, Hateley was full of praise for his striking buddy. He said: 'It was a typical Ally goal and he's been doing that kind of thing ever since I came here. When I first arrived he was just a predator, but he's added so much to his game and now combines and links up well. You never stop learning in this game and Alistair is very smart in that respect. It was nice to have him playing through the middle with me. That has been our forte for a few years and I am sure there are plenty more goals left in him yet.'[4]

McCoist was relegated to the bench for Rangers' next outing, the return leg of the Champions League qualifier against Anorthosis, and he looked on as the Scottish champions ground out a 0-0 draw to qualify for the group stages. The closing stages of a closely fought encounter gave rise to a rather amusing moment. In a bid to run down the clock, McCoist was stripped for action, but as he waited on the touchline for the ball to go dead, Ian Durrant tweaked his hamstring, prompting the Rangers management team to rethink their planned alteration. Instead of introducing McCoist, defensive midfielder Neil Murray took over from Durrant, thus robbing McCoist of the cash bounty on offer to each player should they secure a place in the Champions League. In order to qualify for the bonus payment, a player had to have taken part in the action at some point over the course of the two legs, but with McCoist also an unused substitute at Ibrox, he failed to meet the criteria. He later jokingly referred to Durrant's injury as the most expensive in the history of the game!

McCoist quickly bounced back, however, and was named in the team for the opening league encounter against Kilmarnock, and in the next match against Stirling Albion, in the third round of the League Cup, he demonstrated his continued liking for the competition with another well-taken goal. Having struck the top of the crossbar with a deft chip in the first half, McCoist added to earlier strikes from Hateley and McCall when he finished neatly from 10 yards to put the home side 3-0 ahead. It proved a vital goal too, as Stirling scored twice in the closing ten minutes to set hearts fluttering in the Rangers ranks.

McCoist was rewarded for his goal-scoring start to the season when he was named as the Bell's Player of the Month for August, and he promptly demonstrated why he had won the award by opening his league account for the season in a 4-0 drubbing of Raith Rovers at Ibrox at the start of September. He scored twice against the Kirkcaldy outfit, heading home a fine cross from Laudrup after sixteen minutes before completing the scoring three minutes from time when he poked the ball into the net following good work by Gascoigne. 'Mr Goals' was indeed back with a bang, and his goals must have had the bookmakers in a sweat; at the outset of the season they had quoted staggering odds of 12-1 for the double Golden Boot winner to finish as top scorer in the Premier Division!

The emphatic victory over Raith got what was a hugely important month off to a great start for Rangers. Before the end of September, they were due to travel to Parkhead to face Celtic twice, and Smith's men were also scheduled to rendezvous in Bucharest to take on Romanian champions Steaua Bucharest in their opening Champions League fixture. The latter trip ended in disappointment, with McCoist and his team-mates drawing a blank as the Romanian champions won 1-0, thus avenging the 4-0 pre-season drubbing they had suffered in the Ibrox Tournament three months earlier, but the two journeys to Parkhead proved much more fruitful.

The first visit, on 19 September, was for the quarter-final of the League Cup and marked the first Old Firm clash at the newly renovated Parkhead. Celtic had finished a disappointing fourth in the 1994/95 Premier Division table, and their followers hoped that the new surroundings and hulking great stands would signal a revival in their fortunes, but the 32,789 patrons who turned up hoping to celebrate a triumphant homecoming went home disappointed when the visitors gate-crashed the party.

A keenly fought contest was delicately poised at 0-0 with fifteen minutes remaining when Gascoigne flighted a splendid cross to the far post where the predatory McCoist rose to direct a header beyond Gordon Marshall in the Celtic goal. It was McCoist's twenty-fourth goal against Celtic, edging him yet closer to Jimmy McGrory's record of twenty-seven goals in Old Firm fixtures, and he was quick to pay tribute to the architect after the match, saying: 'It was a brilliant ball from Gazza for the goal. He floated it to the back post and that was the only way the ball could reach me. It was just perfect.'[5]

However, before Rangers returned to the East End to contest the second instalment of the September Old Firm double header, their league challenge suffered a setback when they lost 1-0 at home to Hibernian, a result that toppled them from their perch at the top of the league table. There was disappointment in the Champions League too, when Borussia Dortmund left Glasgow with a point following a 2-2 draw at Ibrox. Rangers twice battled back from a goal down, courtesy of headers from Gough and Ferguson, but Juventus' 3-0 win over Steaua meant that, after the opening two matches, the Light Blues were anchored to the foot of Group C.

McCoist failed to score in both games, but when Rangers returned to the home of their arch-rivals on league business on the last day of the month, he played a significant role in the outcome. The defeat at the hands of Hibernian had allowed Celtic to leapfrog their rivals in the league table, and they enjoyed the better of the first-half exchanges too, with both Pierre van Hooijdonk and Rudi Vata testing Andy Goram early in the match. However, as had so often been the case in this celebrated era, Rangers absorbed everything Celtic could throw at them before striking a killer blow a minute before the interval. The goal came from an unlikely source, full-back Alex Cleland, who got his head on the end of a cross from Salenko to net his first goal in a Rangers jersey.

The timing and execution of the goal was perfect, and it took the wind out of Celtic's sails. They were not as fluent after the interval, and the Light Blues wrapped up the points eleven minutes after the restart. Alan McLaren fielded a Celtic corner with a thumping clearance to the halfway line where McCoist headed the ball on to Salenko. As McCoist's hand had been raised when he met the ball, howls of 'handball' cascaded down from the Parkhead rafters, but referee John Rowbotham allowed play to continue and McCoist latched on to a return pass from Salenko before releasing a delightful through-ball to the on-rushing Gascoigne. The midfielder remained calm and lifted the ball over the diving Marshall to net his first league goal in Light Blue and he celebrated with gusto in front of the delighted travelling support shoehorned into the corner of the new Parkhead grandstand. His strike signalled a mass exodus, as a Celtic support that had spent the afternoon hounding him with chants about his fondness for pies headed for home to nurse the pain of a second Old Firm defeat inside a fortnight.

McCoist's role in Gascoigne's winning goal had showed another side to his game; one which he was very rarely given credit for. Although he had built his reputation on scoring rather than creating goals, he had the ability on occasion to execute a killer pass, as he demonstrated to great effect at Parkhead.

However, just when things were starting to look up for the effervescent striker, the spectre of injury that had haunted him for over two years looked set to strike him down once again. Three days after the success at Parkhead, the newly installed league leaders welcomed Motherwell to Ibrox, and Gascoigne continued where he had left off by grabbing the opening goal after just ten minutes. However, Motherwell, dogged as ever, equalised seven minutes after half-time through Shaun McSkimming. They were on level terms for just sixteen minutes, though, as McCoist ended a four-match goal drought when he met substitute Ian Durrant's free-kick with a wonderful header that flashed into the net to secure all three points for Walter Smith's side. Unfortunately, McCoist's joy was short-lived as, just five minutes after scoring, he injured his abductor muscle and had to be replaced by Neil Murray.

His absence was not a lengthy one, however, and although he missed the next league match, a 1-0 win over Aberdeen at Pittodrie, he was back in action the following weekend when he replaced hat-trick hero Gordon Durie for the final six minutes of a comfortable 4-0 victory against Partick at Firhill. His return was a timely one, with mouth-watering back-to-back clashes with Juventus in the Champions League on the horizon, and when Rangers took to the field in the Stadio Delle Alpi four days after the win over Thistle, McCoist was back in his familiar striking position alongside Oleg Salenko.

Rangers were looking to build on the point they had picked up in their second Group C encounter with Borussia Dortmund and haul themselves off the bottom of the section, but after only twenty-two minutes in Turin humiliation looked to be on the menu as the visitors found themselves 3-0 down. It is often said that 'hell hath no fury like a woman scorned' and Juventus, known as the Old Lady of Italian Football, demonstrated this to devastating effect. Three days before Rangers' visit, Marcello Lippi's men had slipped to their first defeat of the season, going down 2-1 to AC Milan in the San Siro, and the Scottish champions found themselves on the receiving end of a ferocious backlash, as they were torn apart by the lavish talents of Fabrizio Ravenelli and Alessandro Del Piero, with the latter the chief torturer.

Juve's favourite son won the free-kick that was converted by Ravenelli for the opening goal after fourteen minutes, and after Antonio Conte had made it 2-0, Del Piero got in on the act himself, firing in an unstoppable shot that arced into the postage stamp top corner of Andy Goram's goal. Rangers were in disarray, but the introduction of the redoubtable John Brown at half-time helped restore order to the ranks, and although Old Firm hero Alex Cleland was dismissed for a crude foul on Del Piero, Rangers shipped only one more goal in the second half, with Ravenelli netting his second of the evening with seventeen minutes to go. Richard Gough reduced the arrears with a goal in the seventy-eighth minute, but it proved scant consolation on a night when the Scottish champions were completely outclassed.

In the face of such an attacking barrage, McCoist spent most of the evening stiffening up the defensive barrier and had little or no impact on proceedings in an attacking sense. As he was still trying to shake off the effects of the abductor injury, he was relegated to the bench for Rangers' next match, a Gascoigne-inspired 4-1 win over Hearts at Ibrox, and although he returned to the starting eleven for the defeat at the hands of Aberdeen in the last four of the League Cup and a 2-2 draw with Raith in the league, he was back among the substitutes for Rangers' next fixture, the return match against Juventus. The Ibrox encounter with *Lo Bianconneri* (the White and Blacks) gave rise to more humiliation, though, as Rangers, admittedly some way short of their strongest eleven, with the likes of Gascoigne and Laudrup absent through injury, were whipped 4-0 to effectively end any lingering hopes they may have had of qualifying for the next phase of the tournament.

McCoist helped cure the European hangover, though, when he returned to the starting line-up for the visit of Falkirk three days later, netting twice to secure a 2-0 win and taking his tally for the season to eight. His goals in the thirty-third and forty-first minutes helped maintain Rangers' momentum in the chase for their eighth successive championship, but they would have to do so without the services of Mark Hateley.

The Englishman had quit the club at the end of September to link up with former Rangers midfielder Ray Wilkins at Queens Park Rangers, and his exit split what many believe to have been the finest striking partnership in Rangers' rich history. Although both he and McCoist had been blighted by injury in recent times, the years of 1991, 1992 and 1993, when both players were at the peak of their powers, had been a golden period, with the duo netting a remarkable 140 goals between them.

During his time at Ibrox, McCoist partnered over twenty strikers in attack, but his union with Hateley was undoubtedly the most successful. They forged an almost telepathic understanding, and Hateley likened their relationship to being something akin to a marriage, with each player getting to learn each other's habits. Reflecting on the partnership, he said: 'The time that Ally had on the bench [in the 1990/91 season] let him see the way I played. That's why when we did become a partnership we were very successful very quickly. You will never get another striking partnership that will emulate that in the modern game, because players move around so much. To score the goals we did in that space of time won't happen again.'[6]

Both players had benefited from their time together, and McCoist was quick to acknowledge the role Hateley had played in his development as a player. Before he had teamed up with the Englishman, he was widely acknowledged as being a predator, an out-and-out goalscorer who did all his work inside the penalty area. However, as his partnership with Hateley blossomed, McCoist added many more dimensions to his game, such as improving his link-up play and his work-rate outside the box. It was a quid pro quo partnership, though, and by playing alongside McCoist, Hateley became a little more selfish inside the eighteen-yard box, and the barrow load of goals the duo delivered for Rangers helped propel the club through arguably the most successful era in their history.

Two weeks after his double against Falkirk, the second of which left him only five goals short of Bob McPhail's all-time record of 230 league goals for Rangers, McCoist reached yet another milestone in his Rangers career. Appearance number 499 against Kilmarnock at Rugby Park had ended prematurely – with McCoist retiring hurt with four minutes remaining – and as a result he started the match against Aberdeen at Ibrox on the bench. But when he replaced Alexei Mikhailitchenko in the sixty-third minute, he joined luminaries like Dougie Gray, John Greig and Sandy Jardine in the select band of players to have made 500 or more appearances in a Light Blue jersey. 'Not many players can boast playing 500 games at the top level, never mind with Rangers, so I am as proud as punch to reach it,' said McCoist when reflecting on reaching such a momentous milestone.[7]

His 501st game for the club was the third Old Firm match of the season, and it turned out to be quite a game as the old foes served up a six-goal thriller at Ibrox. David Robertson had a goal controversially ruled out before Brian Laudrup marked his return from a lengthy spell on the sidelines when he scored after thirty-nine minutes to equalise Andreas Thom's early strike, but a John Collins penalty put Celtic back in front six minutes into the second half.

McCoist, who had once again started the match on the substitutes' bench, replaced Ian Ferguson sixty seconds after Rangers fell behind and, in typical McCoist style, he maintained his knack of netting against the Hoops when he fashioned an equaliser a matter of minutes after taking to the field. Gascoigne's delivery from a free-kick was, as always, immaculate and McCoist rose above John Hughes to head powerfully into the net and haul the home side level. Remarkably for a player not renowned for his aerial prowess, it was the seventh time McCoist had hit the net with a header since the start of the season.

It was turning out to be a thrilling afternoon at the office, with the pulsating action rolling from end to end and rekindling memories of the epic joust these two titans had served up back in 1986. It had ended 4-4 then, and this contest was every bit as absorbing, with Goram, so often the scourge of Celtic, pulling off a quite outstanding save to keep out a point-blank range volley from van Hooijdonk before Rangers hit the front for the first time with twenty minutes remaining. Salenko's cross from the left was measured for McCoist who, stationed in front of an unguarded goal, would have had a tap-in, but the ball did not reach him, as Tosh McKinlay lunged in to intervene. Alas, although he prevented McCoist from eclipsing Sandy McMahon's total of twenty-five Old Firm goals, McKinlay wound up diverting the ball beyond his own goalkeeper to inadvertently hand Rangers a 3-2 lead.

In the end, the spoils were shared when van Hooijdonk eventually formulated a way of beating Goram to tie the match up at 3-3. The result was enough to keep the home side on top of the league, but their Old Firm rivals were still hanging on to their coat-tails, lying four points behind in second place.

Having spent three games out of the starting line-up, McCoist was reinstated to the first eleven for the visit of Steaua Bucharest for the penultimate Champions League match. Rangers still had an outside chance of making it through to the next phase of the competition, but despite taking the lead through a wonderful solo goal from Gascoigne, a fifty-second-minute goal from Damian Militaru earned the visitors a 1-1 draw. McCoist, still seeking his first-ever Champions League goal, could well have secured the points for Rangers six minutes earlier when he almost netted with yet another header, but he was denied by the Romanian custodian Bogdan Stelea, who managed to get across his goal to parry the Rangers centre-forward's attempt to safety. The 1-1 draw signalled Rangers' elimination from the tournament, but in the end, the result at Ibrox made no impact on the final outcome of the group, as Dortmund's 2-1 victory over a weakened Juventus took them out of the reach of the Scottish champions.

With the passports back in the drawer for another year, Rangers returned to domestic duty the following weekend with a trip to the capital to face Hibernian, and McCoist notched his tenth goal of the season when he opened the scoring after fourteen minutes. An own-goal from Darren Dods and strikes from Charlie Miller and Gordon Durie secured a fine 4-1 victory, and when Rangers journeyed east on the M8 again a week later to face Hearts they completed the 'double' over the Edinburgh sides courtesy of a 2-0 triumph over the Jambos. McCoist, thriving on the supply from the supremely talented boots of Gascoigne and Laudrup, chalked up Rangers' opener at Tynecastle, slotting in a penalty after Stevie Fulton had illegally halted Laudrup's run into the box. It was an important goal for the striker: it marked his 250th goal in Scottish League football.

The goal also took him a step closer to Bob McPhail's landmark total of 230 league goals for Rangers, and although delighted to notch his 250th league goal overall, there was no doubt what record he was gunning for. 'I've made no secret of the fact that Mr McPhail's record is the one I want,' he told the *Rangers News*. 'But to reach the 250 league goal mark is a tremendous boost for me. I'm very pleased with my eleven goals so far this season, and if I can stay clear of injury there is no doubt in my mind that there are plenty more goals left in me.'[8]

However, a calf injury picked up in the 1-0 win over Partick Thistle at Ibrox, interrupted McCoist's quest for McPhail's record. The injury kept him out of the side for four matches, including Rangers' biggest win of the season, a 7-0 thrashing of Hibernian in which Gordon Durie scored four goals, but he was back in the firing line alongside the prolific Durie early in January when Rangers visited bottom-of-the-table Falkirk. After

Durie had given Rangers an early lead, McCoist scored twice and David Robertson added another as Rangers cantered to a 4-0 win and, in the process, racked up their seventh successive clean sheet.

McCoist's second goal, a penalty in the seventy-fourth minute, was his 230th league goal for the club and he had now equalled Bob McPhail's cherished fifty-seven-year-old league goals landmark. It would only take seven days before he made the record his own. The opposition on the historic day were Raith Rovers, and with the current record holder, aged eighty-nine, watching from his vantage point in the director's box, McCoist took a mere twenty-one minutes to score the goal he craved. He received a pass from David Robertson on the left-hand side of the penalty area and unleashed a superb curling shot with his right foot that sailed into the net.

It certainly wasn't a typical McCoist goal (he tended to do his best work somewhat nearer the goal), but it was followed for the 231st time by the characteristic goal-scoring grin as Ibrox rose to acclaim their hero. Thus, he had once again woven his name into the rich fabric that makes up the tapestry of Rangers Football Club, and it is unlikely the record will ever be eclipsed, thus guaranteeing McCoist a permanent place in the annals of this magnificent footballing institution. 'I honestly don't believe I'll fully appreciate holding the record until maybe four or five years down the line when I've stopped playing,' gushed McCoist. 'I don't know if it will be beaten in the near future; it's certainly a record that probably I'm as proud of as I am of anything I've achieved in the game.'[9]

January also marked the end of the short-lived Rangers career of Oleg Salenko. The Russian, who had scored seven times in fourteen appearances for the club, found it difficult to settle in Scotland and was transferred to Istanbulspor in Turkey in exchange for Dutch international Peter van Vossen. The Dutchman made his debut as a substitute when Hearts visited Ibrox, but it was not to be a happy introduction, as Rangers, missing their newly crowned record league goalscorer through a recurrence of his calf injury, were humbled 3-0 by the Tynecastle side. Allan Johnston scored a hat-trick, the first goals Rangers had shipped in the league since 25 November, and the defeat allowed Celtic to slash the gap at the top of the table to only one point.

A week later, Rangers came back with all guns blazing, thumping non-league Keith 10-1 in the third round of the Scottish Cup, with hat-tricks coming from the unlikely sources of Alex Cleland and Ian Ferguson. McCoist was missing once again and he was also absent when a double from Gascoigne secured a 2-1 win over Partick Thistle at Firhill. But he returned to the fold in typical fashion when Motherwell came to Ibrox on 10 February. With the teams locked at 2-2 after seventy-two minutes, McCoist was summoned from the bench, and five minutes after replacing van Vossen, he ensured the three points remained at Ibrox when he scored from the penalty spot, sending Motherwell keeper Scott Howie the wrong way after Gascoigne had been felled in the penalty area. With Celtic spilling two points following a draw with Falkirk, McCoist's penalty ensured the margin at the summit had now stretched to three points with ten games remaining.

McCoist remained on the substitutes' bench for the next two matches, vital away victories at Pittodrie (1-0) and Easter Road (2-0), but off the field he was celebrating the release of his second video. Following on from the success of *Super Ally – The McCoist Phenomenon* – a production that had sold something in the region of 40,000 copies – was *The Real McCoist*, a film that crammed in not only the considerable achievements of his last four years on the field but also gave a fascinating insight into McCoist's private life, featuring a tour of his personal trophy room and interviews with his wife Allison and footage of baby Alexander. The video had actually been due for release in April 1995, but the tragic death of Davie Cooper, who features in the video, saw the project put on hold. Fittingly, the production is dedicated to the memory of McCoist's great friend.

Back on the field, Celtic visited Ibrox in mid-March for the final Old Firm match of the season. With only three points separating the two rivals at the head of the Premier Division title race, the outcome of the game would have a significant bearing on the final destination of the League Championship trophy. McCoist, who had enjoyed his first start since suffering his niggling calf injury eight days earlier in a 3-0 win over Inverness Caledonian Thistle in the last eight of the Scottish Cup, spearheaded the Rangers attack, but it was centre-back Alan McLaren who handed the home side the lead with a header late in the first half.

It was a lead they held until three minutes from time when John Hughes popped up to score a dramatic equaliser for ten-man Celtic – Jackie McNamara had been dismissed for a second bookable offence ten minutes earlier – to leave honours even at 1-1. Rangers perhaps should have won the match, with McCall striking the bar and McCoist blazing a good chance into the stands in a frenetic closing period, but although disappointed to have relinquished their lead so late in the day, Smith and his players knew that the destiny of the championship was now firmly in their own hands. Celtic would have to rely on the other teams taking points from Rangers if they were to end their rivals' quest for eight championships in a row.

By the time Falkirk visited Ibrox the following weekend, Smith had further strengthened his forward line, acquiring the gangly Danish striker Erik Bo Andersen from Aalborg for £1.5 million. The Dane had made his second appearance in Light Blue in the Falkirk match and helped himself to two goals as the home side stuttered their way to a 3-2 victory. The manner of the victory mattered little, though, when news filtered through that Celtic had dropped a further two points in a 0-0 draw with Motherwell at Fir Park. The result meant Rangers had stretched their lead over their nearest challengers to five points with only six games remaining.

With time fast running out for Celtic, their fading title hopes were almost given the kiss of life when Rangers travelled to Starks Park to face Raith Rovers on 30 March. With Celtic facing a tricky home game against third-placed Aberdeen, Rangers travelled to Fife looking to extend their lead yet further, but with seven minutes remaining the opposite scenario looked like being on the cards. Having fallen behind to a goal from Peter Duffield after half an hour, McCoist hauled Rangers level nine minutes later, converting a penalty after Bo Andersen had been impeded in the box, but Raith went in front with a penalty of their own in the sixty-eighth minute and they held the 2-1 advantage as the game entered its final stages. However, just when it looked as if Rangers were going to slip up, McCoist stepped up to the plate. In the eighty-third minute, Gascoigne's corner was met by Petric and his header was knocked into the net by the head of the predatory McCoist to restore parity at 2-2.

With their tails up, Rangers pushed for a winner and McCoist, having been released by a sublime pass from Gascoigne, was denied his hat-trick when Bobby Geddes produced a stunning save to stop his volley, and the home keeper was at it again from the resulting corner, tipping a blistering Petric shot over the crossbar. It looked like the reflexes of the veteran Geddes were going to blow the race for the championship wide open, but this battling Rangers side were not to be denied and when Gascoigne's corner broke in the six-yard box, McCoist pounced to snatch his third goal of the game and seize all three points for Rangers. Durie added some shine to the final score when he notched a fourth from the penalty spot in injury-time, but the afternoon undoubtedly belonged to McCoist. 'Today showed what Ally is all about, he's the best goalscorer around,' reflected Walter Smith after the match. 'If it hadn't been for injuries in the past few seasons, he would always have been in my team.'[10]

It was yet another of those afternoons on which Ally McCoist confounded the critics, as his treble strike kept Rangers on course for the title and took his personal goal tally for the season to eighteen. He also struck it lucky with the bookies, too; his each-way bet for the Grand National, Sir Peter Leley, came home in fourth place at odds of 33-1! The answer to one burning question remained, though: why had a man as goal hungry as he was passed up the opportunity to score his fourth goal of the afternoon when Rangers were awarded a penalty in injury-time? 'The reason is simple,' said McCoist. 'Jukebox [Gordon Durie] and I have both bet Gazza £50 that Durie will win the goal-scoring race between them. And thanks to me Gordon is now three up on him.'[11]

McCoist, who had entered the Scottish Football Association Hall of Fame three days before the Raith match when he won his fiftieth cap for Scotland (the momentous occasion was duly marked with the winning goal against Australia), was rewarded for his heroics in Fife when he was named Player of the Month for March by the league sponsors Bells. Next on the agenda were his favourite opponents, Celtic.

In tandem with their success in the league race, Rangers were also progressing well in the Scottish Cup, and the weekend after roaring back to defeat Raith they faced up against Celtic at Hampden in the semi-final. The match was eagerly anticipated, with both teams in top form: Rangers had only lost three times in domestic competition all season, while Celtic had gone one better, only registering a paltry two defeats thus far. Significantly, though, those two losses had come at the hands of Rangers, with the blue half of Glasgow holding the upper hand in the Old Firm battles, having secured the only win in the four league matches – the other three contests had ended in draws – and having also claimed the scalp of the Bhoys in the League Cup at the quarter-final stage.

After a slow start, the Cup semi-final, played out in front of a crowd of 36,333, certainly lived up to its billing. Rangers enjoyed the early ascendancy, and McCoist should have scored when Gascoigne put him in the clear in the sixteenth minute, but he dwelt on the ball too long and the danger was cleared. He made amends for passing up such a golden opportunity, though, when Rangers drew first blood three minutes before the interval. Gordon Marshall in the Celtic goal could only parry a David Robertson drive and when the ball spun loose into McCoist's domain in the six-yard area, the Rangers number nine reacted quickest and took great delight in rolling the ball into the net.

Twenty-four minutes later, Laudrup effectively ended the contest when he linked up delightfully with Durie before racing clear and lobbing the ball over the out-rushing Marshall to put Rangers two ahead. Although van Hooijdonk scored late in the day to half the winning margin, it was a mere consolation as Rangers deservedly progressed through to the final and kept themselves on course for the Double.

However, perhaps chickens were counted too early in the wake of the success in the semi-final, as Rangers stumbled to only their third league defeat of the season in their very next fixture, going down 2-0 to Hearts at Tynecastle. Mercifully, Celtic missed the opportunity to crank up the pressure at the top, though, as they too slipped up, only managing a 1-1 draw at home to Kilmarnock. Rangers duly took heed of this wake-up call and when they hammered Partick Thistle 5-0 at Ibrox they only needed to secure six points from their remaining three league matches to be crowned champions.

Injury had counted McCoist out of the Thistle match, and he was an unused substitute when the first three of the required six points were gathered at Fir Park, with goals from McCall, Bo Andersen and Gascoigne securing a 3-1 win over Motherwell. It meant that victory over Aberdeen the following Sunday would make matters official and Rangers would be crowned champions of Scotland for the forty-sixth time. The match at Ibrox would be a personal triumph for the wayward genius that is Paul Gascoigne.

His debut season in Glasgow had been a resounding success. Despite incurring the wrath of referees on several occasions (he found his name etched in their little black book a staggering seventeen times), he had captivated audiences the length and breadth of the country with his inspirational displays. He had bobbed and weaved his way beyond countless defenders and laid on innumerable goals for his team-mates, while contributing a sizeable return of sixteen goals himself, and he capped a terrific season by scoring a match-winning hat-trick against the Dons to gift wrap the title.

Although Ibrox had been stunned into silence when Brian Irvine shot Aberdeen ahead after nineteen minutes, Gascoigne cranked up the volume when he drew Rangers level two minutes later. Receiving a corner from Laudrup on the edge of the penalty area, he showed great strength to power his way beyond several challenges before lifting the ball over Michael Watt from six yards. The goal sent Ibrox into the throes of ecstasy, but stout defending from the visitors threatened to spoil the party until Gascoigne stepped forward into the limelight once more with ten minutes remaining.

Although his strength had been sapped by the hot April sunshine, the England midfielder summoned up one last burst of energy, setting off on a run that took him from inside his own half through the heart of the Aberdeen defence and into a position to curl a peach of a goal into the net. The third of his treble, which sealed the victory, was a penalty, won by Gordon Durie, four minutes from the end. McCoist, who had replaced Bo Andersen after an hour and was still unsure if he would be part of the set-up at Ibrox for the next campaign, begged Gascoigne to let him take the spot-kick as it may have represented his last chance to score a goal at Ibrox, but Gascoigne, riding the crest of a wave, refused to be denied his moment of glory and he stroked the ball effortlessly into the net. Gascoigne was celebrating again later that evening when his fellow professionals voted him as Scotland's Player of the Year. Walter Smith's calculated gamble had reaped an instant reward.

With his immediate future still uncertain, McCoist was back in the starting eleven as the newly crowned champions travelled to Rugby Park to face Kilmarnock in their final league fixture of the season. With Goram, Gascoigne and Laudrup rested ahead of the Scottish Cup final against Hearts, Smith tinkered with his line-up, blooding young Greg Sheilds at right-back and including Ian Durrant, who had been a peripheral figure for the majority of the season, in midfield, and the champions warmed up for the Hampden showdown with a comfortable 3-0 win. McCoist opened the scoring after twenty-two minutes when he latched on to an Alan McLaren header to claim his twentieth goal of the season, and he had further reason to celebrate when his strike-partner,

Gordon Durie, also took his total for the season to twenty when he netted a brace later in the game. Durie's double at Killie edged him one goal ahead of Paul Gascoigne as the race to finish top goalscorer: his £50-a-head bounty with Gazza had reached its final furlong.

With the Cup final showpiece against Hearts taking place two weeks after the victory at Rugby Park, Walter Smith took the opportunity to keep his players fresh by fielding a strong line-up as Rangers travelled to Kilbowie to face Clydebank in Ken Eadie's testimonial. McCoist again used the match as a platform to convince Smith that he was worth a place in the starting eleven against Hearts by netting a double in the 3-2 win. He could have had a hat-trick too had his fierce shot not cannoned off the crossbar in the second half, but with his future beyond the end of the season still unresolved, his brace of goals had sent out a message to the Rangers management team that he still had the hunger, desire and ability to succeed at Ibrox.

Discussions on his new contract were shelved until after the final, though, to allow both McCoist and the rest of the management team to concentrate fully on the more pressing matter of securing the domestic Double. The evening before the final, Smith announced his team and McCoist was selected to play alongside Durie in attack. The selection came as a huge boost for McCoist, but his joy was to be short-lived.

As the squad warmed up on the Hampden pitch in the hour leading up to the 3pm kick-off, McCoist picked up an injury and had to relinquish his place in the squad, with Ian Ferguson drafted in to wear the number nine jersey McCoist had vacated and Ian Durrant, who thinking he was not going to be involved had enjoyed a beer in the players' lounge as his mates were warming up, was summoned to take a seat on the substitutes' bench.

Despite having just won the championship, Rangers were by no means overwhelming favourites to win the Cup. Jim Jefferies' men had comprehensively won their last two outings against Rangers, 3-0 at Ibrox in January and 2-0 at Tynecastle in early April, but on Cup final day, Rangers were majestic and simply brushed their opponents aside, securing their fourteenth Double with a resounding 5-1 win.

The match will be remembered for many things, but two in particular will always stand out. The first was the performance of Brian Laudrup: a performance that was both exceptional and breathtaking in equal measure. Indeed, the match is now simply referred to as 'The Laudrup

Final' as a result of the Great Dane's wizardry over the course of a magnificent ninety minutes. He scored Rangers' opening two goals and was then on hand to craft the other magical moment, creating three goals for Gordon Durie, who became the first player to net a hat-trick in the Scottish Cup final for over twenty years.

It was Rangers' first Scottish Cup success for three years and the scenes as the squad paraded the trophy at Ibrox were unforgettable, with Laudrup, Player of the Year Gascoigne and Goram conducting the choruses of the throngs of Rangers fans who had gathered on Edmiston Drive, while sitting on top of the team bus.

While McCoist was disappointed to have missed out on appearing in only his third Scottish Cup final, his frustration was tempered shortly afterwards when two significant announcements were made. Firstly, he was given a just reward for his performances during 1995/96, a season in which he netted twenty goals in thirty-seven appearances, when he was offered a new two-year contract at Rangers. His long-term future had been the subject of much discussion as the sun was setting on another successful season for the club, and he had fuelled press speculation of a return to Sunderland by wearing the club's colours during the victory parade following the title-clinching win over Aberdeen. Money-spinning offers to see out the twilight of his career in Japan had also been tabled for the fans' favourite, but there was no doubt where McCoist's heart lay. 'Everyone knew that I didn't want to leave Rangers,' he said. 'But at this stage in my career I had to weigh up all the options that were available to me. The club were good enough to let me do that, but when I spoke to the manager and chairman I knew signing a new deal was the correct move.'[12]

Thus, one of the club's favourite sons would now be around for the charge towards the record equalling Nine-in-a-Row in the forthcoming season, and he could now travel to the European Championships safe in the knowledge that his Ibrox future was secure. This was the second piece of good news McCoist had received in the wake of the Cup final, as it was announced that he would join club-mates Gordon Durie, Stuart McCall, Andy Goram and Alan McLaren in Craig Brown's Scotland squad for the showpiece tournament. Given that the event was being held just across the border in England, the Scots desire to do well was stoked to an even greater degree.

With the injury problems that had hampered his progress during seasons 1993/94 and 1994/95 now firmly behind him and with his long-term future at Ibrox secure, things were starting to look up again for the effervescent thirty-three-year-old. His epic story had not yet reached its conclusion and, despite approaching veteran status, there were many more chapters still to be written in his fairytale career.

CHAPTER FOURTEEN

EURO '96, RECORDS AND NINE-IN-A-ROW: 1996–97

In the summer of 1996, the European Championships were held in England, the first time a major football tournament had been held on British shores for thirty years. On that previous occasion, the 1966 World Cup, Scotland had failed to qualify, and the Tartan Army had to be content with a watching brief as the host nation defeated West Germany by four goals to two to lift the Jules Rimet trophy. This time around, though, the national team were determined that they would not be watching from the sidelines, and as the qualifying campaign began in earnest in September 1994, they set about ensuring that they would be among the invited guests when the party started.

The Scots embarked on their qualification quest under new management. Following the debacle in Lisbon, the night on which Ally McCoist had suffered his broken leg, the SFA changed the managerial hierarchy following the resignation of Andy Roxburgh, promoting his assistant, Craig Brown, to the role of national team manager. In his playing days, Brown had been on Rangers' books, joining the Ibrox side from Coltness United aged nineteen in 1959, but failure to make the breakthrough into the first-team picture led to a transfer to Dundee, where he won a Scottish League championship medal in 1962. He moved on to Falkirk in 1967, but a number of operations on his knee forced him to retire in 1971 at the age of thirty-one. He joined Motherwell as assistant manager in 1974 before taking over the reins at Clyde three years later.

He was in charge at Shawfield on a part-time basis for ten years, balancing his life in football with his job as headteacher of a primary school, and he guided the club to the Second Division title in 1982. He left to become Roxburgh's assistant following the World Cup in Mexico, and further enhanced his CV when he coached the Scotland Under-16 team to the final of the World Championships in 1989 and the Under-21s to the last four of the European Championships in 1992. He enjoyed a decent start to his reign as national boss too, winning three of the remaining five World Cup qualifying matches and then steering the Scots to a flying start in their push for Euro '96 with a tremendous 2-0 win away from home against Finland.

Joining the Finns and the Scots in Group 8 were Greece, Russia, San Marino and the Faroe Islands, all of whom, with the exception of the latter two, represented formidable opposition and a significant hurdle for Scotland to negotiate if they were to realise their dreams of qualifying for the tournament. The fact the tournament was being held in England gave the Scots an extra incentive to make it into one of the group's two qualifying berths.

The Finnish result came off the back of a series of unconvincing displays in friendly matches, but they were quickly forgotten as Scotland followed their opening success with a comfortable 5-1 victory over the Faroes at Hampden. With McCoist still recovering from his leg break and the subsequent knocks and niggles that hampered his comeback, the likes of Aberdeen's Scott Booth and Bolton's John McGinlay took over his mantle as the squad's recognised goalscorer, and both were on target in the win over the Faroes. Booth found the net again in the third group match, but the Scots spilled their first points in a 1-1 draw with Russia at Hampden and they stumbled again the week before Christmas in 1994 when the Greeks dented hopes of qualification with a 1-0 victory in the white-hot atmosphere of the Olympic Stadium in Athens. However, by the time Greece rolled into town for the return match in August 1995, Brown and his players had managed to get back on course with back-to-back away wins in San Marino and the Faroes (both by two goals to nil) and a brave no-score draw in Russia.

With Scotland and Greece now vying for second spot in the group, Brown was aware this was a must-win game for Scotland, but his plans were thrown into disarray before the match when McCoist's club-mate Andy Goram pulled out of the contest claiming he did not feel he was in the right mental state to play. Veteran goalkeeper Jim Leighton was called upon to win his sixty-eighth cap, and the squad was further swelled by the inclusion of McCoist who had finally shaken off the myriad injuries that had tortured him since that fateful night in Lisbon.

With the match poised at 0-0 after seventy-one minutes, Brown made a double substitution, withdrawing Duncan Shearer and Darren Jackson and pitching McCoist and the pocket dynamo, John Robertson of Hearts, into the action. It proved a masterstroke. Barely a minute after the change, McCoist eluded his marker to get on the end of a cross from John Collins and glance a sweet header out of the reach of Ilias Atmatzidis in the Greek goal. It was his first goal in Scotland colours for two-and-a-half years.

McCoist's glorious return to the international fold netted Scotland a priceless three points, and the stage was now set for an enthralling climax to the charge for England. With the Russians runaway leaders in Group 8, Scotland knew that if they defeated Finland and San Marino in their last two matches, both of which were at home, they would book a place at the European Championships by virtue of finishing runners-up in the group ahead of the Greeks.

McCoist was listed among the substitutes for the Finland match, and he replaced former team-mate John Spencer after seventy-four minutes, by which time Scott Booth had grabbed the only goal of a tight game to net the three points. It had been a tough night for Brown's side, but the final qualifying match against San Marino at Hampden was much more straightforward, ending in a resounding 5-0 win. Goals from Booth and Eoin Jess gave the home side a 2-0 lead, and McCoist added a third in the forty-ninth minute just sixty seconds after replacing Gary McAllister. Pat Nevin made it 4-0 and an own-goal from Fabio Francini completed the rout to secure Scotland's qualification for a second successive European Championship finals.

Given their impressive performances during the previous tournament in Sweden, the Tartan Army expected their troops to perform well again, and when the draw was made for the final stages of the tournament, excitement in the UK reached fever pitch, as Scotland and England were bracketed alongside Holland and Switzerland in Group A. The annual conflict between the Auld Enemy had long since disappeared from the fixture list, so the match at Wembley on 15 June would be the first time the pair had crossed swords since England's 2-0 win at Hampden in 1989. Although the fixtures against the Dutch and the Swiss were eagerly anticipated, the clash with the English was the one everyone was looking forward to, and given that it was the second of the three group matches, the outcome would no doubt be pivotal in determining which of the two nations would progress to the knockout stages.

In order to bridge the gap between the end of the qualifying matches and the start of the tournament, Brown arranged a series of warm-up friendlies and one of those encounters, the Hampden clash with Australia in March 1996, was of great significance for McCoist: he reached the milestone of winning fifty caps for his country. He became only the twentieth player to do so and was presented with a gold medal by the SFA to mark the achievement. He was also given the honour of captaining his country for the evening – the only time he did so in his career – and he celebrated the occasion in characteristic fashion, scoring the only goal of the game with a header in the fifty-third minute.

By the time the championships kicked off in earnest in June, McCoist, voted Scotland's most valuable player during the qualifying campaign by readers of the *Daily Record*, had recovered sufficiently from his Cup final injury to play for an hour of the last warm-up match – a 1-0 defeat at the hands of Colombia – and had high hopes of leading the attack in the Scots opening match of the tournament which, just as it had been in Sweden in 1992, was against Holland. However, his hopes were dashed and he had to be content with a place on the bench as Brown selected Booth and Kevin Gallacher to play from the start alongside Cup final hat-trick hero Gordon Durie.

The Scots turned in a magnificent performance against the Dutch at Villa Park in Birmingham. Although on the back foot for most of the match, they defended resolutely and when the orange tide did breach the Scotland defence they found McCoist's team-mate Andy Goram, now restored to the fold, in inspired form in goal. Goram repelled everything the Dutch forwards could throw at him, and when he was finally beaten, the Scots were afforded some of the luck that had deserted them in Sweden when the Swedish referee missed a blatant handball by John Collins on the goal-line. The game ended 0-0 and praise was rightly heaped upon the Scottish team for their dogged display.

Next up in Group A was the match the Scottish public had been waiting for: the clash with the Auld Enemy. Of the team that had been fielded at Hampden the last time Scotland had played England on 27 May 1989, only McCoist and goalkeeper Jim Leighton were still part of the international squad, so for the majority of the Scotland team this would be their first taste of the fixture. Many observers felt the Scots had a more than even chance of upsetting the host nation's apple cart, for England had struggled to a 1-1 draw in their opening match with Switzerland. Their inept display had been met with widespread criticism in the media, with Rangers' Paul Gascoigne bearing the brunt of the bad press.

Again McCoist failed to start the match, taking his place among the substitutes once more, as Chelsea's John Spencer was the preferred pick to partner Durie for this one. The Scots more than held their own in a scoreless first half, but seven minutes after the restart the home side broke the deadlock when Alan Shearer headed a Gary Neville cross beyond Andy Goram.

However, far from being discouraged by this setback, the Scots fought back and were in the ascendancy late in the game, pushing for an equaliser when Gordon Durie, head swathed in bandages, latched on to a loose ball in the penalty area and was brought crashing to the turf under the challenge of Tony Adams. Referee Pairetto did not hesitate and he pointed immediately to the spot. McCoist, now on the field having replaced Spencer after sixty-six minutes, was an excellent penalty-taker, having scored a high percentage of those he had taken for Rangers, and given his propensity to write fairytale endings he seemed the ideal candidate to take the kick. However, the designated penalty-taker for Scotland at that time was Gary McAllister and it was he who stepped forward to place the ball on the spot. With all eyes fixed on the Leeds United midfielder, an eerie hush suddenly fell over Wembley Stadium, belying the fact that there were 76,864 people packed inside the ground.

The Scotland captain, who had netted a penalty against the CIS at Euro '92, stepped forward and hammered the ball goalward. He struck his kick straight down the middle of the goal but, much to the dismay of the Scots, England goalkeeper David Seaman, who had dived to his left, managed to deflect the ball high over the bar with his right elbow. The English, who were hanging on to their one-goal advantage by their fingertips prior to the penalty incident, were buoyed by Seaman's heroics and immediately sprung into action at the other end. The ball broke to the much-maligned Gascoigne 30 yards from goal and Scotland's Player of the Year proceeded to end the match as a contest with a sublime goal, chipping the ball over the head of Colin Hendry before running in behind him and volleying the ball into the net beyond his Rangers team-mate Andy Goram. Yet again a spirited Scottish display had gone without the reward it richly deserved.

Although disappointed not to emerge from the clash with the Auld Enemy with any points, there was still a chance Scotland could qualify for the knockout stages of the competition. Holland had beaten the Swiss 2-0, which meant that the Dutch and England each had four points, while Scotland and Switzerland both had one. In order to progress, the Scots had to beat the Swiss and rely on either England or Holland to record a handsome victory in their match. Should this transpire, Scotland would be through to the next round on goal difference, although even the most ardent Tartan Army foot soldier would have admitted that such a permutation seemed highly unlikely.

Having played for only twenty-four minutes over the course of the first two matches, McCoist finally made the starting line-up for the game against the Swiss at Villa Park, winning his fifty-fourth cap to earn him another place in the record books. He was now the most capped player in Rangers' history, surpassing the fifty-three caps garnered by George Young forty years earlier.

McCoist almost justified his inclusion twice in the opening seven minutes of the match. In the fifth minute the Swiss goalkeeper, Marco Pascolo, denied him, clawing his shot away for a corner, and two minutes later he passed up an even better opportunity when he somehow failed to score from just two yards. In the opinion of journalist Bill Leckie, McCoist had 'time to paint the goalposts', but instead of finding the back of the net, his shot struck Pascolo and rebounded to safety. It was a gilt-edged opportunity, but as ever he refused to let the missed chances dent his resolve, and in the thirty-seventh minute he found the net with an exceptional strike to register the Scots' first goal of the tournament. Coming in from the left flank, McCoist played a delightful one-two with McAllister before lashing an unstoppable right-foot drive high into the net from about twenty-five yards. It was his first goal for his country in a major international championship.

With their noses in front, the Scots had now succeeded in fulfilling their part of the unlikely pre-match bargain and midway through the second half it looked as though England were about to provide the other vital ingredient necessary to edge Scotland into the next round. News filtered through from Wembley that Paul Gascoigne and co had romped into a 4-0 lead against a bewildered Holland, and there was a sudden realisation that, if the results remained as they were, Scotland would qualify for the knockout stages of a major competition for the first time. Never before had the tidings of an English success been greeted with such pleasure by the Tartan Army!

Inevitably, though, all hopes would be cruelly dashed. The Scots defeated Switzerland 1-0, but Patrick Kluivert managed to score a late consolation goal in London to book Holland's place in the quarter-finals at Scotland's expense. The Scots were left to rue the missed chances in the games with England and Switzerland, as the conversion of just one of them would have been enough to knock the Dutch out of the tournament on goal difference. Instead, Scotland were consigned to a third-place finish in Group A and yet another chapter was written in the nation's catalogue of glorious failures. 'Ally scores two, we go through' was the chant from the Scotland squad as the team bus made its way back to the hotel, as McCoist's team-mates playfully teased him about the two clear-cut chances he had passed up against the Swiss. Had one of them gone in then the make-up of the last eight would have been different, with Scotland taking on France, but the charismatic striker, so often the joker himself, was thick-skinned enough to see the funny side of the banter and to laugh it off.

The Scots' early exit from Euro '96 meant McCoist had over a month to rest and recuperate before the rigours of the new season unfolded. Yet again Scotland's poor UEFA co-efficient meant Rangers had to kick-off their season before everyone else, as the first leg of their European Champions League qualifying tie with Russian champions Alania Vladikavkaz at Ibrox was due to take place on 7 August, three days before the curtain was raised on the Premier Division campaign.

Walter Smith and his management team prepared the troops for this monumental season – Rangers were on the verge of equalling Celtic's run of nine successive league titles that they had achieved between 1966 and 1974 – by embarking on a pre-season tour of Denmark, a trip that included three warm-up matches at the end of July. Two new faces joined the party in Scandinavia, with Smith once again taking the opportunity to flesh out an already formidable squad by adding Hamburg's German midfielder Jorg Albertz for a fee of £4 million and acquiring centre-back Joachim Bjorklund from Italian Serie A side Vicenza at a cost of just over £2 million.

When the action started in the warm-up matches, McCoist continued where he had left off at Villa Park and Euro '96. After replacing Gordon Durie sixty-eight minutes into the opening tour match against FC Copenhagen, a match that Rangers lost 1-0, McCoist was included in the starting eleven when the tourists faced Aalborg in their second match two days later, and it took him just thirteen minutes to break the deadlock. Brian Laudrup's corner picked out Gordan Petriç, and when the goalkeeper parried the Serb's header, McCoist feasted on the scraps to notch his first goal of the season. It was a typical McCoist goal, showing that he had lost none of his sharpness in the danger area despite his advancing years. Further goals from Bo Andersen and Petric handed Rangers a 3-2 victory, and the Light Blues completed their Scandinavian visit with a 9-1 mauling of amateur outfit Fremad Amager. McCoist, now the longest-serving player at Ibrox, was among the goals in this game too, netting a hat-trick, but for once he had to play second fiddle as Peter van Vossen grabbed the headlines by finding the back of the net on four occasions.

Understandably, McCoist was delighted with the form he had shown in Denmark, and his goals once again served notice that he was far from finished with the goal-scoring game that had become almost second nature to him since the fledgeling years of his career at St Johnstone. 'I'm here to score goals and that's what I intend to do,' he said. 'People can say what they want about my age, but I feel good and I know I have the ability. I scored a few goals in Denmark and that's always good, but the real test will start against the Russians and in the league.'[1]

However, the excellent start that both player and club had enjoyed to the campaign was clouded when the team returned to Scotland: news emerged that the legendary figure of Jock Wallace had passed away. 'Big Jock' had been fighting Parkinson's Disease for some years and died at the age of sixty after suffering a heart attack while visiting his daughter at her home in Basingstoke. During his time at Ibrox, Wallace, a giant of a man who never hid his passion for Rangers, won two Trebles, a League Championship and a Scottish Cup during his first stint in the manager's chair, and two further League Cup successes during a second spell at the helm in the mid-eighties. McCoist was one of the first to pay tribute to a man who he credited as being arguably the most influential figure in his career. He pointed to the time Wallace had spent with him in his early days at Ibrox when times were troubled for the striker, motivating him and cajoling him, convincing him he had what it took to be a success in a Rangers jersey. After Wallace left Ibrox in 1986, the pair remained close friends, with McCoist a regular visitor to the Wallace family home in Bothwell. 'I knew Jock for so long and it was distressing to see him deteriorate with ill health,' reflected McCoist. 'However, that doesn't detract from what a great man he was. He will go down in Ibrox folklore as he spent a huge part of his life with the side. But it was his way with people and the way he motivated them which I'll remember.'²

An emotional tribute was paid to Wallace before Rangers' first home fixture of the season, Richard Gough's testimonial match against Arsenal. The players all wore black armbands as a mark of respect, and a minute's silence was impeccably observed by the 41,245 crowd before kick-off. Fittingly, the home side won the match, the final friendly before the serious business got underway against Alania, by three goals to nil. The name 'McCoist' once again found its way on to the scoresheet, with the striker scoring from three yards in the fifteenth minute following good approach play involving Laudrup and Trevor Steven. The resurgent Dutchman, Peter van Vossen, who was finally beginning to show his true form after having endured a difficult first six months at Ibrox, also grabbed a goal, before Jorg Albertz capped off a fine day with what would become a trademark left-foot rocket from the fringes of the penalty area.

Four days later, on 7 August, when the Russian champions Alania Vladikavkaz arrived in Glasgow for the Champions League qualifier, an air of caution enveloped Ibrox. Having had the Russians watched by his network of spies, Walter Smith was quick to point out that Alania would be no pushover and that it would take a first-rate performance over the two legs to see Rangers through to the riches of the group stages.

Initially it seemed that the players had heeded their manager's warning, as the new-look Rangers started the match well and carved out the first chance of the night after only eight minutes. Alex Cleland fashioned it with a cross from the right, but McCoist's header was errant and flew over the bar. However, the Russians were creating chances too, and although Goram made a fine one-handed save to prevent Igor Yanovsky breaking the deadlock in the twenty-third minute, the Alania player enjoyed better fortune six minutes later when his low shot beat the Rangers goalkeeper and silenced the 44,799 fans inside Ibrox.

The patrons should have been back in full voice sixty seconds later, though, when McCoist was presented with an opportunity to equalise, but the striker was once again unusually profligate, with goalkeeper Dmitry Kramarenko saving his effort with his legs. And on the stroke of half-time, McCoist's miserable first-half display was compounded when he passed up his third chance of the evening, meekly heading a cross from Laudrup into the arms of Kramerenko.

The Scottish champions looked destined for a humbling early exit, but on the back of a few harsh words at the interval, they rallied and were level within five minutes of the restart when substitute Derek McInnes netted a rebound after Gough had a header blocked on the line. Sighs of relief were audible around the ground, and the Light Blues got their noses in front nine minutes later when McCoist finally found his range, cleverly volleying a Durie cross into the net. The goal was his thirteenth in Europe, which meant he had shattered the jointly held record of Ralph Brand and Alex Scott, and was now Rangers' all-time top scorer in European competition.

Eleven minutes from the end, Rangers extended their lead with a third goal when Petric headed a cross from McInnes into the net, but within a minute the Russians were given a chance to halve the deficit when the German referee awarded them a penalty following a foul by Goram on substitute Oleg Sergeev. Yanovsky took the kick, but to the delight of the home fans, he blazed his effort wide of the post. Thereafter, the visitors tried to find a way through a tiring Rangers rearguard, but the home defence held firm and preserved their two-goal lead to give them a good cushion to take to Russia.

Ahead of the return leg in Vladikavkaz, Rangers began their quest for nine league championships in a row by fashioning two wins, a 1-0 victory in the curtain-raiser against Raith Rovers, and 5-2 triumph against Dunfermline Athletic at East End Park, with the latter match memorable for the return from injury of Paul Gascoigne. They also defeated Clydebank by three goals to nil in the opening round of the League Cup, and the latter two matches demonstrated that McCoist, now aged thirty-three, had lost none of his desire to continue scoring goals for Rangers.

He came off the bench at Firhill to score Rangers' third goal against Clydebank in the fifty-fourth minute, and he followed that with a terrific treble in the match at East End Park to take his total for the season to five in only four matches. His first of the afternoon arrived in the forty-sixth minute, a calmly struck penalty awarded after Charlie Miller had been felled in the box, and he completed his hat-trick with two goals inside five minutes late in the game, taking passes from Miller on each occasion and expertly beating Ian Westwater in the Dunfermline goal. With competition for the strikers' jerseys as hot as ever, with van Vossen, Bo Andersen and Durie prominent in the early part of the season, McCoist knew he would have to maintain his scoring streak if he wanted to retain his place in the starting eleven. He said: 'It's important to stick the ball in the back of the net and make it difficult for the gaffer to replace you. With so many quality players around it's the only way to guarantee a place in the side this season.'[3]

Next up was the crucial second leg in Russia. It could not be over-emphasised just how important these ninety minutes were for Smith's men. While most identified annexing the championship (and clinching 'Nine-in-a-Row') as the primary objective for the season, a place in the Champions League was also imperative, as it brought with it a huge financial jackpot, estimated at £10 million, and a chance for Rangers to test themselves against the cream of the continent's club sides.

McCoist, having netted in three of his last four outings, was looking to continue his purple patch of form in Vladikavkaz and, after a mere thirty-three seconds, he got Rangers off to a flying start, nodding a stunning header beyond Zaur Khapov to stretch Rangers' aggregate lead to 4-1. His strike had added importance too, as it cancelled out the crucial away goal Alania had scored at Ibrox, but Rangers, who had set their stall out to attack by naming Laudrup, McCoist and van Vossen in a three-pronged strikeforce, did not use the early counter as an excuse to sit back. Instead they pushed for more goals, and ten minutes after scoring the opening goal, McCoist was at it again. On this occasion, Jorg Albertz was the provider, picking out McCoist on the right-hand side of the penalty area, and the number nine again used his head to fire the Scots into a two-goal lead.

Rangers now looked home and dry and they pressed home their superiority for the remainder of a match that is generally regarded as one of their finest displays away from home in continental competition. Although Alania pulled a goal back through Yanovsky after fourteen minutes, Rangers' in-form hit man completed a quick-fire hat-trick – his first in Europe – after seventeen minutes when good work again by Albertz left him with an easy tap-in. An incredible evening in Rangers' history was complete when later strikes from van Vossen, Charlie Miller and a double from the exceptional Laudrup left the final score at 7-2, a result that took Rangers through to the group stages by an emphatic ten goals to three on aggregate.

McCoist's three goals took his European tally to sixteen, equalling the total of the Celtic great, Jimmy Johnstone, who held the record for the most goals scored in European competition while with one Scottish club. Ally was now just two shy of Willie Wallace's milestone of eighteen goals, the record number scored by a Scottish player in Europe, and his scintillating start to the season led to him being crowned Bell's Player of the Month for August. He was also named as one of the new captains on the popular, long-running BBC quiz show *A Question of Sport*, following such sporting luminaries as Emlyn Hughes, Henry Cooper, Bill Beaumont and Ian Botham into the job.

The happiness borne from his fine early season form and his appointment as team skipper on *A Question of Sport* was tempered somewhat, though, when he found himself in trouble off the field. As he was returning home after a party at a Glasgow nightclub to celebrate Rangers' 3-0 win over Arsenal in Richard Gough's testimonial, the police stopped his car in Glasgow's Waterloo Street at 4am and he was promptly breathalysed. The results of the test showed the alcohol content in McCoist's bloodstream to be above the legal limit and he was charged with drink-driving. He was later convicted and served with a £2,500 fine and a fifteen-month driving ban. It was not his only off-field indiscretion in 1996; in April, McCoist was clocked doing 101mph on the A69 in Northumberland, and when his case was heard in Hexham in October, he earned a further driving ban. His plea that he was rushing to Sunderland to comfort his wife who was at her dying father's bedside failed to find favour with the magistrate who fined McCoist £360 and disqualified him from driving for five months.

Back on the field, McCoist picked up a hamstring injury in the 1-0 win over Dundee United, which meant he missed the victory over Ayr United in the League Cup. He returned to the squad when Rangers travelled to Motherwell in the league, but was an unused substitute in a match the Light Blues won 1-0 thanks to a thirty-eighth-minute header from Richard Gough.

The victory at Fir Park was Rangers' eighth in succession, and they carried that unblemished record to Zurich for their opening Champions

League match against Grasshopper. Joining Rangers and Grasshopper in Group A were French side Auxerre and Dutch cracks Ajax Amsterdam, but given the emphatic nature of their result in the qualifying round, the Scottish champions were among the favourites not only to qualify from the section but also to win the trophy itself.

However, at the end of the ninety minutes in the Hardturm Stadium, Walter Smith's side were left with faces as red as the new change kit they were sporting, as they were humbled 3-0 by the Swiss champions to leave their unbeaten start to the season in tatters. Indeed, had it not been for a series of terrific saves from Andy Goram, the result could have been even more humiliating. McCoist, fit again and restored to the starting line-up, did not play well on the night and was substituted after sixty-eight minutes. The European malaise continued two weeks later when Auxerre visited Ibrox on matchday two and returned to France with a 2-1 win, a result that left 'favourites' Rangers firmly anchored to the bottom of the group.

Although the European assignment was not quite going to plan, the mission to snare the championship trophy was proving much more fruitful. Rangers continued to sweep aside all before them, following the result in Switzerland with three wins and eleven goals and then curing the hangover from the Auxerre match by emerging victorious from the first Old Firm match of the season, with goals from Gough and Gascoigne securing a 2-0 win and opening up a five-point lead at the top of the table.

McCoist, who scored Rangers' third goal in a tempestuous 3-0 win over Hearts at Ibrox three days after the debacle in Zurich (the Edinburgh side had *four* players dismissed), missed the Celtic match and also the two matches prior to it with a recurrence of his old calf injury. He sustained the injury in a 4-0 victory over Hibernian in the quarter-final of the League Cup (a match that saw Ray Wilkins, aged forty, make an emotional return to Ibrox wearing the green jersey of the visitors), and it necessitated a spell on the sidelines. He would not return to action until the end of October when he replaced Brian Laudrup twelve minutes from the end of a resounding 5-0 win over Motherwell at Ibrox.

The victory over the Lanarkshire side marked a welcome return to form for a Rangers side that had struggled during the month of October. It followed hard on the heels of a 6-1 hammering of Dunfermline in the semi-final of the League Cup, with McCoist's deputy, Erik Bo Andersen, netting a double to secure a result that ended a run of three matches without a win. In that spell, the Light Blues had surrendered their unbeaten record in the league, losing 2-1 to Hibernian at Easter Road in a match that saw Laudrup miss two penalties, and spilled another two points when they relinquished a two-goal lead to draw 2-2 at home against Aberdeen. Domestic woe was compounded in the European arena, with the lights going out on the club's Champions League hopes for another season following back-to-back defeats at the hands of Ajax. Smith's men were thrashed 4-1 in Amsterdam and had Paul Gascoigne ordered off after the maverick Geordie had aimed a petulant kick at Winston Bogarde, and although they performed much better in the return match at Ibrox, a 1-0 defeat left them win-less and pointless after four of the six games.

McCoist had replaced Derek McInnes for the final nine minutes of the second Ajax defeat, and was back in the starting eleven for the next league match, a trip to Kirkcaldy to take on Raith Rovers. However, it looked as if Rangers' wretched European form was manifesting itself in the league, as Iain Munro's side snatched a point when Scott Thomson levelled the match at 2-2 with fifteen minutes remaining. McCoist had netted his tenth goal of the season to fire Rangers into a 2-1 lead ten minutes earlier, pouncing on a rebound to shoot the ball beyond former Rangers goalkeeper Colin Scott, but once again Smith's men failed to consolidate their advantage, and the dropped points allowed Celtic, their next opponents, to assume the leadership of the title race on goal difference.

Prior to the trip to Parkhead to take on the new league leaders, McCoist won his fifty-sixth cap for Scotland when he replaced goal hero John McGinlay five minutes from the end of an excellent 1-0 win over Sweden at Ibrox, a victory that kept the Scots on course for a place at the World Cup finals in France, and he was on the bench again when Rangers travelled to the east end of Glasgow four days later. Inevitably it turned out to be an evening of high drama.

Brian Laudrup, October's Player of the Month, opened the scoring in the seventh minute when he capitalised on a slip by Brian O'Neill to drill a shot into the net from the edge of the penalty area to kickstart a thrilling contest that witnessed two penalties saved – Gascoigne's weak effort for Rangers was smothered by Stewart Kerr and Pierre van Hooijdonk's late strike for Celtic was parried to safety by Goram – and innumerable opportunities missed. Peter van Vossen spurned the easiest of them; the Dutchman guilty of a glaring eighty-third-minute gaffe when he ballooned the ball over a gaping goal after an Albertz pass had taken out the Celtic defence. At the end of a breathtaking ninety minutes, Rangers emerged victorious to stretch their unbeaten Old Firm record to eight matches and claim back the lead in what was once again unfolding into a monumental race for the title.

The following Wednesday, Rangers restored some pride when they chalked up their first Champions League points of the season, beating Grasshopper 2-1 at Ibrox. It was a special night for McCoist, who finally broke his duck in the group stages. Remarkably, he had failed to score in his thirteen previous Champions League outings, but he brought that barren spell to an end when he scored from the penalty spot in the sixty-seventh minute. Peter van Vossen attempted to chip the ball between two defenders, and when the ball ricocheted off them, the Hungarian referee saw a handball offence and awarded a penalty-kick. McCoist took the responsibility and confidently sent the goalkeeper the wrong way to net his landmark goal. 'I wanted to score on Wednesday [against Grasshopper] more than anything,' McCoist said a few days later. 'It's a matter of pride in your own performance. I was slightly disturbed that I had never scored in the Champions League. It wasn't a case of me doubting my own ability because I always thought I was good enough to score in the Champions League. It wasn't a question of confidence, either. It was a question of achievement and I'm delighted to have got that out of the way now.'[4]

Champions League goals it seems are just like buses – you get one and then another follows almost immediately – for just six minutes after scoring his first, McCoist grabbed his second when he took a pass from Albertz and thundered a shot through the legs of Zuberbuhler in the Grasshopper goal. He clearly enjoyed the moment, but was promptly booked by the Hungarian referee when he removed his shirt as he celebrated the goal. 'It was the best booking I will ever suffer,' said McCoist afterwards, 'but I won't be doing it again.'[5]

His brace of goals finally silenced team-mate Ian Durrant who had been dishing out spade-loads of stick in the dressing room over McCoist's lack of European goals. Durrant himself had three strikes to his name in the Champions League, including the late consolation in the Amsterdam Arena in October, but McCoist at last had a couple of his own, allowing him the chance to deliver a defiant riposte to the acerbic jibes from his good friend.

The victory over the Swiss allowed Rangers to gain a crumb of consolation in Group A, and it also helped wreak revenge on a number of the Grasshopper players who had made disparaging remarks following the clash in Zurich, labelling the Rangers party as 'holidaymakers' in the wake of their inept display in the Swiss capital. The triumph also acted as the perfect preparation for Smith's side, as just four days later they faced Hearts at Parkhead in the League Cup final. McCoist, who appeared to have put his recent injury worries behind him, was understandably buoyant after his midweek exploits, and he took to the field for his tenth appearance in a League Cup final looking to claim an unprecedented haul of nine winners' medals.

Rangers went ahead after just ten minutes. Laudrup, coming in from the right-hand touchline, slipped a pass into the feet of McCoist, who sprang the offside trap and netted with a low shot from eighteen yards. Fifteen minutes later, the elder statesman had the Rangers fans on their feet once more when he collected a sublime cross-field pass from Albertz and sent in a rasping drive that stung the palms of Hearts' keeper Rousset. The save only delayed the inevitable, though, as from the resulting corner McCoist, unguarded inside the six-yard box, stooped to direct a Craig Moore header over the line to give Rangers a 2-0 lead and resurrect memories of the previous season's Scottish Cup final when Rangers had mauled Hearts 5-1. With Rangers and McCoist in such irresistible form, it looked likely that a similar punishment was about to be dealt, but Hearts rallied as Rangers relaxed, pulling a goal back on the stroke of half-time through ex-Celtic midfielder Stevie Fulton.

From a position of overwhelming ascendancy, Rangers now found themselves pegged back and their situation was not helped when McCoist and Gascoigne had a fierce tête à tête, the result of a breakdown in communication after a Rangers attack had broken down. The argument was still raging as the teams went up the tunnel and into the dressing room at the interval. 'Our dressing room was like a war zone,' recalled captain Richard Gough. The incident seemed to be totally out of character for a player who always gave the impression that he was larger than life and the joker in the pack, but it was a side that his team-mates, and Gough in particular, had seen at close quarters many times on the training field. Gough, who called McCoist a 'born winner' in the lead-up to the final said: 'I've had one or two flashpoints in training and Ally McCoist has been the man involved. He has the reputation of being a happy-go-lucky guy, but he has a depth of desire and hunger that got him two more Cup final goals.'[6]

An irascible Walter Smith, who arrived in the dressing room annoyed that his troops had become lackadaisical and allowed Hearts a passport back into the game, eventually restored calm before rollicking his troops for their relaxed demeanour in the closing stages of the first half.

His words appeared to have had little effect, though, as fifteen minutes after the restart Hearts levelled the match when Neil McCann, who was beginning to become more and more prominent since the departure of his marker, Alex Cleland, at half-time with a groin injury, sped down the left wing and delivered a low cross that Hearts' goal king John Robertson diverted behind Goram. It was now pandemonium, but before Hearts could get up a head of steam and forge ahead, they were facing a two-goal deficit once more thanks to the genius that is Paul Gascoigne.

The last few months had not been a pleasant time for the Geordie on a personal level, with his off-the-field problems ultimately costing him his marriage and plunging him deep into the throes of alcoholism. On the field he could find no escape from his off-field angst, as he had been sent off in Rangers' 4-1 defeat to Ajax in the Champions League for a retaliatory kick aimed at Winston Bogarde. He was slaughtered in the media, with Gerry McNee from the *News of the World* particularly vociferous in his unequivocal condemnation of the Rangers midfielder.

Gascoigne was still on edge on the day of the Cup final at Parkhead. Fifteen minutes prior to kick-off, he had appeared in one of the lounges decked out in his match kit and downed a double brandy in an attempt to quell his nerves. The medicinal beverage did not appear to have delivered the desired effect, though, as Gascoigne did not seem to be at his best in the first half, which may explain why he and McCoist had become embroiled in their heated discussion after another Gascoigne pass had gone astray.

However, just when it looked as if the roof was going to cave in on Rangers, Gascoigne grabbed the match by the scruff of the neck and dominated the second half in much the same way as McCoist had done in the first. He netted a quick-fire double, with both goals worthy of winning any Cup final. In the sixty-third minute, he received a throw-in from David Robertson on the touchline and proceeded to weave his way through the Hearts rearguard before passing the ball with unerring accuracy into the bottom right-hand corner of the net from the edge of the penalty area. It was a terrific piece of skill and, two minutes later, he scored again with another exquisite strike, bursting into the box and linking superbly with Charlie Miller before stabbing a right-foot shot behind Gilles Rousset.

Rangers eventually won a rousing contest by four goals to three, with Gascoigne and McCoist showing they had patched up their first-half differences as they posed for the cameras during the lap of honour. McCoist and his manager, who had just picked up his eleventh trophy out of a possible sixteen since he had taken over in April 1991, were given more reason to celebrate when they were named November's Bell's Player of the Month and Manager of the Month respectively, the second time that season the duo had picked up the monthly gongs.

Shortly after the final, Rangers' European challenge petered out when they went down 2-1 to Auxerre in France. Guy Roux's side stormed into a 2-0 lead in the opening half-hour, but Gough reduced the deficit ten minutes before the interval with a fine header. McCoist took to the field in the sixty-second minute, replacing Gordan Petrič, but he failed to add to the goals he had netted last time out against Grasshopper, and Rangers limped to yet another Champions League defeat. The result left the Scottish champions with a quite abysmal record of one win and five defeats from six matches. They scored a paltry five goals and conceded thirteen, a damning statistic that once again illustrated that a side that were masters of all they surveyed in Scotland were still some way short of the standard required to achieve success in Europe's premier competition.

In order to gain a passport back into the Champions League for the 1997/98 season and silence their critics, Rangers had to capture a ninth successive Premier Division title, and Smith's men were firing on all cylinders, leading Celtic by five points after fourteen matches. Match fifteen brought fifth-placed Hibernian to Ibrox, and it turned out to be yet another landmark day for Ally McCoist.

The league goal he notched against Raith Rovers in November was his 263rd in Scottish League football (consisting of a remarkable 241 in a Rangers shirt and twenty-two in the fledgeling years of his career at St Johnstone), which took him to within touching distance of Gordon Wallace's post-war league goals record. Wallace had accrued a total of 264 league goals during spells with Montrose, Raith Rovers, Dundee and Dundee United in the 1960s and '70s, but McCoist drew level and then eclipsed his record within the space of five minutes against a battling

Hibernian side. A goal from Keith Wright fired the visitors ahead in the twentieth minute, and although Ian Ferguson equalised, Darren Jackson scored with a header five minutes short of the interval to give the Edinburgh side a 2-1 lead, an advantage they still clung on to when the clock ticked on to the seventieth minute.

In an attempt to redress the balance, Walter Smith had pitched the gangly Erik Bo Andersen into the fray at the outset of the second half, and the Dane was heavily involved when the home side eventually fashioned an equaliser. His attempt on goal was blocked by a Hibernian defender, and although a desperate goal-line clearance defied Scott Wilson from Gascoigne's flag-kick, Rangers restored parity when Laudrup's delivery from the resulting corner found the head of McCoist, who duly ruffled the rigging for the 264th time in his illustrious Scottish league career.

Five minutes later, the record was his. Gascoigne bobbed and weaved his way into the penalty area before shooting towards goal. The ball may have gone in of its own accord, but McCoist thrust out a leg to ensure that it found its destination. Initially there was some confusion as to who had actually scored the goal that edged Rangers 3-2 ahead, with Gascoigne running with arms aloft to celebrate in front of the Main Stand, while McCoist sank to his knees to rejoice with the patrons of the Govan Stand on the opposite side of the pitch. However, a quick glance at the television monitor verified that the ball had deflected into the net via McCoist's leg, thus confirming that he had overtaken Wallace's total and had established himself as the most prolific striker in Scottish football since the end of the Second World War. 'This was one I really wanted,' he told the *Rangers News*. 'I actually played against Gordon Wallace when I was at St Johnstone and I'm sure it will be a difficult record to beat now.'[7]

It turned out to be a fine afternoon for Rangers too, as Celtic were beaten 2-1 by Motherwell at Fir Park, but Smith's side enjoyed the newly established eight-point cushion for just three days. An own-goal from Richard Gough handed his former club Dundee United a 1-0 win at Tannadice, Rangers' first league reverse since Hibernian's 2-1 victory at Easter Road in October. They were soon back on track, though, with McCoist setting them on the road to seven successive league wins when he opened the scoring with a header in the fifth minute of a 3-1 win over Dunfermline. He was on the mark again on Boxing Day when he scored a fine goal against Raith Rovers, Rangers' fourth in a 4-0 win, to take his tally for the season to eighteen in only twenty-two appearances, and it looked as though he was on course for another goal-laden season. However, after starting the first match of the New Year, a 3-1 victory over Celtic at Ibrox on 2 January, he only appeared in the starting eleven in four of Rangers' last sixteen league matches.

On 2 January, despite being ridden with a flu virus, McCoist took to the field to face Celtic for the traditional New Year Old Firm clash. Clearly toiling, he was replaced by Erik Bo Andersen with fifteen minutes remaining, and the Dane proceeded to grab all the headlines, scoring a quickfire brace to give Rangers a 3-1 victory and hand them an eleven-point lead in the title race.

Still suffering from the effects of flu, McCoist was listed among the substitutes for Rangers' next two matches, but he enjoyed a brief return to the first eleven in a 1-1 midweek draw against Kilmarnock on 15 January. However, the normally deadly marksman was strangely lethargic in front of goal, passing up several good opportunities to net all three points for Rangers, and he returned to the bench for the next league fixture at Motherwell. Rangers won 3-1, with new £4 million Chilean striker Sebastian Rozental making his debut as a seventy-seventh-minute substitute for Bo Andersen. The extravagant purchase of the twenty-year-old South American swelled what was already a talented contingent of strikers at Ibrox, but his arrival did not unduly concern McCoist, who said: 'There's no way I feel threatened by Seb's arrival, although the competition for places up front will now be even tougher.'[8]

In a bid to hone his match fitness and ready himself for the youthful challenge to his berth in the team, McCoist turned out for the reserves against Motherwell at Bathgate towards the end of January, but neither he nor fellow first-team regulars Durie, Durrant, van Vossen and Ferguson could prevent the second string slipping to a 2-1 defeat. A brief ten-minute cameo appearance for the first team followed, as Rangers kicked off their Scottish Cup campaign with a 2-0 win over St Johnstone, and he returned to the starting eleven for the next league match, a drab 0-0 draw against Hearts.

McCoist was also part of the squad that travelled to Amsterdam to take part in the inaugural European Super Sixes tournament. Liverpool, AC Milan and hosts Ajax joined Rangers at the event, and McCoist was among the goalscorers when the Scots thumped Liverpool 7-3 in their second match, firing Walter Smith's side 4-2 ahead with a quickly taken free-kick and adding a second in the midst of a late avalanche of goals. Having lost 6-2 against Ajax in their opening fixture, the Light Blues needed to defeat an AC Milan side boasting the talents of Edgar Davids and Roberto Baggio in their last match to reach the final, but despite clawing themselves back to 3-3 after falling three goals behind, it was the Italians who progressed to take on Ajax in the final. Rangers had to be content with a third/fourth-place shootout against Liverpool, with six players from each side charged with the responsibility of embarking on a run from the halfway line and scoring within a timeframe of five seconds. After three players from both sides, including both goalkeepers, had missed, it was left to McCoist, who along with Durie and Durrant had netted one of Rangers' regulation penalties, to slot home Rangers' winner in sudden death.

On their return from Holland, Rangers maintained their relentless push for the Treble, comfortably defeating Dunfermline in the league and East Fife in the fourth round of the Scottish Cup. Both matches ended 3-0, with McCoist enjoying a rare start in the latter. He got himself on the scoresheet too, netting his first goal since Boxing Day when he diverted a cross from Trevor Steven into the net with his chest in the thirty-seventh minute.

Four days earlier, he had picked up his fifty-seventh cap for Scotland against Estonia at the Stade Louis II in Monaco. This was a World Cup qualifier that had been re-arranged after the Estonians had failed to show up for the original tie, but although he replaced John McGinlay with seventeen minutes remaining, McCoist could not add the necessary potency to a sterile Scottish attack, and Craig Brown's men could only muster a no-score draw, thus shedding two vital points in the race to qualify for the forthcoming World Cup in France.

Although still very much in the frame at international level, McCoist's lack of regular game time in the Rangers top team had served to stoke the fires of the rumour mill once again, with some newspapers speculating that the veteran hitman would be among a host of players deemed surplus to requirements at Ibrox in the close season. With Walter Smith set to be rewarded with a significant summer transfer kitty following the £40 million investment made in the club by Bahamas-based billionaire Joe Lewis, McCoist and other members of the old guard – such as Ian Durrant, Ian Ferguson and Gordon Durie – were believed to be on their way to pastures new in a bid to create room for a clutch of new arrivals. Walter Smith was quick to pour cold water on such speculation, however, and McCoist seemed set to stay in Govan to complete the final year of his existing contract.

Try as he might, though, McCoist could not force his way into the starting eleven, managing just seven minutes of action as Rangers won 3-1 against Hibernian at Easter Road and drew 2-2 against Aberdeen at Pittodrie. The latter result saw Rangers' lead over Celtic at the summit of the Premier Division cut to five points, and the match was a precursor to a vital period in the season, with an Old Firm double-header sandwiching a crucial league meeting against third-placed Dundee United at Ibrox. The results of all three matches would have a huge bearing upon whose sideboard the remaining domestic silverware would be resting come the end of the season.

The first of the trio of matches was the Scottish Cup quarter-final against Celtic at Parkhead on 6 March. Tommy Burns' side were on a good run of form, but they hadn't registered a win over Rangers since May 1995, a winless sequence of nine matches. However, they soon rectified that on what turned out to be a dire night for a ragged Rangers side. Smith's men simply did not perform over the course of the match and were comprehensively beaten by two goals to nil. The defeat emphatically extinguished any notion that the season would end with the second domestic Treble of the Smith era, and McCoist, who had replaced Erik Bo Andersen in the thirty-eighth minute after the Dane had fractured his skull in a sickening collision with Alan Stubbs, rated the display as being 'the worst Rangers performance in an Old Firm game I've ever experienced'. He added: 'I can offer no excuses for the performance of the team at Parkhead. It beggared belief that we could actually play that badly.'9

It was a devastating blow for Rangers at a vital juncture in the season, and the hangover induced by the inept display was still lingering when Dundee United arrived at Ibrox six days later on league business. Remarkably, Rangers lost again, turning in a performance that was even shoddier than the one served up on their previous outing. Goals from Robbie Winters and Kjell Olofsson extended United's unbeaten run to fifteen matches and threatened to blow the title race wide open. Thankfully, Rangers' five-point lead was sustained by virtue of the fact that Kilmarnock had beaten Celtic at Rugby Park twenty-four hours earlier.

With Rangers lolling around on the ropes, something had to be conjured up to restore stability to foundations that were buckling under the strain associated with the pursuit of nine-in-a-row. The anxiety around Ibrox was palpable, but Walter Smith waved his magic wand ahead of the return visit to Parkhead in the league to coax yet another rabbit out of the hat. Mark Hateley was tempted back to Glasgow just forty-eight hours before the titanic clash, and the Englishman played a significant role in what turned out to be yet another tempestuous entry in the Old Firm logbook.

There were no fewer than nine bookings and two red cards over the course of the ninety minutes, with Celtic's Italian firebrand Paolo Di Canio having to be restrained at full-time as he attempted to go toe-to-toe with Ian Ferguson. By then, Rangers had all but clinched the title thanks to a goal from Brian Laudrup on the stroke of half-time. Jorg Albertz shelled a free-kick forward towards the head of Hateley, and although he made no contact with the ball, his presence unsettled the Celtic defence and allowed Ian Durrant to nip in and loft a shot over Stewart Kerr in the home goal. The ball may well have reached the net of its own accord, but Laudrup slid in at the far post to nudge the ball over the line and secure the first-ever clean sweep of Premier Division Old Firm victories.

Thereafter the match descended into a series of ugly skirmishes, with Hateley dismissed in the sixty-seventh minute following an altercation with Kerr, and Malky Mackay also invited to take an early bath when he picked up his second caution ten minutes before the end of the match. Amid the mayhem, McCoist replaced Durrant with two minutes remaining, just in time to soak up the atmosphere on another momentous day in Rangers' history.

Although they contrived to lose their next league match 2-1 at home against Kilmarnock, Rangers eventually secured their ninth successive championship, finishing five points ahead of nearest challengers Celtic. After the champagne fell flat when Motherwell gate-crashed the first opportunity to clinch the record-equalling title by winning 2-0 at Ibrox, a rare Brian Laudrup header secured a 1-0 win over Dundee United at Tannadice and sparked scenes of unbridled joy and elation.

The burden on this squad of players to deliver the ninth title had been immense throughout the campaign, with McCoist later putting that pressure into context by saying that had Rangers not won the championship then this celebrated squad would forever have been remembered as the group of players that had failed to clinch nine titles in a row, rather than the team that had accumulated eight in succession. Thus, against this backdrop, the achievement was even more extraordinary, and Richard Gough, bedecked in his club suit and set to quit the club at the conclusion of the campaign and wind down his career in the US, wept tears of joy as he received the championship trophy. Injury had robbed him of the chance of policing the central defensive beat that he had patrolled with such great distinction since arriving at Ibrox in 1987, but it was fitting that he was the first man to cup his hands around the trophy on this momentous evening. It was the fourteenth and last piece of silverware he had raised aloft since being appointed team captain in 1990, a remarkable achievement for arguably one of the finest Rangers captains of all time.

As had been the case since the turn of the year, McCoist's role on the night of the celebrations had been a supporting one. He replaced the goal hero Laudrup in the final minute, but despite a recent lack of regular action, his contribution to the championship charge was sizeable. A goal against Raith Rovers in an emphatic 6-0 win four games from the end of the campaign took his tally for the season to twenty, which meant he finished as club's joint-top goalscorer alongside Scotland's Player of the Year Brian Laudrup.

McCoist's contribution to the considerable effort required to annex nine successive titles had also been colossal. He appeared in 231 of the 348 league games that Rangers contested (only Richard Gough and Gary Stevens played more often) and he delivered an awesome scoring return of 136 goals. Alongside Gough and Ian Ferguson, McCoist also became a member of an elite club; the trio were the only players to participate actively in each of the nine league campaigns that made up the nine-in-a-row, and at a ceremony held to mark the tenth anniversary of the achievement in 2007, his dedication to the club during that distinguished era was recognised when he was awarded the 'Greatest Contribution to Nine-in-a-Row' honour.

However, some question marks were hanging over the club record goalscorer's Ibrox future as the curtain closed following the final act of the 1996/97 season. Despite his advancing years – he was approaching his thirty-fifth birthday – McCoist still had enough confidence in his ability that he could score goals on a consistent basis for Rangers. He was keen to

Above: Celebrating lifting the Scottish League Cup with the irrepressible Paul Gascoigne in 1996. During Gascoigne's three-year stay in Glasgow, the pair forged a close friendship. © *SNSPIX*

Below: Netting his first-ever goal in the Champions League group stages against Swiss side Grasshopper Zurich in 1996. © *SNSPIX*

Above: Celebrating clinching a ninth successive Premier Division title with
Richard Gough. Along with Ian Ferguson, McCoist and Gough were the only
Rangers players to play an active part in each of the nine title-winning seasons.

© *SNSPIX*

Below: Saluting the Rangers supporters for the last time following the Scottish
Cup final in 1998. © *SNSPIX*

Pictured with Kilmarnock manager Bobby Williamson after signing for the
Ayrshire side in August 1998.   © *SNSPIX*

Above: Playing against Rangers during the 1998/99 season. © *SNSPIX*

Below left: With Fred MacAulay and guests Paul Gascoigne, Nigel Benn and Jayne Middlemiss ahead of another edition of *McCoist and MacAulay*. The chat show ran for three series between 1998 and 2001. © *PA Photos*

Below right: Pictured after receiving the Sports Presenter of the Year award from the Television & Radio Industry. © *PA Photos*

Promoting ITV's coverage of Euro 2000 with Des Lynam. McCoist was an
integral part of the channel's match analysis team. © *ITV/REX Features*

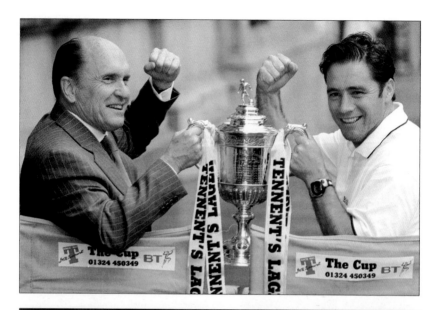

Above: With legendary Hollywood actor Robert Duvall at a publicity shoot for *A Shot at Glory*. Although the film enjoyed little box office success, McCoist was lauded for his performance on his silver screen debut.   © *Mirrorpix*

Below: Pictured alongside Walter Smith and the late Tommy Burns after taking up a position on the backroom staff of the Scottish national team following the departure of Berti Vogts in 2004.   © *PA Photos*

Above: Arriving back 'home' in January 2007 to take up the role of assistant manager at Ibrox. Also pictured are Walter Smith (centre) and first-team coach Kenny McDowall.   © *SNSPIX*

Below: Ally salutes the crowd after Rangers' heartbreaking UEFA Cup final defeat in 2008.   © *SNSPIX*

2008/9 was another incredible season for Ally and Rangers, as they clinched an
SPL and Scottish Cup double.

stay on and aid the club in its quest to win the championship for the tenth year in a row, an unprecedented achievement for a Scottish side, and he was also a mere four strikes short of notching 250 league goals for Rangers and only eleven short of 350 goals in all competitions. However, with the World Cup finals looming large on the horizon, McCoist knew he required regular action in order to safeguard his place in the international set-up, and if that meant a move to pastures new, then the gut-wrenching decision to leave his spiritual home would have to be taken.

Fortunately such a course of action was not necessary. Three days after completing their league programme with a 3-1 defeat against Hearts at Tynecastle, Rangers travelled to Highbury to take on Arsenal in a testimonial match for the Gunners long-serving full-back, Nigel Winterburn. An enthralling match in which David Unsworth, John Moncur and former Ranger Steven Pressley appeared as guests for the Ibrox side, ended 3-3, with McCoist opening the floodgates in the fifth minute when he thundered home an exquisite pass from Gascoigne with his right foot. Immediately after the final whistle, a meeting was convened with Walter Smith, which ended with a definitive resolution on McCoist's immediate future. 'I am delighted to confirm I will be staying at Rangers next season,' a thrilled McCoist told the *Rangers News*. 'We [McCoist and Walter Smith] had a long meeting and all I asked him was to judge me not on the last few months of the season, when I've had a few niggling injuries, but on how I look as a player in pre-season training. He agreed that if I go away, have a good rest and come back fully fit, I'll figure in his plans.'[10]

In addition to seeing out the final year of his existing contract, it was also agreed that McCoist would take on a more active role within the club's commercial department. He would be working under the watchful eye of commercial manager Bob Reilly, and with his sharp wit and infectious personality, the affable striker, who had dabbled in some commercial ventures during the 1996/97 season that included helping to unveil the club's new '1873' Superstore, seemed to be tailor-made for the role.

The twilight was beginning to descend on the remarkable Rangers career of Ally McCoist, and the party was almost over for the Light Blues' resident goal-getter. The collective decision to allow him to remain at Ibrox, however, meant that he would at least be granted one last curtain call.

CHAPTER FIFTEEN

THE FINAL HURRAH: 1997–98

When the dust had settled on the historic achievements of the 1996/97 season and the Rangers players and fans had had the chance to drink in what they had been a part of, the focus shifted towards a new target. At that point in time, no club side had ever won their domestic championship for ten years in succession: it left Walter Smith's men standing on the cusp of history.

Ally McCoist, a few months shy of his thirty-fifth birthday, was entering his fifteenth season in a Rangers shirt and the last of his current contract. He had enjoyed a renaissance in the previous two seasons, finding the net regularly, and with his Rangers future beyond the end of 1997/98 uncertain, he was intent on ensuring that should he be bidding a fond farewell at the end of the campaign then he would be doing so clutching a tenth successive championship medal in the palm of his hand.

Walter Smith and David Murray certainly made their intentions for the forthcoming season pretty clear, splashing out transfer fees in the region of £12 million on eight new recruits. Among them were central defender Lorenzo Amoruso from Fiorentina who, at £4 million, was perceived to be a replacement for departing captain Richard Gough, and the moody but prolific striker Marco Negri, who arrived from Perugia for £3.75 million. A young eighteen-year-old Italian midfield dynamo by the name of Gennaro 'Rino' Gattuso was also welcomed into the fold alongside fellow Italian Sergio Porrini, Australian Tony Vidmar, Norwegian Staale Stensaas and Swedish midfielder Jonas Thern. Finnish goalkeeper Antti Niemi completed the set to add a cosmopolitan look to a Rangers squad that looked to be gearing up for an assault on all fronts in the season ahead.

McCoist knew that twenty-eight-year-old Negri, in particular, was not travelling to Scotland merely to warm the substitutes' bench and cool his heels on the sidelines. Despite the fact that Perugia had become entangled in the lower reaches of Serie A for most of the previous season, Negri had finished as one of the top goalscorers in Italy's top division. He had found the net fifteen times, which was a splendid record in a division that had given birth to the *cattenacio* (door-bolt) style of defending, an approach through which defenders regularly prevailed by suffocating the attacking notions of the opposition.

Thus, for the first time since he had arrived at Ibrox, McCoist was aware that he would no longer be a guaranteed first pick when fully fit. It was a case of choose one from five, as the veteran marksman would be battling it out with Gordon Durie, Erik Bo Andersen, Peter van Vossen and Sebastian Rozental to partner Negri in attack.

McCoist staked his claim for that role with an impressive showing in the pre-season matches, racking up six goals, including a hat-trick in the showpiece match at the Nike Family Day held at Ibrox when the supposedly second-string 'Whites' trounced the first-choice 'Blues' by six goals to one. And when the serious business started just a few weeks later, the thirty-four-year-old carried that goal-scoring form into the early season confrontations, booking himself yet another place in the history books in the process.

The first competitive fixture of the campaign took place in the surreal surroundings of a cliff-top stadium in Toftir when Rangers came face to face with part-timers Gotu Itrottarfelag (GI) from the Faroe Islands in the first qualifying round for the Champions League. This was the first season of a ground-breaking new era for the continent's premier club competition. In addition to the champions from the leading European nations such as England, Germany, Holland, France, Italy, Spain, and Portugal making it into the competition, the teams that had finished second in each of those country's leagues during 1996/97 would also be granted an invitation to join the party; it made a mockery of the 'Champions League' label.

The champions would join holders Borussia Dortmund as direct entries into the group stages, while the runners-up would enter into the second of two qualifying rounds. Each of the other countries were then ranked based on the performances of their teams in the various European competitions over the previous five years. The middle-ranked teams, such as Sparta Prague, IFK Gothenburg and Norwegian champions Rosenborg BK, were exempt from the first qualifying round, while the remaining teams with the lowest coefficient had to battle their way through two qualifying rounds in order to make it to the promised land of the Champions League.

Unfortunately for Walter Smith and his expensively assembled squad, Scotland's UEFA co-efficient had now dipped to the extent that they were ranked twenty-seventh on the list, and thus the Scottish champions would have to play in both qualifying rounds, the first of which was scheduled to take place on 23 July, twelve days before Rangers were due to kick off their defence of their Premier Division title against Hearts at Ibrox.

Thus, despite reaching the group stages of the tournament in three of the previous five seasons, Rangers were penalised for the inept performances of the other Scottish clubs over the years, while Newcastle United, who had finished runners-up to Manchester United in the English Premiership the previous season and who were debutants in the competition, were afforded a 'bye' to the final qualifying round by virtue of the fact they were representing one of European football's heavyweight countries.

McCoist started the first leg of the clash with Gotu on the substitutes' bench – Durie was given the nod to partner Negri in attack – but when new team captain Brian Laudrup's involvement in the game was ended prematurely, after thirty-seven minutes due to a back injury, McCoist was pitched into the action. By the time he arrived, Rangers were already 2-0 up thanks to a debut goal from Negri and another strike from Durie. McCoist then notched his first goal of the season with a fine finish after sixty-seven minutes to extend Rangers' advantage before turning provider ten minutes from time when he set up Durie's second goal of the evening.

Another McCoist counter on the stroke of full time completed the 5-0 rout, and his brace of goals took his European tally to twenty, marking him out as the top goalscorer for a Scottish club in European competition. He had now eclipsed the total Willie Wallace had accrued when representing Hearts and Celtic, and he was understandably elated to seize yet another record. 'I just couldn't believe I'd actually done it – that's another one for the hall of fame in my house!' he said. 'I knew about it before, but I didn't really want to talk much about it, but I think you could tell from my reaction that I loved every second.'[1]

In the return leg at Ibrox a week later, McCoist took his place in the starting eleven, and he nudged his European tally to twenty-one when he found a way beyond the Gotu goalkeeper Jens Martin Knudsen, again with a header from a Jorg Albertz cross in the forty-eighth minute. That strike, added to first-half efforts from Durie and Negri, took Rangers into a 3-0 lead on the night, and McCoist could have further swelled his European goals total just after the hour mark when the Latvian referee awarded Rangers a penalty after Negri had been brought down by Rasmussen. However, his spot-kick was poor and Knudsen saved with ease. His miss was a mere blip, though, and further goals from Albertz, Ian Ferguson and Negri ensured that Rangers strolled through to the final qualifying round where they would face sterner opposition in the shape of Swedish giants IFK Gothenburg.

With this crucial match in mind, Walter Smith took the opportunity to rest some of his big guns in the opening round of the League Cup due to be contested ahead of the trip to Scandinavia, and the match against Hamilton Academical presented McCoist with the opportunity to register more goals and shatter another long-standing record into the bargain. After being left out of the squad when Rangers raised the curtain on the new domestic season with a Negri-inspired 3-1 win over Hearts in the opening league fixture, McCoist returned to warm the substitutes' bench when a second-string Rangers made the short journey to Fir Park to take on Hamilton, who were managed by McCoist's former strike-partner, Sandy Clark. McCoist was introduced to the action in the thirty-second minute after Staale Stensaas sustained an eye injury, and his presence and experience proved vital as a stodgy Rangers side struggled against their gutsy First Division adversaries.

After having a goal ruled out for offside three minutes before the half-time interval, McCoist eventually broke the deadlock in the sixty-second minute when he turned inside the penalty area and fired a fine shot out of the reach of Allan Ferguson and into the net. Although it had been rather more uncomfortable than many observers had expected, McCoist's goal was enough to see the cup-holders through to the next round and also earned the veteran striker another club goal-scoring record. He had now amassed fifty-one goals in a tournament that had been kind to him many times over the years, and that surpassed Jim Forrest's half-century of League Cup goals to make McCoist Rangers' top marksman in the competition. 'This tournament has been lucky for me,' he said on learning that he had overtaken Forrest's total. 'I have nine winners' medals and now to overtake Jim Forrest's goal-scoring record is very special.'[2]

Six days after the Hamilton match, Rangers' season spectacularly imploded. Walter Smith took his side to the Ullevi Stadium in Gothenburg to face a side that were smarting after suffering a humiliating 6-0 drubbing at the hands of Halmstads in the Swedish league, their biggest reverse for five years. Clearly Rangers felt the full force of the backlash, as Gothenburg, who despite the heavy defeat still topped the Swedish league table on goal difference from Helsingborg, dealt a hammer blow to Rangers' hopes of reaching the Champions League for a third successive season by winning 3-0. McCoist replaced the ineffectual Negri for the final twenty-two minutes when Rangers were 2-0 behind, and although he almost fashioned a crucial away goal when he flashed a header a fraction wide of the target, he could only watch as Gothenburg substitute Peter Eriksson rubbed salt into the wounds by scoring a third goal for the hosts in the final minute. Although Rangers had been denied the services of Brian Laudrup – the Dane was out of action following a bout of chickenpox – their display left little room for excuses, with lamentable defending costing them dearly.

Clearly, the shooting boots would have to be unearthed ahead of the return leg, and McCoist and Negri seemed to have found theirs when they hit the goal trail in the two domestic matches Rangers played following the Gotheburg debacle. Falkirk were first to fall victim to the razor-sharp duo, with the Bairns reduced to tears when a hat-trick from McCoist ushered them out of the League Cup at Ibrox. The home side fell behind in the thirty-seventh minute through a goal from Kevin James, before McCoist restored parity with a thundering shot from a free-kick two minutes before the interval and added two more goals in the final eight minutes, completing his hat-trick from the penalty spot after Negri had fallen following an aerial joust with James.

Although the Italian failed to find the net against Falkirk, he duly resumed normal service when Rangers entertained Dundee United in the league match the following weekend. With McCoist again watching from the substitutes' bench, Negri turned in an awesome display of finishing that the Ibrox master would have been proud of himself; the moody Italian scored five times as United were hammered by five goals to one. Unfortunately neither marksmen could reproduce their form when Gothenburg came visiting four days later. Both were included in the starting line-up, but drew a blank as the Swedes secured a 1-1 draw and progressed to the lucrative league stage 4-1 on aggregate.

The Gothenburg match had been a rare start for McCoist, and despite a prolific opening to the new season that had yielded seven goals in only four appearances, he gradually found his involvement in the first team diminishing. Over the course of the next eleven league fixtures, McCoist made it onto the field of play only four times, playing a sum total of just forty-two minutes.

The reason for his exclusion from the starting eleven was simply down to the sensational form of new boy Negri. The Italian blazed an electrifying trail in his first ten league matches, adding to his five-goal haul against United with doubles against Hearts, Hibernian, St Johnstone and Kilmarnock, four goals in a 7-0 demolition of Dunfermline at Ibrox, and a hat-trick in the 4-1 home victory over Kilmarnock. This amazing run earned him a place in the record books: the Italian became the first player to score in ten successive league matches since the inception of the Premier Division back in 1975.

By Christmas, the moody Italian had racked up a staggering total of thirty-four goals, and the record-book writers were readying their pens for plenty of rewriting. Although Negri displayed the same predatory instincts in front of goal that had become synonymous with McCoist throughout his reign at Ibrox, the strike pair were polar opposites in terms of the way they chose to celebrate getting on the scoresheet. McCoist had made a career out of flashing a goal-scoring grin that would have put a Cheshire cat to shame, but the sullen Negri could barely raise a smile to acknowledge despatching the ball into the opposition net.

Negri's mannerisms were of no real significance to the hordes of Rangers fans, though. They yearned for that tenth successive title and were acutely aware that if Negri could manage to stretch his early season hot streak into the New Year then any pretenders to Rangers' crown would be brushed aside with ease, meaning that the championship flag would be fluttering in the Ibrox breeze come the end of the season. McCoist could only watch in admiration as the man eight years his junior cut a swathe through the Premier Division defences, threatening in the process to obliterate goal-scoring records that McCoist had spent years building up.

In addition to Negri's glut of goals, McCoist's lack of game time was also down to the fact Walter Smith had tweaked his system, opting to deploy the Italian as a solo striker, ably supported by Brian Laudrup, playing in his familiar free role. He did, however, earn his first start since the Gothenburg match in late August when he replaced the suspended Gordon Durie for the visit to Motherwell on 22 November, and despite donning the unfamiliar number ten jersey, he duly netted his first league goal of the season when he fired Rangers into the lead in the twenty-first minute. However, a late defensive lapse allowed Motherwell to equalise and earn a share of the spoils. This was Rangers' third successive draw, and allowed league leaders Hearts to stretch their lead to four points.

Unfortunately for McCoist, any hopes he may have held that his goal at Fir Park would help cement a return to regular first-team action were dashed when he suffered a hamstring injury that sidelined him for a fortnight. However, when he managed to shake off his ailment, opportunities to break into the first eleven were still at a premium, with McCoist's only appearances before the end of the year being a six-minute cameo against Dundee United at Ibrox on 27 December and a run-out in a closed-doors match against Raith Rovers in which he netted twice from the penalty spot.

With the forthcoming World Cup in France looming large, McCoist knew he had to secure regular first-team action in some way, shape or form in order to remain at the forefront of national coach Craig Brown's mind. It left him with little option other than to contemplate a future away from his beloved Ibrox.

His affection for Rangers meant that seeking employment in Scotland at another Scottish Premier League club was never going to be entertained, but a move to England presented an attractive alternative. McCoist's goal-starved spell with Sunderland at the outset of his career had always raised question marks in some quarters over whether he was deserving of a place in the pantheon of great goalscorers to have graced the British game, so this opportunity, albeit late in his career, presented a chance to definitively silence the doubters once and for all.

A three-month loan deal was widely touted, with a host of potential suitors voicing an interest in luring the experienced hitman south of the border. Former team-mates Trevor Francis and Ray Wilkins, in charge of Birmingham City and Fulham respectively, both registered their interest, as did Howard Kendall at Everton and Kenny Dalglish at Newcastle United, with McCoist expected to fill the striking berth vacated by Alan Shearer, who had succumbed to a long-term injury, should he pursue the latter option.

A return to Sunderland was also mentioned. The Wearsiders' manager, Peter Reid, was keen to add McCoist's experience to his player pool, but with Reid unlikely to split his first-choice striking duo of Niall Quinn and Kevin Phillips – a pairing that had helped fire Sunderland to a fourteen-match unbeaten run in the First Division – it was difficult to see how a move to Wearside would satisfy McCoist's desire to secure the regular action in the first team he craved. Three teams from across the Atlantic, including Tampa Bay Rowdies, were also reported to be in the running for his signature.

In the end, no transfer, temporary or otherwise, materialised. Early in the New Year, any potential moves were scuppered when McCoist injured his knee ligaments following an innocuous challenge on the training ground. The initial diagnosis was a lay-off of at least six weeks, and it appeared that this injury, rather than a lack of footballing action, was going to rob the veteran of the chance to bring the curtain down on his international career at the World Cup.

McCoist, never one to take kindly to being written off, was not finished yet in his quest to make it to France, and he made a scoring return from his knee injury on 3 March when he netted the only goal of the game in a 1-0 win over Liverpool at Ibrox. The Merseysiders had travelled north to take part in a testimonial match for Walter Smith who, at the club's Annual General Meeting in October, had announced that the 1997/98 season would be his last in charge at Ibrox. A crowd of 50,009 turned out to pay a fitting tribute to a man whose successful tenure in Govan marked him out as one of the finest managers of the post-war era. Since taking over the reins from Graeme Souness in 1991, Smith had guided the Light Blues to thirteen domestic honours in addition to steering the club into what was effectively the semi-final of the European Cup in 1992/93. He will always have an indelible place in Rangers folklore.

Six days after the Liverpool victory, McCoist was back in competitive action when he replaced Finnish striker Jonatan Johansson nine minutes from the end of a drab 0-0 draw against Dundee in the last eight of the Scottish Cup. His return was a timely one, as Rangers found themselves in something of a rut as they strove to ensure that the departing Smith would leave clutching yet more silverware. Although Rangers had replaced Hearts at the summit of the Premier League in December, thanks mainly to a resounding 5-2 victory over the Gorgie outfit at Tynecastle, a series of poor results since the turn of the year – Rangers won just three of their first eight Premier Division matches in 1998 and lost 2-0 to Celtic at Parkhead – had resulted in both Celtic and Hearts leapfrogging the Light Blues in the league table.

Rangers were suffering from a lack of goals, with the prolific Negri sustaining an eye injury while playing squash with team-mate Sergio Porrini that ruled him out of action for six weeks. When he returned to the fold, an unsavoury attitude problem surfaced and the morose Italian only added a further two goals to his phenomenal pre-Christmas tally in the remainder of the campaign.

Thus, with the charge towards the tenth league title now almost at a standstill, Walter Smith elected to round up the old guard in the hope that they could help mount a salvage mission and inject new life into his flagging forces. One of the elder statesmen he called upon was McCoist, and the legendary goal-grabber seized the opportunity with relish.

He made his first league start since November, ironically it was at the same venue as his first, Fir Park in Motherwell, and it took him just eleven minutes to etch his name onto the scoresheet. Captaining the side in the absence of Richard Gough, who had returned to Rangers in November following an SOS from Walter Smith, McCoist broke the deadlock when he sent a stunning low right-foot shot into the net from twenty yards, but despite a stellar display that earned him the Man of the Match award, he was unable to prevent Motherwell fighting back to win by two goals to one. That defeat allowed Celtic to extend their lead at the summit to five points, and it seemed that dreams of 'Ten-in-a-Row' were evaporating with each passing week.

Despite the defeat, McCoist's return to the team was the shot in the arm Rangers needed. His presence injected some much-needed passion and fighting spirit back into the side, and this newfound desire served Rangers well when they visited Dens Park four days after the Fir Park defeat to take on Dundee in the Scottish Cup quarter-final replay.

Having delivered a listless performance in the 0-0 draw at Ibrox, the visitors looked to be in trouble again when they fell behind early in the game after James Grady scored in the tenth minute, but parity was restored eight minutes later when McCoist maintained his perfect record of finding the net in each of the matches he had started that season, bravely heading a throw-in from Tony Vidmar behind Rab Douglas. Rangers now had one eye on the last four of the competition, and the winning goal duly arrived thirteen minutes into the second half when McCoist fizzed a free-kick into the net from the edge of the penalty area.

His two-goal salvo took his tally for the season to eleven in just eight appearances, and took his overall goals total for Rangers to a magnificent 350. Thus, he had now achieved one of the two goals he had set himself at the outset of the campaign, and that achievement was the crowning glory on an excellent day for the irrepressible striker. He had also cleaned up at the bookmakers, with his bet for the Queen Mother Champion Chase, One Man, streaking to victory at odds of 7-2, while his prediction of a 1-1 draw in the Champions League match between Monaco and Manchester United also panned out!

One week after the win at Dens Park, the focus of the media spotlight was once again trained on the Ibrox club when it was announced that Paul Gascoigne would be leaving Rangers to join Middlesbrough for a fee of £3.45 million. The news of the Geordie genius' departure at such a critical juncture in the season was met with widespread condemnation by the Rangers support. They were at a loss to understand why the board would sanction the sale of such an important player at a stage of the season when the championship crown and the Scottish Cup were still very much up for grabs. Although Gascoigne's campaign had been interrupted by injury – he had made only twenty-eight appearances, scoring three goals – many friends of Rangers felt he still had a huge part to play in the run-in and that by agreeing to let him leave the club, the board was effectively raising the white flag in the title race.

In truth, the transfer had to be immediate, as the offer from Teeside would not have been on the table in the summer when it was widely expected that Gascoigne would be leaving Govan. It was unlikely the wayward genius would figure in the long-term plans of new manager Dick Advocaat, a renowned disciplinarian, so an immediate parting of the ways was the best course of action for both parties.

McCoist, like the club's supporters, was also saddened when he heard the news of Gascoigne's exit. Not only was he losing a first-class team-mate, he was also bidding farewell to a great friend. He reflected:

> *He was the one player out of all the guys I've played with that could take a game by the scruff of the neck and go and win it for you. I was probably as close to him at Rangers as anybody. I've laughed with Gascoigne, I've fought with Gascoigne, played golf, you name it we've done the lot. I feel honestly very thankful that Gascoigne was in my life. I look on him as a friend. He's an amazing character.*[3]

Gascoigne's time in Glasgow gave rise to countless stories of the shenanigans that took place within the bowels of Ibrox Stadium. Many remain untold, but two that did make it into the public domain deserve to be recounted here for their comedic value.

The first took place at a time when Gascoigne had spent in the region of £12,000 to have some dental work carried out. After years of decay precipitated by the amount of sugary sweets he ate as a youngster, Gascoigne decided to have his teeth capped to re-align them, but while the work was being carried out, his dentist fitted him with a set of temporary caps. The only problem was that the caps were a little too large and, as a result, protruded from Gascoigne's mouth, giving him something of an equine disposition, and when he arrived for training one morning, his team-mates could not resist the opportunity to have a laugh at his expense.

On arrival in the dressing room, Gascoigne threw his bag onto the floor and flashed a beaming grin at those already gathered to prepare for that day's training session, which stimulated an extended bout of uproarious laughter as the players noticed his new dental work. When the initial spell of hilarity subsided, McCoist took the opportunity to set everyone off again by informing his team-mate that his new teeth would now allow him to chew an apple through a letterbox!

For the second incident, Gascoigne enlisted the help of McCoist. The Geordie arrived for training one morning still dressed in his fishing gear (with the exception of the mandatory collar and tie that players were required to wear when they arrived at the stadium for training) carrying two fish he had caught after a successful morning's angling. He and McCoist both happened to be injured at the same time, and when the rest of the team departed for training, the duo went to work. Gascoigne decided that it would be fun to hide the fish inside one of the players' cars and Gordon Durie's club-sponsored Honda was selected. Armed with the fish, McCoist and Gascoigne located Durie's car, hoisted up the boot, unscrewed the spare wheel and lay one of the fish in the bay underneath before re-attaching the wheel in its original position.

Delighted with the job they had done, McCoist set off towards the dressing room only to be beckoned back to the car by the mischievous Gascoigne. Sure that Durie would eventually locate the fish, Gascoigne found a compartment inside the car that few knew existed and laid the second fish to rest there.

Within a few days, Durie began to notice a rather unpleasant odour developing in his car. After failing to get rid of the smell with the aid of a multitude of 'Magic Tree' air fresheners, the striker took his car to be valeted, and during the cleaning process, the remnants of the first fish were found under the spare wheel. Thinking he had finally solved the mystery of the source of the malodorous miasma, Durie continued to use his car to travel to and from training, but the stink of the decaying second fish remained until a perplexed Durie eventually had to admit defeat and get rid of the car!

Although his presence may have been missed in the dressing room, the departure of Gascoigne, for the time being at least, did not seem to have an adverse affect on Rangers' push for supremacy in Scotland. The team notched up three successive victories, with St Johnstone and Hibernian defeated at Ibrox (2-1 and 3-0 respectively) while Dunfermline were beaten 3-2 away from home. These results re-ignited the Light Blues' championship challenge, and inevitably McCoist was at the hub of the successes, adding a further three goals to his season's tally.

After drawing a blank against St Johnstone, he bagged a brace against Dunfermline, with the second of his two goals ringing up yet another milestone in his Rangers career. He opened his account with a typical McCoist finish in the twenty-sixth minute, feasting on the scraps after Ian Westwater had parried a shot from Laudrup, and he fired Rangers into a 2-1 lead three minutes after the interval with almost an exact replica, profiting on this occasion after Westwater had made a fine block to deny Negri his thirty-seventh goal of the season. The latter strike was his 250th league goal in Rangers' colours, and he grabbed his 251st, and ultimately final, Premier Division counter for the club four days later when he thumped a header into the net as Rangers motored into top gear with a convincing win over relegation-haunted Hibernian.

That sequence of events represented a stunning turnaround in McCoist's fortunes. Seemingly on his way out of Ibrox just two months earlier and out of the running for a place in Scotland's World Cup squad, the 'old-timer' had yet again dished up a generous helping of humble pie for the numerous 'experts' who had called time on his career at the top level. His return had galvanised Rangers, and he was justly rewarded for his contribution when he picked up the Player of the Month trophy for March, the fifth time he had laid his hands on the award. Inevitably that earned him yet another record, as no other player in the Scottish game had picked up the accolade on five separate occasions.

Buoyed by the recent renaissance that had hauled them back into contention for the main prizes, McCoist and Rangers travelled to Parkhead on Sunday, 5 April to face Celtic in the semi-final of the Scottish Cup. McCoist was in the starting line-up, wearing the number eight jersey and leading the line with support being provided by Brian Laudrup, who occupied his usual roving role. On the bench was Lorenzo Amoruso, who had yet to kick a ball in anger for the first team as he had been injured since his arrival the previous summer. He only had to wait nineteen minutes before he made his Rangers bow, as he was pitched into the white-hot heat of the Parkhead cauldron when an injury to Gordan Petric necessitated an early substitution.

Celtic dominated the first half, but found Andy Goram, so often the scourge of the Hoops, in inspired form. Time after time he repelled Celtic's advances on the Rangers goal and when referee Jim McCluskey signalled the end of the first half, he did so with the scoresheet still blank.

Rangers emerged for the second period with renewed vigour, roused by a lively half-time discussion and the heroics of Goram. Inspired by the promptings of Jonas Thern and Jorg Albertz, the Light Blues enjoyed their own spell of concerted pressure, pinning their rivals back in their own half, and their pressure was rewarded fifteen minutes from the end.

Thern, who had been plagued by injuries since joining the club, gathered the ball on the right flank, immediately in front of the dugouts, from where he floated a delightful sixty-yard diagonal pass with his right foot into the stride of Albertz, who had popped up on the opposite wing. The big German looked up and arrowed a left-footed cross into the danger area. Lurking there was a veteran predator still hungry to snare more goals, and as the ball bounced once on the sodden turf, McCoist stole in between Celtic keeper, Jonathon Gould, and his marker, Alan

Stubbs, to launch himself at the ball. He directed a diving header out of the reach of Gould and despatched it into the back of the net to send the Rangers fans behind the goal into raptures.

The goal was McCoist's twenty-seventh against Celtic and he now had a share of yet another record, as he now stood alongside Celtic legend Jimmy McGrory as the top goalscorer in Old Firm matches. There was no hiding McCoist's delight as he sank to his knees in front of the Rangers legions, many of whom had no doubt backed their hero to net the first goal at staggeringly long odds of 7-1.

A few minutes later, the Light Blues booked their place in the final when Albertz doubled their advantage with a quite splendid solo goal. Picking up the ball on the halfway line, the German powerhouse carved his way through the Celtic defence, leaving a trail of defenders in his wake, before lashing an unstoppable shot into the net. Celtic rallied thereafter, but their only reward was a late strike from Craig Burley in stoppage time.

Rangers won 2-1, and the dream of the Double, one that had seemed dead in the water just a few weeks earlier, had suddenly been resuscitated, with McCoist the man who had undoubtedly supplied the kiss of life. His vital counter at Parkhead was his seventh in his last six games, a spell during which Rangers had reduced the gap at the top of the table to three points and overcome the challenges of Dundee and Celtic to take their place at the end-of-season showpiece, the Scottish Cup final, where they would meet Hearts.

Praise for the veteran's recent endeavours rained in from all angles in the wake of the Old Firm triumph. Team-mate Joachim Bjorklund called him 'incredible'[4], while Stuart McCall lauded his determination to win back his place in the team and produce the goods to drag Rangers out of the mire. 'He kept going and going and we're all so proud of him,' said the flame-haired midfielder. 'I still get surprised by him and what he can do. After all these years you would have thought I would have wised up, wouldn't you?'[5] 'The Ranger', a weekly columnist in the *Rangers News*, also heaped praise on McCoist's shoulders saying: 'Ally McCoist injected urgency into the side at a time when many gave the distinct impression of self-pity. His goals have ignited our challenge and the team has visibly taken a lift from his irrepressible enthusiasm and love for Rangers. I believe that he has also rallied the dressing room and what once looked a dispirited squad can really go on and make this season memorable.'[6]

THE FINAL HURRAH: 1997–98

Seven days after locking horns at Parkhead, the titans clashed again, with league points at stake this time. Having failed to capitalise on Rangers' mid-season form slump and construct a sizeable advantage in the championship, Celtic arrived in Govan just three points ahead of their arch-rivals. Thus, a win by two clear goals would take Rangers back to the top of the pile on goal difference, and they duly obliged in front of a packed house, with goals from Thern and Albertz securing a 2-0 win.

The goals were magnificent. Thern's was a rasping volley from twenty-five yards reminiscent of the goal Ray Wilkins had scored against Celtic back in August 1988, while the Albertz strike was almost a carbon copy of his semi-final wonder goal. Rangers were streets ahead of their rivals and should have won more emphatically, but the golden touch of McCoist that had propelled the Light Blues back into the ring as championship contenders was conspicuous by its absence on this occasion. He passed up three openings to mark his final Old Firm match by notching up his twenty-eighth goal in this fixture, with the last of them in the final few minutes providing his most glaring miss of all; McCoist somehow failed to hit the target when teed up in front of goal by the unselfish Albertz.

The victory now put Rangers in charge at the top of the league with only four games left to play. Although Smith's side had the harder run-in – they faced trips to Pittodrie, Tynecastle and Tannadice, while Celtic would have to go on their travels just once when they faced Dunfermline in their penultimate fixture – the ball was in their court, with four wins likely to be enough to secure a tenth consecutive title.

However, just when it seemed as though the championship bandwagon was beginning to purr beautifully, it was dramatically derailed the following weekend when Rangers were dumped 1-0 at Pittodrie by Aberdeen. Despite fielding the same eleven that had outplayed Celtic, Rangers chose the wrong time to return to the dire form that had plagued them in the early months of 1998. Stephen Glass scored the only goal of the game, and Rangers' misery was compounded when Lorenzo Amoruso, who had shown signs of just how good a player he was in his first two games for the club, was sent off in the fifty-eighth minute by referee Willie Young for a push on Eoin Jess. McCoist was starved of the service that had reaped so many rewards in recent matches and his afternoon also came to a premature ending when he was replaced by Marco Negri in the seventy-second minute after picking up a muscle strain. Celtic duly took advantage of Rangers' lacklustre display, defeating Motherwell 4-1 at Parkhead to regain their three-point advantage at the top of the table.

Rangers' title hopes looked to have evaporated, but remarkably fortunes see-sawed again the following weekend, as Celtic dropped two points in a 0-0 home draw with bottom-of-the-table Hibernian, while Rangers hammered Hearts 3-0 at Tynecastle. Gennaro 'Rino' Gattuso, who would subsequently find fame, fortune, two Champions League-winners' medals and a World Cup-winners' medal as a world-class midfielder with AC Milan and Italy, chose the perfect moment to notch his first double for Rangers, and Jorg Albertz completed the scoring with the type of left-foot drive with which he had become synonymous. Gattuso was sporting the number eight jersey McCoist had graced in each of the previous eight matches, with the veteran hitman having to content himself with a place on the substitutes' bench this time after failing to shake off the injury that had curtailed his involvement at Pittodrie six days earlier.

With just two fixtures remaining, it could scarcely have been tighter at the top. Celtic led by a solitary point with respective goal differences identical, but on the penultimate weekend of the season, the advantage looked to be with the blue half of Glasgow. On the Saturday, Rangers were due to host Kilmarnock at Ibrox with the knowledge that a win would see them overtake Celtic, who were faced with a tricky fixture away at Dunfermline the next day.

Alas, on an emotionally charged day that saw McCoist and so many other great Rangers players performing on the Ibrox stage for the last time, it turned out to be an opportunity missed for the reigning champions. Their leaving party was sensationally gate-crashed by the Ayrshire visitors, who won a poor game by one goal to nil thanks to a goal from Ally Mitchell in injury-time.

It was an afternoon when the creativity and guile of Paul Gascoigne was sorely missed, and even the half-time introduction of McCoist failed to spark Rangers into life. The club's chief sharpshooter was again starved of any decent openings, with the only one of note arriving four minutes after the interval when he manoeuvred himself into position to receive a pass from Laudrup. For once, though, the Danish wizard failed to conjure up the perfect assist, with his pass falling behind his unguarded team-mate, and by the time McCoist had adjusted his body to shoot for goal, he was closed down and the chance had gone.

THE FINAL HURRAH: 1997–98

It seemed such a heartbreaking way to end arguably the most successful era in the club's history. This team should have gone out with a resounding bang not a silent whimper, and as the players re-emerged to take a final bow in front of the crowd for a final time, the realisation that his time at Ibrox was at an end finally hit home for McCoist. 'When I looked around at the final whistle it suddenly dawned on me that I would soon be leaving all this behind,' he said. 'So many memories came flooding back, the highs and the lows, and I just broke down.' He went on to say: 'When Rangers has been part of your life for so long, it's very difficult to let go and I'm now realising that. I feel privileged to have been at a club like Rangers for such a lengthy spell of my career. And I would like to think that I've played my part in the great run of success which the club has enjoyed since Graeme Souness first took charge.'[7]

The 290 goals he had scored in 454 appearances since Souness' arrival in the summer of 1986 tended to suggest that the role he had played had almost been as significant, arguably more so, than that of any of the other legends to have donned the Light Blue jersey in that timeframe.

Although Celtic kept the title race alive for another week by drawing 1-1 at East End Park, they duly denied their rivals the coveted tenth title when they beat St Johnstone 2-0 on the last day of the season. Disappointment clouded the blue skies that enveloped Tannadice where Rangers had completed their season with a 2-1 victory over Dundee United. Goals from Laudrup and Albertz turned out to be academic in the end, as strikes from Henrik Larsson and Harald Bratbakk ensured that the championship trophy would reside in the Parkhead trophy room for the first time since 1988. It was the end of an era for Rangers, with the likes of McCall, Gough, Durrant, Goram and Laudrup, established stars and iconic figures from the previous decade, about to join McCoist in leaving Ibrox in order to make way for the next generation of players under Dick Advocaat.

While downcast at not having secured a record tenth successive title, these legends, who had rightly secured their place in Rangers folklore, still had the opportunity to go out on a high with the chance of silverware still very much alive. Seven days after the championship had been snatched away from their grasp, Rangers faced up to Hearts at Parkhead in the Scottish Cup final. McCoist, who had replaced Brian Laudrup in the sixty-sixth minute of the win over Dundee United, started a match that would turn out to be his last in a Rangers jersey on the bench, as Smith favoured the partnership of Durie and Laudrup up front.

Barely two minutes into a match watched by a crowd of 48,946, Hearts claimed the lead. Ian Ferguson was adjudged to have fouled Colin Cameron on the right of the penalty area, and although television evidence suggested the offence had taken place outside the area, referee Willie Young awarded a penalty. Cameron dusted himself down and duly converted the spot-kick.

Hearts, mauled 5-1 by Rangers in their last Cup final appearance in 1996, had not captured a major trophy since winning the League Championship in 1960, and the early goal allowed them to dictate the play. The Edinburgh side simply retreated and invited Rangers to find a way through a rearguard that was superbly marshalled by former Ranger Dave McPherson and future Ranger David Weir. Rangers pushed and probed for the remainder of the first half, but they failed to find the combination required to pick the lock holding the Hearts defence together.

Changes were made at the interval in a bid to engineer an equaliser. With hopes of securing one last piece of silverware in his final match in charge looking increasingly forlorn, Smith once again turned to his old guard, and McCoist was introduced to the fray, taking over from the ineffectual Staale Stensaas. It was an opportunity for McCoist to pen one last entry in his capacious tome of fairytales, and his impact on this his 581st appearance in Light Blue was almost immediate, as he fashioned two opportunities in the opening moments of the second period, firing into the side netting before squandering a good opening when he failed to beat Gilles Rousset when well placed.

At last Rangers seemed to be making some headway, but they were rocked in the fifty-second minute when Hearts doubled their lead. Amoruso was caught in possession by Stephane Adam, and the French forward duly capitalised by rifling the ball behind Goram. It was all turning into something of a damp squib. Hearts had clearly failed to adhere to the pre-match script, and the glorious send-off for the greatest of all Rangers teams seemed certain to end, uncharacteristically, with failure.

McCoist was not about to toss in the towel just yet, though. The enthusiasm that had acted like a shot in the arm in the dying embers of the title bid was showing no signs of waning, and it took a save from Rousset from point-blank range to deny him a goal that would have put a completely different complexion on the match.

The veteran sharpshooter was not to be denied, however, and he set up a grandstand finish when he got his name on the scoresheet nine minutes from the end. Young Gattuso was the architect, receiving the ball in the heart of the pitch and executing the most delightful slide-rule pass that prised open the Hearts defence. For McCoist, this kind of service was manna from heaven and he needed no second invitation, taking Gattuso's pass in his stride before sweeping the ball beyond Rousset in the Hearts goal to drag Rangers back into the match. Surely he wasn't going to do it again? Was he?

With four minutes left on the clock and with Rangers pinning Hearts to the ropes, McCoist received the ball on the edge of the penalty area. He eluded his marker and suddenly the chance was on. The Rangers fans rose from their seats in anticipation as McCoist drew back his right leg in preparation for the execution of his 356th goal for the club. However, in the act of shooting he was impeded and brought crashing to the ground by the challenge of David Weir. It had to be a penalty, and for a moment Hearts' hearts stopped beating. All eyes were now transfixed on referee Willie Young awaiting his decision with baited breath. Young, who had awarded Hearts a controversial spot-kick earlier in the match, did indeed spot the infringement and for a moment it looked as though he was pointing towards the twelve-yard mark and awarding Rangers a penalty. Hearts leapt but soon sank, as it turned out that his judgement was to award Rangers a free-kick right on the edge of the box and not the penalty they were so desirous of. Young deemed that the foul had been committed outside the penalty area.

There were howls of frustration from fans and players alike. The earlier award for Hearts carried the same sort of dubiety as to whether it had taken place inside or outside the penalty box, but in this instance Young declined to listen to the protests. Laudrup took the free-kick, but Rousset saved his effort and the last chance to force the final into extra-time was gone, as did the chance for this glorious era in Rangers history to end with a touch of silverware.

It was hardly fitting that perhaps the greatest of all the eras in Rangers' history should end in such a manner. Smith, McCoist and the many others who were turning out for Rangers for the last time deserved to retire with a roar rather than with a trophy-less whimper, and as the players trooped round Parkhead on their final lap of honour, there were tears shed, not only by the supporters in the stands but also by the players who had been the beating heart of the club throughout a period of unparalleled success.

The Cup final defeat and the fact that he had just played his last match for his boyhood heroes only served to compound a gut-wrenching week for Ally McCoist. A few days before the match with Hearts, the veteran striker had found out that he would not be part of Craig Brown's twenty-two-man Scotland squad to travel to France to compete in the 1998 World Cup. He had looked upon the World Cup as being the ideal platform upon which to bring to an end an international career that had seen him amass fifty-nine caps and score nineteen goals for his country, but despite the fact that his Cup final goal illustrated he could still cut the mustard at the top level, it was not to be.

His omission perplexed many observers (former Rangers striker Derek Johnstone called it 'utterly scandalous'[8]), as despite his advancing years, he had enjoyed a fine run of scoring form in the latter part of the season and was in far more prolific form than the strikers who had been included. He had notched sixteen goals in twenty-six appearances in the season just past, but Brown instead favoured Gordon Durie, Scott Booth, Darren Jackson and Kevin Gallacher as his attacking options. 'To miss out on being picked for the World Cup squad was bad enough, but defeat at Celtic Park on Saturday [in the Cup final] was catastrophic,' said McCoist. 'I was inconsolable when Willie Young blew the final whistle and hard as I tried I just couldn't prevent the tears from flowing. It was possibly the worst week in my life and it was a disappointing end to a disappointing season.'[9]

McCoist's team-mate Stuart McCall was also overlooked, and some years later in his autobiography, *The Real McCall*, he alluded to the reasons why the duo were left at home. He said: 'Craig [Brown] said he feared that Coisty and I, if we weren't picked [for the games], were going to treat the trip like a party.'[10] This was a remarkable statement to make. Although both McCoist and McCall were fully paid-up members of the 'work hard, play hard' gang, their lifestyle had never compromised their performances on the field, so to use this as a means of reasoning why neither were selected for France seemed preposterous. Whatever Brown's actual reasons were (he hinted that he felt McCoist was perhaps lacking the level of fitness required to play at such a level), McCoist would not be gracing the world's premier tournament, thus robbing him of the chance to bring the curtain down on his international career on the greatest stage of all.

McCoist could at least take consolation from the fact that his place in the realm of great Rangers players was secure. Since signing in 1983, he had pulled on a Rangers shirt 581 times, a total surpassed only by John Greig and Sandy Jardine in the post-war era, and his remarkable tally of 355 goals marked him out as Rangers' top goalscorer of all time. (Incidentally, Jimmy Smith, a wonderful centre-forward who graced the Ibrox turf between 1928 and 1946, would have rivalled McCoist's total, but a portion of his goals were scored during wartime matches, goals which are discounted from the official records.)

In fifteen full seasons at Ibrox, Ally McCoist won a total of twenty winners' medals, ten of which were from the League Championship, with the others being one Scottish Cup badge and a record nine League Cup baubles. He is also part of an elite group of Rangers players, having been one of only three – Richard Gough and Ian Ferguson are the others – who actively participated in each of the Nine-in-a-Row championship seasons between 1989 and 1997. He claimed a surfeit of personal accolades and records in that timeframe too, the most noteworthy of which were his two European Golden Boots and the double Player of the Year award picked up in the 1991/92 season.

His goal-scoring feats are unsurpassed and provide clinical proof that disproves the theory that was often perpetuated about McCoist being a 'lucky' player. In addition to being Rangers' top goalscorer of all time, McCoist has the distinction of being the club's top marksman in the League Championship (251 strikes in 418 games), Rangers' leading scorer in the Scottish League Cup (a phenomenal fifty-four goals in sixty-two games) and the club's top scorer in European competition (twenty-one goals in fifty-four games, a tally that stood as a record for all Scottish clubs until Celtic's Henrik Larsson broke it in 2002).

Are such statistics the hallmark of a 'lucky' footballer? McCoist undoubtedly enjoyed his fair share of fortune on occasion, but it is impossible to attribute all of his success to a plethora of kisses from 'Lady Luck'. McCoist had a talent few footballers are blessed with, a razor-sharp goal-scoring instinct, and his heightened awareness and alertness inside the penalty area gave rise to a glut of goals and a career tally that, in today's post-Bosman era where long periods spent with the same club are a rarity, is unlikely to be matched, far less beaten.

All good things must come to an end, though, and after fifteen glorious years it was time for 'The King of Goal-scoring' to abdicate his Ibrox throne. With Rangers about to embark on a new era under the stewardship of their first-ever foreign manager, the Dutch disciplinarian

ALLY McCOIST

Dick Advocaat, Ally McCoist was given a free transfer in the summer of 1998. His departure from Ibrox closed the longest and most successful chapter in his football career, but the old dog still believed he had a few tricks left in the locker. Despite a burgeoning media career – his role as team captain on *A Question of Sport* was earning him rave reviews and he would now be an integral part of the BBC coverage of the forthcoming World Cup, acting as a pundit, a role that with his quick wit and sharp, wise-cracking sense of humour was tailor-made for him – McCoist still wanted to keep playing football.

Time would tell whether or not he would get his wish, but for the moment it was all about looking back and reflecting on one of the truly great Rangers careers, as the followers of the Light Blues bid farewell to the greatest goalscorer of his generation.

CHAPTER SIXTEEN

FOOTBALL IN PERSPECTIVE

In the summer of 1998, Ally McCoist was smiling again. Following the heartbreaking end to his Rangers career and his exclusion from the Scotland World Cup squad, he had not had his troubles to seek of late, but on 2 June, two days before he was due to travel to France to take up his role as a pundit with the BBC at the World Cup, McCoist's wife Allison gave birth to twin boys at Paisley's Royal Alexandra Hospital. Mitchell and Argyll, weighing in at 5lb 7oz and 6lb 2oz respectively, were born twenty minutes apart, and the McCoist clan had now swelled to five, with three-year-old Alexander waiting to greet his wee brothers when they returned to the family home in Bridge of Weir. There was also a degree of sentiment in the naming of the two babies. Both took the middle name Cooper, a tribute to McCoist's great friend, the late Davie Cooper.

The arrival of his newborn sons more than made up for the anguish McCoist had been suffering in the wake of leaving Rangers and missing out on an international swansong with Scotland at the World Cup. He even joked that it was fortunate he had not been selected, as he would have had to return home from the Scots' training camp to be present at the birth.

Less than one week after the birth, the McCoists were back in hospital, but this time it was for an altogether different reason. Mitchell was admitted to the cardiac unit at Glasgow's Yorkhill hospital for tests on a suspected heart defect. The doctors were concerned that the newborn tot had a leaking heart valve, a defect that can lead to the lungs filling up with fluid and precipitate breathing difficulties. The results of tests carried out confirmed the initial diagnosis, and also revealed that Mitchell had been born with a hole in his heart and would require surgery at the age of six months to seal it.

However, the heart operation had to be brought forward following complications, and over the next four months the McCoist family were put through the emotional wringer, as Mitchell fought for his life. In that timeframe, he flitted between intensive care and the high dependency unit at Yorkhill Sick Children's hospital in Glasgow, undergoing a series of operations to rectify his heart defect and also a stomach condition. The baby's troubles suddenly put everything into perspective for McCoist, making the quandary over where his footballing future lay superfluous. 'You think with all your years on the big stage you are geared up to handle anything,' he said in the wake of Mitchell's first operation, 'but nothing can prepare you for coping with seeing your wee boy so helpless.'[1]

However, Mitchell's condition steadily improved, and although he spent much of the first year of his life undergoing surgery in hospital, he was eventually released the day before his first birthday. A series of operations have since followed, including a major procedure that gave his heart one chamber to replace two, but the youngster has shown remarkable strength to pull through, earning the admiration of his father in the process. 'He's a baby, but I call him a man, because he's been through more than any of us will go through in a lifetime,' said McCoist during an interview for his video *The Real McCoist*.[2]

My mum phoned me up the other day and my old school had been on looking to fill out one of these questionnaires. My mum usually fills them in, but there was one question that she couldn't answer, because she had forgotten my answer. It was 'Which person in the world do you most admire?' and I said she should just have put Mitchell. A lot of people would maybe find that that's a strange thing to say about a sixteen-month-old baby, but I've become so much a better person within myself for the experiences I've had with Mitchell than I could ever have wished for in any other walk of life. He's a remarkable person for what he has been through.

With Mitchell on the road to recovery after the first series of operations in the early months of his life, Ally McCoist was able to concentrate his efforts on finding a new club for the 1998/99 season. As expected, the arrival of Dick Advocaat at Ibrox heralded the end of the Rangers careers of so many of their greatest players. Club captain Richard Gough returned to America and Kansas City Wiz, Stuart McCall went back to his first club, Bradford City, and Ian Durrant joined Kilmarnock. Goalkeeper Andy Goram was also freed as Advocaat's revolution really started to take shape.

McCoist now had a decision to make. He could have easily hung up his boots and concentrated on his mushrooming career in the sporting media, but recollections of a conversation some years earlier with the late Davie Cooper convinced him to extend his playing career. Cooper had himself faced a similar choice when he had left Rangers in 1989, but instead of quitting, he signed for Motherwell and enjoyed a hugely successful spell with the Lanarkshire side, winning a Scottish Cup medal in 1991 and earning a recall to the national team for a World Cup qualifier with Norway. Indeed, had he not been injured towards the end of the 1989/90 season, he would also have been part of the Scotland squad to take part in the World Cup in Italy.

Cooper's adventures proved there was life after Rangers and prompted McCoist to consider the options on offer. Five clubs – Kilmarnock, Raith Rovers, Airdrie, Hibernian and Queens Park Rangers – registered an interest in securing his signature, with Kilmarnock seemingly the front-runners. The presence of McCoist's close friend Ian Durrant in the Rugby Park dressing room was a major factor in tipping the scales in favour of the Ayrshire side, although Raith manager Jimmy Nicholl, a former team-mate at both Ibrox and Roker Park, was also confident of acquiring the services of the veteran hitman.

One week before the 1998/99 season officially kicked off, McCoist played in a bounce game for Kilmarnock at Rugby Park and scored in a 3-2 win. His performance was of a sufficient standard to convince the Ayrshire side's hierarchy to offer him a contract, and on 4 August 1998, he was officially unveiled as a Kilmarnock player. He penned a one-year contract and became the highest paid player in Kilmarnock's history on a wage that was reported to be worth in the region of £5,000 per week.

Although the midnight hour of McCoist's football career was fast approaching, the call for time had not come just yet. It may have been last orders, but there were a few more goals left to be added to the McCoist collection, a prospect that no doubt struck fear into the hearts of defenders all over the country.

CHAPTER SEVENTEEN

THE FINAL CHAPTER: 1998–2001

Kilmarnock Football Club was formed in 1869. In common with other football clubs founded at this time, it was a group of cricketers who instituted the club, as they sought a wintertime alternative to their fair-weather pursuit. They played their cricket on Barbados Green, and the venue they chose for their football club was a mere stone's throw from there, with Rugby Park located a matter of yards away on South Hamilton Street. Incidentally, Rugby Park got its name from the type of football the new club played at that time. It was a hybrid of football and rugby – hence Rugby Park – and it took some time for Kilmarnock to adopt purely football tactics.

When the Scottish Football Association was founded, four years after Kilmarnock's formation in 1873, the Ayrshire side were named as one of the original members, and when the SFA devised the Scottish Cup competition, Kilmarnock paid one pound towards the cost of the grand old trophy. Unfortunately, their first experience of the tournament was a rather unpleasant one: they lost their inaugural match against Renton by two goals to nil.

However, despite that early setback, the Scottish Cup was kind to Kilmarnock in their formative years and the club enjoyed a great deal of success in the tournament. They soon built up a formidable reputation as a fearsome cup side, and were the one team outside the Old Firm the other clubs wanted to avoid when the draw was made.

After reaching the final in 1898, where they lost 2-0 to Rangers, Kilmarnock enjoyed their first success in the competition in 1920 when they defeated Albion Rovers 3-2 in the final. However, their second triumph, nine years later, was arguably more satisfying: they claimed the scalp of Cup-holders Rangers, defeating the league champions 2-0 in the final at Hampden Park in front of 114,708 supporters. The game became famous when Rangers left-half, Thomas 'Tully' Craig, earned an unwanted place in the history books by becoming the first player in history to miss a penalty in the Scottish Cup final. Kilmarnock took the lead in the forty-eighth minute when their outside-left John Aitken fired the ball beyond Tom Hamilton and doubled their advantage in the seventy-seventh minute when centre-forward Harry Cunningham scored. They held on to their two-goal advantage until the final whistle, but another slice of history was made two minutes from time, when Jock Buchanan became the first player to be ordered off in the Cup final, the Rangers right-half being given his marching orders by referee Tom Dougray for dissent. Incidentally, Gordon 'Mattha' Smith, grandfather of Gordon Smith, SFA chief executive at the time of writing, played for Kilmarnock in this game.

In the League Championship, the Ayrshire side began life in Division Two, and their supporters had to wait until 1899 before they got their first taste of action in the top tier of the Scottish game. Kilmarnock won promotion as Second Division champions at the end of the 1898/99 season, and they rubbed shoulders with the elite for the next forty-seven years.

Kilmarnock were never serious contenders for the title in that timeframe, but neither were they regulars in the relegation dogfight. For much of the 1920s, '30s and '40s they finished mid-table and rose as high as third in 1917/18, but in the first full season contested after the end of the Second World War, Kilmarnock finished fifteenth and were relegated to Division B along with Hamilton Academical.

During their seven-season stay in the lower division, they reached the final of the Scottish League Cup in 1953, defeating Rangers 1-0 in the semi-final before losing by the same scoreline to Dundee in the Hampden final. The following season, they won promotion back to the First Division and, in 1957, they finished third in the league behind

Rangers and Hearts. The club also reached the Scottish Cup final where they lost to Falkirk.

This was the beginning of the most successful era in the club's history and, as the world swung into the sixties, the Ayrshire side finished as runners-up in Division One, four points behind champions Hearts, with Rangers, who defeated Kilmarnock in the Scottish Cup final, eight points adrift in third. They finished second again the following season and also reached the League Cup final, only to lose out to champions Rangers. Two more runners-up spots followed in the next three seasons, before the club celebrated its finest hour in the 1964/65 season when Kilmarnock won the Scottish Division One Championship for the first time in quite thrilling circumstances.

On the final day of the season, Kilmarnock, managed by Rangers legend Willie Waddell, were at Tynecastle to face league-leaders Hearts. The Edinburgh side led their Ayrshire counterparts by two points and needed only a draw to clinch the title; Kilmarnock, on the other hand, needed to win by two clear goals to snatch the championship on goal average (goals scored divided by goals conceded). That is exactly what they did, with goals from David Sneddon and Brian McIlroy securing the requisite 2-0 victory. The league trophy was bound for Rugby Park, with the margin of victory just 0.041 of a goal!

Kilmarnock failed to build on their success, though. Despite enjoying several thrilling nights on the European stage, notably at Rugby Park against Real Madrid with whom they drew 2-2 in 1965 and Eintracht Frankfurt, who were beaten 5-1 to overturn a 3-0 deficit from the first-leg in West Germany, they gradually began to slither down the league ladder until they were relegated at the end of the 1972/73 season. They did reach the semi-final of the League Cup in 1965/66, but were edged out in a thrilling match against Rangers that finished 6-4 in the Glasgow giants' favour.

However, their stay in the lower league was a brief one, and they bounced straight back up the following season, but when the Scottish League underwent reconstruction at the end of 1974/75, Kilmarnock found themselves two points short of gaining a place in the new Premier Division and had to settle instead for a berth in the First Division. The Ayrshiremen contested their maiden season in the Premier Division in 1976/77, but the season ended with relegation once again, as they finished bottom of the league, thirteen points adrift of safety.

Thereafter, the club was sucked into a downward spiral, and although they did have a three-season flirtation with the top flight in the early eighties, Kilmarnock were relegated from the First Division in 1988, forcing them to play in the third tier of Scottish football, the Second Division, for the first time in their history. With the club at its lowest ebb, they were rescued when a consortium including Bobby Fleeting and James Moffat launched a takeover bid. They provided much needed revenue for manager Jim Fleeting and with the help of star signings Tommy Burns and Davie MacKinnon, the club won the Second Division title in 1988/89 and gained promotion back to the First Division at the first time of asking.

Burns, a real favourite with the Rugby Park crowd, took over from Fleeting in the manager's chair and guided the club back to the Premier Division in 1992/93, with a 0-0 draw at home to Hamilton sufficient to clinch a place in Scottish Football's top twelve for the first time in ten years. Burns' men made a successful fist of their first season back in the top flight too, winning 2-1 at Ibrox early in the campaign and staying up on goal difference. The Ayrshire side also reached the semi-finals of the Scottish Cup, but Rangers, who went on to clinch the championship that year, made amends for their early season defeat to Kilmarnock by beating them 2-1 in a replay.

With Rugby Park now beautifully refurbished into an all-seated 18,128 capacity stadium, Kilmarnock maintained their place in the Premier Division with three successive seventh-place finishes. Tommy Burns left the club in 1994 to take over the reins at his beloved Celtic, while Alex Totten took over and continued Burns' good work. When Totten moved to Falkirk in December 1996, Bobby Williamson, a member of the playing staff at Rugby Park, took charge of team affairs and led Kilmarnock to the Scottish Cup final in 1997. Their opponents at Ibrox on 24 May were ironically Alex Totten's Falkirk, but a first-half strike from Paul Wright took the Cup back to Ayrshire for the first time since 1929. Williamson built on this triumph, and in the season prior to McCoist's arrival, Kilmarnock finished fourth in the title race and won a place in the UEFA Cup for the next season.

Williamson was a former team-mate and strike-partner of McCoist's at Ibrox. Signed by Jock Wallace in December 1983 from Clydebank for a fee of £100,000, his Rangers career was badly compromised when he suffered a broken leg on a pre-season tour of Australia. He recovered and partnered McCoist in attack for much of the 1985/86 season, and in his three years at Ibrox netted twenty goals in fifty-two appearances, but his time with Rangers came to an end in 1986 when he was part of the exodus driven by the arrival of Graeme Souness. He moved to West Bromwich Albion and then enjoyed a successful spell with Rotherham United before returning north of the border to spend the twilight of his career with Kilmarnock.

In addition to tempting Ally McCoist to Rugby Park, Williamson had also managed to persuade McCoist's best friend, Ian Durrant, to sign for the club. Durrant, approaching his thirty-second birthday, had also been given a free transfer from Rangers at the end of the 1997/98 season, but despite his advancing years, he was still considered to be one of the best midfielders in the SPL and his signing was a major coup for the Ayrshire club. He had never really fully recovered from the horrendous knee injury he had suffered in 1988 at a time when he was perhaps the most talented player in Scottish football. He showed glimpses of his former glories when he played an integral part in the Rangers side that had come within touching distance of the European Cup final in 1993, but he had become more and more marginalised during the last few years of his Rangers career. With first-team opportunities limited, he had a spell on loan at Everton in 1994, and in the final three years of his contract at Ibrox he only managed to make fifty-four appearances.

Five days after he had been introduced to the media, McCoist was the main attraction as his new club held an Open Day at a sun-drenched Rugby Park on 9 August. It soon became apparent that Ayrshire had been gripped by 'McCoist Mania', as a crowd of around 20,000 people, twice Kilmarnock's average home attendance during the 1997/98 season, turned up to acclaim his signing. Sales of McCoist memorabilia were sky rocketing and over one thousand replica shirts replete with 'McCoist' and his squad number of thirteen – Paul Wright was already in possession of McCoist's favourite number nine shirt – were sold on the day, along with countless T-shirts and other artefacts. It was clear, even at this early stage, that attracting McCoist to Rugby Park would be a major benefit to the club, both on and off the field. In just one day, the club coined in over £100,000, which corresponded to the amount they would normally expect to raise over the course of a year! 'It's absolutely fantastic,' said McCoist when asked about the rapturous reception he had received. 'The welcome here has been unbelievable and the people are like the weather – sensational.'[1]

Having been signed after the 1 August European signing deadline, McCoist was not eligible to take part in Kilmarnock's UEFA Cup campaign, a campaign which started positively with a 2-1 aggregate win over NK Zeljeznicar of Sarajevo but which ended abruptly when SK Sigma Omolouc dumped Williamson's side out of the competition in the second preliminary round, winning 4-0 on aggregate.

McCoist eventually pulled on Kilmarnock's blue-and-white striped shirt for the first time in the second league match of the season, coming on as a substitute in a no-score draw against his first club St Johnstone on 15 August at McDiarmid Park. He made another substitute appearance the following midweek, this time replacing veteran winger Pat Nevin to make his home debut in the League Cup third-round tie against First Division outfit Livingston, and marked the occasion by scoring his first goal for his new club, thus maintaining the love affair he had enjoyed with this competition during his time with both St Johnstone and Rangers. Paul Wright, who scored twice, joined McCoist on the scoresheet as Kilmarnock progressed to the fourth round by virtue of a 3-1 win after extra-time.

Despite suffering that early exit from the UEFA Cup, the Ayrshire men made an excellent start to their SPL campaign, losing only one of their opening twelve matches. The solitary defeat was a 3-1 reverse against Rangers at Rugby Park, a match in which McCoist was in the Kilmarnock starting eleven for the first time. Much of the press coverage ahead of the fixture centred on the fact that McCoist and Durrant were set to come face to face with their former side, with McCoist saying: 'I really don't know what it's going to be like playing against them, although I know it's going to be a little strange. I never thought I'd see the day when I would play against Rangers, but it's happened and I just have to be professional enough to get on with it.'[2]

Unfortunately for Kilmarnock, McCoist was unable to repeat what had happened the last time he had faced Rangers (on that occasion he had scored for St Johnstone at Ibrox in a Scottish Cup replay), as goals from Rod Wallace and Charlie Miller and a penalty from Jorg Albertz handed a Rangers side that had been given an expensive facelift in the close season all three points. Paul Wright netted Kilmarnock's goal. McCoist, who was afforded a standing ovation by the visiting supporters when he was replaced by Pat Nevin two minutes from time, had little in the way of scoring opportunities, partly due to poor service, but also because of the sterling marking job done by Rangers' Australian central defender, Craig Moore. 'They [Rangers] will take some stopping this season,' was McCoist's post-match reflection.[3]

Kilmarnock bounced back emphatically from that defeat. Eight days later, they welcomed Scottish Cup-holders Hearts to Rugby Park, with the Edinburgh side seeking the three points they required to overtake Rangers at the summit of the SPL table. They failed to achieve their objective, though, as they were put to the sword by a performance from McCoist that rolled back the years.

He broke the deadlock after only eight minutes, scoring his first league goal for Kilmarnock when he eluded his marker, Thomas Flogel, and slid in to thump a cross from Jerome Varielle beyond Giles Rousset, and he almost added a second four minutes later when he robbed David Weir and unleashed a drive from 18 yards that drew a fine reflex save from the Hearts goalkeeper. McCoist duly doubled his tally in the sixty-second minute when he ruthlessly punished hesitancy in the Hearts defence with a fine volleyed finish with his left foot, and he completed a splendid hat-trick four minutes from time when he fired a left-foot shot through the legs of Rousset after Durrant had carved open the visitors' defence with a sublime through-ball.

It was a devastating display of finishing from McCoist and one that provided clinical proof that he still had more to offer at the highest level. He certainly impressed one onlooker in the audience of 10,376, with Craig Brown deciding that his performance merited a recall to the international squad for the forthcoming European Championships qualifying match against Lithuania. 'Ally was very impressive out there and the situation has changed from the summer,' said the national team manager. 'He [McCoist] is fitter now than he was then and we are thin on the ground with strikers after Gordon Durie's injury.'[4]

Having thought his international career had reached a conclusion following his omission from Scotland's World Cup squad, McCoist was understandably elated by his surprise recall, and he was selected to start the match in Vilnius on 5 September, winning his sixtieth cap in the process. He had last tugged a Dark Blue jersey over his head almost a year earlier when the Scots had defeated Belarus 4-1 in a World Cup qualifier at Pittodrie, but his inclusion this time around failed to inspire Scotland, who delivered an insipid display against the plucky Lithuanians. The match featured the debut appearance of future Rangers and Scotland captain Barry Ferguson, who replaced Celtic's Darren Jackson in the fifty-sixth minute, and the youngster, a star turn for Rangers in the opening matches of the season, gave the Scots some much needed impetus and almost fashioned a goal for McCoist in the closing stages.

The midfielder, who had broken into the Rangers first team during McCoist's final season at Ibrox, darted to the bye-line before cutting the ball towards the front post, territory he knew from experience that McCoist tended to prowl. However, McCoist's advancing years had perhaps blunted his razor-sharp instinct and the ball drifted harmlessly to safety. 'In training you always expect Ally to make the near-post run, but he admitted to me later he was a little slow to react,' revealed Ferguson after the match. 'I'm used to him making those runs and I'd watched him do it on Sunday [during Kilmarnock's 3-0 win over Hearts] when he came across his marker to score. I thought it would happen again, but it wasn't to be.'[5]

McCoist was eventually withdrawn seven minutes from the end of the match, with another debutant, Hearts winger Neil McCann, taking over in a bid to inject some pace into the Scotland attack. The change was of no avail, though, and the match ended goal-less. It represented a hammer blow to the nation's hopes of qualifying for a third successive European Championships.

The following weekend, McCoist was listed among the Kilmarnock substitutes when the Ayrshire side travelled to Parkhead to take on reigning champions Celtic. A goal from Jerome Vareille secured a creditable 1-1 draw, which more than made up for a disappointing League Cup exit at the hands of Airdrie four days earlier.

McCoist remained on the bench for Kilmarnock's next SPL encounter, a 0-0 draw against Motherwell at Fir Park, but was reinstated to the starting eleven when Dundee visited Rugby Park on 23 September, the day before his thirty-sixth birthday. McCoist collected the best possible present when he scored a quite splendid goal, stepping away from his marker 30 yards from goal before curling a sumptuous effort into the net with his left foot. The goal silenced the travelling support that had spent most of the evening heckling McCoist and making disparaging remarks about his thickening waistline. Kevin McGowne was also on the scoresheet in a match Killie won 2-1.

A victory over Aberdeen and a 0-0 draw at home to Dunfermline followed (McCoist started both matches but failed to add to his tally of goals for the season) before McCoist won his sixty-first and final cap for Scotland on Saturday, 10 October 1998. The Scots faced Estonia at Tynecastle and recovered from a goal down on two occasions to eke out a 3-2 victory. Dundee United's Billy Dodds, who replaced McCoist in the sixty-ninth minute, was the hero, netting twice on this his fifth appearance for his country.

The match brought to an end Ally McCoist's twelve-year international career. With sixty-one caps to his name, he is currently ranked eighth (alongside David Weir and former team-mate Richard Gough) in the top ten appearance-makers for Scotland, and his tally of nineteen goals is the fifth highest in the national team's history. Only Denis Law (with thirty), Kenny Dalglish (thirty), Hughie Gallacher (twenty-four) and Lawrie Reilly (twenty-two) have scored more goals in Dark Blue, and although often criticised in some quarters for a poor scoring return, McCoist's scoring ratio of one goal in every 3.2 international appearances betters that of the revered Dalglish, who comes in with an average of one goal in every 3.4 internationals. Indeed, there is considerable weight to the argument that had McCoist not sustained a broken leg while at the zenith of his goal-scoring career in 1993, an injury that kept him out of the national side for over two years during which time Scotland played seventeen international matches, he may even have gone on to leapfrog the four players above him to become Scotland's top goalscorer of all time. Already a member of the SFA's Hall of Fame, by virtue of the fact that he had amassed over fifty caps for his country, McCoist was inducted into the Scottish Football Hall of Fame in November 2007, a fitting reward for one of Scotland's finest footballing servants.

Back at Rugby Park, Kilmarnock were making excellent progress in the SPL, lying in second place after fifteen matches, five points adrift of leaders Rangers. They had even claimed the scalp of Celtic, defeating Dr Jozef Venglos' side 2-0 at Rugby Park on Hallowe'en, a match McCoist missed as a result of an injury sustained while representing Scotland against Estonia. He missed a total of six matches before he made his return to the side when he replaced Vareille during a 3-0 win over Dunfermline at East End Park, the highlight of which was a brace of goals from the revitalised Ian Durrant.

Further substitute appearances followed against Aberdeen – a fixture in which Killie chalked up an emphatic 4-0 win – and Rangers, with the latter match marking the return of McCoist and Durrant to their old stomping ground. Both were afforded a fantastic ovation, particularly McCoist, who graced the hallowed Ibrox turf as an opposition player when he replaced Paul Wright for the closing sixteen minutes. The home supporters even launched into a few choruses of 'Super Ally', which added to a surreal experience that McCoist admitted 'felt strange'.[6] Although the visitors acquitted themselves well, a Rod Wallace goal in the tenth minute gave the home side a 1-0 win and consigned Kilmarnock to only their third defeat of the season. The result allowed Rangers to move three points ahead of the Ayrshiremen with a game in hand, but McCoist refused to rule his side out of the title chase. He said: 'We're lying second in the league now so we must have a chance of winning it.'[7]

Home victories over Dundee United and Hearts served to reinforce McCoist's assessment, and when Kilmarnock won at Fir Park on New Year's Day, they moved to within three points of Rangers. The match against Motherwell was beamed live across the nation on satellite television and McCoist scored Kilmarnock's first goal of 1999, linking well with Durrant before slotting the ball into the net from eighteen yards. It was his first goal for the top team since September, and the return of McCoist, allied to the exceptional form of Durrant, suggested that Kilmarnock were building up a head of steam.

However, after the 2-1 win at Fir Park, Williamson's side embarked on a wretched spell of form that effectively killed off any hopes they may have had of mounting a realistic championship challenge. They won only one of their next eight matches and suffered a 5-0 drubbing at the hands of Rangers at Rugby Park in late February. They had the misfortune of running into the Light Blues at a stage of the season when they were in rampant form. Dick Advocaat's side had scored six times in each of their two previous matches, and a hat-trick from the pint-sized Rod Wallace, plus goals from McCann and Johansson, helped to sustain their hot streak. McCoist was part of the Kilmarnock starting eleven, but failed to find the net against his former employers, although he did pass up a good opportunity to level the score in the sixty-third minute when he shot meekly at Stefan Klos when well placed.

Kilmarnock could find little solace in the Scottish Cup either. McCoist was afforded his first taste of an Ayrshire derby when Killie travelled to Somerset Park to face bitter rivals Ayr United in the third round, but the home side extinguished any hopes Williamson's side may have harboured of annexing the Cup they had won just two years earlier by inflicting an emphatic 3-0 defeat upon them. McCoist's fellow veteran, Andy Walker, stole the show with an impudent chipped penalty-kick.

This spell ironically represented McCoist's longest run in the starting eleven. He started seven of the eight league matches in the dire sequence before being relegated to the bench for the visit to Tynecastle in April. Kilmarnock's miserable run looked set to continue in the capital when Gary McSwegan shot the home side into a 2-0 lead, but an inspirational double substitution in the sixty-fourth minute rescued a point for the Ayrshire side. McCoist and John Henry were thrown into the fray, and Henry's impact was immediate, as he took a pass from Durrant and struck a shot beyond Giles Rousset from the edge of the penalty area. Twelve minutes later the scores were tied when Man of the Match Durrant surged through the midfield and played Gary Holt in on goal. Holt's effort was blocked by Rousset, but the ball broke to McCoist, who was stationed a matter of inches from the goal-line rammed a shot into the net to claim his sixth league goal of the season.

A fine 4-2 win over Aberdeen followed, and McCoist was among the goals yet again as Killie recorded a comprehensive 6-0 hammering of Dunfermline at East End Park on 17 April. John Henry scored twice for the visitors, and further goals from Mitchell, Vareille, Durrant and McCoist earned Killie their biggest win of the season. It proved their last success of the campaign, though, as they drew three and lost two of their final five fixtures, eventually finishing the season in fourth place, having accumulated fifty-six points from thirty-six games. They were a colossal twenty-one points adrift of champions Rangers, who crowned a fantastic debut season for Dick Advocaat by winning their sixth domestic Treble. Although their title plans had been scuttled by that miserable run of form at the turn of the year, Kilmarnock could at least take consolation from the fact that the top-four finish meant European football would be played at Rugby Park during the 1999/2000 season.

McCoist had enjoyed a fine debut season in Kilmarnock colours. He finished the campaign as the club's joint top goalscorer, joining Paul Wright at the head of the scoring charts with eight goals (seven in the SPL) in twenty-nine appearances.

However, the season ended amid some controversy when McCoist and Durrant were sighted in the Rangers end at Parkhead on the day their former club beat Celtic 3-0 to clinch the SPL title. Much was made in the media about the fact that two employees of one SPL club had been celebrating the triumph of another, and many Kilmarnock followers were among the dissenting voices. The situation was simply blown out of proportion because of who the players involved were and the matter was placed firmly in perspective just twenty-four hours later. McCoist explained: 'We went into the Kilmarnock dressing room on the Monday where there was a big sign up on the notice board, and it was 'Celtic 6, Rangers 3.' There were six of the Kilmarnock boys up the Celtic End and there were three up the Rangers End! That was fantastic. That's humour and that's what you need in dressing rooms. The bottom line is that there will be players from all over Scotland at that game wanting one of the two teams to win.'[8]

McCoist's attendance at Parkhead did not seem to irk Bobby Williamson. Although his allegiance to Rangers was a strong one, Williamson knew that, when he donned their blue-and-white striped jersey, McCoist's loyalty lay with Kilmarnock and that, coupled with his fine form over the course of the season, was enough to convince his manager that he merited a new contract. Although his media commitments were placing more of a demand on his time and despite the fact that he was a couple of months short of his thirty-seventh birthday, Ally McCoist signed a one-year deal to stay at Rugby Park for the 1999/2000 season.

An injury picked up during pre-season training ruled McCoist out of Kilmarnock's first three league matches – the Ayrshire side had a rather uneven start to the campaign, sandwiching a 2-0 win against Aberdeen with defeats at Ibrox and McDiarmid Park – but he was back in the starting line-up for the visit of Motherwell at the end of August. His return failed to lift Kilmarnock out of their early season lethargy, though, and the Fir Park side recorded a 1-0 win, but Williamson's men cast aside their poor start in the league when KR Reykjavik visited Rugby Park for the second leg of the qualifying-round tie in the UEFA Cup. McCoist made his European debut for Kilmarnock against the Icelanders and helped the home side overturn a 1-0 deficit from the first leg, with Paul Wright's penalty taking the tie into extra-time, during which David Bagan netted the winner to grant Kilmarnock passage into the first-round proper and a lucrative tie with German cracks Kaiserslautern. The European adventure ended there, however, as the Germans, inspired by French World Cup-winner Youri Djorkaeff, romped to a convincing 5-0 aggregate victory.

In the SPL, Kilmarnock were finding it difficult to string together any sort of winning run. A 3-0 win over Hibernian at Easter Road – a game that featured a first goal of the season for McCoist, from the penalty spot – ended a run of four matches without a victory, but a 2-0 win for Dundee at Rugby Park left Killie marooned in the bottom half of the table, with just seven points on the board after eight matches.

In their ninth league fixture, they welcomed champions Rangers to Rugby Park, and many predicted another difficult afternoon for the home side. Thanks to their 100 percent winning record in the league, Dick Advocaat's side arrived in Ayrshire a staggering *seventeen* points ahead of their opponents, and they took the lead after twenty-six minutes when Dutch midfielder Giovanni van Bronckhorst lobbed Michael Watt. Rather than bow to the inevitable and collapse under the early onslaught, Kilmarnock dug in and fought back into contention, with McCoist, buoyed by the two goals he had netted in Kilmarnock's 3-2 League Cup win over Hibernian four days earlier, troubling the Rangers central defensive pairing of Lorenzo Amoruso and Craig Moore. Five minutes before the interval, he almost hauled the home side level, but his header from Martin Baker's cross fell wide of target. However, just on the half-time whistle, McCoist's afternoon was ended prematurely when he collided innocuously with Amoruso and suffered the second broken leg of his career. He was replaced by close-season signing Michael Jeffery, and the new boy rescued a crucial point for Williamson's charges seventeen minutes from the end when he headed Ally Mitchell's cross beyond Stefan Klos.

McCoist now faced up to a long spell on the sidelines. The one consolation he could take from his enforced absence from duty at Rugby Park was that he could now dedicate more time to his increasingly successful media career and to young Mitchell, who was now well on course to making a full recovery from his heart and abdominal problems. The injury inevitably prompted the resurfacing of stories heralding the end of McCoist's football career but, six months later, he was back in action, making his seventh appearance of the season in a 1-0 win over Hibernian at Rugby Park.

Kilmarnock had struggled in his absence. Although they managed to reach the last four of the League Cup (where they lost to eventual winners Celtic by one goal to nil), they had toiled badly in the SPL and suffered a humiliating exit from the Scottish Cup at the hands of Alloa

Athletic. Williamson's side won just three of their first twenty-six league matches and such form predictably meant they were sucked into the relegation dogfight.

Unfortunately, McCoist was unable to aid the quest to avoid the drop. The comeback from his leg break had to be aborted when he suffered a calf injury, and he only made two further appearances before the season's end, replacing Andy Smith in matches against Rangers at home (lost 0-2) and Aberdeen away (lost 1-5). Kilmarnock eventually survived the drop, though, hitting form at the right time to win five of their last ten fixtures and stave off the spectre of relegation by finishing in ninth position. In the end, Kilmarnock would in fact have been safe even if they had finished bottom of the heap. The SPL underwent reconstruction that summer, with the top flight expanded to twelve clubs for the 2000/01 season, which meant that the SPL's bottom side, Aberdeen, dodged the ignominy of their first-ever demotion since the inception of the Premier Division back in 1975.

With his second twelve-month contract at Rugby Park due to expire and the filming of his debut Hollywood movie, *A Shot at Glory*, imminent, it looked likely that, after twenty-one years, the top-flight football career of Ally McCoist would come to an end. There was interest from Raith Rovers, managed by Peter Hetherston, a co-star in the movie, and Carlisle United, but after an intensive pre-season work out, McCoist did enough to convince himself and Bobby Williamson that he still had something to give, and he was offered another deal to stay in Ayrshire with Kilmarnock. 'Despite other expressions of interest, I'm determined to finish on a high in the Scottish Premier League with Kilmarnock,' said McCoist. 'I'm delighted to have pre-season training behind me. I've had a great time at the club since joining from Rangers and I want to repay them with a positive contribution to the campaign.'[9]

On signing his third one-year contract at Kilmarnock, McCoist confirmed that this was almost certainly going to be his last season as a professional. He would finally hang up his shooting boots at the end of the 2000/01 season and bring an illustrious twenty-three-year career to an end. It was a prospect he was dreading: he knew he would miss the day-to-day involvement of being part of a football club, the games and the dressing-room banter, but he was determined to finish on a high note.

McCoist started the new campaign well. Although he failed to score in his first nine league appearances, he did net the winning goal in the opening round of the League Cup, a 2-1 extra-time win over First Division Clyde, and added another match winner in the next round against former club, St Johnstone. His goal against Clyde was Kilmarnock's 500th in the League Cup tournament, while his strike at McDiarmid Park represented yet another landmark moment in his career: it was his sixty-third goal in the League Cup, equalling the record held by Bobby Lennox, who had played for Celtic in the sixties and seventies. As has been noted, Lennox played a significant part in McCoist's football career when his intervention in the Parkhead player's lounge had stopped McCoist from walking out on Rangers post-Cheltenham in 1991 when his feud with Graeme Souness was at its height. 'I've been fortunate enough to pick up nine winners' medals and one losers' medal [in the League Cup],' said McCoist after the match. 'It's been an incredible, unbelievable competition. I'm delighted to equal the Lennox record. Scoring goals always means a lot to me. It does not matter if it's a 20-yarder or a tap-in off my knee.'[10]

In early September, McCoist and his wife, Allison, stepped out on the red carpet when *A Shot at Glory* premiered in Canada. The movie, directed by Michael Corrente and written by Denis O'Neill, was the brainchild of acclaimed and respected Hollywood actor Robert Duvall. It is a film in which the underdog is championed, as the plot follows the fortunes of a small, unfashionable (and fictitious) Scottish football club named Kilnockie. At the outset of the film, the club are struggling in the lower tier of the Scottish game and, with attendances and interest in the local community dwindling, they are taken over by an ambitious American tycoon called Peter Cameron, played by Michael Keaton, the star of *Batman*. Cameron is intent on making money out of the club, but to do this he knows the team have to start winning again to raise their profile. He and manager Gordon McLeod, played by Duvall, target success in the Scottish Cup as their number one goal, and in order to help achieve this, Cameron signs Jackie McQuillan, a washed-up former Celtic player played by McCoist.

The action scenes in the film are rather surreal. They show McQuillan scoring goals in his Parkhead heyday, but the footage is actually of McCoist scoring goals for Rangers, but with a green jersey superimposed on top of Rangers' royal blue equivalent.

The recruitment of McQuillan is against the wishes of McLeod, as he still holds a grudge against the wayward striker. He was previously married to his daughter before vices such as womanising, drinking and gambling got to grips with him and signalled the end of the marriage. One of the sub-plots of the movie is the rivalry between McLeod and McQuillan and how the two attempt to patch up their differences for the good of the club.

Very soon, Kilnockie's stock is on the rise and McQuillan's goals help the minnows sweep the opposition aside to set up their date with destiny in the Scottish Cup final against the mighty Rangers. Rangers are managed by Martin Smith, played by Brian Cox, whose previous job was assistant manager alongside McLeod at Kilnockie. Both had vowed to resist any offers from Scotland's larger clubs in order to stay and help make Kilnockie a team to be proud of once again, but when Rangers came calling, the lure of the big time proved too much and Smith abandoned his post at Kilnockie, a move that tarnished his friendship with McLeod.

The grand finale of the movie is set at the scene of a great many of McCoist's triumphs, Hampden Park on Cup final day, as Kilnockie go toe to toe with their illustrious opponents in their quest for Cup glory. The plucky minnows give a good account of themselves, and McQuillan's equaliser takes the match into extra-time and penalties before Kilnockie finally surrender when they go down valiantly on penalties.

Although the film itself received mixed reviews, McCoist's debut as an actor drew praise from many, with most of the critics recognising his role as being the one shining light in a movie that failed to sparkle at the box office. These glowing reviews repaid the faith that Duvall had shown in the inexperienced movie star when he was casting for the role of McQuillan. Despite interest from many established members of the Hollywood glitterati and advice from friends who tried to dissuade him, Duvall felt there was only one man capable of playing the role: McCoist. He and director Michael Corrente met with McCoist and decided to hire the Kilmarnock striker there and then, even though he had not been screen tested. Duvall called it 'positive blind faith', but his gamble paid off.

Just over a year later, McCoist was back on the red carpet to attend the UK premiere of the film in London. The occasion would be one of the last public engagements for McCoist and his wife Allison. Their marriage broke up a few months later and they reached a divorce settlement in early 2004.

A recurrence of an old calf injury, an ailment that had dogged him since the latter days of his time with Rangers, forced McCoist onto the sidelines in October, but he was back in contention for selection in December as he looked to aid Kilmarnock's push in what was developing into a fascinating three-way fight with Rangers and Hibernian for second place in the SPL.

Celtic, under new management in the shape of Martin O'Neill, were runaway leaders in the SPL, but the race for second and a place in the Champions League was much more keenly contested. Kilmarnock provided ample illustration that they would not be cast in the role of also-rans when they travelled up the M77 to Ibrox on 28 October and hammered Rangers by three goals to nil, a result that represented the third successive league defeat for Dick Advocaat's deflated defending champions. In addition to their fine run in the league, Williamson's men were also going well in the League Cup, having seen off the challenge of Hibernian to set up a semi-final date with St Mirren in February.

Although they had endured something of a lukewarm start to the New Year, including a 6-0 hammering by champions-elect Celtic at Parkhead, Kilmarnock comfortably saw off St Mirren by three goals to nil in the League Cup showdown and, in doing so, booked a date with Celtic in the final at Hampden Park on Sunday, 18 March. For McCoist, who had been linked with a loan move to Morton in January after making just two brief substitute appearances against Dundee and Celtic since returning from his calf injury, the match represented the opportunity to take his collection of League Cup-winners' medals into double figures. Celtic were overwhelming favourites and when Kilmarnock's talisman Ian Durrant retired injured in the first half, any hope the Ayrshire men had of causing an upset went with him. Celtic won the first leg of the domestic Treble convincingly, as McCoist, an unused substitute, watched Swedish striker Henrik Larsson notch a hat-trick as he powered his way towards a half-century of goals for the season.

McCoist had not scored since that record-equalling League Cup goal in September, so he was glad to end his goal famine two weeks after the final when he netted the opening goal in a 2-1 SPL home win over Dunfermline. The goal was significant as it meant McCoist had now scored at least one league goal in each of the seasons in which he had been a professional, save the first two campaigns of his career when he was making fleeting appearances for the first team as he attempted to make the breakthrough at St Johnstone.

The following Wednesday, Rangers were the visitors to Rugby Park, with the teams set to do battle for the first time since Kilmarnock had rampaged to a shock 3-0 win at Ibrox in October. With rivals Celtic running away with the championship and Kilmarnock falling out of contention, Dick Advocaat's men were now fighting it out with Hibernian for second place and the one remaining Champions League slot for the 2001/02 season.

The visitors took the lead through record signing Tore Andre Flo, but Kilmarnock were given an opportunity to get back on level terms when they were awarded a penalty-kick shortly afterwards. McCoist, still keen to notch a goal against his former club before he ended his playing days, grabbed the ball, but although he struck his kick firmly enough, Rangers' goalkeeper Stefan Klos touched his effort on to the post.

Rangers went on to win the game 2-1 and the following day McCoist was greeted with suggestions that he had deliberately missed his penalty in order to aid his old club in their push for second place. The rumour mongers were pointing to the fact that McCoist had spoken to Klos before taking his kick, and in this conversation he had allegedly told the Rangers number one to which side of the goal he was going to place his penalty. These allegations were preposterous and disappointed McCoist greatly but, in characteristic fashion, he tried to make a joke of the whole affair, saying that he had no need to aid the opposing goalkeeper in his quest to stop his spot-kick as he had been more than capable of failing to score from twelve yards throughout his career! Bobby Williamson was also quick to leap to the defence of his striker, saying: 'There will be the people who look at it [the penalty miss] and say things like that [that McCoist missed on purpose], but they are mindless and don't deserve the time of day. He is a Killie man and is desperate to score all the time, not just against Rangers.'[11]

Having fallen away in their push to finish in the top three, Kilmarnock now faced a battle with Hearts to finish fourth and secure the one remaining European slot for the next campaign. A crucial point in a 1-1 home draw with the Tynecastle side kept Williamson's men ahead, but back-to-back defeats at Dens Park (1-2) and Ibrox (1-5) meant it was a 'win-or-bust' scenario on the last day of the season with champions Celtic due to visit Rugby Park. The match against Martin O'Neill's side would be Ally McCoist's final appearance as a professional footballer.

The previous weekend he had been an unused substitute in Kilmarnock's defeat at Ibrox. As the minutes ticked away, and with Rangers firmly in control of the match, the home supporters turned their attention to the visitors' dugout and collectively implored Bobby Williamson to pitch McCoist into the action to give him one last bow at the stadium where he had made his name. Williamson stubbornly refused to introduce him to the fray though, and it looked like the home audience were to be denied the opportunity to pay homage to a player who had been their icon for fifteen years.

However, at the end of the game, Dick Advocaat persuaded McCoist to go back on to the field to take one final bow and the ovation he received was startling, with Ibrox rising in unison to acclaim their hero. 'I felt a bit sorry for the gaffer as he was being put under a bit of pressure,' said McCoist. 'His job isn't to entertain 46,000 Rangers fans, although he did his best on Saturday.' The departing striker also paid tribute to Advocaat saying: 'I want to thank him because I don't think I would have gone out there to say cheerio and that would have been something I regretted for the rest of my life.'[12]

With so much at stake on the final day, McCoist was keen to play his part against Celtic. He was also desperate to make up for the disappointment of what had happened at Ibrox a week earlier. After performing well in training in the week leading up to the game, Williamson handed him a place in the starting line-up and he more than played his part as Kilmarnock got the win they required, with Alan Mahood's goal enough to secure a 1-0 win.

When the final whistle sounded at Rugby Park on that sunny May afternoon it signalled not only the end of the season but also the conclusion of Ally McCoist's playing career. In his three seasons at Rugby Park, he had scored fourteen goals in sixty-three appearances, which took his career grand total at club level to 405 goals in 777 appearances.

At his final press conference, McCoist reflected on a glittering twenty-three-year career that had brought a plethora of emotions, although the many, many great times far outweighed the dark periods. 'Overall I have no right to look back with regret or remorse,' he said. 'It has been like being on the biggest and best rollercoaster ride ever for twenty-three years. I have had the chance to live out every schoolboy's dream. Sure, it has not been plain sailing all the way, but it's been some experience and the good times have far outnumbered the bad ones. The great thing is I have probably learned more from the downs than I have from the ups. So there is no way I can stand here and say I wish I was just starting out again. I have thoroughly enjoyed every minute of it.'[13]

ALLY McCOIST

Ally McCoist is the finest exponent of the art of goal-scoring Scotland has produced since the Second World War. His footballing roll of honour is without doubt comparable to the greats of Association Football: ten Scottish League Championship medals, nine winners' medals from the Scottish League Cup, a solitary Scottish Cup-winners' badge and, of course, two European Golden Boot awards. Add to this the profusion of Rangers and Scottish League goal-scoring records he holds, many of which are unlikely ever to be matched, never mind broken, and sixty-one Scotland caps, and it is safe to say that his place among the esteemed figures in football history is secure. Scottish Football would undoubtedly be duller without him, but in a fashion that had typified McCoist throughout his playing career, he was not quite finished making his mark on 'The Beautiful Game' in this country just yet.

CHAPTER EIGHTEEN

AFTER THE BALL: 2001–07

Often when a footballer ends his playing career he is at a loss to know what to do with himself. Having known nothing other than the routine of training and playing games for a large chunk of his early adult life, a newly retired footballer often finds it difficult to make the transition of going back to living a 'normal' life. In the sixties and seventies, in the days when players' salaries were not at the inflated level they are today, most ex-professionals became publicans or progressed into a football management role of some sort, but from a very early stage it was apparent that a job in the media was always going to be Ally McCoist's chosen vocation when he hung up his golden boots for the last time. He was after all made for the job, a natural one might say, with his charisma, sharp wit and sense of humour that had made him so popular with his colleagues in the dressing room through the years making him perfect for television work.

He took his first fledgeling steps in the media world in 1996 when he was appointed as one of the team captains on the legendary and long-running BBC sports quiz show *A Question of Sport*. The show is hugely popular and has been running since it was first aired in 1970. The first-ever episode, presented by David Vine, was filmed in a BBC studio that was actually a converted church, with two teams, captained by British heavyweight boxing champion Henry Cooper and Welsh rugby union star Gareth Edwards, competing against each other. Now, almost forty years later, it is a sporting institution, boasting audience figures of over 200 million.

McCoist first appeared on the show as a guest in 1987, and was such a success that he became something of a regular thereafter. He became extremely popular with the viewers to the extent that when long-serving captains Bill Beaumont and Ian Botham decided to step down in 1996, the programme's producers did not have to look far for their replacements.

The other appointment was 1991 world snooker champion John Parrott, and McCoist called the fusion of a 'daft Scouser and a daft Jock', 'a marriage made in heaven'[1]. The question master also changed early in McCoist's reign, with the legendary David Coleman replaced by former French Open tennis champion Sue Barker, and the wise-cracking banter between McCoist, Parrott, Barker and the show's guests proved to be a real highlight. The trio managed to blend together a mixture of fun and frolics, while still retaining the focus on the quiz show element of the programme. This resulted in a positive upturn in the show's popularity, and in 1999 and 2001, A Question of Sport was awarded the Royal Television Society's Sports Entertainment Programme of the Year accolade.

Parrott vacated his chair in 2002 to pursue a career as a pundit on the world snooker circuit, and was replaced by the diminutive jockey Frankie Dettori. He lasted a further two years before England's rugby union scrum-half, Matt Dawson, took over, but the show's popularity never waned despite the changes.

McCoist's return to Ibrox in 2007 as Walter Smith's assistant manager precipitated the end of his illustrious Question of Sport career, and he made his final appearance on the show on Friday, 18 May 2007. It is testament to the quality of the job McCoist had done that he remained an integral part of the team for eleven years, and his final appearance tally of 363 eclipsed the previous record number of appearances held by former England rugby union captain Bill Beaumont, who appeared on the show 319 times. Fittingly, McCoist's last show ended with a victory, but it also left the departing skipper a little red-faced. In one of the show's most famous rounds, Mystery Guest, McCoist's team failed to identify their guest from the clips shown, and when their true identity was revealed, McCoist was stunned: it was none other than his new gaffer, Walter Smith!

However, despite his undoubted success on *A Question of Sport*, it was in his role as a football pundit that McCoist made his biggest impression on the television audience. Having assumed the role on several occasions when he was still an active player, it was inevitable that he would pursue it as a career when he stopped playing.

His first big 'gig' came in the twilight of his playing career. Having been snubbed by Craig Brown for a place in the Scotland squad for the 1998 World Cup in France, the BBC recruited McCoist as part of their match-analysis team, and he compensated for not playing by running the rule over the matches alongside the likes of Desmond Lynam, Alan Hansen, Mark Lawrenson and David Ginola. His on-screen performances showed just what a natural he was in front of the television cameras, with his humour, charm and charisma all coming to the fore. What was also evident, though, was that he had a wealth of knowledge on the game he had graced for twenty years, and his informed and educated opinions won him a new army of fans.

With his playing career winding down in the early years of the new millennium, and his television star ascending, McCoist was recruited by ITV in 1999 to form part of their match-analysis panel, and when the channel won the battle with the BBC to screen highlights from the English Premiership in 2001, McCoist was an integral part of their team, joining forces once again with Desmond Lynam, who presented the Saturday evening show *The Premiership*.

McCoist made an instant impact, beating off competition from more established and experienced pundits to win the Television Radio Industry Club's 'Sports Presenter of the Year' in 2002, and he also played a large part in spin-off shows such as *On the Ball*, screened on Saturday lunchtimes, and *The Premiership Forum*, shown late on Monday evenings. With ITV also securing the rights to screen live coverage of Europe's premier club competition, the Champions League, McCoist was never short of work.

When the BBC won back the right to show Premiership highlights in 2004, many expected McCoist to defect from ITV and join the *Match of the Day* team, but he remained loyal to his employers at ITV and continued to be a prominent member of their team, working on the channel's extensive Champions League coverage and also the show that offered a highlights package from matches in the Coca-Cola English Championship. McCoist can also count the Irish satellite channel Setanta among his employers after joining them in 2006 to help analyse the live action they screen from the Scottish Premier League.

McCoist's television successes have not simply been confined to quiz shows and work as a pundit. He also hosted his own television chat show, which aired for the first time on 13 August 1998. He teamed up with Scottish comedian Fred MacAulay, a follower of Ally's first club, St Johnstone, to present a programme that took the hosts rambling around the British Isles, with the broadcast coming from a different city each week. The opening act was a short sketch that was specific to the location of the show, followed by the duo interviewing a number of celebrity guests. The guest list over the course of the three years was varied and diverse and was littered with many of the pre-eminent figures of the time, with luminaries such as Meatloaf, Paul Gascoigne, the late Donald Dewar and Melanie C of Spice Girls fame all making an appearance.

The programme was a massive hit and ran for three series between 1998 and 2000, and in the BBC's Annual Report of 1997/98, McCoist and MacAulay were recognised in the Broadcasting Council of Scotland section as being 'hugely popular talk-show hosts'.[2] The burgeoning popularity of a show that was only broadcast in Scotland initially resulted in it being networked throughout the UK, although screening south of the border did tend to be in a late-night slot. Eventually viewing figures averaging around 960,000 were posted, and McCoist drew praise for his performances. 'I went on to *McCoist and MacAulay* and I noticed then what a good professional he's become,'[3] commented Desmond Lynam, a colleague at ITV and one of the most celebrated sports presenters of his generation. 'He can do a piece straight to camera; he wears an earpiece so he's listening to all the garbage you get in your ear at the same time. That takes some doing. He hasn't been doing it that long. He's funny and asks the right questions when he's interviewing you too, embarrassingly so in my case.'

However, despite all his newfound stardom in the movies and the media, McCoist was never too far away when an opportunity to pull on the football boots presented itself. For instance, he became a regular participant in the Sky Sports Masters Football tournament; a six-a-side competition held indoors and made up of UK league teams full of a galaxy of stars from the past. It commences with a series of regional heats, with the winners of each of the stages qualifying for the grand final held at the NEC Arena in Birmingham, where the winners are crowned the Masters of British Football.

Rangers first took part in the event's inaugural year in 2000, and McCoist, still an active player in the SPL with Kilmarnock, was part of a Light Blues squad that also included Andy Goram, Trevor Steven and Mark Hateley. In the Scottish heat, Rangers came up against past masters from Celtic, Hearts, Hibernian and Dundee United and, inspired by the promptings and sublime ball skills of Mark Walters and the goals of the irrepressible McCoist, they triumphed and went on to represent Scotland in the grand final. They were denied the inaugural British Masters title, though, by Nottingham Forest, who edged home by three goals to two in the final. McCoist was a winner, however, finishing as the tournament's top goalscorer with ten goals, including one in the final against Forest, giving him yet another Golden Boot to add to his collection.

Although Rangers failed to qualify for the grand final in 2001 and 2002 (McCoist was a winner in the latter when he won the Slendertone 'Body of the Tournament' award!), McCoist and Rangers were back in Birmingham in 2003, but were again losing finalists, this time going down to Manchester City. McCoist was voted Player of the Tournament in the Scottish heat, scoring goals against Hearts, Hibernian and Celtic (two), to claim the top goalscorer accolade, and he added a further two strikes to his Masters tally in the opening match of the grand final, a 7-2 drubbing of West Bromwich Albion. Television commitments saw him miss out in 2004, but he was back in blue in 2005 and 2006, although he missed out when Rangers eventually laid their hands on the trophy when they thumped Chelsea by eight goals to two in the 2006 grand final. His exploits since his inaugural appearance in 2000 have secured his place alongside the likes of Ian Rush, Glenn Hoddle and Gianfranco Zola in the competition's Hall of Fame, with McCoist the only player from north of the border to figure in that elite group.

McCoist turned out in the odd eleven-a-side game, too. In January 2001, he was presented with an opportunity to play in front of a capacity crowd at Ibrox for one last time in a Rangers shirt. The match was against old foes Celtic with the gate receipts going to charity. A capacity crowd turned out to watch the teams made up of players who had graced both clubs in the past. In the crowd that afternoon were McCoist's three sons, Alexander, Mitchell and Argyll. It was the first time they had seen their daddy play for Rangers, and McCoist didn't let his boys down, proving he was still the scourge of Celtic by bagging a hat-trick as Rangers ran out convincing 4-1 winners.

When the veterans crossed swords again in March 2005, this time for a 1-1 draw at Hampden, with charities such as The Davie Cooper Centre and Motor Neurone Research benefiting, McCoist was back in blue and, despite failing to get on the scoresheet, he was still afforded a prolonged standing ovation by the Rangers fans. His most recent bow in a blue jersey came in the challenge match arranged to mark the tenth anniversary of Rangers' achievement of capturing nine league titles in a row. An array of Rangers heroes from that era donned the Light Blue jersey once again and took on a Scottish League Select comprising of players that had turned out against Rangers during their record-equalling title sequence. The match ended 2-2, with Rangers' goals coming from Brian Laudrup and Pieter Huistra.

There have also been appearances in testimonial matches for, among others, John Lambie, Stuart McCall and Ted McMinn, in addition to an appearance in an Auld Enemy match when a team of Scotland legends met their English counterparts at McDiarmid Park, Perth in May 2005. Furthermore, when Terry Venables was asked to pick a European select side consisting of the continent's top twenty most representative players aged between thirty-five and forty-five to take part in the inaugural EFPA (European Former Players' Association) match in Eindhoven a year later, McCoist was the only Scot included.

At the time of writing, McCoist's last tour of duty came at the City of Manchester Stadium in December 2007 when he was part of a Rest of the World select side that took on a team of England legends to mark the 100th anniversary of the Professional Footballers' Association (PFA). The Rest of the World team triumphed by three goals to two, with Ally inevitably getting his name on the scoresheet, grabbing what proved to be the winning goal with twelve minutes of the match remaining.

Not content with returning to the football field, McCoist even turned his hand to a bit of rugby too, playing his part in the British and Irish XV that took on the Rest of the World XV in a testimonial match for Scott Quinell and Rob Howley at the Millennium Stadium in Cardiff in June 2005. Having initially planned only to make an appearance to take goal-kicks for Quinell's British and Irish side, McCoist ended up playing on the wing for a full thirty minutes of the second half. Inevitably, his name ended up on the scoresheet, as he successfully kicked four conversions and added a fine solo try of his own, as Howley's Rest of the World side triumphed by 67 points to 57.

Aside from his promising media career and occasional football outings, McCoist also dabbled in football journalism, penning a weekly column in the *Daily Record* newspaper. He signed up as part of the *Record*'s sports team in 2004, having previously held a similar role with the *Daily Express* and the *News of the World*. His column often made for interesting reading, as it presented him with a platform to talk about Scottish football, a privilege he was not too often afforded, with his work with ITV primarily focusing on the English scene. His editorial was, as one would expect, highly amusing on occasion, but no punches were pulled either and no bias was shown towards his beloved Rangers. Indeed, the Light Blues were regularly slated in his articles, particularly between 2005 and 2006 when the Glasgow giants lurched through a traumatic time on the field in the latter days of the Alex McLeish era and during the ill-fated reign of Paul Le Guen.

Thus, it appeared that the scene was set for McCoist to remain in the public eye as a respected media pundit, although it was also suggested that he would become a football agent after his golden boots had completed their final tour of duty. McCoist and Ian Durrant were directors of a firm called MAD (McCoist and Durrant) that represented footballers, and although McCoist's good friend, Andrew McCormick, did much of the day-to-day running of the business while the major shareholders were still active players, McCoist had intimated a desire to become more involved when he ceased playing, thus allowing him to retain an association with the game he was passionate about. He maintained an involvement with the agency for a number of years after he wound down his playing career, but he yearned for involvement at the sharp end of the football world, and in late January 2005, McCoist was tempted back into the fray.

Having attended the requisite courses and passed the examinations required to obtain his SFA coaching badges and his 'A' licence under the watchful eye of Jimmy Sinclair, one of Scotland's most capped footballers was recruited to join the coaching staff of the national team under new manager Walter Smith, who was appointed following the ill-fated reign of Berti Vogts.

During Vogts' time in charge, Scotland had plummeted swiftly towards football oblivion. Failure to qualify for the European Championships in 2004 was compounded by a rapid descent down the world rankings and a less than inspiring start to the qualifying campaign for the 2006 World Cup, prompting Vogts to leave his post amid reports that most of the players had lost faith in him. Smith was earmarked by the SFA as the man to drag Scotland out of the mire, and he immediately pinpointed McCoist as the ideal man to help him and his assistant Tommy Burns in their quest to restore the battered and bruised pride of the beleaguered Scottish team.

The first match for the new management team could hardly have been more daunting, a real baptism of fire in the San Siro against Italy in March. With results in Group Seven less than inspiring up to this point and after a number of embarrassing defeats in friendly matches, many feared the worst for Scotland, but although they were beaten by two goals to nil, they gave a good account of themselves and it was clear that the fighting spirit that had been missing in the Vogts era was back with a vengeance.

Further promising results followed, including a win over Norway in Oslo and excellent draws with Italy at Hampden and Belarus in Minsk, results which re-ignited Scotland's World Cup qualification hopes. Unfortunately defeat at home against the Belarusians extinguished dreams of a trip to Germany in the summer of 2006, but pride and stability had at least been restored, with the sights now readjusted and trained on qualification for the 2008 European Championships in Austria and Switzerland.

Accomplishment of that objective was dealt a seemingly fatal blow, though, when the Scots were bracketed in the most demanding qualifying section. In addition to drawing the new world champions Italy and runners-up France, the dangerous Georgians and Ukrainians were also included in Scotland's section. Finishing in the top four of this 'Group of Death', never mind in either of the two qualifying slots, seemed beyond the Scots, but galvanised by the spirit that Smith, McCoist and Burns had instilled in the squad, Scotland proceeded to stun the football fraternity with a series of astonishing results.

The most notable was the tremendous 1-0 victory over the French at Hampden. Smith got his tactics spot on, with Scotland absorbing all the blows that Thierry Henry and co could rain down on them before, in a rare forward foray, Gary Caldwell stole in at the far post to force the ball into the net and give the Dark Blues three priceless points. Although the Smith and McCoist era ultimately ended with a disappointing 2-0 defeat in the Ukraine, the solid foundations they had laid served Smith's replacement, Alex McLeish, well, with the former Rangers manager picking up the reins and leading the Scots to an awe-inspiring 1-0 win over France in Paris in September 2007 that took them to the brink of qualification for the finals of a major international tournament for the first time in ten years. Dreams of qualifying for Euro 2008 were cruelly dashed, however, in the final minute of the final fixture against Italy at Hampden.

The role Ally McCoist played in the nation's renaissance cannot be underestimated. Undoubtedly, his jovial personality and presence at squad gatherings helped raise spirits in the camp, but his knowledge of the game and, in particular, the art of goal-scoring came to the fore, with the misfiring Kenny Miller the main beneficiary.

Miller had first burst on to the scene in the 1999/2000 season while plying his trade at Hibernian, and his goal-scoring prowess was soon attracting interest from clubs all over the country. In the end it was Rangers who snared the youngster for a fee of £2 million in the summer of 2000 and many expected him to flourish under the tutelage of Dick Advocaat. Unfortunately things did not quite proceed as planned, and despite a promising start that saw him net five goals in a 7-1 league win over St Mirren and the opening goal in the 2-2 Champions League draw with Monaco at Ibrox, Miller found a regular place in the first team hard to come by and was eventually shipped out to Wolverhampton Wanderers, initially on loan and then on a permanent basis following the appointment of Alex McLeish to the Rangers manager's office.

It was during the spell at Molineux that Miller began to mature into a regular goalscorer. In the 2002/03 season, Wolves won promotion to the Premiership via the playoffs and Miller was an integral part of that success, netting nineteen league goals over the course of the campaign. Unfortunately, he failed to transfer his prolific club form onto the international arena, which attracted a fair amount of criticism.

Miller had made his first appearance for Scotland as a substitute in a friendly against Poland in 2001 while still a Rangers player but, after almost two years in the international wilderness, he was recalled to the squad in 2003. However, his return did not turn out to be the answer to the Scots' goal-scoring problem. In his first twenty appearances in Dark Blue, he found the net on just two occasions, and after a series of glaring misses in important matches, Miller was widely criticised in the Scottish media, with many journalists questioning whether or not he had the ability to cut it at that level.

However, working on the training field with McCoist and listening to his pearls of wisdom proved the perfect tonic for Miller's ailing Scotland career, giving it a shot in the arm and sharpening his striking instincts to such an extent that he embarked on a run that yielded four goals in his next three internationals. The media, quick to chide when things were going wrong, were swift to bless, with some declaring the striker a national hero after his brace against Norway in Oslo helped re-establish Scotland as genuine contenders for the World Cup playoff spot in Group Seven. McCoist showered his protégé with praise too, saying after Miller's goal had earned Scotland a 1-1 draw against Italy at Hampden that his performance ranked 'alongside the very best I've seen in the position'.[4]

Working with Miller was just one example that illustrated McCoist's aptitude for coaching, and his name was soon being touted when managerial vacancies arose throughout the country. He was strongly linked with the Dunfermline Athletic job when Jim Leishman stood down at East End Park, and he emerged as the number one candidate when Inverness Caledonian Thistle sought a replacement for Craig Brewster in January 2006. Brewster had left the Highlands to take up the reins at Dundee United, and although Charlie Christie took charge as caretaker manager, McCoist was identified as the man the Inverness board wished to assume the role on a permanent basis.

McCoist's considerable media commitments were initially perceived as being a major stumbling block, but it appeared that would be overcome with an arrangement whereby McCoist would strike the balance by working in tandem with Charlie Christie. Talks were held with the club's director of football, Graeme Bennett, and McCoist was eventually offered the job, but after careful consideration, he rejected the offer of the post. 'Inverness are a fantastic club and I was sorely tempted by their wonderful offer, but unfortunately this came at the wrong time for me,' he said. 'I have three young kids and another one on the way [his fourth son, Arran Ross, was born on 18 February 2006]. To work full time up there and not see them all week would be too hard to bear... It's only down to geography. That's not Inverness' fault and it is certainly no slight on them because they are a fantastic club, one of the best in Scotland. If it was a bit closer to home then I would have jumped at this opportunity.'[5]

Almost a year later, the opportunity that was 'closer to home' presented itself. McCoist's first football love, Rangers, were in dire trouble as the world welcomed 2007, lurching through a calamitous season in Scotland, while being ripped asunder by internal rifts between the manager, Paul Le Guen, and a number of the club's principal characters, notably the captain, Barry Ferguson. At the behest of chairman Sir David Murray, a major salvage operation was mounted in order to restore stability to the quaking foundations of this proud institution. Le Guen agreed to a parting of the ways by 'mutual consent' and Murray made an impassioned plea to two legendary figures from one of the most successful spells in Rangers' history to help rescue the Light Blues from slithering even further into the mire.

In January 2007, after almost ten years away, it was time for Ally McCoist to come home.

CHAPTER NINETEEN

COMING HOME

When Paul Le Guen arrived in Scotland to become the thirteenth manager of Rangers Football Club in the summer of 2006, the appointment was met with widespread approval within the Rangers community. On the back of a hugely impressive CV, many Rangers supporters anticipated that the Frenchman would revolutionise their club, returning them to the summit of the Scottish game, while boosting their ailing reputation on the European stage. However, just seven months later, the dreams lay in tatters after a tortuous time that left Rangers' fortunes flat-lining and in dire need of resuscitation and the reputation of one of Europe's most sought-after coaches somewhat tarnished.

It had been known for some time that 2005/06 would be Alex McLeish's last season in charge at Ibrox. The likeable flame-haired Scotsman, who had made his name as a stalwart centre-half in Alex Ferguson's all-conquering Aberdeen side in the 1980s, had succeeded Dick Advocaat at the Ibrox helm in December 2001 and proceeded to lead the side to seven domestic trophies, including two dramatic SPL championship triumphs. He had also made history by steering Rangers into the knockout stages of the Champions League, with the Light Blues becoming the first Scottish club to achieve such a feat. However, his past glories failed to buy him any time when Rangers found themselves trapped in the mire of a decidedly mediocre domestic season in 2005/06.

Having won the SPL title in dramatic fashion in the 2004/05 season, and with a new manager in the shape of McLeish's friend and former team-mate Gordon Strachan taking control at arch-rivals Celtic, the expectation at the outset of the new campaign was that Rangers would once again reign supreme in Scotland. The reality was somewhat different, though, as the Scottish giants lurched through the worst series of results in their history – at one juncture they went nine matches without registering a win – and this doleful period prompted the board to act and agree a mutual parting of the ways with the ever-dignified McLeish.

Le Guen's remit when he arrived in Glasgow was simple: prompt a swing in the balance of power in Scottish football away from Celtic and back towards Rangers. There was also an expectation, given his impressive track record in the Champions League while in charge of Olympique Lyonnais, that he could also mastermind a prolonged presence in European competition.

Such a task appeared, even from the outset, to be a tall order for the Frenchman, who became only the second non-Scot to take control at Ibrox since the inception of the club back in 1873. He had inherited a group of players from Alex McLeish that were regarded by friend and foe as the worst Rangers side in their long and distinguished history. The amiable Scot had been starved of any semblance of a transfer kitty during his four-year tenure thanks to the precarious financial position in which Rangers found themselves in the wake of the frivolous spending that had marked out the latter days of the Dick Advocaat era. As a result, McLeish had to cut his cloth accordingly and fish for talent in the notoriously murky waters of the Bosman market. Although he managed to unearth a few gems, like the Croatian warhorse Dado Prso and the French centre-back Jean Alain Boumsong – whom he sold six months later to Newcastle United for £8 million – all too often he was left with players of a substandard quality, which was reflected in Rangers' woeful and abject domestic performances during 2005/06.

Some funds were made available for Le Guen, and although not the same exorbitant amount that had been afforded to Advocaat, there was still sufficient to inject fresh blood into the ailing squad. With a number of new faces added to the player pool and a punishing pre-season training schedule drawn up, the Rangers community, who were already rejoicing over the recruitment of the Frenchman, were positively salivating at the prospect of a return to greatness for Rangers in the 2006/07 season.

However, before the competitive action got underway, the cracks that would eventually develop into chasms began to surface. En route to South Africa for a pre-season tour, Dutch full-back Fernando Ricksen, a man who was hardly noted for his angelic ways during an eventful six-year stay in Glasgow, allegedly verbally abused an air steward. Le Guen's response to his behaviour was immediate. Ricksen was sent back to Scotland and transfer-listed, and he eventually linked up with his former manager Dick Advocaat in Russia, moving to Zenit St Petersburg on loan before making the move permanent a few months later. The prompt despatching of the unruly Ricksen seemed to give an early indication that insubordination of any sort would not be tolerated under the new regime. Seven months later, attempts to deal with other acts of rebellion effectively ended Le Guen's ill-fated spell in Glasgow.

Minus Ricksen, Rangers kicked off the Le Guen era with a fine 2-1 victory over Motherwell at Fir Park. The margin of victory should have been more emphatic, as Rangers breached Motherwell's defensive barrier time and time again only to be denied by profligate finishing when the goal beckoned. Nonetheless, the football Le Guen's side, playing in a 4-2-3-1 formation, had exhibited was quite breathtaking, with many critics stating that the Rangers juggernaut would be almost impossible to stop once the shooting boots had been sourced from the hamper.

Six days later, amid much pomp and pageantry, Le Guen was paraded before the excited Ibrox legions ahead of his first home league match against Dundee United. By the end of the ninety minutes, though, two points had been spilled, with the visitors exposing the defensive frailties that would manifest themselves in the months ahead. United led 2-0 at one stage before a strike from Chris Burke and an unfortunate own-goal rescued a point for Rangers, who had once again showcased some stunning football only for their finishing ability to desert them for the second successive match.

Further lax defending accounted for another two points lost in Le Guen's third league outing – an error from goalkeeper Lionel Letizi allowed Owen Morrison to equalise Thomas Buffel's opening goal in a 1-1 draw against Dunfermline – but when Rangers returned to a sun-kissed Ibrox the following weekend, they shot to the summit of the SPL table, producing a scintillating performance to defeat Hearts 2-0. Both wingers, Chris Burke and Lee Martin, were in devastating form, with the latter teeing up Kris Boyd for his second goal of the game with a wonderful delivery from a free-kick. Thus, within the space of just four fixtures, Le Guen had taken Rangers into pole position in the title race. Unfortunately for him, this would be the first and last weekend of his reign that would culminate with the Glasgow giant sitting on top of the SPL pile.

The rot set in almost immediately. Rangers won just three of their next nine league matches before plummeting to the nadir of the Le Guen era when they exited the League Cup at the hands of First Division St Johnstone. All the talk prior to the match was of how Rangers were now red-hot favourites to win the tournament (most of the perceived 'big guns', including holders Celtic, had already bowed out of the competition), but the Saints won 2-0 at Ibrox, a result that actually flattered the home side. The defeat also handed Le Guen an unwanted place in the history books: he had just become the first manager to oversee Rangers being eliminated from a domestic cup competition on their own patch at the hands of a team from a lower division.

In the midst of that wretched spell, rumblings of discontent within the Ibrox dressing room had become worryingly audible, with the dissatisfaction centred around the treatment of two players in particular, Kris Boyd and Allan McGregor. Despite continuing the prolific goal-scoring form that had shone like a beacon in the latter days of the McLeish era, Boyd was often overlooked for selection, with Le Guen citing his lack of work-rate and application outside the penalty area as the reasons for leaving the most natural goalscorer on the club's books on the bench. Given that Rangers were struggling to score goals and win football matches, the decision baffled an increasingly beleaguered Rangers support, but when Le Guen followed it up by dramatically dropping goalkeeper Allan McGregor, Rangers' season began to spiral out of control.

Lionel Letizi, one of Le Guen's close-season acquisitions, had made a less than inspiring start to his Rangers career. Aside from his error at East End Park that had gifted Dunfermline a point, his hesitancy and indecision had done little to inspire confidence in a defence that was already showing signs of strain. When the Frenchman sustained a calf muscle injury during the victory over Hearts, Allan McGregor, who had been understudy to both Stefan Klos and Ronald Wattereus, was handed the gloves, and the young Scot acquitted himself superbly during what was fast becoming a difficult time for the club.

However, when Letizi was passed fit to play against Inverness Caledonian Thistle at Ibrox on Saturday, 14 October, McGregor was cast aside, with Le Guen telling the press corps that Letizi was first choice and would always be on the team sheet when fit to play, irrespective of how well any replacement had being playing. The decision understandably irked McGregor to the extent that he began to contemplate a future away from Ibrox, and Le Guen's reasoning did little to placate a clutch of his players and also the Rangers supporters, many of whom were beginning to fear the worst as Rangers consistently failed to discover some sort of winning formula. Inevitably, Letizi's return to the team ended in disaster when the former Paris Saint-Germain goalkeeper spilled a long-range shot and allowed Graham Bayne to net the winning goal for Inverness. To say the Ibrox patrons were not amused would have been a gross understatement.

There were also problems with Phil Bardsley, a young right-back on loan from Manchester United. Apart from a rather stupid ordering off at Easter Road, Bardsley had been in impressive form since arriving at Ibrox, but his time in Govan ended when he was dismissed from the training field by Le Guen in the lead-up to a vital UEFA Cup clash against Livorno. Le Guen had introduced a style of training through which tackling was banned (an approach that is reportedly common in France), and when Bardsley was guilty of a wild and robust challenge on Thomas Buffel, he was jettisoned and never donned a Light Blue jersey again.

Commenting on the incident in his weekly newspaper column, Ally McCoist, who had urged for patience as the supporters began to turn on the Rangers manager, admitted to being 'a bit surprised' at what had come to pass with Bardsley, stating that Le Guen would have struggled had he attempted to implement training methods such as this during the Nine-in-a-Row era. He said: 'The absence of tackling in training may be the French way, but Rangers are a passionate club with passionate players. I liked to train as I played because I reckoned I needed that competitive edge to take into matches. Le Guen's approach wouldn't have worked with me – and certainly not the likes of John Brown and Richard Gough. The fans will accept new methods, managers and ideas, but they will not accept their side falling even further behind Celtic and Hearts so early in the season.'[1]

Perhaps the saving grace for Le Guen during this time of domestic toil was the fact that the club finally appeared to be making inroads on the European stage. Having comfortably defeated the Norwegian outfit Molde to qualify for the UEFA Cup group stages, Rangers became the first Scottish side to win on Italian soil when they defeated Livorno 3-2 in their opening fixture, and two further victories over Maccabi Haifa and Partizan Belgrade, coupled with a 2-2 draw against Auxerre in France, saw the Scots progress smoothly to the knockout stages as group winners. As attractive as success on the continent was, though, the yardstick against which Rangers managers are generally judged has been their ability to win, or at least sustain a prolonged challenge for, domestic honours, an arena within which Le Guen and his players had thus far been found wanting.

For a short spell, however, a chink of light appeared to be visible at the end of what had threatened to become a long and desperately dark tunnel. After enduring another doleful away day when they lost 1-0 at Falkirk, Rangers somehow found a performance that was befitting the club's great name and tradition when Hibernian visited Glasgow. Some weeks earlier, the young Easter Road outfit had comprehensively outplayed Le Guen's side during a 2-1 victory in Edinburgh, but on this occasion, the tables were turned as Rangers racked up three goals in the first half and cantered to a 3-0 victory. They played well again the following weekend, drawing 1-1 at home with runaway leaders Celtic, and the apparent upturn continued when Nacho Novo and Libor Sionko scored to help record a 2-1 victory over Aberdeen at Pittodrie, a venue that Rangers had found notoriously difficult to take points from in recent years. There were notes of caution, though, with McCoist among those wary of getting carried away. 'Talk of turning the corner, as I have continually stated over the past few weeks, is premature and will be until Rangers remedy the defensive problems that have afflicted them this season,' he said.[2]

McCoist's observations turned out to be prophetic, as just when they appeared to be reaching the apex of the corner, Rangers once again rumbled off the rails when, four days later, they meekly surrendered to an Inverness Caledonian Thistle side that had not registered a victory in their previous seven league outings. Despite taking an early lead courtesy of Novo's penalty-kick, Le Guen's side were pegged back to 1-1 as half-time approached and were beaten in injury-time when John Rankine lashed home a terrific shot from twenty-five yards. The 'Caley Curse' had struck again, and the result heralded the beginning of the end for Rangers' flagging Frenchman. More points were tossed away as the year was rounded off with a 1-1 draw at home against struggling St Mirren, before Le Guen effectively signed his ticket out of Ibrox on New Year's Day.

Countless Rangers supporters must have been questioning the amount of alcohol they had consumed as they brought in the New Year the previous evening, or whether they were still in a state of inebriation when they awoke on the opening day of 2007 to banner headlines proclaiming the news that club captain Barry Ferguson, the apple of the Rangers supporters' eye and the one consistent performer in the dreadful opening gambit of the 2006/07 season, had been sensationally dropped for that day's match against Motherwell, stripped of the captaincy and placed on the transfer list. Surely this couldn't be true? Had Le Guen truly lost his way and managed to plumb new depths in his turbulent Ibrox reign?

The pair had been at loggerheads for some weeks following comments attributed to Le Guen regarding the importance of the captain's armband. He had intimated that the role of the captain was much more diminished and less important in his homeland, a statement that irked Ferguson who, as a born-and-bred Rangers supporter, regarded the honour of captaining Rangers to be one of the most distinguished bestowed upon him in his career. The pair had also clashed following the matches against Inverness and St Mirren, with Ferguson allegedly failing to adhere to his manager's instructions as he tried to rescue Rangers from the state of mediocrity in which they were now firmly ensconced.

The fixture against Motherwell was played against the backdrop of supporters protests requesting Le Guen bid 'au revoir' and return to France, and even some of the players got in on the act too, with Kris Boyd, who himself enjoyed a less than amicable relationship with his manager, saluting Ferguson after he netted the winning goal from the penalty spot. He held six fingers in the air, a less than veiled gesture signifying support for Ferguson, who wore the number six jersey, a shirt that meant a great deal to him.

After the match, Le Guen was grilled over the whole affair. He told the press corps that he felt as though his captain had too much authority, which undermined his own influence and left him, in his opinion, with no option but to relieve Ferguson of his duties. Asked if he felt that Ferguson had tugged on a Rangers jersey for the last time, the Frenchman stated that he did not know, but that it would be 'difficult' for the Scotland skipper to return to the team under his stewardship, although he did seem to offer an olive branch to the now-former captain by suggesting that he could well be accommodated again should he show 'other behaviour'.

As is the case in such personality clashes, there is often only one winner, and in this instance it was Ferguson. A summit involving the warring factions and chairman Sir David Murray was held, but the war was ended before any ceasefire could be declared. Five days after the news broke regarding the decision to discard Ferguson, an agreement was reached that saw Le Guen and Rangers go their separate ways. Le Guen returned to France to take charge of Paris Saint-Germain, while Sir David Murray sent out an SOS to Walter Smith to come back to Ibrox and save the club from drifting into oblivion.

Smith had performed a minor miracle in rescuing the Scottish national team from the stupor induced by the ill-fated Berti Vogts era, and Murray had high hopes that he could do something similar at Ibrox. A dream team comprising of Smith and Ally McCoist was concocted, with the dynamic duo enticed away from their posts with the national side. Smith returned to his first love for a second spell as manager and McCoist joined up as his assistant. The move represented yet another fairytale entry in the McCoist storybook, and he said he was like a 'kid in a sweetie shop'[3] after Walter Smith approached him to join his management team at Ibrox.

Speaking to the *Rangers News* on the day of his return 'home', McCoist could not conceal his delight. 'It's a dream come true,' he said. 'I spent so many great years at this football club and to be back as assistant manager under Walter and to work with Kenny [McDowall, the first-team coach who had been lured to Ibrox from Celtic after guiding the Parkhead youngsters to five successive Under-21 league titles] is amazing. It's a big job, let's make no mistake about it. The lads have under-performed to a certain degree. Hopefully we can rectify that.'[4]

The legendary striker had actually rebuffed an opportunity to return to Ibrox in the latter days of the Alex McLeish era, citing the coaching role offered as being 'too big' to take up on a part-time basis while he juggled his ever-increasing media commitments. Almost eighteen months later, though, the goalposts had moved somewhat and McCoist was only too glad to return to the club that had stolen his heart during his glittering playing career.

Although he had left Ibrox in 1998, he was still hugely popular in the Rangers community. In 1999, Rangers canvassed opinion among their own supporters in a bid to find out who they thought were the legendary figures in the club's history. Fans were invited to cast their votes in categories ranging from Greatest-Ever Striker to Greatest-Ever Foreign Player and Greatest-Ever Goal, and were also asked to select their Greatest-Ever Rangers XI.

The winners were announced at an exclusive black-tie dinner, and McCoist won two awards on the night. He was voted the club's top striker, fending off competition from the likes of Bob McPhail, Derek Johnstone and Mark Hateley to win the award, and he was also included in the Greatest-Ever Rangers team, a galaxy of stars that included former team-mates Andy Goram, Terry Butcher, Richard Gough, Paul Gascoigne, Brain Laudrup, Mark Hateley, the late, great Davie Cooper and star turns from the 1960s and '70s, Jim Baxter, John Greig and Sandy Jardine. The ultimate award of the evening, 'The Greatest Ever Ranger', went to John Greig, but McCoist was honoured to finish as runner-up, with Davie Cooper third. 'In my opinion, the right man won it,' said a magnanimous McCoist afterwards. 'Greigy is known as a legend, always has been, always will be, but to come second to a man of that stature made me very proud.'[5]

McCoist had also been involved at Ibrox as one of the patrons of the Rangers Charity Foundation, and in early 2005, it was announced that he had been elected to the Rangers Hall of Fame committee, a role which involved deciding which of the players who have graced the club with distinction over the years would be the next to be included in the Rangers Hall of Fame. This is a log of luminaries that have been recognised for their significant contribution to the history of Rangers and their names are etched in gold on an oak panel that is hung above the famous marble staircase just inside the Ibrox foyer. When the Hall of Fame was inaugurated in 2000, it came as no surprise that McCoist was one of the first inductees.

The new management team certainly hit the ground running. In front of a packed house that included the entire McCoist clan, Rangers got the second Smith era off to a stunning start by registering a thumping 5-0 home victory over a Dundee United side that had taken four points out of a possible six during the previous regime. The result was the platform from which Rangers launched their bid to secure second place, with

Smith and McCoist slowly restoring and rebuilding the club. The remnants of the Le Guen era were quickly off-loaded, with a mixture of young and experienced Scottish players drafted in to plug the gaps that had been all too evident in the opening months of the season. The potion that the new regime brewed both on and off the park turned out to be a winning one, and the inconsistency that had ravaged Rangers in the opening months of the season swiftly vanished, as Smith's side progressed smoothly towards Champions League football for the 2007/08 season.

The emphatic win over United was followed by wins over Dunfermline, Kilmarnock, Falkirk and Hibernian and a 0-0 draw at home against Hearts. For a club the size of Rangers, victories over these sides does not normally register much of a reading on the Richter Scale, but these were the types of matches the Light Blues were carelessly spilling points in under the previous regime.

As always, though, the acid test for any new Ibrox administration comes in the shape of performances against Celtic, and Smith took his troops to Parkhead on 11 March for his first taste of the Old Firm conflict since April 1998. When he arrived for his second spell in charge, Celtic were a mere dot on the horizon, as they stormed unchallenged towards a second successive SPL crown, but Rangers won the match 1-0 thanks to a stunning goal from one of Smith's early acquisition's, former England centre-back Ugo Ehiogu. Although the victory did little to disrupt Celtic's championship charge, it was vital for Rangers, as it laid down a marker for the months ahead. Indeed, when Celtic came to Ibrox in May after the SPL split, Smith worked his magic again, with Rangers scoring a 2-0 victory thanks to goals from Boyd and Charlie Adam.

The result confirmed that Rangers would end the season as runners-up in the SPL and would thus have a crack at Europe's premier competition, the Champions League, in 2007/08. Although the final two league fixtures against Kilmarnock and Aberdeen were lost – results that brought to an end a magnificent thirteen-match unbeaten run domestically – sufficient evidence had been provided since January that the arrival of Smith, McCoist and McDowall had steadied the listing ship and steered her back onto the right course.

Further confirmation was delivered at the outset of the 2007/08 campaign too, with Rangers flying out of the blocks and sprinting to the summit of the SPL table in the early months of the season. Smith,

McCoist and McDowall guided a solid-looking Rangers squad, swelled by the addition of no fewer than thirteen new faces in the close season, to an excellent start to the season.

After claiming a morale-boosting victory over Chelsea in a pre-season friendly at Ibrox, the Light Blues won their first five SPL fixtures to sit on top of the table at the end of August. The highlight in that run was a thrilling 7-2 home win over Falkirk, with three of the strikers in the squad, Kris Boyd, Daniel Cousin and Jean-Claude Darcheville, contributing five of the goals, and although Rangers won just one of their next four league fixtures, this brief decline was arrested by a comprehensive 3-0 victory over Celtic at Ibrox in the campaign's first Old Firm encounter. Barry Ferguson was in inspirational form, imperiously commanding the midfield and scoring one of the goals. The other two were netted by the livewire Spanish forward Nacho Novo, who said afterwards: 'In the last few weeks I haven't even been on the bench which was hard to take. But you need to think about the team as well and the gaffer is doing a great job. Ally McCoist has also been brilliant and when I score I think of him. He's a legend. When you score you want to celebrate with your team-mates and particularly with Coisty.'[6]

It was clear that the players and the striking fraternity, in particular, had developed an underlying respect for the new regime, with the forwards undoubtedly benefiting from training alongside McCoist, the club's greatest-ever goalscorer. One player who profited more than most was the much-maligned Kris Boyd, perceived to be the heir-apparent to the goal-scoring throne McCoist had vacated ten years earlier.

Having fallen out of favour with Paul Le Guen despite an enviable goal-scoring return – the Frenchman was openly critical of the former Kilmarnock striker's work ethic – Boyd found himself revitalised after the arrival of the managerial dream team in January 2007. He was suddenly back in the team and scoring on a regular basis, with hat-tricks against Kilmarnock and Aberdeen and an elusive first goal against Celtic helping to swell his total goal count for the season to twenty-six.

McCoist, who trained alongside Boyd when the youngster was making waves at Kilmarnock in the fledgeling years of his career, had clearly taken the heir-apparent under his wing, as illustrated by Boyd's reaction when his left-foot volley beat Artur Boruc in May to give the striker his first-ever goal against Celtic. As the ball hit the net and the Ibrox stands erupted, Boyd made a bee-line for McCoist in the technical area and the resulting embrace showed how much Boyd appreciated the help he has received from the assistant manager. 'I ran to Ally because he has really helped me since he has come to the club,' said a delighted Boyd after the match. 'It is probably the most significant goal in my career and I wanted to celebrate it with him.'[7]

Boyd was also swamped by his team-mates as he celebrated, giving an indication that the togetherness that had been conspicuous by its absence in the dark, doleful days of the early part of the season had returned. This was another by-product of the Smith-McCoist-McDowall reconstruction job. During his playing days, McCoist had always spoken of the importance of having a happy and contented dressing room, and it was apparent that this was the mantra to which he and Smith were adhering as they attempted to restore Rangers back to the pinnacle of the Scottish game. 'I see bonds developing and relationships getting stronger,' said McCoist when reflecting on the early months of his second stint at Ibrox:[8]

> When I first came here I got the impression that a lot of the lads were not 100 percent enjoying their work. The body language didn't appear to be the greatest and there was a need to get quite a few of them smiling again. That's something we addressed and there is an improvement. In the nine-in-a-row team we had friendships as well [as] being team-mates. I can see that now with the current team. There's a work ethic and a desire to do well. That comes from enjoying being at your work.

That enjoyment of being at work soon began to reap handsome rewards, with the early success in the SPL subsequently augmented by qualification for the lucrative 2007/08 Champions League group stages.

Once again a solid defensive base reaped handsome dividends, with Rangers keeping clean sheets in each of their four qualifying matches. FK Zeta were beaten 3-0 on aggregate in the second qualifying round, and a last-gasp Nacho Novo goal at Ibrox followed by a stoic and disciplined defensive performance in the hostile cauldron of the Marakana in Belgrade was sufficient to see off the challenge of Crevzena Zvedza (Red Star) and book a place alongside the continent's elite.

Therein Rangers were handed the toughest possible assignment. Bracketed with FC Barcelona, French champions Olympique Lyonnais and reigning Bundesliga champions VfB Stuttgart in Group E, it was understandably labelled a fearsome 'Group of Death' immediately after the draw was made in Monaco. Rangers stunned many onlookers, though, by getting off to an astonishing start.

The Light Blues fought back from a goal down to defeat Stuttgart by two goals to one at Ibrox on matchday one, but if that result caused a minor tremor among the European heavyweights, their triumph in the Stade Gerland against Lyon on matchday two made a significantly higher impact on the Richter Scale, as Rangers thumped Alain Perrin's side by three goals to nil. The opulent French city of Lyon is recognised as being the culinary capital of France, but it was the throng of visiting supporters who gorged themselves on the fare dished up by Walter Smith's side. Goals from McCulloch, Cousin and Beasley inflicted upon Lyon their heaviest home defeat in the Champions League, and propelled Rangers, seeded fourth in the group, into contention for a place in the last sixteen of the competition. 'It was a wonderful performance from our boys against a very, very good European team,' said an elated McCoist in the wake of the contest. 'The result was probably beyond our wildest dreams, but I always thought we could get something as there was a bit of confidence in the squad prior to the match. In saying that, to win 3-0 was fantastic and full credit goes out to the players as they did a terrific job.'[9]

Back-to-back matches against arguably the best side in the competition, Barcelona, yielded a further point (a terrific 0-0 draw at Ibrox against Ronaldinho, Henry, Messi and company was followed by a 2-0 reverse in the Nou Camp), and although Rangers lost narrowly in their penultimate fixture against Stuttgart, their fate lay in their own hands ahead of the do-or-die final fixture against Lyon at Ibrox in mid-December.

Ultimately, the quest for the last sixteen of the tournament foundered in the final fixture, with the French champions chalking up the victory they needed to eliminate Rangers from the competition. However, although defeat was a bitter pill to swallow, the fact that the Light Blues performed to a sufficient standard to parachute into the UEFA Cup by finishing third in such a taxing group was yet another endorsement for the excellent job the new management team had done since their appointment. They had helped to restore the club's credibility, manufacturing a well-oiled footballing machine and putting a smile back on the face of an outfit that was left horribly disfigured by the chaotic events of the Paul Le Guen era.

Ally McCoist's personality and emerging talent as an excellent coach was undoubtedly a major factor in the revolution in Rangers' fortunes. Indeed he made such an impression that it soon became apparent that he was serving his apprenticeship under Walter Smith with the ultimate aim of one day assuming the position of manager of the club that he loves, a position that as recently as 1992 McCoist did not reckon would hold much interest for him. Back then he said: 'At this moment in time, I don't see myself in football management. I suppose that could change, but deep down I doubt it. I would enjoy coaching youngsters – the same mentality, you might say – but I can't see myself as your official team boss giving my side a Souness-type rollicking. I couldn't get myself as emotionally angry as that.'[10]

Times have changed, though, and McCoist has since taken a different perspective on the situation. 'In terms of coaching I'm still a baby. I just hope I develop into a man,' he said in 2007. 'I enjoy the tactical side of things, going to watch teams and learning about shapes and formations. It's a great education, but I'm a novice. As a player I feel I made a good contribution to Rangers. Now I want to make things happen as part of the management team.'[11]

And McCoist and the management team certainly did 'make things happen' during the latter part of what proved an incredible 2007/08 season, as they led Rangers in their pursuit of unprecedented success at home and abroad.

CHAPTER TWENTY

RIDING THE ROLLERCOASTER

When Walter Smith and Ally McCoist accepted the mission to revive the flagging fortunes of Rangers in January 2007, few could have forecast the drama and excitement that would unfold over the course of the next eighteen months. Even if you had quizzed the eternal optimists in the Rangers family, it is certain that none of them would have dared predict that by the end of the duo's first full season in charge, a red, white and blue convoy would be embarking on a journey down the M6 motorway to watch their heroes contest a European final. After all, Rangers had not scaled such dizzying heights for almost forty years, and squads of players that were infused with more quality than the one that gathered at the outset of the 2007/08 season had tried and failed to reach what many experts reckoned to be an insurmountable peak. But shortly before 10.30pm on the evening of 1 May 2008, a stoic Light Blue Brigade, under the command of Smith and his trusted lieutenants McCoist, McDowall and Durrant, defied the odds and climbed to the seemingly unreachable summit of that mountain.

The voyage to the City of Manchester Stadium and the final of the UEFA Cup began in February 2008 when Rangers were drawn against Panathinaikos in the last 32 of the competition. After a goalless first leg at Ibrox, the Light Blues, who had parachuted into the tournament after finishing third in their Champions League group, looked to be heading for an early exit when a stunning volley from Panathinaikos skipper Ioannis Goumas broke the deadlock in the opening minutes of the return leg, but a goal from first-leg sinner Nacho Novo seven minutes from time carried them into the next round on the 'away' goals rule. Although under the cosh for much of the first half, a tactical readjustment from the trusted 4-5-1 formation to a more positive 4-4-2 allowed Rangers to take a grip of proceedings after the restart, and Novo, who had missed a handful of chances in the no-score draw at Ibrox, redeemed himself by netting the priceless late leveller.

Rangers' opponents in the last sixteen were one of the tournament favourites, Werder Bremen. The Germans were riding high in the Bundesliga – they would eventually finish as runners-up behind Bayern Munich – but Rangers profited from two horrendous goalkeeping errors from Tim Weiss to establish a 2-0 lead after the first leg at Ibrox. Daniel Cousin, restored to the side after his proposed £3,000,000 transfer to Fulham collapsed, scored the first shortly before the interval when Weiss fumbled his speculative long-range shot into the net, and the German stopper was fishing the ball out of the net again minutes after the restart after Steven Davis, a dynamic midfielder who had arrived on loan from Fulham during the January transfer window, slid in to poke the ball home after the hapless Weiss had spilled another shot from Cousin. The result was completely unexpected, as many observers had expected Rangers to face a sterner examination from the 2006 Bundesliga champions, but a disciplined and professional display, aided by Weiss' butterfingers, gave Smith's side a platform upon which they could launch their bid to make the last eight of the UEFA Cup for the first time in their history.

As one would expect, the Light Blues were the subjected to an attacking barrage in the second leg, as their German hosts attempted to turn around the two-goal deficit that they faced. However, despite taking a pummelling from the first minute to the last – the Germans registered a total of thirty-five shots on goal – the resolute Rangers rearguard once again stood firm. All Werder could muster was a goal from their Brazilian playmaker, Diego, although it took a superlative save from the Rangers custodian Allan McGregor, one of many on the night, in the closing stages to ensure that the Scots progressed to the next stage.

Old foes Sporting Lisbon, who had been beaten en route to Rangers' last European triumph in 1972, were accounted for in the quarter-final – following a blank score-sheet at Ibrox, Rangers played textbook, counter-attacking football to win 2-0 in Portugal thanks to goals from Jean-Claude Darcheville and a sublime solo effort from Steven Whittaker – and suddenly Rangers were within touching distance of the final. Standing in their way were Serie A high-flyers Fiorentina, who were chasing Champions League football, and the Italians were immediately installed as overwhelming favourites to eliminate Rangers. However, despite dominating both matches, La Viola failed to prise open a tight-knit Rangers defence that was superbly marshalled by thirty-seven-year-old David Weir and the indomitable Carlos Cuellar over the course of 210 minutes of largely uninspiring action.

Thus, with no goals on the scoreboard, an anxiety-ridden penalty shoot-out was necessary to decide the Light Blues' European fate, and once again this Rangers side showed their mettle. They bounced back after skipper Barry Ferguson missed their first spot kick – his well-struck shot drew a fine save from Sebastian Frey – and when Fabio Liverani and Christian Vieri failed to score for Fiorentina, Nacho Novo was presented with the opportunity to fire Rangers into their first European final since 1972. Suddenly the hopes of a footballing community rested on the shoulders of the livewire Spaniard, but he held his nerve and calmly stroked the ball into the net to spark wild and emotional celebrations among those of a red, white and blue persuasion.

Ally McCoist, who had no doubt kicked every ball over the course of the match and wished that he had been able to take one of the spot-kicks in the shoot-out, was overcome by the emotion of the whole occasion, and he wept tears of joy as he joined the players on their lap of honour. Reaching a European final was one of the few achievements that was absent from the extraordinary CV of McCoist's playing career, but now he had the satisfaction of further boosting his promising coaching resume having played a significant role in helping to navigate this Rangers side through rough seas en-route to a date with Zenit St Petersburg at the City of Manchester Stadium.

It was a startling achievement for the Light Blues considering the state of flux that they had been in just eighteen months earlier when Smith and McCoist returned to Govan, yet despite the journey to Manchester being a hugely memorable one, the road on which Rangers travelled to get there was paved with stiff opposition, both on and off the park. Not only did the Glasgow giants have to overcome four top drawer outfits, they also had to withstand a barrage of criticism from football purists and sections of the media, with many deeming the Light Blues' perceived aversion to attacking (particularly in the semi-final clashes with Fiorentina) to be 'anti-football'.

However, this was simply a Rangers team playing to their strengths. The management team were acutely aware of the limitations of their troupe – the squad lacked sufficient guile and cutting edge to sparkle on this stage in an attacking sense – but they were also quick to recognise that they were proficient in one of the games other fine arts, that of defending. Thus, they became very difficult to break down and played a style of counter-attacking football that reaped a handsome reward. Those who are swift to criticise the 'backs-to-the-wall' displays against Fiorentina are quick to forget the excellent display against the much-fancied Werder Bremen at Ibrox in the last sixteen and the terrific performance in Lisbon when Rangers produced one of their finest results of the European run.

'If we win [the UEFA Cup] it will be as good as anything I've ever experienced in football. As good as anything I'm ever likely to experience in football,' said McCoist on the eve of the Final. 'Playing is the best thing but I can't do that any more and neither can Ian Durrant. So what's the next best thing? We're involved with our team, a team we both supported from when we were kids, and we're in a European final. We lived the dream as players and now we're living a second dream as part of Walter's team.'[1]

Ultimately, the quest for European glory was ended by an expensively assembled and extremely gifted Zenit St Petersburg side, who were under the charge of former Rangers manager, Dick Advocaat. The Russians were in the ascendancy for much of the contest and they prodded and probed before the game's outstanding player, Andrei Arshavin, succeeded where others had failed, as he finally managed to pick the lock that had held Rangers' unyielding defensive line together in all but two of their eight UEFA Cup fixtures. His precise pass allowed Igor Denisov to break the deadlock in the seventy-second minute, and the goal forced Rangers to break free from their defensive cocoon and onto the front foot as they sought a route back into the game. However, they failed to restore parity - substitute and European talisman Nacho Novo squandered a good opportunity to level the match in the final minute – and the Russians made sure of their victory with a clever breakaway goal in stoppage time.

Prior to the defeat in the UEFA Cup Final, talk had buzzed around the football world about Rangers completing an unprecedented Quadruple, which consisted of the League Championship, Scottish Cup, Scottish League Cup and UEFA Cup. The Russians had quashed that dream, but the Light Blues were still on course to snare the domestic Treble for the eighth time in their history.

In March, the first leg had been completed when Rangers edged out Dundee United in an epic final to win the League Cup for the twenty-fifth time. Smith's side were lethargic for much of the match – their strength perhaps sapped by a heroic defensive display that had repelled a flurry of blows and an attacking barrage from the Werder Bremen attack three days earlier as the Light Blues eliminated the Germans from the UEFA Cup – and a vibrant United side dominated the first half, claiming the half-time advantage when Noel Hunt squeezed the ball over the line after ten minutes. However, the introduction of the pacey Darcheville at the interval reinvigorated Rangers, with the Frenchman's attacking thrusts ruffling the feathers of the United defence, but it was another substitute, Kris Boyd, who made the decisive contribution when he seized upon a defensive error to restore parity with just six minutes of normal time remaining.

United edged ahead once again in extra-time through Mark de Vries, but Boyd, who was enduring another prolonged spell of absence from the starting eleven, forced a penalty decider when he knocked home a header at the back post following good work from Steven Davis. The Ayrshireman was the hero in the shoot-out too: he netted the winning penalty after Allan McGregor had produced two excellent saves to swing the tie back in Rangers' favour after Darcheville had struck the crossbar and Lee McCulloch had seen his weak penalty saved by the United keeper.

For the much-criticised Boyd, it was a similar type of storybook ending to the ones that his mentor, McCoist, had been involved in on countless occasions throughout his playing career, and his contribution delivered the first piece of silverware of the Smith-McCoist era, ending a three-year trophy famine for Rangers in the process. It was perhaps fitting that the League Cup, a tournament in which he had claimed nine winners' medals as a player, should present McCoist with the first gong of his coaching career, and he was also quick to lavish praise on the match-winning hero. 'He [Boyd] is probably the only Rangers player who could have scored those two goals. I have the greatest sympathy with him over being out the team. He's the best goal-scorer at the club, arguably the best goal-scorer in the country. But scoring goals does not guarantee you a game. I like to think Boydy will handle it with the same desire to get back into the team as I did [in 1990/91 when McCoist was almost a permanent resident on the substitutes' bench]. I'm sure he will.'[2]

For a long spell it seemed that the second part of the Treble, the SPL Championship, would also be Ibrox bound. After losing 2-1 against Dundee United at Tannadice in October, the team embarked on an electrifying run of success that took Rangers on a twenty-match unbeaten run. A miserly four points were yielded in that golden spell – score draws against Aberdeen (1-1) and Dundee United (3-3) – and with Celtic also accounted for in the season's second Old Firm match – a Kevin Thomson goal gave the Light Blues a 1-0 victory at Ibrox in March – Smith's side found themselves in a commanding position at the head of the table.

During that sequence, the superstitious side of McCoist's character came to the fore; fearing he would jinx the run, Ally refused to have his club suit cleaned until Rangers lost a league match! The suit was eventually dispatched to the dry cleaners when the run was halted by Jan Venegoor of Hesselink's goal deep into stoppage time at the end of the season's third Old Firm encounter at Parkhead, but from there on in, no amount of superstitious gestures could stop the Light Blues' title charge, which had been largely trouble free until that point, from hitting the skids. In the midst of a glut of fixtures spread across three competitions – the final seven matches of the campaign were played out inside just seventeen days – Rangers failed to recover enough poise, and won just three of their last eight league matches.

Celtic's last, desperate throw of the dice provoked a run of seven successive league victories, which allowed them to overhaul Rangers' advantage at the top of the table. A Rangers side that had responded so magnificently to each gauntlet that was thrown down to them over the course of a marathon season suddenly began to buckle under the physical and mental strain brought about by a congested conclusion to the campaign. Four priceless points were spilled at Easter Road and Fir Park on the weekends that immediately followed a draining European trip, and with another defeat at Parkhead following the first-leg of the

UEFA Cup semi-final against Fiorentina, Rangers surrendered their seven-point advantage to leave the Old Firm level on points going into the final fixture of the SPL season, but with Celtic holding all the aces thanks to a vastly superior goal difference. A 2-0 defeat at Pittodrie hammered the final nail into the Light Blue coffin, but although the victory spoils of the SPL trophy went to the east end of Glasgow, Smith's men undoubtedly deserved recognition for gallantry and valour. The team had just completed their sixty-seventh fixture of the season, yet still managed to take the title race into the final furlong, and there is considerable weight in the argument that had Rangers' schedule not been quite so hectic at the business end of the campaign, they would have resisted the late charge from Celtic, maintained their advantage at the top of the table and claimed the silverware themselves.

As it was they were left with two trophies on the sideboard, with the Scottish Cup collected at the end of May to sit alongside the League Cup. The latter triumph was arguably the most satisfying for Ally McCoist, as the tournament witnessed the sternest test yet of his managerial credentials. Although not quite given carte blanche by Walter Smith, Ally was effectively handed the reins for the Cup run and charged with objective of attempting to successfully negotiate the road to Hampden. He was responsible for devising the tactical approach to each tie and administering the team talks, and he played a leading role in team selection too, although the latter required rubber stamping by Smith.

McCoist's team certainly hit the ground running; a Kris Boyd hat-trick and a final goal in Light Blue for the soon-to-be-departing Alan Hutton were among the six goals racked up in their opening fixture, albeit against an East Stirling side that carried the ignominy of finishing bottom of the heap in the Scottish Third Division in each of the previous five seasons. They escaped unscathed too from a visit to Easter Road in the next round, holding out for a 0-0 draw against Hibernian in a match that saw goalkeeper Allan McGregor ordered off in the dying moments. A Ranger saw red in the replay too – Nacho Novo taking an early bath after a dreadful two-footed challenge on Thierry Gatthusei – but Chris Burke's goal was enough to steer the Light Blues into the last eight, at which stage it seemed that the engraver should ready himself to etch Rangers' name on the trophy for the thirty-first time.

Thanks to a series of shock results, a number of the big guns, including holders Celtic, had been silenced by the time Rangers got around to tackling Partick Thistle in their quarter-final tie on 19 March. The Light Blues were now installed as overwhelming favourites to win the trophy, but they almost joined their Old Firm rivals on the Scottish Cup scrapheap when they faced Thistle at Ibrox. The plucky Maryhill outfit shot into a shock lead twenty minutes from time, and it took a Kris Boyd goal seconds later to rescue a draw from what had been a stale and lacklustre Rangers performance. There was no stumble in the replay four weeks later, though; goals from Novo and Burke being sufficient to take Rangers into the last four. 'We have given ourselves a chance of winning the Scottish Cup because we are still in it,' was McCoist's post-match reflection. 'The result was always going to be more important than the performance. There's always a bit of a worry when you come to a place like this. But I thought, over the 90 minutes, we deserved the win.'[3]

The reward for the victory over Thistle was a Hampden showdown with another First Division side, McCoist's first club, St Johnstone, and they too almost upset Rangers' applecart. The match came in the heart of a flood of fixtures for the Light Blues, and they delivered an insipid performance in front of a sparsely populated National Stadium. After a goalless ninety minutes, the tie was brought to life when Daniel McBreen capitalised on hesitancy in the Rangers rearguard to shoot The Saints ahead, but Nacho Novo forced a penalty decider when he netted from the penalty spot after Daniel Cousin had been impeded inside the six-yard box. Brahim Hemdani missed one of Rangers' penalty quota, but Steven Milne and Jody Morris did likewise for St Johnstone, which allowed Cousin, who had been almost anonymous throughout the match, to step forward and net the decisive penalty that took Rangers into the final.

For the third successive round, First Division opposition stood in the path of glory. Queen of the South, managed by McCoist's former Sunderland team-mate Gordon Chisholm, had defied the odds to defeat Aberdeen by four goals to three in the semi-final, and they almost caused a huge upset in the final when they clawed back a two-goal deficit to restore equilibrium in a contest that Rangers had threatened to run away with. A thunderous free-kick from Boyd, who was establishing himself as something of a Cup Final talisman, and a clever finish from the returning DaMarcus Beasley put the Light Blues into what seemed a commanding 2-0 interval lead, but that advantage was wiped out inside five second-half minutes when the Doonhamers stormed back to 2-2. Mercifully, Boyd restored Rangers' lead when he headed home a corner kick with eighteen minutes remaining to ensure that the silverware was heading to Govan and not Dumfries.

Ally McCoist had thus, albeit unofficially, led Rangers to another trophy, and he lapped up the applause of the Rangers supporters as he led a group of leg-weary players on a deserved lap of honour following the presentation of the trophy. Remarkably the Light Blues had taken to the field at Hampden less than 48 hours after trudging despondently off the field at Pittodrie following the heartbreaking end to their quest for the SPL title, yet the players still managed to summon up the energy required to edge out their dogged opponents and snare the Cup.

'It felt great to win the Cup on Saturday,' said McCoist after the match. 'Before the game, I was nervous and in the end I was so pleased for the players and the fans. The disappointment after Thursday [when Rangers lost out on the SPL title] was a factor, but I think even more of an issue was the time we had to prepare. It was ridiculous. We had 38 hours – just 38 hours to prepare for a Scottish Cup Final. But the boys still did it. For 10 months we've kept asking them questions and they kept coming up with answers. [The 2007/08 season has] been a rollercoaster ride I'll never forget. We've reached the UEFA Cup Final, the Scottish Cup Final, the CIS Cup Final and took the league right down to the wire. That is tremendous.'[4]

For McCoist, the Cup campaign had afforded him another opportunity to climb a few more rungs on the managerial ladder, and he took further steps in the close season when he travelled to Salzburg in Austria to complete his Uefa Pro Licence, a qualification that is widely regarded as being the highest coaching qualification in Europe. The overall Pro Licence course focuses more on the management side of things rather than purely coaching and comprises sixteen modules, which deal with a variety of diverse topics, including the handling of players, contracts and agents, sports medicine, and business management. Managerial luminaries such as Arsene Wenger and Rafa Benitez hold a Uefa Pro Licence, and during his studies, McCoist was able to glean valuable hints and tips from the likes of Kevin Keegan and Kenny Dalglish, while also gaining a grasp of subjects such as accountancy and media relations. By achieving his licence, McCoist has demonstrated not only an aptitude for coaching but also an ability to manage a football club, which leaves him perfectly positioned to take on a managerial role in his own right anywhere in Europe.

A number of learned observers postulated that that managerial role would be at Ibrox, but at the outset of the 2008/09 season, Ally remained content to work under the wing of Walter Smith. He told the Evening Times: 'Walter has been my mentor since I was in the Scotland under-17s, which is the best part of thirty years. That's how highly I'd take his advice. The gospel truth is that I enjoy working with him so much that I'd be happy to stay here and do this for as long as he wants me.'[5]

In addition to continuing to work with and learn from Smith in the new season, McCoist was also reunited with one of his old sparring partners from his playing days ahead of the new campaign. Ian Durrant, who had had one match in charge of the club in a caretaker capacity before Smith and McCoist arrived in January 2007, was promoted to the role of first-team coach after a successful spell working with the club's reserve and U-19 sides to form a four-man management team at Ibrox.

The revamped coaching team would be working with some new faces too. Despite enjoying a relatively successful season in 2007/08, Rangers elected to flesh out their squad ahead of the new campaign, investing a sizeable proportion of the money they accrued from the run to the UEFA Cup Final to recruit new players. £6,000,000 was splashed out to attract strikers Kenny Miller, Andrius Velicka and Kyle Lafferty to Glasgow, while a further £2,500,000 was spent to bring in Madjid Bougherra from Charlton Athletic.

The signing of Miller, who became the first player since Dr Willie Kivlichan to cross the Old Firm divide twice, was a high risk strategy on the part of the management team, as his signing was not embraced with any kind of warmth by a significant majority of those of a red, white and blue persuasion. With the exception of a fickle minority, the Rangers supporters' aversion to the arrival of Miller had little to do with his recent allegiance with Celtic, though; the groundswell of opinion was in fact that the player was simply not good enough to wear the light blue jersey. Compared with the other striking options on the Ibrox books, Miller's scoring return was dreadful – in his previous sixty-three league games, he had netted just eleven goals – but Smith and McCoist, who, as we have seen in an earlier chapter, had reinvigorated the player's international career, knew the gamble they were taking was a calculated one.

Initially it seemed that their confidence was somewhat misplaced. Miller was barracked by a section of the supporters in both the pre-season friendlies and the early competitive encounters, as the Light Blues stumbled their way through the early part of the season. They were hammered 4-0 by Liverpool in a glamour friendly at Ibrox, and that was followed by a humbling early exit from Europe at the hands of the Lithuanian minnows, FBK Kaunas. Miller was guilty of passing up a handful of decent scoring opportunities over the two legs, which saw him cast as a scapegoat in some quarters for what was a cataclysmic fall from grace for Smith's side.

In truth, the entire team had been shambolic over the course of the tie, and the early exit threatened to blow a huge hole in the club's finances. With no guaranteed income to be sourced from European football, money had to be raised elsewhere in order to fund further acquisitions to strengthen the player pool. This inevitably meant that prized assets would have to be sold, and one of them, Spanish stalwart and 2007/08 Scottish Football Writers' Player of the Year Carlos Cuellar, elected to invoke a release clause in his contract just days after the Kaunas defeat. He left to join Martin O'Neill's Aston Villa for 10 million euros, and his departure brewed up an almighty storm among the Rangers supporters. Disillusioned about the direction in which their club were heading, sections of the support called for the heads of Sir David Murray and Walter Smith, and for the first time since their return to Ibrox, Smith, McCoist and the players were faced with a mutinous mob demanding rapid solutions to restore stability and control to what had become, in their eyes, a rudderless ship.

'I had a chat with the lads last week and I wouldn't say it is easy as such but it's a lot easier to be a Rangers player when things are going well,' McCoist told the Rangers News in the wake of the Kaunas defeat. 'You find out plenty about people when things aren't going so well and we've certainly had a testing week. It is time for our players to come up to the plate and stand up. That's when you find out who is a Rangers player.'[6]

His words seemed to have the desired effect. After a mundane showing in the opening league fixture against Falkirk, the playing squad was bolstered with the creative player that the fans had craved when Pedro Mendes arrived from Portsmouth for £3,000,000. The little Portuguese lit up Ibrox with a dazzling debut against Hearts, and his arrival supplemented by the words of the management team galvanised Rangers. Hearts were beaten 2-0, and when further quality was added in the shape of Spanish teenager Aaron Niguez, American starlet Maurice Edu and Steven Davis, who finally made his loan move from Fulham permanent, the defeat in Lithuania seemed a distant memory. A point was gleaned from a trip to Pittodrie – an appalling error from assistant referee Billy Baxter denied Rangers a legitimate winning goal in stoppage time – before Rangers travelled to Parkhead and pummelled reigning champions Celtic by four goals to two. The script was written for the much-maligned Miller to break his scoring duck, and he didn't disappoint; he scored a brace of goals on his return to his old stomping ground to add to others scored by Daniel Cousin and Pedro Mendes.

Miller's double strike finally stilled the dissenting voices among the Rangers support, and also vindicated the decision of the management team to bring him back to Glasgow. Ally McCoist was understandably delighted, and told the *Rangers News*: 'It was brilliant for Kenny. It was a tough afternoon for him. For Kenny to go to Parkhead and score two goals must be beyond his wildest dreams. He even had a wee chance to make it a hat-trick in the last minute! Well, maybe I'm getting greedy.'

McCoist also drew parallels with Miller's achievements to that of his close pal Maurice Johnston almost two decades earlier. '[Miller's goals] brings back memories of Mo Johnston nearly twenty years ago,' he said. 'I can remember him scoring against Celtic at Ibrox as if it was yesterday. If I close my eyes I can see wee Mo hitting it down low to the keeper's right side on 88 minutes down at the Rangers end, the Copland Road end.

'The thing about Mo and Kenny is that they are both terrific players and good team players. And when you work as hard as they do then you are always going to win the fans over.'[7]

The hard work of Miller and the squad was sustained too. Rangers followed the Parkhead victory with narrow home wins over Kilmarnock and Motherwell and a resounding 3-0 victory over Hibernian at Easter Road, with Miller rattling in two goals in the latter match to maintain the habit he had developed of scoring when coming up against former employers.

Although a surprise defeat against St Mirren and draws against Dundee United and Motherwell upset the apple cart somewhat, Rangers were still clinging to Celtic's coat-tails as the season moved into the festive period. And it was during this pivotal spell in the campaign that the Rangers Chairman, Sir David Murray, confirmed what the public had suspected all along: Ally McCoist would be the next manager of Rangers Football Club. Murray chose the media conference arranged to commemorate his twenty-year anniversary as Rangers Chairman to announce that Ally was effectively the heir to the Ibrox throne, saying: 'I would have thought, all things being equal, that he [McCoist] will become manager. It hasn't been discussed, but it is an understanding among us.'[8]

However, Murray did stipulate that in order for McCoist to ascend to the top job at Ibrox, the management team would have to ensure that they were successful on the field, which meant that delivery of the SPL Championship for the first time in four years was of paramount importance. He said: 'It will be success driven. If we are successful, if Walter is successful, then the natural successor would be McCoist. But if we go another two or three years without winning the league, then we will be under the same pressure as any club. You wouldn't have thought [McCoist could be a manager] 20 years ago but he's a very strong boy. He has a strong mentality. He and Kenny [McDowall] are a good team.'[9]

McCoist's mentor, Smith, echoed the Chairman's sentiments. 'I hope that that will be the case [that McCoist would succeed him as manager],' he said. 'Ally will have the opportunity if we are successful, and I hope he gets that opportunity to become the manager. I've said before that, when I do leave, I hope that he will take over. I'll make it clear to you that if we gain a level of success at Rangers, then Ally will take over. If we don't, then there's the possibility that he won't. That's the way it is. I don't think there is anything complicated about it. Ally is my assistant manager. I was the assistant manager when Graeme Souness was here. If Rangers hadn't won anything back then, I wouldn't have been made manager. So if we are successful, then Ally's got a better opportunity than anyone else – if I decide to leave. But, if I get the sack, then his chances diminish.'[10]

Thus, for McCoist to secure his dream job it was imperative that Rangers embarked on a successful season and stopped rivals Celtic making it four league titles in a row. Their mission was dealt a hefty blow when the transfer window opened in January, though, when the global credit crunch seemed set to force Rangers to sell one of their prize assets to balance the books. Kris Boyd, who had already registered twenty goals in just twenty-three appearances, was the player earmarked for the exit door, and a fee of £3,750,000 looked set to reunite the Club's top marksman with former Rangers manager Alex McLeish at Birmingham City. Understandably moves to sell Boyd at a pivotal point in the season caused uproar among the Rangers followers, but while empathising with the supporters, McCoist was quick to point out that the loss of Boyd would not necessarily signal the death knell for Rangers' hopes of winning the SPL.

He said: 'I totally understand the fans' views. They just see the fact we're in the middle of the title race and may be selling our top scorer. I appreciate that. All I can ask the supporters is to look at the facts – we have to sell. I know the fans aren't interested in balancing books. All they want is a good team and to win the league. I don't agree with anyone who says if Boyd goes we can't win the title or we can't win without him. I'd say that about whoever goes. Please do not look on this situation as a sign we're giving up on anything. If that was the case I may as well get my bag from my locker, throw away the key, jump in my car, drive off and never come back. That's just ridiculous and I hope they don't think like that because it's not the case at all. No matter who leaves we'll be doing everything we can to make sure we're successful on the park.'[11]

In the end the sale of Boyd or any other prized assets did not materialise. Boyd's move to Birmingham collapsed when he failed to agree personal terms and the squad remained intact as the race for honours began to hot up after the transfer window slammed shut. Although defeat at home to Celtic before the end of 2008 had thrust Rangers' archrivals seven points clear at the top of the table, the Light Blues managed to capitalise on a number of stumbles by the Hoops to eventually overhaul them and take over at the summit of the SPL table towards the end of February.

'It's a great view [from the top of the table], it really is', said a delighted McCoist after Rangers assumed pole position. 'I'm thrilled to be there. It seems a long, long time since we have been there [it was actually the first time that the Light Blues had led the title race since November 2008]. But we know what the most important thing is – and that's staying there. He continued: 'The players, since the defeat against Celtic, have been great, they really have. They've knuckled down and got some good results. I think they felt a little bit harshly treated in the Celtic game in terms of the result and I'd probably go along with them. But, having lost the game, all you can ask is that the players react in the right manner and that is to go out and get results and keep the pressure on Celtic. So far, they've answered all the questions, but it's important that they keep doing it.'[12]

And the squad did keep answering the questions that were asked of them. Although Celtic got their noses back in front after Rangers gathered just one point from home matches against Inverness and Hearts – The Hoops also claimed the first silverware of the season when they defeated Rangers 2-0 in the League Cup Final in March – the pendulum continued to swing back and forth as the title race turned the corner and entered the home straight. It was Rangers who held their nerve, though, racking up six successive league victories – a run that included a 1-0 win over Celtic at Ibrox, which dislodged their Old Firm rivals from the SPL summit – and gleaning 25 points from their final nine SPL matches to take the title by four points.

It was a stunning achievement when one considers that the Light Blues were seemingly dead and buried at the turn of the year when they languished seven points adrift of Celtic, and McCoist, who was also celebrating off the field when he became a father for the fifth time (the arrival of fifth son Harris finally giving Ally the five-a-side team he craved!), was understandably elated. His first title win as assistant manager was just as sweet and satisfying as any of the ten he had claimed during his playing days, and he milked the applause of the Light Blue followers at Tannadice where Rangers clinched the title and was at his effervescent best when the squad brought the trophy home to Ibrox where they were welcomed by 30,000 rapturous fans.

In tandem with aiding their pursuit of glory in the league, McCoist also ensured that Rangers successfully negotiated the road to Hampden, and just six days after clinching the title he led the Light Blues to victory in the Scottish Cup Final. Having effectively taken charge of the team throughout the triumphant campaign in 2007/08, Ally once again assumed the responsibility of looking after the team in a bid to further develop his managerial skills as part of the process of readying him for the top job on a full-time basis. And on the eve of the 2009 Final, Walter Smith gave an insight into what McCoist's role actually entailed. He said: 'Publicly I've handed the reins to Alastair, to allow him to get the general experience of taking the team. All the staff still prepare the team but Alastair is trying to get a wee bit of experience of what it's like to take the team talk before the game and at half-time etc and it's been an excellent opportunity for him to do that. It was a very simple thing, I just felt that the cup competition gave him a great opportunity to build up his experience. He did it last year and he's been doing it this year and obviously he's been making a good job of it.'[13]

In contrast to twelve months earlier where progress had been laboured

– replays were required in two of the four rounds played ahead of the Final and a penalty shoot-out was necessary to despatch St Johnstone in the semi-final – McCoist guided the Light Blues through much calmer waters this time around. Vanquished semi-final opponents St Johnstone were the first team put to the sword – McCoist's men managed to avoid slipping on the proverbial banana skin thanks to an own goal and a late strike from Nacho Novo – and successive four-goal victories over Forfar Athletic (4-0) and Hamilton Academical (5-1) took Rangers into the last four where they faced St Mirren. The Saints had defeated Celtic in the previous round, but any chance of securing a rare Old Firm 'double' were scuppered inside the opening two minutes when Andrius Velicka fired Rangers in front. Further goals from Kris Boyd and Kenny Miller cemented Rangers' place in the Final, with Boyd's goal carrying him into the history books alongside Ally McCoist.

Despite enduring another topsy-turvy season that saw him flit in and out of the starting eleven, Boyd had still managed to rack up an impressive goal tally, and his strike at Hampden, his fourth in four games, took him into triple figures in a Rangers jersey. He became only the thirtieth player in the Club's history to notch up 100 goals, achieving the landmark in 145 appearances, thirty-three fewer than McCoist who scored his 100th Rangers goal during his 178th appearance in Light Blue, against Clydebank in April 1987. Undoubtedly Boyd had developed as a player through working with McCoist on the training ground and also at the embryonic stage of his career when the two played together at Kilmarnock, but when paying tribute to Rangers' latest centurion, Ally was quick to play down his role in Boyd's haul. 'It's a sensational record,' he said when interviewed after the St Mirren game. 'I thought he earned his goal today. His overall play was unselfish. He linked up well with people, took his fair share of kicks and won his fair share of headers against two big strong centre-backs. I'm delighted for him. I watch him in training and I might be able to tell him where to go, how to handle defenders and with his movement but I do not think I could tell Kris Boyd how to score a goal.'[14]

Although Boyd didn't add to his goal tally when Rangers took on Falkirk in the Final, a stunning strike from Nacho Novo was sufficient to grant the Light Blues a 1-0 victory. The ebullient Spaniard had only been on the field a mere twenty-eight seconds having replaced Boyd at the half-time interval when he thundered in a sumptuous dipping volley from thirty yards that arced up and over the despairing dive of Dani Mallo in the Falkirk goal. In truth Rangers were poor on a day of searing heat at the National Stadium, but Novo's touch of brilliance edged them home to another trophy triumph.

'It just feels magic,' said a delighted McCoist afterwards. 'I thought Sunday [when Rangers defeated Dundee United 3-0 at Tannadice to clinch the SPL title] was one of the best days of my football life but watching the players with the cup was fantastic. Walter gave me his medal and it will mean so much. I'll cherish it and no doubt will have a few looks at it during the coming days.'[15]

Thus, the success that Sir David Murray said was a pre-requisite if Ally McCoist was to become the next manager of Ranges Football Club had been achieved. However, with Walter Smith keen to keep his hands on the tiller for another year to have one more crack at the Champions League, it appears that McCoist will have to continue to bide his time before he claims the manager's job in his own right. For the time being, he is content to remain as second in command, the apprentice learning from the master craftsman. 'I'm a little bit biased but I think he's the best in the business and it's safe to say the manager has transformed the club since he came back,' said McCoist in the wake of the Scottish Cup Final. 'If you're asking me I hope he stays as manager for the foreseeable future. His record is wonderful and from our club's point of view he has been brilliant. He gives us stability and pride in our club. I would be very disappointed if he was not here for the foreseeable future. If I was given the option [of becoming Rangers manager] I would rather he [Smith] stayed on and I hope he does. The club deserves somebody like Walter. We're in good shape at the moment and I wouldn't want to break it.'[16]

Prior to returning to Rangers as assistant manager in January 2007, Ally McCoist's razor-sharp goal-scoring prowess and glut of goals meant that his place in the pantheon of great Rangers was already secure. Now he is carving yet another niche in the history books as part of Walter Smith's successful backroom team, and it seems certain that he will one day replace 'Mr Rangers' in the Ibrox manager's office. It is an appointment that is sure to be welcomed with open arms by a Rangers community who will always have a place in their hearts reserved for 'Super Ally'.

GOAL-SCORING RECORD AND CAREER MILESTONES

COMPETITIVE APPEARANCES (1978–2001)

Total	**838 appearances, 424 goals**
League Championship	584 appearances, 290 goals
Scottish Cup/FA Cup	58 appearances, 30 goals
Scottish/English League Cup	79 appearances, 64 goals
European competition	56 appearances, 21 goals
International Caps	61 appearances, 19 goals (for Scotland)

(Note: this total excludes appearances and goals scored in non-competitive matches, such as friendlies and testimonials)

ST JOHNSTONE FOOTBALL CLUB (1978–81)

Total	**68 appearances, 27 goals**
League Championship	57 appearances, 22 goals
Scottish Cup	4 appearances, 1 goal
Scottish League Cup	7 appearances, 4 goals

SUNDERLAND FOOTBALL CLUB (1981–83)

Total	**65 appearances, 9 goals**
League Championship	56 appearances, 8 goals
FA Cup	4 appearances, 0 goals
English League Cup	5 appearances, 1 goal

ALLY McCOIST

RANGERS FOOTBALL CLUB (1983–98)

Total	**581 appearances, 355 goals**
League Championship	418 appearances, 251 goals
Scottish Cup	47 appearances, 29 goals
Scottish League Cup	62 appearances, 54 goals
European competition	54 appearances, 21 goals

KILMARNOCK FOOTBALL CLUB (1998–2001)

Total	**63 appearances, 14 goals**
League Championship	53 appearances, 9 goals
Scottish Cup	3 appearances, 0 goals
Scottish League Cup	5 appearances, 5 goals
European competition	2 appearances, 0 goals

GOAL-SCORING RECORD AND CAREER MILESTONES

ALLY McCOIST – SEASON BY SEASON

(Figures in brackets denote appearances as substitute)

SEASON	CLUB	LEAGUE		CUP		LEAGUE CUP		EUROPE		TOTAL	
		A	G	A	G	A	G	A	G	A	G
1978–79	St Johnstone	4	0	-	-	-	-	-	-	4	0
1979–80	St Johnstone	9(6)	0	1	0	-	-	-	-	10(6)	0
1980–81	St Johnstone	38	22	3	1	2	0	-	-	43	23
1981–82	St Johnstone	-	-	-	-	5	4	-	-	5	4
1981–82	Sunderland	19(9)	2	3	0	1	0	-	-	23(9)	2
1982–83	Sunderland	19(9)	6	0(1)	0	4	1	-	-	23(10)	7
1983–84	Rangers	29(1)	8	3(1)	3	10	9	2(1)	0	44(3)	20
1984–85	Rangers	22(3)	12	3	0	6	5	3(1)	1	34(4)	18
1985–86	Rangers	33	25	1	1	4	1	2	0	40	27
1986–87	Rangers	44	34	1	0	5	2	6	2	56	38
1987–88	Rangers	40	31	2	1	5	6	6	4	53	42
1988–89	Rangers	18(1)	9	7(1)	5	4	4	2	0	31(2)	18
1989–90	Rangers	32(2)	14	2	0	4	4	-	-	38(2)	18
1990–91	Rangers	5(11)	11	1(1)	1	4	3	2(2)	3	22(14)	18
1991–92	Rangers	37(1)	34	5	4	1(3)	1	2	0	45(4)	39
1992–93	Rangers	32(2)	34	4	5	5	8	9	2	50(2)	49
1993–94	Rangers	16(5)	7	4(2)	3	0(1)	1	-	-	20(8)	11
1994–95	Rangers	4(5)	1	-	-	-	-	-	-	4(5)	1
1995–96	Rangers	18(7)	16	2	1	4	3	4(2)	0	28(9)	20
1996–97	Rangers	13(12)	10	1(2)	1	2(1)	3	4(2)	6	20(17)	20
1997–98	Rangers	7(8)	5	2(2)	4	1(2)	4	2(2)	3	12(14)	16
1998–99	Kilmarnock	16(10)	7	1	0	1(1)	1	-	-	18(11)	8
1999–2000	Kilmarnock	5(4)	1	-	-	1	2	2	0	8(4)	3
2000–2001	Kilmarnock	11(7)	1	0(2)	0	1(1)	2	-	-	12(10)	3
TOTALS		481	290	46	30	70	64	46	21	643	405
		(103)		(12)		(9)		(10)		(134)	

ALLY McCOIST

HONOURS (ALL WITH RANGERS)

10 League Championship medals: 1987, 1989, 1990, 1991, 1992, 1993, 1994, 1995, 1996, 1997

9 Scottish League Cup-winners' medals: 1983/84, 1984/85, 1986/87, 1987/88, 1988/89, 1990/91, 1992/93, 1993/94, 1996/97

1 Scottish Cup-winners medal: 1992

FIRST AND LAST

St Johnstone Football Club

First Appearance: St Johnstone 3 Raith Rovers 0, Scottish First Division, 07/04/79
Last Appearance: Hibernian 2 St Johnstone 1, Scottish League Cup, 22/08/81
First Goal: Dumbarton 0 St Johnstone 3, Scottish First Division, 16/08/80
Last Goal: Celtic 4 St Johnstone 1, Scottish League Cup, 19/08/81

Sunderland Football Club

First Appearance: Ipswich Town 3 Sunderland 3, English First Division, 29/08/81
Last Appearance: Sunderland 1 West Bromwich Albion 1, English First Division, 14/05/83
First Goal: Sunderland 2 Nottingham Forest 3, English First Division, 25/11/81
Last Goal: Everton 3 Sunderland 1, English First Division, 23/10/82

Rangers Football Club

First Appearance: Rangers 1 St Mirren 1, Scottish Premier League, 20/08/83
Last Appearance: Hearts 2 Rangers 1, Scottish Cup Final, 16/05/98
First Goal: Queen of the South 1 Rangers 4, Scottish League Cup, 27/08/83
Last Goal: Hearts 2 Rangers 1, Scottish Cup Final, 16/05/98

Kilmarnock Football Club

First Appearance: St Johnstone 0 Kilmarnock 0, Scottish Premier League, 15/08/98
Last Appearance: Kilmarnock 1 Celtic 0, Scottish Premier League, 20/05/2001
First Goal: Kilmarnock 3 Livingston 1, Scottish League Cup, 18/08/98
Last Goal: Kilmarnock 2 Dunfermline Athletic 1, Scottish Premier League, 07/04/2001

Scotland

First Appearance: Holland 0 Scotland 0, Friendly, 29/04/86
Last Appearance: Scotland 3 Estonia 2, European Championships Qualifier, 10/10/98
First Goal: Scotland 2 Hungary 0, Friendly, 09/09/87
Last Goal: Scotland 1 Switzerland 0, European Championships 1996, 18/06/96

GOAL-SCORING RECORD AND CAREER MILESTONES

RANGERS CAREER MILESTONES

100th Competitive Goal for Rangers	v Clydebank, Scottish Premier League, 18/04/87
200th Competitive Goal for Rangers	v Dunfermline, Scottish Premier League, 24/08/91
300th Competitive Goal for Rangers	v Morton, Scottish League Cup, 19/08/95
1st League Goal for Rangers	v Celtic at Parkhead, 03/09/83
100th League Goal for Rangers	v Dundee at Ibrox, 26/12/87
128th League Goal for Rangers	v Motherwell at Ibrox, 09/12/89

(overtakes Frank McGarvey's total of 127 Premier League goals to become top goalscorer in the history of the Scottish Premier Division.)

132nd League Goal for Rangers	v Celtic at Ibrox, 01/04/90

(surpasses Derek Johnstone's tally of 131 league goals to become Rangers' top post-war league goalscorer.)

200th League Goal for Rangers	v Hearts at Tynecastle, 21/11/92
231st League Goal for Rangers	v Raith Rovers at Ibrox, 13/01/96

(becomes Rangers' top league goalscorer of all time, beating Bob McPhail's total of 230 league goals.)

250th League Goal for Rangers	v Dunfermline at East End Park, 28/03/98
Last League Goal for Rangers	v Hibernian at Ibrox, 01/04/98

RANGERS FOOTBALL CLUB'S TOP TEN GOAL-SCORERS OF ALL TIME

Player	Year Joined	Year Left	Appearances	Goals Scored
Ally McCoist	1983	1998	581	355
Bob McPhail	1927	1940	408	261
Jimmy Smith	1928	1946	259	249
Jimmy Fleming	1925	1934	267	220
Derek Johnstone	1970	1986	546	210
Ralph Brand	1954	1965	317	206
Willie Reid	1909	1920	230	195
Willie Thornton	1937	1954	308	194
Robert C Hamilton	1897	1908	209	184
Andy Cunningham	1915	1929	389	182

Note: the above only includes goals scored in the Scottish League Championship, the Scottish Cup, the Scottish League Cup, or in European competition. It does not include goals scored in competitions such as the Glasgow Merchant's Charity Cup or the Glasgow Cup. It also does not take into account goals scored during the Second World War.

RECORDS HELD BY ALLY McCOIST

- Most capped Rangers player with 59 international caps. McCoist was capped 61 times in total but two of these were gained while with Kilmarnock.

- Rangers' top League goal-scorer of all time with 251 goals. This assumes that goals scored during wartime are discounted. This means that Jimmy Smith, who netted 74 times during the Second World War, had a final total of 226 league goals for Rangers.

- Rangers' top goal-scorer in European competition with 21 goals. McCoist was top goalscorer for any Scottish club in European competition until Henrik Larsson overtook his total in October 2002.

- Top goal-scorer in the history of the Scottish Premier Division with 251 goals

- Scottish League top goal-scorer (post-war) with 282 goals

- Top goal-scorer in the Scottish League Cup with 63 goals, a record held jointly with Bobby Lennox.

- Top goal-scorer in the history of Old Firm matches with 27 goals, a record held jointly with Jimmy McCrory of Celtic. Robert Cumming Hamilton netted a total of 36 goals against Celtic, but a number of his goals came in non-competitive matches.

- Most winners' medals in the Scottish League Cup with 9

- Fourth top Scottish League goal-scorer of All-Time with 282 goals

- Fifth top goal-scorer of all time for Scotland with 19 goals

GOAL-SCORING RECORD WITH RANGERS AGAINST SENIOR SCOTTISH LEAGUE TEAMS

With the exception of Queen's Park, Ally McCoist scored at least one goal against each of the opposition teams he faced in domestic football during his fifteen-year career with Rangers. Below is a complete club-by-club breakdown of the 355 goals Ally scored in a Light Blue jersey.

ALLY McCOIST

ABERDEEN FOOTBALL CLUB – 49 APPEARANCES, 14 GOALS

League Championship   42 app/ 11 goals
Scottish Cup   1 app/1 goal
Scottish League Cup   6 app/2 goals

SEASON	COMPETITION	VENUE	RESULT	GOALS
1986/87	League Championship	Ibrox	Rangers 2 - Aberdeen 0	1
1987/88	League Championship	Pittodrie	Aberdeen 1 - Rangers 2	1
1988/89	Scottish League Cup Final	Hampden Park	Rangers 3 - Aberdeen 2	2
1989/90	League Championship	Ibrox	Rangers 2 - Aberdeen 0	1
1990/91	League Championship	Ibrox	Rangers 2 - Aberdeen 2	2
1991/92	League Championship	Pittodrie	Aberdeen 2 - Rangers 3	1
1991/92	Scottish Cup Third Round	Pittodrie	Aberdeen 0 - Rangers 1	1
1991/92	League Championship	Pittodrie	Aberdeen 0 - Rangers 2	2
1992/93	League Championship	Ibrox	Rangers 3 - Aberdeen 1	1
1992/93	League Championship	Ibrox	Rangers 2 - Aberdeen 0	1
1994/95	League Championship	Ibrox	Rangers 1 - Aberdeen 0	1

AIRDRIE FOOTBALL CLUB – 7 APPEARANCES, 6 GOALS

League Championship   6 app/5 goals
Scottish Cup   1 app/1 goal

SEASON	COMPETITION	VENUE	RESULT	GOALS
1991/92	League Championship	Broomfield	Airdrie 0 - Rangers 4	2
1991/92	League Championship	Ibrox	Rangers 4 - Airdrie 0	1
1991/92	Scottish Cup Final	Hampden Park	Airdrie 1 - Rangers 2	1
1992/93	League Championship	Ibrox	Rangers 2 - Airdrie 2	2

ALLOA ATHLETIC FOOTBALL CLUB – 1 APPEARANCE, 3 GOALS

Scottish Cup   1 app/3 goals

SEASON	COMPETITION	VENUE	RESULT	GOALS
1993/94	Scottish Cup Fourth Round	Ibrox	Rangers 6 - Alloa Athletic 0	3

ARBROATH FOOTBALL CLUB – 2 APPEARANCES, 4 GOALS

Scottish Cup   1 app/1 goal
Scottish League Cup   1 app/3 goals

SEASON	COMPETITION	VENUE	RESULT	GOALS
1989/90	Scottish League Cup Second Round	Ibrox	Rangers 4 - Arbroath 0	3
1992/93	Scottish Cup Quarter-Final	Gayfield	Arbroath 0 - Rangers 3	1

AYR UNITED FOOTBALL CLUB – 1 APPEARANCE, 1 GOAL

Scottish Cup   1 app/1 goal

SEASON	COMPETITION	VENUE	RESULT	GOALS
1992/93	Scottish Cup Fourth Round	Somerset Park	Ayr United 0 - Rangers 2	1

ALLY McCOIST

CELTIC FOOTBALL CLUB – 53 APPEARANCES, 24 GOALS

League Championship	43 app/17 goals	
Scottish Cup	6 app/3 goals	
Scottish League Cup	4 app/4 goals	

SEASON	COMPETITION	VENUE	RESULT	GOALS
1983/84	League Championship	Parkhead	Celtic 2 - Rangers 1	1
1983/84	Scottish League Cup Final	Hampden Park	Celtic 2 - Rangers 3	3
1984/85	League Championship	Parkhead	Celtic 1 - Rangers 1	1
1985/86	League Championship	Parkhead	Celtic 1 - Rangers 1	1
1985/86	League Championship	Ibrox	Rangers 3 - Celtic 0	1
1985/86	League Championship	Ibrox	Rangers 4 - Celtic 4	1
1986/87	League Championship	Parkhead	Celtic 1 - Rangers 1	1
1986/87	League Championship	Ibrox	Rangers 2 - Celtic 0	1
1986/87	League Championship	Parkhead	Celtic 3 - Rangers 1	1
1987/88	League Championship	Ibrox	Rangers 2 - Celtic 2	1
1988/89	League Championship	Ibrox	Rangers 5 - Celtic 1	2
1989/90	League Championship	Ibrox	Rangers 3 - Celtic 0	1
1990/91	League Championship	Parkhead	Celtic 1 - Rangers 2	1
1991/92	League Championship	Ibrox	Rangers 1 - Celtic 1	1
1991/92	League Championship	Parkhead	Celtic 1 - Rangers 3	1
1991/92	Scottish Cup Semi-Final	Hampden Park	Celtic 0 - Rangers 1	1
1993/94	League Championship	Ibrox	Rangers 1 - Celtic 2	1
1995/96	Scottish League Cup Quarter-Final	Parkhead	Celtic 0 - Rangers 1	1
1995/96	League Championship	Ibrox	Rangers 3 - Celtic 3	1
1995/96	Scottish Cup Semi-Final	Hampden Park	Celtic 1 - Rangers 2	1
1997/98	Scottish Cup Semi-Final	Parkhead	Celtic 1 - Rangers 2	1

GOAL-SCORING RECORD WITH RANGERS AGAINST SENIOR SCOTTISH LEAGUE TEAMS

COWDENBEATH FOOTBALL CLUB – 2 APPEARANCES, 1 GOAL

Scottish Cup   1 app/1 goal
Scottish League Cup   1 app/0 goals

SEASON	COMPETITION	VENUE	RESULT	GOALS
1990/91	Scottish Cup Fourth Round	Ibrox	Rangers 5 - Cowdenbeath 0	1

CLYDE FOOTBALL CLUB – 2 APPEARANCES, 1 GOAL

Scottish League Cup   2 app/1goal

SEASON	COMPETITION	VENUE	RESULT	GOALS
1985/86	Scottish League Cup Second Round	Ibrox	Rangers 5 - Clyde 0	1

CLYDEBANK FOOTBALL CLUB – 11 APPEARANCES, 12 GOALS

League Championship   7 app/7 goals
Scottish League Cup   4 app/5 goals

SEASON	COMPETITION	VENUE	RESULT	GOALS
1983/84	Scottish League Cup Section 2	Ibrox	Rangers 4 - Clydebank 0	2
1983/84	Scottish League Cup Section 2	Kilbowie	Clydebank 0 - Rangers 3	1
1985/86	League Championship	Ibrox	Rangers 4 - Clydebank 2	1
1986/87	League Championship	Kilbowie	Clydebank 1 - Rangers 4	2
1986/87	League Championship	Ibrox	Rangers 5 - Clydebank 0	2
1986/87	League Championship	Kilbowie	Clydebank 0 - Rangers 3	2
1988/89	Scottish League Cup Third Round	Ibrox	Rangers 6 - Clydebank 0	1
1996/97	Scottish League Cup Second Round	Kilbowie	Clydebank 0 - Rangers 3	1

DUMBARTON FOOTBALL CLUB – 6 APPEARANCES, 4 GOALS

League Championship   4 app/3 goals
Scottish Cup   1 app/0 goals
Scottish League Cup   1 app/1 goal

SEASON	COMPETITION	VENUE	RESULT	GOALS
1984/85	League Championship	Boghead	Dumbarton 1 - Rangers 2	1
1984/85	League Championship	Ibrox	Rangers 3 - Dumbarton 1	2
1992/93	Scottish League Cup Second Round	Hampden Park	Dumbarton 0 - Rangers 5	1

ALLY McCOIST

DUNDEE FOOTBALL CLUB – 37 APPEARANCES, 30 GOALS

League Championship	30 app/27 goals
Scottish Cup	5 app/2 goals
Scottish League Cup	2 app/1 goal

SEASON	COMPETITION	VENUE	RESULT	GOALS
1984/85	League Championship	Ibrox	Rangers 1 - Dundee 3	1
1985/86	League Championship	Dens Park	Dundee 3 - Rangers 2	2
1985/86	League Championship	Ibrox	Rangers 5 - Dundee 0	3
1985/86	League Championship	Dens Park	Dundee 2 - Rangers 1	1
1986/87	League Championship	Ibrox	Rangers 2 - Dundee 1	1
1986/87	League Championship	Dens Park	Dundee 0 - Rangers 4	2
1986/87	League Championship	Ibrox	Rangers 2 - Dundee 0	1
1987/88	League Championship	Ibrox	Rangers 2 - Dundee 1	1
1987/88	League Championship	Ibrox	Rangers 2 - Dundee 0	2
1987/88	League Championship	Dens Park	Dundee 0 - Rangers 1	1
1988/89	Scottish League Cup Quarter-Final	Ibrox	Rangers 4 - Dundee 1	1
1988/89	League Championship	Ibrox	Rangers 3 - Dundee 1	1
1989/90	League Championship	Ibrox	Rangers 2 - Dundee 2	2
1989/90	League Championship	Ibrox	Rangers 3 - Dundee 0	1
1992/93	League Championship	Dens Park	Dundee 4 - Rangers 3	2
1992/93	League Championship	Ibrox	Rangers 3 - Dundee 1	2
1992/93	League Championship	Dens Park	Dundee 1 - Rangers 3	1
1992/93	League Championship	Ibrox	Rangers 3 - Dundee 0	1
1993/94	League Championship	Ibrox	Rangers 3 - Dundee 1	2
1997/98	Scottish Cup Quarter-Final Replay	Dens Park	Dundee 1 - Rangers 2	2

GOAL-SCORING RECORD WITH RANGERS AGAINST SENIOR SCOTTISH LEAGUE TEAMS

DUNDEE UNITED FOOTBALL CLUB – 54 APPEARANCES, 26 GOALS

League Championship	45 app/22 goals
Scottish Cup	3 app/2 goals
Scottish League Cup	6 app/2 goals

SEASON	COMPETITION	VENUE	RESULT	GOALS
1983/84	League Championship	Tannadice	Dundee United 1 - Rangers 2	1
1984/85	League Championship	Tannadice	Dundee United 2 - Rangers 1	1
1985/86	League Championship	Ibrox	Rangers 1 - Dundee United 0	1
1985/86	League Championship	Tannadice	Dundee United 1 - Rangers 1	1
1985/86	League Championship	Ibrox	Rangers 1 - Dundee United 1	1
1985/86	League Championship	Tannadice	Dundee United 1 - Rangers 1	1
1986/87	League Championship	Ibrox	Rangers 2 - Dundee United 3	2
1986/87	Scottish League Cup Semi-Final	Hampden Park	Dundee United 1 - Rangers 2	1
1986/87	League Championship	Ibrox	Rangers 2 - Dundee United 0	1
1987/88	League Championship	Ibrox	Rangers 1 - Dundee United 1	1
1987/88	League Championship	Ibrox	Rangers 1 - Dundee United 0	1
1988/89	Scottish Cup Quarter-Final	Ibrox	Rangers 2 - Dundee United 2	1
1988/89	Scottish Cup Quarter Final Replay	Tannadice	Dundee United 0 - Rangers 1	1
1988/89	League Championship	Ibrox	Rangers 2 - Dundee United 0	1
1989/90	League Championship	Ibrox	Rangers 2 - Dundee United 1	1
1989/90	League Championship	Ibrox	Rangers 3 - Dundee United 1	1
1990/91	League Championship	Ibrox	Rangers 1 –Dundee United 2	1
1991/92	League Championship	Ibrox	Rangers 1 - Dundee United 1	1
1991/92	League Championship	Tannadice	Dundee United 3 - Rangers 2	2
1991/92	League Championship	Ibrox	Rangers 2 - Dundee United 0	2
1992/93	Scottish League Cup Quarter-Final	Tannadice	Dundee United 2 - Rangers 3	1
1992/93	League Championship	Tannadice	Dundee United 0 - Rangers 4	1
1992/93	League Championship	Ibrox	Rangers 3 - Dundee United 2	1

ALLY McCOIST

DUNFERMLINE ATHLETIC FOOTBALL CLUB – 21 APPEARANCES, 22 GOALS

League Championship   17 app/17 goals
Scottish Cup   2 app/1 goal
Scottish League Cup   2 app/4 goals

SEASON	COMPETITION	VENUE	RESULT	GOALS
1983/84	Scottish Cup, Third Round	Ibrox	Rangers 2 - Dunfermline 1	1
1987/88	Scottish League Cup Third Round	East End Park	Dunfermline 1 - Rangers 4	3
1987/88	League Championship	Ibrox	Rangers 4 - Dunfermline 0	3
1987/88	League Championship	East End Park	Dunfermline 0 - Rangers 4	1
1987/88	League Championship	Ibrox	Rangers 2 - Dunfermline	1
1987/88	League Championship	East End Park	Dunfermline 0 - Rangers 3	1
1989/90	Scottish League Cup Semi-Final	Hampden Park	Dunfermline 0 - Rangers 5	1
1989/90	League Championship	East End Park	Dunfermline 1 - Rangers 1	1
1989/90	League Championship	Ibrox	Rangers 3 - Dunfermline 0	1
1989/90	League Championship	Ibrox	Rangers 2 - Dunfermline 0	1
1991/92	League Championship	Ibrox	Rangers 4 - Dunfermline 0	1
1991/92	League Championship	East End Park	Dunfermline 0 - Rangers 5	1
1996/97	League Championship	East End Park	Dunfermline 2 - Rangers 5	3
1996/97	League Championship	Ibrox	Rangers 3 - Dunfermline 1	1
1997/98	League Championship	East End Park	Dunfermline 2 - Rangers 3	2

EAST FIFE FOOTBALL CLUB – 2 APPEARANCES, 1 GOAL

Scottish Cup   1 app/1 goal
Scottish League Cup   1 app/0 goals

SEASON	COMPETITION	VENUE	RESULT	GOALS
1996/97	Scottish Cup Third Round	Ibrox	Rangers 3 - East Fife 0	1

FALKIRK FOOTBALL CLUB – 22 APPEARANCES, 25 GOALS

League Championship	20 app/22goals
Scottish League Cup	2 app/3goals

SEASON	COMPETITION	VENUE	RESULT	GOALS
1986/87	League Championship	Ibrox	Rangers 1 - Falkirk 0	1
1986/87	League Championship	Brockville	Falkirk 1 - Rangers 5	1
1986/87	League Championship	Brockville	Falkirk 1 - Rangers 2	2
1987/88	League Championship	Ibrox	Rangers 4 - Falkirk 0	3
1987/88	League Championship	Brockville	Falkirk 0 - Rangers 5	2
1991/92	League Championship	Brockville	Falkirk 1 - Rangers 3	1
1991/92	League Championship	Ibrox	Rangers 4 - Falkirk 1	3
1992/93	League Championship	Ibrox	Rangers 4 - Falkirk 0	4
1992/93	League Championship	Brockville	Falkirk 1 - Rangers 2	1
1995/96	League Championship	Ibrox	Rangers 2 - Falkirk	2
1995/96	League Championship	Brockville	Falkirk 0 - Rangers 4	2
1997/98	Scottish League Cup Third Round	Ibrox	Rangers 4 - Falkirk 1	3

HAMILTON ACADEMICAL FOOTBALL CLUB – 10 APPEARANCES, 5 GOALS

League Championship	6 app/4 goals
Scottish Cup	1 app/0 goals
Scottish League Cup	3 app/1 goal

SEASON	COMPETITION	VENUE	RESULT	GOALS
1986/87	League Championship	Douglas Park	Hamilton 0 - Rangers 2	1
1986/87	League Championship	Ibrox	Rangers 2 - Hamilton	1
1986/87	League Championship	Ibrox	Rangers 2 - Hamilton 0	1
1988/89	League Championship	Douglas Park	Hamilton 0 - Rangers 2	1
1997/98	Scottish League Cup Second Round	Fir Park	Hamilton 0 - Rangers 1	1

ALLY McCOIST

HEART OF MIDLOTHIAN FOOTBALL CLUB – 49 APPEARANCES, 28 GOALS

League Championship	40 app/20 gaols
Scottish Cup	4 app/3 goals
Scottish League Cup	5 app/5 goals

SEASON	COMPETITION	VENUE	RESULT	GOALS
1983/84	League Championship	Tynecastle	Hearts 2 - Rangers 2	1
1984/85	League Championship	Ibrox	Rangers 3 - Hearts 1	1
1985/86	Scottish Cup Third Round	Tynecastle	Hearts 3 - Rangers 2	1
1985/86	League Championship	Tynecastle	Hearts 3 - Rangers 1	1
1986/87	League Championship	Ibrox	Rangers 3 - Hearts 0	1
1986/87	League Championship	Tynecastle	Hearts 2 - Rangers 5	1
1986/87	League Championship	Ibrox	Rangers 3 - Hearts 0	3
1987/88	Scottish League Cup Quarter-Final	Ibrox	Rangers 4 - Hearts 1	2
1990/91	League Championship	Tynecastle	Hearts 1 - Rangers 3	2
1990/91	League Championship	Ibrox	Rangers 4 - Hearts 0	1
1991/92	Scottish League Cup Quarter-Final	Tynecastle	Hearts 0 - Rangers 1	1
1991/92	League Championship	Ibrox	Rangers 2 - Hearts 0	1
1991/92	League Championship	Tynecastle	Hearts 0 - Rangers 1	1
1991/92	League Championship	Ibrox	Rangers 1 - Hearts 1	1
1992/93	League Championship	Ibrox	Rangers 2 - Hearts 0	1
1992/93	League Championship	Tynecastle	Hearts 1 - Rangers 1	1
1992/93	League Championship	Ibrox	Rangers 2 - Hearts 1	1
1992/93	Scottish Cup Semi-Final	Parkhead	Hearts 1 - Rangers 2	1
1993/94	League Championship	Tynecastle	Hearts 1 - Rangers 2	1
1995/96	League Championship	Tynecastle	Hearts 0 - Rangers 2	1
1996/97	League Championship	Ibrox	Rangers 3 - Hearts 0	1
1996/97	Scottish League Cup Final	Parkhead	Rangers 4 - Hearts 3	2
1997/98	Scottish Cup Final	Parkhead	Hearts 2 - Rangers 1	1

HIBERNIAN FOOTBALL CLUB – 47 APPEARANCES, 22 GOALS

League Championship	42 app/21 goals
Scottish League Cup	5 app/1 goal

SEASON	COMPETITION	VENUE	RESULT	GOALS
1985/86	League Championship	Easter Road	Hibernian 1 - Rangers 3	1
1985/86	League Championship	Ibrox	Rangers 3 - Hibernian 1	3
1986/87	League Championship	Easter Road	Hibernian 2 - Rangers 1	1
1988/89	League Championship	Easter Road	Hibernian 0 - Rangers 1	1
1989/90	League Championship	Ibrox	Rangers 3 - Hibernian 0	2
1991/92	League Championship	Ibrox	Rangers 4 - Hibernian 2	2
1991/92	League Championship	Easter Road	Hibernian 1 - Rangers 3	2
1991/92	League Championship	Ibrox	Rangers 2 - Hibernian 0	1
1991/92	League Championship	Easter Road	Hibernian 1 - Rangers 3	1
1992/93	League Championship	Ibrox	Rangers 1 - Hibernian 0	1
1992/93	League Championship	Easter Road	Hibernian 3 - Rangers 4	1
1992/93	League Championship	Ibrox	Rangers 3 - Hibernian 0	1
1993/94	Scottish League Cup Final	Parkhead	Rangers 2 - Hibernian 1	1
1995/96	League Championship	Easter Road	Hibernian 1 - Rangers 4	1
1996/97	League Championship	Ibrox	Rangers 4 - Hibernian 3	2
1997/98	League Championship	Ibrox	Rangers 3 - Hibernian 0	1

INVERNESS CALEDONIAN/INVERNESS CALEDONIAN THISTLE – 2 APPEARANCES, 2 GOALS

Scottish Cup	2 app/2 goals

SEASON	COMPETITION	VENUE	RESULT	GOALS
1983/84	Scottish Cup Fourth Round	Caledonian Stadium	Inverness 0 - Rangers 6	2

ALLY McCOIST

KILMARNOCK FOOTBALL CLUB – 12 APPEARANCES, 1 GOAL

League Championship	9 app/1 goal
Scottish Cup	2 app/0 goals
Scottish League Cup	1 app/0 goals

SEASON	COMPETITION	VENUE	RESULT	GOALS
1995/96	League Championship	Rugby Park	Kilmarnock 0 - Rangers 3	1

MEADOWBANK THISTLE FOOTBALL CLUB – 2 APPEARANCES, 3 GOALS

Scottish League Cup	2 app/3 goals

SEASON	COMPETITION	VENUE	RESULT	GOALS
1984/85	Scottish League Cup Semi Final First Leg	Ibrox	Rangers 4 - Meadowbank 0	2
1984/85	Scottish League Cup Semi Final Second Leg	Tynecastle	Meadowbank 1 - Rangers 1	1

(Note that Meadowbank Thistle is the former name of Scottish First Division side Livingston)

MORTON FOOTBALL CLUB – 10 APPEARANCES, 12 GOALS

League Championship	7 app/11 goals
Scottish Cup	2 app/0 goals
Scottish League Cup	1 app/1 goal

SEASON	COMPETITION	VENUE	RESULT	OALS
1984/85	League Championship	Ibrox	Rangers 2 - Morton 0	1
1984/85	League Championship	Cappielow	Morton 0 - Rangers 3	3
1987/88	League Championship	Ibrox	Rangers 7 - Morton 0	3
1987/88	League Championship	Cappielow	Morton 0 - Rangers 3	1
1987/88	League Championship	Ibrox	Rangers 5 - Morton 0	3
1995/96	Scottish League Cup, Second Round	Ibrox	Rangers 3 - Morton 0	1

GOAL-SCORING RECORD WITH RANGERS AGAINST SENIOR SCOTTISH LEAGUE TEAMS

MOTHERWELL FOOTBALL CLUB – 43 APPEARANCES, 27 GOALS

League Championship	40 app/25 goals
Scottish Cup	2 app/2 goals
Scottish League Cup	1 app/0 goals

SEASON	COMPETITION	VENUE	RESULT	GOALS
1983/84	League Championship	Ibrox	Rangers 1 - Motherwell 2	1
1983/84	League Championship	Ibrox	Rangers 2 - Motherwell 1	1
1985/86	League Championship	Fir Park	Motherwell 0 - Rangers 3	2
1985/86	League Championship	Ibrox	Rangers 1 - Motherwell 0	1
1985/86	League Championship	Ibrox	Rangers 2 - Motherwell 0	1
1986/87	League Championship	Ibrox	Rangers 1 - Motherwell 0	1
1987/88	League Championship	Ibrox	Rangers 1 - Motherwell 0	1
1987/88	League Championship	Fir Park	Motherwell 0 - Rangers 2	1
1988/89	League Championship	Ibrox	Rangers 1 - Motherwell 0	1
1989/90	League Championship	Ibrox	Rangers 3 - Motherwell 1	1
1990/91	League Championship	Ibrox	Rangers 2 - Motherwell 0	1
1991/92	League Championship	Ibrox	Rangers 2 - Motherwell 0	1
1992/93	League Championship	Fir Park	Motherwell 1 - Rangers 4	3
1992/93	League Championship	Ibrox	Rangers 4 - Motherwell 2	3
1992/93	Scottish Cup Third Round	Fir Park	Motherwell 0 - Rangers 2	2
1992/93	League Championship	Fir Park	Motherwell 0 - Rangers 4	1
1993/94	League Championship	Fir Park	Motherwell 2 - Rangers 1	1
1995/96	League Championship	Ibrox	Rangers 2 - Motherwell 1	1
1995/96	League Championship	Ibrox	Rangers 3 - Motherwell 2	1
1997/98	League Championship	Fir Park	Motherwell 1 - Rangers 1	1
1997/98	League Championship	Fir Park	Motherwell 2 - Rangers 1	1

ALLY McCOIST

PARTICK THISTLE FOOTBALL CLUB – 5 APPEARANCES, 1 GOAL

League Championship   4 app/1 goal
Scottish League Cup   1 app/0 goals

SEASON	COMPETITION	VENUE	RESULT	GOALS
1993/94	League Championship	Firhill	Partick Thistle 1 - Rangers 2	1

QUEEN OF THE SOUTH FOOTBALL CLUB – 2 APPEARANCES, 1 GOAL

Scottish League Cup   2 app/1 goal

SEASON	COMPETITION	VENUE	RESULT	GOALS
1983/84	Scottish League Cup Second Round, Second Leg	Palmerston Park	Queen of the South 1 - Rangers 4	1

RAITH ROVERS FOOTBALL CLUB – 17 APPEARANCES, 16 GOALS

League Championship   11 app/10 goals
Scottish Cup   4 app/1 goal
Scottish League Cup   2 app/5 goals

SEASON	COMPETITION	VENUE	RESULT	GOALS
1984/85	Scottish League Cup Third Round	Ibrox	Rangers 4 - Raith Rovers 0	2
1987/88	Scottish Cup Third-Round Replay	Ibrox	Rangers 4 - Raith Rovers 1	1
1990/91	Scottish League Cup Quarter-Final	Ibrox	Rangers 6 - Raith Rovers 2	3
1993/94	League Championship	Ibrox	Rangers 4 - Raith Rovers 0	1
1995/96	League Championship	Ibrox	Rangers 4 - Raith Rovers 0	2
1995/96	League Championship	Ibrox	Rangers 4 - Raith Rovers 0	1
1995/96	League Championship	Starks Park	Raith Rovers 2 - Rangers 4	3
1996/97	League Championship	Starks Park	Raith Rovers 2 - Rangers 2	1
1996/97	League Championship	Ibrox	Rangers 4 - Raith Rovers 0	1
1995/96	League Championship	Starks Park	Raith Rovers 0 - Rangers 6	1

STENHOUSEMUIR FOOTBALL CLUB – 1 APPEARANCE, 1 GOAL

Scottish League Cup   1 app/1 goal

SEASON	COMPETITION	VENUE	RESULT	GOALS
1986/87	Scottish League Cup Second Round	Ochilview	Stenhousemuir 1 - Rangers 4	1

STIRLING ALBION FOOTBALL CLUB – 2 APPEARANCES, 2 GOALS

Scottish League Cup   2 app/2 goals

SEASON	COMPETITION	VENUE	RESULT	GOALS
1987/88	Scottish League Cup, Second Round	Brockville	Stirling Albion 1- Rangers 2	1
1995/96	Scottish League Cup Third Round	Ibrox	Rangers 3 - Stirling Albion 2	1

STRANRAER FOOTBALL CLUB – 2 APPEARANCES, 5 GOALS

Scottish Cup   1 app/2 goals

Scottish League Cup   1 app/3 goals

SEASON	COMPETITION	VENUE	RESULT	GOALS
1988/89	Scottish Cup 4th Round	Ibrox	Rangers 8 - Stranraer 0	2
1992/93	Scottish League Cup Third Round	Stair Park	Stranraer 0 - Rangers 5	3

ALLY McCOIST

ST JOHNSTONE FOOTBALL CLUB – 23 APPEARANCES, 14 GOALS

League Championship   17 app/9 goals
Scottish Cup   5 app/2 goals
Scottish League Cup   1 app/3 goals

SEASON	COMPETITION	VENUE	RESULT	GOALS
1983/84	League Championship	Ibrox	Rangers 6 - St Johnstone 3	2
1983/84	League Championship	Muirton Park	St Johnstone 1 - Rangers 4	1
1988/89	Scottish Cup Semi-Final Replay	Parkhead	St Johnstone 0 - Rangers 4	1
1991/92	League Championship	McDiarmid Park	St Johnstone 2 - Rangers 3	2
1991/92	Scottish Cup Quarter-Final	McDiarmid Park	St Johnstone 0 - Rangers 3	1
1992/93	League Championship	Ibrox	Rangers 1 - St Johnstone 0	1
1992/93	Scottish League Cup (Semi-Final)	Hampden	Rangers 3 - St Johnstone 1	3
1992/93	League Championship	McDiarmid Park	St Johnstone 1 - Rangers	1

ST MIRREN FOOTBALL CLUB – 29 APPEARANCES, 20 GOALS

League Championship   28 app/18 goals
Scottish League Cup   1 app/2 goals

SEASON	COMPETITION	VENUE	RESULT	GOALS
1983/84	Scottish League Cup Section Two	Ibrox	Rangers 5 - St Mirren 0	2
1984/85	League Championship	Love Street	St Mirren 2 - Rangers 1	1
1985/86	League Championship	Love Street	St Mirren 2 - Rangers 1	1
1985/86	League Championship	Ibrox	Rangers 2 - St Mirren 0	1
1986/87	League Championship	Love Street	St Mirren 1 - Rangers 3	3
1987/88	League Championship	Love Street	St Mirren 2 - Rangers 2	2
1987/88	League Championship	Love Street	St Mirren 0 - Rangers 3	1
1988/89	League Championship	Ibrox	Rangers 3 - St Mirren 1	1
1988/89	League Championship	Love Street	St Mirren 0 - Rangers	1
1989/90	League Championship	Love Street	St Mirren 0 - Rangers 2	1
1990/91	League Championship	Ibrox	Rangers 5 - St Mirren 0	2
1990/91	League Championship	Ibrox	Rangers 1 - St Mirren 0	1
1991/92	League Championship	Love Street	St Mirren 1 - Rangers 2	1
1991/92	League Championship	Ibrox	Rangers 4 - St Mirren 0	2

APPENDIX C

GOAL-SCORING RECORD FOR RANGERS IN EUROPEAN COMPETITION

54 APPEARANCES, 21 GOALS

SEASON	COMPETITION	VENUE	RESULT	GOALS
1984/85	UC, First Round, First Leg	Dalymount Park, Dublin	Bohemians 3 - Rangers 2	1
1986/87	UC, First Round, First Leg	Ibrox Stadium	Rangers 4 - Ilves Tampere 0	1
1986/87	UC, Second Round, First Leg	Ibrox Stadium	Rangers 2 - Boavista 1	1
1987/88	EC, First Round, Second Leg	Ibrox Stadium	Rangers 2 - Dynamo Kiev 0	1
1987/88	EC, Second Round, First Leg	Ibrox Stadium	Rangers 3 - Gornik Zabrze 1	1
1987/88	EC, Second Round, Second Leg	Stadio Gornik Zabrze	Gornik Zabrze 1 - Rangers 1	1
1987/88	EC, Quarter-Final, Second Leg	Ibrox Stadium	Rangers 2 - Steaua Bucharest 1	1
1990/91	EC, First Round, First Leg	Ta'Qali Stadium, Valletta	Valletta 0 - Rangers 4	1
1990/91	EC, First Round, Second Leg	Ibrox Stadium	Rangers 6 - Valletta 0	1
1990/91	EC, Second Round, Second Leg	Ibrox Stadium	Rangers 1 - Red Star Belgrade 1	1
1992/93	EC, Second Round, First Leg	Ibrox Stadium	Rangers 2 - Leeds United 1	1
1992/93	EC, Second Round, Second Leg	Elland Road, Leeds	Leeds United 1 - Rangers 2	1
1996/97	EC, First Round, First Leg	Ibrox Stadium	Rangers 3 - Alania 1	1
1996/97	EC, First Round, Second Leg	Spartak Stadium, Vladikavkaz	Alania 2 - Rangers 7	3

ALLY McCOIST

1996/97	ECL, Group A, Match Five	Ibrox Stadium	Rangers 2 - Grasshoppers Zurich 1	2
1997/98	EC, First Round, First Leg	Svangaskard, Toftir	GI Gotu 0 - Rangers 5	2
1997/98	EC, First Round, Second Leg	Ibrox Stadium	Rangers 6 - GI Gotu 0	1

(KEY: UC = UEFA Cup, EC = European Champions Cup, ECL = European Champions League)

ALLY McCOIST'S INTERNATIONAL RECORD WITH SCOTLAND

UNDER-18 LEVEL 10 CAPS, 7 GOALS

COMPETITION	DATE	VENUE	RESULT	GOALS
European Youth Championships Qualifier, First Leg	06/10/80	Reykjavik	Iceland 0 - Scotland 1	1
European Youth Championships Qualifier, Second Leg	16/10/80	Parkhead, Glasgow	Scotland 3 - Iceland 1	1
Friendly	29/10/80	Somerset Park, Ayr	Scotland 3 - Northern Ireland 1	1
Monaco Youth Tournament	13/11/80	Monaco	Scotland 0 - West Germany 1	0
Monaco Youth Tournament	15/11/80	Monaco	Scotland 2 - Switzerland 0	1
Monaco Youth Tournament	17/11/80	Monaco	Scotland 1 - France 1	1
Friendly	05/05/81	Harelbeke	Belgium 0 - Scotland 0	0
European Youth Championships	25/05/81	Nattenberg Stadium, Ludenscheid, West Germany	Scotland 1 - Austria 0	0
European Youth Championships	27/05/81	Tivoli Stadium Aachen, West Germany	Scotland 1 - England 0	1
European Youth Championships	29/05/81	Duren, West Germany	Scotland 1 - Spain	1

ALLY McCOIST

UNDER-21 LEVEL 1 CAP, 0 GOALS

COMPETITION	DATES	VENUE	RESULT	GOALS
European U-21 Championships Qualifier	11/10/83	Tannadice Park, Dundee	Scotland 0 - Belgium 0	0

SENIOR LEVEL 61 CAPS, 19 GOALS

COMPETITION	DATE	VENUE	RESULT	GOALS
Friendly	29/04/86	Philips Stadoin, Eindhoven	Holland 0 - Scotland	0
*European Championships Qualifier	12/11/86	Hampden Park, Glasgow	Scotland 3 - Luxembourg 0	0
*European Championships Qualifier	18/02/87	Hampden Park, Glasgow	Scotland 0 - Republic of Ireland 1	0
European Championships Qualifier	01/04/87	Constant Van den Stock Stadion, Brussels	Belgium 4 - Scotland 1	0
Sir Stanley Rous Cup	23/05/87	Hampden Park, Glasgow	Scotland 0 - England 0	0
Sir Stanley Rous Cup	26/05/87	Hampden Park, Glasgow	Scotland 0 - Brazil	0
Friendly	09/09/87	Hampden Park, Glasgow	Scotland 2 - Hungary 0	2
European Championships Qualifier	14/10/87	Hampden Park, Glasgow	Scotland 2 - Belgium 0	1
Friendly	22/03/88	Ta/Qali Stadium, Valletta	Malta 1 - Scotland	0
Friendly	27/04/88	Estadio Santiago Bernabeu, Madrid	Spain 0 - Scotland	0
Sir Stanley Rous Cup	17/05/88	Hampden Park, Glasgow	Scotland 0 - Colombia 0	0
Sir Stanley Rous Cup	21/05/88	Wembley Stadium, London	England 1 - Scotland 0	0
*World Cup Qualifier	19/10/88	Hampden Park, Glasgow	Scotland 1 - Yugoslavia 1	0
World Cup Qualifier	08/03/89	Hampden Park, Glasgow	Scotland 2 - France 0	0
World Cup Qualifier	26/04/89	Hampden Park, Glasgow	Scotland 2 - Cyprus 1	1
Sir Stanley Rous Cup	27/05/89	Hampden Park, Glasgow	Scotland 0 - England 2	0
World Cup Qualifier	06/09/89	Maksimir Stadion, Zagreb	Yugoslavia 3 - Scotland 1	0
World Cup Qualifier	11/10/89	Parc des Princes, Paris	France 3 - Scotland 0	0
World Cup Qualifier	15/11/89	Hampden Park, Glasgow	Scotland 1 - Norway 1	1
*Friendly	25/04/90	Hampden Park, Glasgow	Scotland 0 - East Germany 1	0
Friendly	16/05/90	Pittodrie Stadium, Aberdeen	Scotland 1 - Egypt 3	1
Friendly	19/05/90	Hampden Park, Glasgow	Scotland 1 - Poland 1	0
*Friendly	28/05/90	Ta'Qali Stadium, Valletta	Malta 1 - Scotland	0
*World Cup Finals Italia '90	11/06/90	Stadio Luigi Ferraris, Genoa	Costa Rica 1 - Scotland	0

ALLY McCOIST'S INTERNATIONAL RECORD WITH SCOTLAND

*World Cup Finals Italia '90	16/06/90	Stadio Luigi Ferraris, Genoa	Sweden 1 - Scotland 2	0
World Cup Finals Italia '90	20/06/90	Stadio Delle Alpe, Turin	Brazil 1 - Scotland 0	0
European Championships Qualifier	12/09/90	Hampden Park, Glasgow	Scotland 2 - Romania 1	1
European Championships Qualifier	17/10/90	Hampden Park, Glasgow	Scotland 2 - Switzerland 1	0
European Championships Qualifier	14/11/90	Vasil Levski Stadion, Sofia	Bulgaria 1 - Scotland	1
Friendly	06/02/91l	brox Stadium, Glasgow	Scotland 0 - USSR 1	0
European Championships Qualifier	27/03/91	Hampden Park, Glasgow	Scotland 1 - Bulgaria 1	0
European Championships Qualifier	11/09/91	Wankdorf Stadion, Berne	Switzerland 2 - Scotland	1
European Championships Qualifier	13/11/91	Hampden Park, Glasgow	Scotland 4 - San Marino	1
Friendly	19/02/92	Hampden Park, Glasgow	Scotland 1 - Northern Ireland 0	1
*Friendly	25/03/92	Hampden Park, Glasgow	Scotland 1 - Finland 1	0
Friendly	17/05/92	Mile High Stadium, Denver	USA 0 - Scotland 1	0
Friendly	20/05/92	Varsity Stadium, Toronto	Canada 1 - Scotland 3	1
Friendly	03/06/92	Ullevaal Stadion, Oslo	Norway 0 - Scotland 0	0
Euro '92	12/06/92	Ullevi Stadion, Gothenburg	Holland 1 - Scotland 0	0
Euro '92	15/06/92	Idrottsparken, Norrkoping	Germany 2 - Scotland	0
Euro '92	18/06/92	Idrottsparken, Norrkoping	CIS 0 - Scotland 3	0
World Cup Qualifier	09/09/92	Wankdorf Stadion, Berne	witzerland 3 - Scotland 1	1
World Cup Qualifier	14/10/92	Ibrox Stadium, Glasgow	Scotland 0 - Portugal	0
World Cup Qualifier	18/11/92	Ibrox Stadium, Glasgow	Scotland 0 - Italy	0
World Cup Qualifier	17/02/93	Ibrox Stadium, Glasgow	Scotland 3 - Malta 0	2
World Cup Qualifier	28/04/93	Estadio da Luz, Lisbon	Portugal 5 - Scotland 0	0
*European Championships Qualifier	16/08/95	Hampden Park, Glasgow	Scotland 1 - Greece	1
*European Championships Qualifier	06/09/95	Hampden Park, Glasgow	Scotland 1 - Finland 0	0
*European Championships Qualifier	15/11/95	Hampden Park, Glasgow	Scotland 5 - San Marino 0	1
Friendly	27/03/96	Hampden Park, Glasgow	Scotland 1 - Australia	1
*Friendly	24/04/96	Parken Stadion, Copenhagen	Denmark 2 - Scotland 0	0
Friendly	29/05/96	Orange Bowl, Miami	Colombia 1 - Scotland 0	0

ALLY McCOIST

*Euro '96	15/06/96	Wembley Stadium, London	England 2 - Scotland	0
Euro '96	18/06/96	Villa Park, Birmingham	Scotland 1 - Switzerland 0	1
World Cup Qualifier	31/08/96	Ernst Happel Stadion, Vienna	Austria 0 - Scotland 0	0
*World Cup Qualifier	10/11/96	Ibrox Stadium, Glasgow	Scotland 1 - Sweden 0	0
*World Cup Qualifier	11/02/97	Stade Louis II, Monaco	Estonia 0 - Scotland	0
World Cup Qualifier	02/04/97	Parkhead, Glasgow	Scotland 2 - Austria 0	0
World Cup Qualifier	07/09/97	Pittodrie Stadium, Aberdeen	Scotland 4 - Belarus 1	0
European Championships Qualifier	05/09/98	Zalgiris Stadion, Vilnius	Lithuania 0 - Scotland 0	0
European Championships Qualifier	10/10/98	Tynecastle Park, Edinburgh	Scotland 3 - Estonia 2	0

Note: asterisks denote appearances made as a substitute

NOTES

CHAPTER ONE – THE EARLY YEARS

Daily Record, 24/09/99, p. 25.
Ally McCoist Testimonial Year 1993–94 Brochure, Section 4.
Ally McCoist Testimonial Year 1993–94 Brochure, Section 4.
Rangers News, 15/06/83, p. 5.
Ally McCoist, *My Story*, Mainstream Publishing, 1992, p. 14.

CHAPTER TWO – THE SAINTS

Ally McCoist, *My Story*, Mainstream Publishing, 1992, p.19.
McCoist, *My Story*, Mainstream Publishing, 1992, p.20.
Daily Record, 26/05/81, p. 35.
Evening Times, 13/08/81, p. 30.
Evening Times, 13/08/81, p. 30.
Daily Record, 14/08/81, p. 43.
Daily Record, 14/08/81, p. 43.
Glasgow Herald, 26/08/81, p. 20.
Daily Record, 26/08/81, p. 31.

CHAPTER THREE – ROKER DAYS

The Times, 26/08/81, p. 13.

Rangers News, 28/07/93, p. 11.

McCoist, *My Story*, Mainstream Publishing, 1992, p.167.

Ally McCoist Testimonial Year 1993-94 Brochure, Section 2.

Ally McCoist Testimonial Year 1993-94 Brochure, Section 2.

Video – *Super Ally – The McCoist Phenomenon*, Pickwick, 1991.

CHAPTER FOUR – A DREAM COME TRUE

Glasgow Herald, 09/06/83, p.18.

Rangers News, 15/06/83, p. 4.

Ally McCoist, *My Story*, Mainstream Publishing, 1992, p. 29.

McCoist, *My Story*, Mainstream Publishing, 1992, p. 30.

McCoist, *My Story*, Mainstream Publishing, 1992, p. 32.

McCoist, *My Story*, Mainstream Publishing, 1992, p. 32.

Rangers News, 07/09/83, p. 2.

The Glasgow Herald, 26/03/84, p. 16.

McCoist, *My Story*, Mainstream Publishing, 1992, p. 34.

Glasgow Herald, 26/03/84, p. 16.

Stanley Paul, *Playing for Rangers, No.16*, 1984, pp.42-43.

CHAPTER FIVE – ALMOST THE END OF THE ROAD

Stanley Paul, *Playing for Rangers, No.17*, 1985, p. 27.

Stanley Paul, *Playing for Rangers, No.17*, 1985, p. 31.

Stanley Paul, *Playing for Rangers, No.17*, 1985, p. 58.

Rangers News, 11/12/84, p. 1.

McCoist, *My Story*, Mainstream Publishing, 1992, p. 39.

McCoist, *My Story*, Mainstream Publishing, 1992, p .40.

Evening Times, 18/02/85, p. 32.

McCoist, *My Story*, Mainstream Publishing, 1992, pp. 40-41.

Ian Durrant, *Blue & White Dynamite*, First Press Publishing, 1998 p. 9.

Stanley Paul, *Playing for Rangers, No.17*, 1985, p. 32.

Video – *Super Ally – The McCoist Phenomenon*, Pickwick, 1991.

McCoist, *My Story*, Mainstream Publishing, 1992, p. 44.

NOTES

CHAPTER SIX – THE AWAKENING

Ally McCoist, *My Story*, Mainstream Publishing, 1992, p. 44.

McCoist, *My Story*, Mainstream Publishing, 1992, pp.44 and 45.

McCoist, *My Story*, Mainstream Publishing, 1992, p. 46.

McCoist, *My Story*, Mainstream Publishing, 1992, p. 51.

McCoist, *My Story*, Mainstream Publishing, 1992, p. 161.

Sunday Mail, 10/08/86, p. 43.

McCoist, *My Story*, Mainstream Publishing, 1992, p. 54.

McCoist, *My Story*, Mainstream Publishing, 1992, p. 56.

CHAPTER SEVEN – GOALS, GOALS, GOALS

Rangers News, 05/08/87, p.12.

Rangers News, 23/09/87, p. 5.

Roddy Forsyth, *Blue and True, Unforgettable Rangers Days*, Mainstream Publishing, 1996, p. 121.

Rangers News, 09/03/88, p. 4.

Rangers News, 09/03/88, p. 5.

Rangers News, 03/02/88, p. 1.

Rangers News, 03/02/88, p. 1.

Rangers News, 11/08/88, p. 1.

Rangers News, 03/11/88, p. 1.

Graeme Souness, *A Manager's Diary*, Mainstream Publishing, 1989, p. 114.

CHAPTER EIGHT – MO JOHNSTON AND ITALIA '90

Video – *Super Ally – The McCoist Phenomenon*, Pickwick, 1991

Rangers News, 08/06/89, p. 1.

Rangers News, 08/06/89, p. 1.

Rangers News, 13/12/89, p. 4.

Ally McCoist, *My Story*, Mainstream Publishing, 1992, p. 100.

McCoist, *My Story*, Mainstream Publishing, 1992, p. 107.

Rangers News, 13/06/90, p. 1.

McCoist, *My Story*, Mainstream Publishing, 1992, p. 109.

McCoist, *My Story*, Mainstream Publishing, 1992, p. 105.

McCoist, *My Story*, Mainstream Publishing, 1992, p. 109.

McCoist, *My Story*, Mainstream Publishing, 1992, p. 105.

CHAPTER NINE – THE JUDGE

Ally McCoist, *My Story*, Mainstream Publishing, 1992, p. 65.
McCoist, *My Story*, Mainstream Publishing, 1992, p. 67.
McCoist, *My Story*, Mainstream Publishing, 1992, p. 64.
McCoist, *My Story*, Mainstream Publishing, 1992, p. 68.
McCoist, *My Story*, Mainstream Publishing, 1992, pp. 68-9.
McCoist, *My Story*, Mainstream Publishing, 1992, p. 69.
McCoist, *My Story*, Mainstream Publishing, 1992, pp. 72-3.
Daily Record, 19/03/91, p. 44.
Rangers News, 27/02/91, p. 1.

CHAPTER TEN – A PAIR OF GOLDEN BOOTS

Walter Smith, *Mr Smith*, Mainstream Publishing, 1994, p. 87.
Daily Record, 16/08/91, p. 40.
Rangers News, 11/09/91, p. 13.
Rangers News, 08/01/92, pp. 12-13.
Rangers News, 05/02/92, p. 2.
Rangers News, 06/05/92, p. 6.
McCoist, *My Story*, Mainstream Publishing, 1992, p. 133.
McCoist, *My Story*, Mainstream Publishing, 1992, p. 135.
Rangers News, 29/07/92, p. 21.
Video – *5-in-a-row – There's No Limit*, Cameron Williams, 1993.
Rangers News, 07/10/92.
Rangers News, 04/11/92, p. 9.
Video – *5-in-a-row – There's No Limit*, Cameron Williams, 1993.
Rangers News, 10/02/93, p. 10.

CHAPTER ELEVEN – INJURY HELL

Video – *McCoist – Still Having A Ball*, John Williams Productions, 1999.
Rangers News, 06/10/93, p. 4.
Video – *6-in-a-row – The Bluebells are Blue*, Cameron Williams, 1994.
Video – *6-in-a-row – The Bluebells are Blue*, Cameron Williams, 1994.
Rangers News, 03/11/93, p. 6.
Rangers News, 23/02/94, p. 6.
Rangers News, 23/02/94, p. 7.
Rangers News, Summer Special '94, p. 13.

NOTES

Ian Durrant, *Blue & White Dynamite*, First Press Publishing, 1998 p. 12.
Rangers News, 19/10/94, p. 3.
Daily Record, 18/11/94, p. 3.
Video – *The Real McCoist*, Cameron Williams, 1995.
Daily Record, 26/01/95, p. 3.

CHAPTER TWELVE – COOP

Graham Clark, *Davie Cooper – Tribute to a Legend*, Mainstream
 Publishing, 1995, pp.134-135.
The Herald, 24/03/95, p. 48.
Graham Clark, *Davie Cooper – Tribute to a Legend*, Mainstream
 Publishing, 1995, pp.134-135.
Daily Record, 28/03/95, p. 43.
Daily Record, 28/03/95, p. 43.
Daily Record, 28/03/95, p. 43.
The Herald, 28/03/95, p. 1.
Rangers News, 24/03/99, p. 3.

CHAPTER THIRTEEN – THE LAST CHANCE SALOON

Rangers News, 09/08/95, p. 7.
Rangers News, 23/08/95, p10.
Daily Record, 18/08/95, p. 71.
Rangers News, 23/08/95, p8-9.
Rangers News, 27/09/95, p7.
Iain King, *Rangers – The 100 Greatest*, First Press Publishing, 1998, p.53.
Rangers News, 15/11/95, p. 18.
Rangers News, 06/12/95, p11.
Video – *The Real McCoist*, Cameron Williams, 1995.
Sunday Mail, 31/03/96, p. 63.
Sunday Mail, 31/03/96, p. 64.
Rangers News Summer Special 1996, p. 3.

CHAPTER FOURTEEN – EURO '96, RECORDS AND NINE-IN-A-ROW

Rangers News, 31/07/96, p. 13.
Rangers News, 31/07/96, p. 20.

ALLY McCOIST

Rangers News, 21/08/96, p. 10.
The Daily Record, 22/11/96, pp. 78-9.
The Herald, 21/11/96, p. 40.
The Daily Record Winner, 25/11/96, p. 2.
Rangers News, 11/12/96, p. 12.
Rangers News, 15/01/97, p. 10.
Rangers News, 12/03/97, p. 8.
Rangers News, 21/05/97, p. 8.

CHAPTER FIFTEEN – THE LAST HURRAH

Rangers News, 30/07/97, p. 12.
Rangers News, 13/08/97, p. 12.
Video – *The Real McCoist,* Cameron Williams, 1995.
Rangers News, 08/04/98, p. 7.
Rangers News, 08/04/98, p. 11.
Rangers News, 08/04/98, p. 46.
Rangers News, 06/05/98, pp. 26-7.
Rangers News, 20/05/98, p.17.
Rangers News, 20/05/98, p. 6.
Stuart McCall, *The Real McCall,* Mainstream Publishing, 1998, p. 178.

CHAPTER SIXTEEN – FOOTBALL IN PERSPECTIVE

Daily Record, 13/10/98, p. 9.
Video – *McCoist – Still Having a Ball,* John Williams, 1999.

CHAPTER SEVENTEEN – THE FINAL CHAPTER

Daily Record, 10/08/98, p. 3.
Rangers News, 19/08/98, p. 6.
Rangers News, 27/08/98, p. 9.
Daily Record, 31/08/98, p. 40.
Sunday Mail, 06/09/98, p. 72.
Rangers News, 16/12/98, p. 16.
Rangers News, 16/12/98, p. 16.
Video – *Blue and White, Dynamite – The Ian Durrant Story,* Sports, Business and Leisure, 2002.

BBC Sport website (www.bbc.co.uk/sport), 03/08/2000.
Daily Record, 06/09/2000, p. 49.
Evening Times, 12/04/2001, p. 66.
Daily Record Winner, 14/05/2001, p. 7.
Daily Record, 21/05/2001, p. 43.

CHAPTER EIGHTEEN – AFTER THE BALL

Video – *The Real McCoist*, Cameron Williams, 1995.
BBC Annual Report, 1997/98.
Video – *The Real McCoist*, Cameron Williams, 1995.
Daily Record, 09/09/2005, p. 76.
Daily Record, 26/01/2006, p. 63.

CHAPTER NINETEEN – COMING HOME

Daily Record, 19/10/2006, p. 65.
Daily Record, 14/12/2006, p. 64.
Daily Record, 13/01/2007, p. 66
Rangers News, 12/01/2007, pp. 8-9.
Video – *McCoist – Still Having A Ball*, John Williams Productions, 1999
Sunday Mail, 21/10/2007, p. 100.
Rangers News, 09/05/2007, p. 9.
Sunday Mail, 30/09/2007, p. 72.
www.rangers.co.uk
McCoist, *My Story*, Mainstream Publishing, 1992, p. 185.
Sunday Mail, 30/09/2007, p. 72.

CHAPTER TWENTY – RIDING THE ROLLERCOASTER

Daily Record (www.dailyrecord.co.uk), 14/05/08
The Herald, 19/03/08, Sport p.4
BBC Sport website (www.bbc.co.uk/sport), 13/04/08
Daily Record (www.dailyrecord.co.uk), 28/05/08
Evening Times, 07/10/08, p.59
Rangers News, 13/08/08, p.9
Rangers News, 03/09/08, p.10
BBC Sport website (www.bbc.co.uk/sport), 21/11/08

ALLY McCOIST

The Times Online (www.timesonline.co.uk), 21/11/08
The Times Online (www.timesonline.co.uk), 22/11/08
Sunday Mail, 11/01/09, p.70
Evening Times, 26/02/09, pp. 47-48
The Homecoming Scottish Cup Final Official Programme, p.20
BBC Sport website (www.bbc.co.uk/sport), 24/04/09
Sunday Mail, 31/05/09, p.88
Daily Record, 01/06/09, p.47